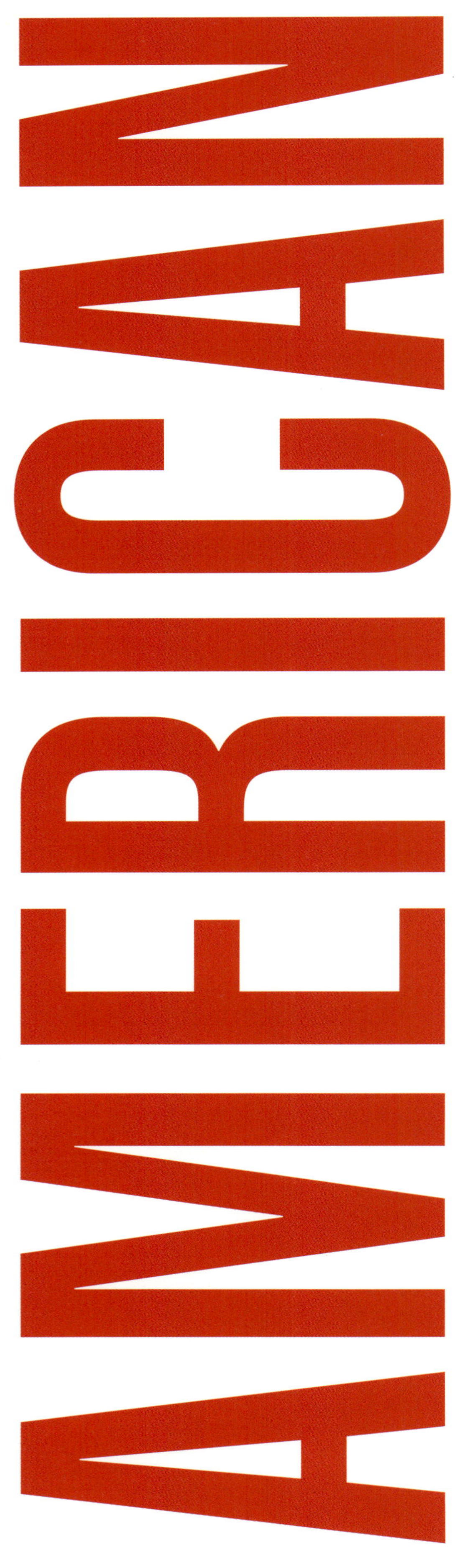

# AMERICAN ART

## ART

### 1961–2001

# THE WALKER ART CENTER COLLECTIONS

edited by
Vincenzo de Bellis
Arturo Galansino

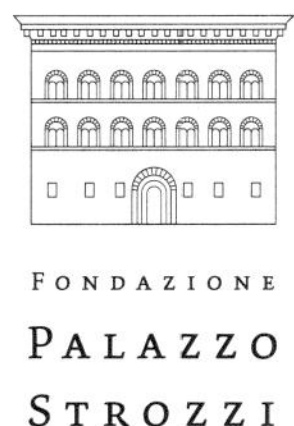

FONDAZIONE
PALAZZO
STROZZI

WALKER

Marsilio

**AMERICAN ART 1961–2001**
THE WALKER ART CENTER COLLECTIONS

Palazzo Strozzi, Florence
28 May – 29 August 2021

*With the Patronage of*

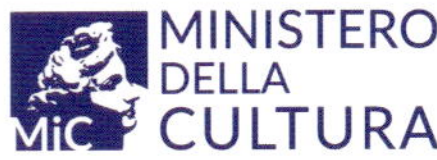
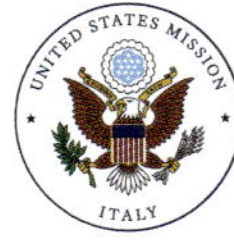

*Promoted and organized by*

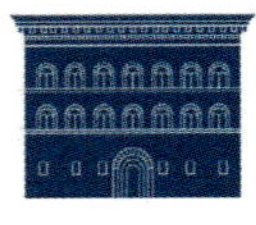
WALKER

*Supported by*

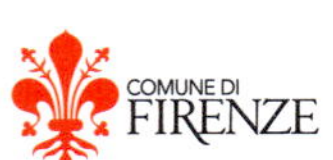
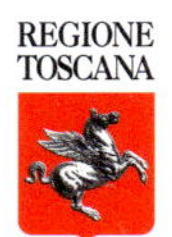
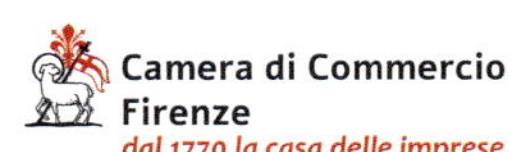

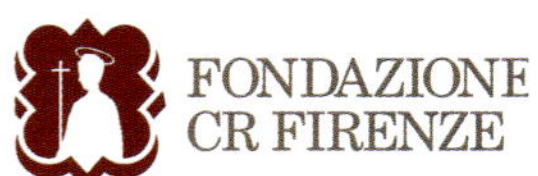
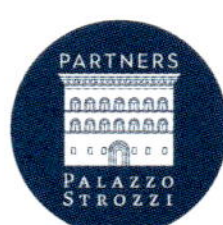
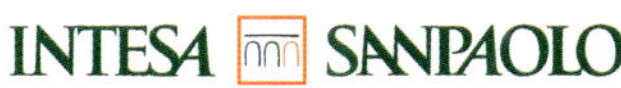

*Premium sponsor*

GUCCI

*With the support of*

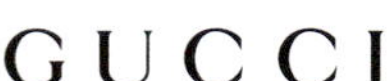

*Technical Sponsors*

*Educational partner*

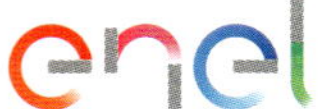
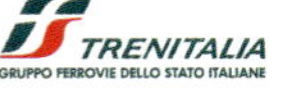
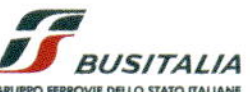
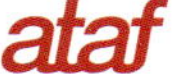
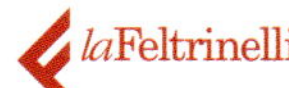
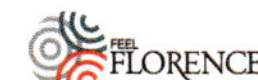
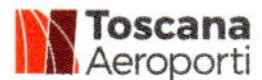
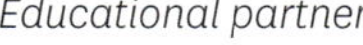
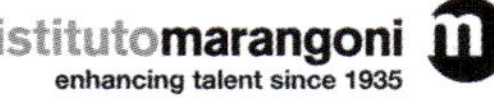

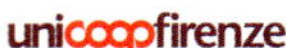
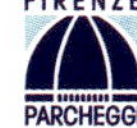
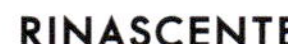
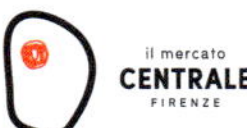
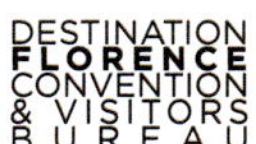
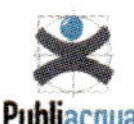

*Exhibition curated by*
Vincenzo de Bellis
Arturo Galansino

*Exhibition layout*
Luigi Cupellini
*in collaboration with*
Carlo Pellegrini

*Consultant for the installation*
Rita Scrofani

*Exhibition design*
Avuelle
Carmagnini s.n.c.
ERCO
Galli Allestimenti
Stampa in Stampa s.r.l.

*Exhibition graphics and
communication design*
RovaiWeber design

*Accompanying texts
in the exhibition*
Ludovica Sebregondi

*Accompanying texts in the
exhibition translated by*
Stephen Tobin
(Italian-English)

*Communication and promotion*
Susanna Holm
CSC SIGMA

*Press Office*
Antonella Fiori
(National press)
Sutton PR
(International press)

*Support for educational
activities*
Marianna Di Rosa
Chiara Martini
Anna Ricciardi
Nicoletta Salvi
Azzurra Simoncini

*Photographer*
Elzbieta Bialkowska,
OKNO Studio

*Website*
Vertical Media

*Technological coordination*
Matteo Lotti Margotti

*Individual visitor and groups
tours*
CSC SIGMA

*Exhibition reservations office*
CSC SIGMA

*Exhibition and box office staff*
TML Service s.r.l.

*Multichannel box office*
Vivaticket S.p.A.

*Audio guide*
Orpheo Group

*Palazzo Strozzi app*
Hidonix

*Insurance*
Huntington T. Block Insurance
Agency

*Transport and installation*
Arterìa

*Head of security DM569*
Ulderigo Frusi

*Head of prevention
and protection*
Filippo Galletti

*Electrical system*
Bagnoli s.r.l.

*Alarm system*
Professional Security s.r.l.

*Air conditioning system*
Soc. E. Palchetti & C. s.r.l.

*Cleaning service*
Cooplat

Walker Art Center
Nikki Kane,
*Exhibition Researcher*
Erin McNeil,
*Exhibition Coordinator*
Joe King, *Registrar*
Kayla Nordlund,
*Associate Registrar*
David Bartley, *Installation*

*Opificio delle Pietre Dure*
Marco Ciatti, *Superintendent
Department of Preventive
Conservation and Climate
Control*
Monica Galeotti, *Director*
Sandra Cassi, *Assistant
Department for the Restoration
of Mural Paintings, Department
for the Restoration of Paintings
on Canvas and Wood,
Department for the Restoration
of Polychrome Wooden
Sculptures, Department for
the Restoration of Paper and
Parchment Documents*
Sandra Rossi, *Director
Department for the Restoration
of Bronzes and Antique
Weapons, Department for the
Restoration of Ceramic and
Plastic Materials*
Laura Speranza, *Director*

*Condition reports*
Alessandra Ramat
(coordination),
Stefania Agnoletti, Sara Bassi,
Francesca Bettini, Annalena
Brini, Barbara Cattaneo,
Gabriele Coccolini, Maria
Cristina Gigli, Chiara Modesti,
Letizia Montalbano, Claudia
Napoli, Maria Luisa Reginella,
Luciano Ricciardi, Chiara Sforzi

*Aknowledgements*

This exhibition was made
possible thanks to the
many people who, in their
different capacities, offered
their generous contribution.
Fondazione Palazzo Strozzi
expresses its gratitude to them
all, and is especially grateful to
its colleagues at the Walker Art
Center for their generosity and
professionalism. Special thanks
go to Mary Ceruti, Executive
Director, who made this
collaboration possible.

Vincenzo de Bellis wishes
to thank his colleagues Erin
McNeil, Joe King, Siri Engberg,
Nikki Kane, Jadine Collingwood,
William Hernandez-Luege,
as well as Matthew C. Lange,
Matthew Barney Studio, Kara
Walker Studio, Meg Malloy, Gary
Simmons Studio, Robert Gober
Studio, Sherrie Levine Studio.

For the program *Fuorimostra*,
we wish to thank all the people
and institutions who made it
possible to hold these events
in Florence and throughout the
Tuscany region. For the program
*Palazzo Strozzi alle Oblate* and
at Florence's libraries we wish to
thank Tiziana Mori and the staff
of the Biblioteca delle Oblate
and of the other Biblioteche
Comunali in Florence.

We are grateful to the University
of Florence for its collaboration,
and special thanks go to the
University's Rector Luigi Dei.
For their collaboration on
*Glossario* and *Seminario
sulle culture visive della
contemporaneità*, we wish to
thank SAGAS, the Department
of History, Archeology,
Geography, Art, Performing
Arts, and especially Professors
Tiziana Serena, Giorgio Bacci,
and Silvia Bruni.

We wish to thank the Academy
of Fine Arts in Florence, and
especially Director Claudio
Rocca for their collaboration.
For their collaboration
on the project *Instagram
Accademia*, we are grateful
to the Department of the
Communication and Teaching

of Art, especially Professors
Federica Chezzi, Luca Farulli,
and Cristina Frulli.

We wish to thank the Cinema
Compagnia di Fondazione
Sistema Toscana for the online
display of the video works in the
exhibition.

For their collaboration on
the project *Perenne attualità*
dedicated to the students
of Italian and international
academies, we wish to thank
the tutors Davide Daninos,
Walter Conti, Franco Fiesoli,
Matteo Innocenti, Lucia
Minunno, Marco Raffaele,
Marsha Steinberg, and
Francesca Giulia Tavanti.
We also wish to thank Istituto
Marangoni Firenze and the
director Lorenzo Tellini for their
essential support.

We are grateful to Luca Carli
Ballola and Michela Mei
(Associazione Anna) for *A
più voci*, a project devoted to
people with Alzheimer's and
to their carers. We are also
grateful to Autismo Firenze for
the project *Sfumature* devoted
to young people with autism.
We wish to thank the Fresco
Parkinson Institute for the
project *Corpo libero* and Dance
Well for its collaboration.

For its participation in the
project *Plurals* devoted to
adolescents, we are grateful to
the Istituto Ernesto Balducci of
Pontassieve and in particular to
Cristiana Canali. For the project
*Giovedì per i giovani*, we are
grateful to the International
School of Florence and, in
particular, to the director Simon
Murray and Morgan Fiumi.

For the photos of Matthew
Barney at Pitti Immagine, we
wish to thank Lapo Cianchi,
Fondazione Pitti Immagine
Discovery. Heartfelt thanks to
Maria Gloria Conti Bicocchi and
Gianni Melotti.

For the Palazzo Strozzi
staff uniforms thanks to
Save The Queen.

*Lighting partner*

**ER**CO

*The new ticket office
at Palazzo Strozzi
was designed by*

**ARCHEA ASSOCIATI**

*In these difficult and troubled times in the throes of the pandemic, Fondazione Palazzo Strozzi has fo-cused its commitment—a natural one for this place of culture—to promoting and increasing its cultural offer. It has done so by renewing and restructuring its own digital identity, thereby paving the way for agile and educational types of long-distance access to culture, fully aware that the digital revolution increasingly tends to valorize the social dimension of art and culture. In the meantime, the traditional planning of exhibitions and the related research activities have continued. Although this period has been marked by the closure of the exhibition devoted to Tomás Saraceno for three months, when it was reopened in June it was hugely successful despite the limited access. Moreover, it allowed us to try new ways of visiting the works. The Fondazione then presented to the public the installations* We Rise by Lifting Others *by Marinella Senatore and* La Ferita (The Wound) *by JR, which gave us the opportunity to recreate a sense of connectedness between the physical and the digital.*

*In spite of the situation, while guaranteeing all the safety precautions, the Fondazione also decided to resume its exhibition activity with an event titled* American Art 1961–2001. *The common thread of this exhibition is identified in a diachronic reading going back over four of the most intense decades in the history of art in the United States, history that is at the same time a mirror and a mouthpiece for politi-cal, military, and social events that had crucial relevance around the world. In 1961 John F. Kennedy was elected president, and in December of the same year the Vietnam War broke out as the first American helicopters arrived in Saigon. On September 11, 2001, during the presidency of George W. Bush, almost three thousand people died in the deadliest attack on US soil since Pearl Harbor. Those two dates mark a watershed in the historical and political context, but they also characterize an unprecedented era of experimentation in the arts, in which the United States became a point of reference around the world. As a result, this exhibition offers the chance to reflect on the idea of the "American Dream," to revisit the iconic and colorful images of Pop Art, but also to rethink Minimalism as an answer to the brutality and violence of the Vietnam War and to the more or less explicit forms of discrimination that swept through the various segments of American society via the freezing of forms and geometric reduction. It is also possible to grasp the reaction of the artists themselves. Indeed, their works express the perception of distance between society and politics, and not just in terms of military policies, but also in the attention paid to themes that are still relevant in the United States and the world today. Once again, the fact that art is a crucial driver with which to build the future is confirmed. The works exhibited at Palazzo Strozzi compel us to reflect on the role of women, on the safeguarding of minorities, on the struggle for civil rights and against inequality, on integration policies. The dramatic events of 2020—which, beginning Minneapolis, triggered race-related protests throughout the US, thus drawing the media's attention to the Black Lives Matter movement—bear out the importance of the demand to put an end to discrimi-nation, which many of the artists present in this exhibition rework and express through works that move between passion, irony, and drama.*

*The exhibition allows us to reflect on the past and the present on both sides of the Atlantic. To this end, the splendid and fruitful collaboration with the Walker Art Center of Minneapolis has proved to be deci-sive: I wish to thank all those who work there with enthusiasm and competence, starting from Vincenzo de Bellis, co-curator of the exhibition and Curator and Associate Director of Programs, Visual Arts at the American institution. I am also grateful to the institutional backers of Fondazione Palazzo Strozzi: the City of Florence, the Region of Tuscany, and the Chamber of Commerce. I would also like to thank Fon-dazione CR Firenze and Intesa Sanpaolo for their constant support for our activity, and the Committee of the Partners of Palazzo Strozzi, a body that brings together private parties that supply funding to our institution on an annual basis. I would also like to express thanks to the members of the organs of the Fondazione Palazzo Strozzi—the Board of Administration, the Advisory Board, the General Director, who is also the co-curator of the exhibition—as well as to all the staff members of the Fondazione for having worked skillfully and passionately, making this new and challenging as well as exciting venture possible.*

**GIUSEPPE MORBIDELLI**
President Fondazione Palazzo Strozzi

*This past year has proven to be one of the most complex, unexpected, and dramatic in the history—and not just recent history—of the world, with a devastating impact on a city like Florence that has always thrived on tourism and has suddenly found itself not just without foreign visitors, but local visitors as well. The Covid-19 restrictions have to a great extent had an impact on cultural activities, which were among the first to be shut down. Fondazione CR Firenze intervened immediately by sending financial aid to the health system, fulfilling the fundamental needs of the population, without, however, overlooking the world of culture, which has been brought to its knees by the pandemic.*

*The Palazzo Strozzi also had to respond to the traumatic situation and was forced to close its* Tomás Saraceno. Aria *exhibition only a few days after it opened. But the installation* Thermodynamic Constellation, *consisting of three large suspended reflecting spheres, was still visible in the courtyard. This large-scale and poetic site-specific work proved to be prophetic, speaking as it does of the problems of humanity today, but even more importantly of a better, sustainable future in which we strike a new harmony with the ecosystem. The installation suggests future perspectives, and for this reason the doors leading to the palazzo courtyard are never closed: It is one of the few places that stays open in the city during total lockdown. In a deserted Florence, the few Florentines who wandered around the city during the first lockdown were afforded a sign of hope, and it is also for this reason that our Institution was pleased to contribute to its realization.*

*A new sign of a return to social and cultural life—and not just in Florence and Tuscany—is now represented by the exhibition* American Art 1961–2001, *a rereading of the trajectory of the arts during a crucial period in the history of art, and history tout court, not just in the United States. Two dates, 1961 and 2001, that encompass a vision of the great American dream of the early 1960s, but also the time of the protests against the Vietnam War, racial segregation, and sexual and gender discrimination: four decades that can now be viewed in all their complexity thanks to the collaboration of the Walker Art Center of Minneapolis.*

*This event also fulfills the primary mission of the Fondazione CR Firenze, which is to contribute to bringing to Florence a type of art that is seldom found here, and to allow for a greater openness toward the present and the future by proposing the works of artist who have already established themselves as historical artistic figures—artists such as Andy Warhol, Mark Rothko, Roy Lichtenstein, Claes Oldenburg, Robert Mapplethorpe, and Cindy Sherman, along with artists belonging to a new, contemporary generation such as Mark Bradford, Mike Kelley, Gary Simmons, and Kara Walker. Though all of these are artists whose work has been shown at major events around the world, seeing them in Florence offers a special opportunity, all the more so in an exhibition that encourages the general public to appreciate their work thanks to the contextualization of the cultural, social, and historical origins of their work.*

*The exhibition therefore wants to communicate with a broad audience, and particularly a young audience, to whom the Fondazione CR Firenze pays close attention in its aim to support the adults of tomorrow. Indeed, if the health emergency has affected the whole population, students have been especially subjected to its effects during a very delicate moment in their education, and not just in terms of formal schooling.*

**LUIGI SALVADORI**
President, Fondazione CR Firenze

*graphic design*
Carmen Malafronte

*copy editing*
Lemuel Caution

*translation*
Sylvia Notini

© 2021 by
Marsilio Editori® s.p.a., Venice

*first edition* May 2021
ISBN 978-88-297-0928-1
www.marsilioeditori.it

Available through ARTBOOK | D.A.P.
75 Broad Street, Suite 630
New York, NY 10004
www.artbook.com

# CONTENTS

ARTURO GALANSINO

# AMERICAN ART IN FLORENCE

The exhibition *American Art 1961–2001 from the Walker Art Center of Minneapolis* consolidates the research carried out by Palazzo Strozzi on modern American art, and brings to a close a trilogy of exhibitions devoted to the key moments in the history of art in the United States.

The two previous exhibitions underscored the relationship between European and American culture, especially to the advantage of the former. *Americani a Firenze* (2012)[1] focused on the painters of the late nineteenth and early twentieth centuries, and included names such as John Singer Sargent, or the Ten American Painters, who embraced the Impressionist language and spent long periods of time in Italy; *La grande arte dei Guggenheim* (2016),[2] which showcased masterpieces of European and American art from the 1920s to the 1960s, reconstructing the links—and not just the cultural links—between the two Atlantic shores through the life and collections of Peggy and Solomon Guggenheim.

In this sort of passing of the baton, the first part of the current exhibition, with works by Joseph Cornell, Mark Rothko, and Louise Nevelson, connects us once again to the world of Peggy Guggenheim. As this remarkable patron left Europe in 1941 to escape Nazism, taking her collection with her, she made it possible for many European artists and intellectuals to flee the horrors of war, thus conveying to the New World the avant-gardes of the Old Continent. One of the highlights of the exhibition devoted to Peggy Guggenheim, Marcel Duchamp's *Boîte-en-valise* (1941)[3]—a box in a suitcase where the French artist placed miniature reproductions of the works he had made up until then so that their story could be transported—symbolizes this passage.

Although there are no works by Duchamp in the current selection, his revolutionary spirit can still be perceived in the rooms of Palazzo Strozzi as he was a major reference point for the new generations of American artists. This can be seen in some of the exhibition's pivotal links, with works such as *Walkaround Time* (1968) by Jasper Johns [2.3]—the transposition of Duchamp's *The Large Glass* into the plastic stage décor for a ballet by Merce Cunningham, with music by David Behrman and costumes also by Johns—or *Fountain* (1991) [7.8], a gilt bronze urinal by Sherrie Levine, a replica of and homage to Duchamp's 1917 and most iconic readymade. However, beyond these direct citations, the father of Conceptual art is, in the broadest and most profound way, the noble father of the new generations of the artists of the new world.

The words of the great artist-*cum*-chess player can help us to understand the cultural difference between the two worlds, especially with respect to the weighty comparison with tradition that was so distinctive of European art:

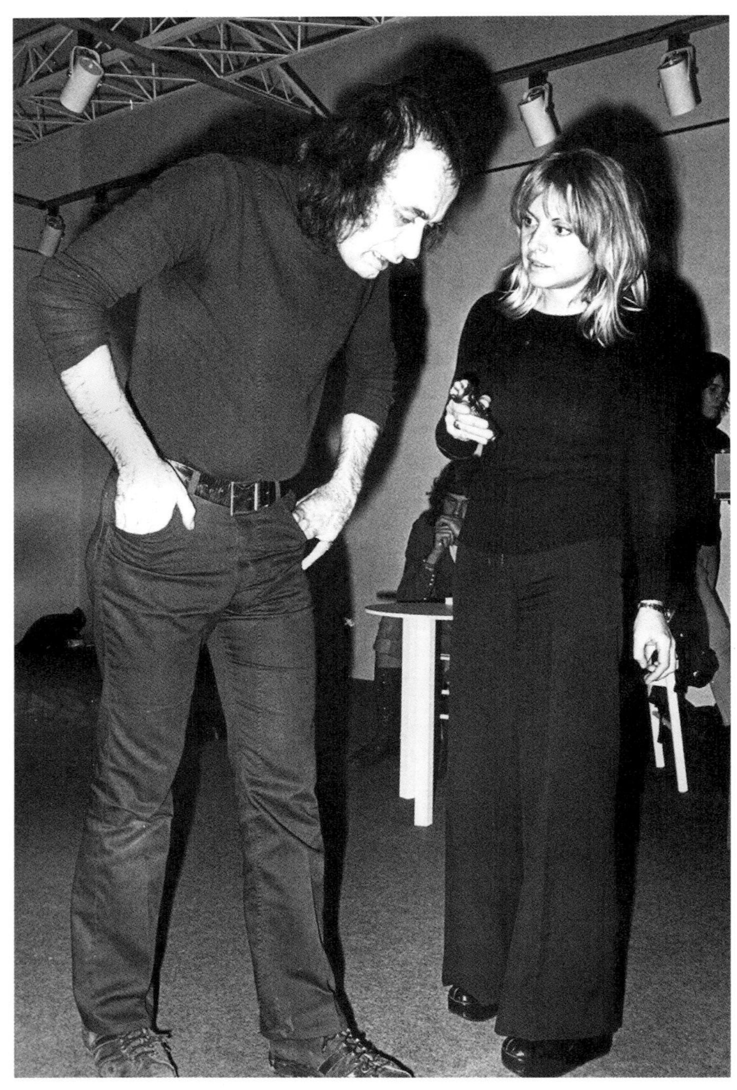

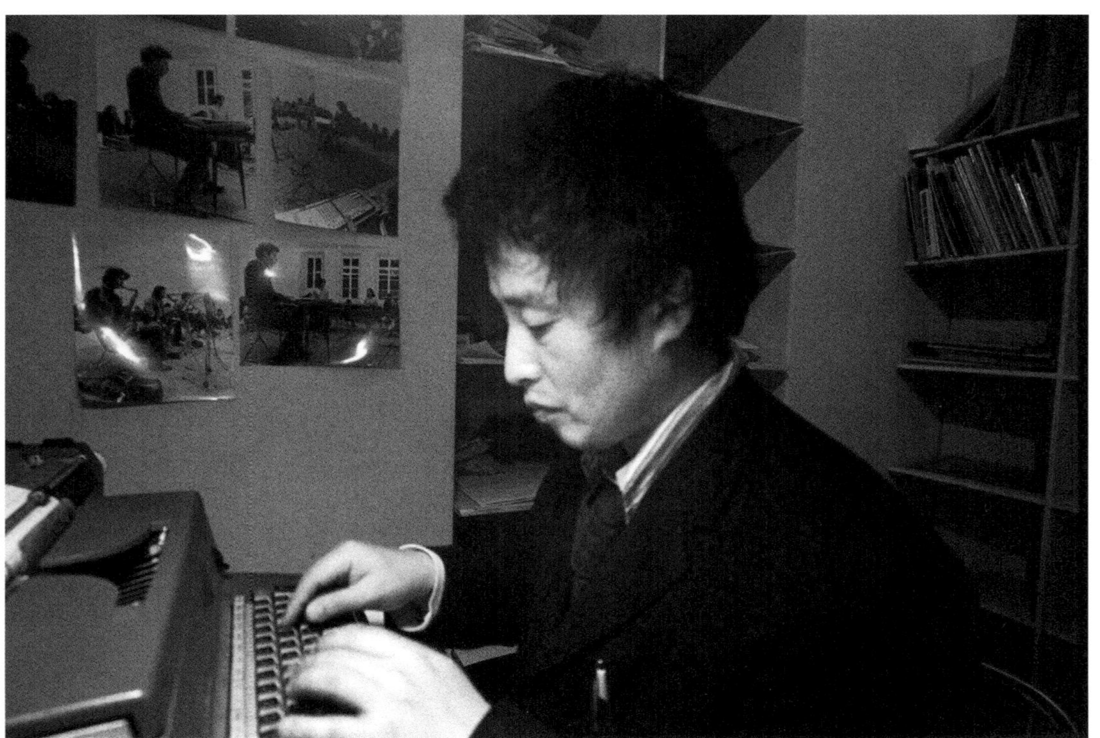

> In France, in Europe [. . .] young artists of any generation always act as grandsons of some great man—Poussin, for example, or Victor Hugo. They can't help it. Even if they don't believe in that, it gets into their system. And so when they come to produce something of their own, the tradition is nearly indestructible. This doesn't exist over here [in the United States]. You really don't give a damn about Shakespeare, you're not Shakespeare's grandsons. So it's a better terrain for new developments.[4]

The name Duchamp also emerges when we examine the relationship between Florence in the post-World War II period, a city that was still closely bound to its passéist identity, and American art of the second half of the twentieth century, to find the persistence of the profound reservations that had already accompanied the exhibition of works from the Peggy Guggenheim collection at Palazzo Strozzi's Strozzina in 1949.[5] Something similar occurred in 1953 at the *Mostra di arazzi di Cy Twombly/Scatole e costruzioni contemplative di Robert Rauschenberg* held at the Galleria d'Arte Contemporanea Lungarno delle Grazie in Florence, which aroused nothing short of the irritation of the art historian and connoisseur Carlo Volpe, one of Roberto Longhi's best students. Volpe used colorful ekphrastic prose to lambast Rauschenberg's works, which he saw as nothing more than mere and "conceptuous" Duchampian deviation:

> Refined knick-knacks to be used as highly intellectual incantations against unkind nature. It was easy to recognize some of the most chilling idioms of the barbarian metaphysics, presented with a facile attention to detail that does not hide the discovered commonality of the terms and the evidence of their purpose: the eye (glass) in the dust, the newborn child surrounded by the twine and debris left by the woodworm: why these are the excrements of time! There were masks and fetishes, horse tails and, lastly, fragrant objects without a name. So that they could truly be identified by sniffing. [. . .] "Very bold cross-overs from Surrealism," they say. The inventions of Duchamp in the most refined "epigonic" involution [. . .] objects of stupidity. To think of it, it would have been great fun, a madness advantageous to our health, to throw all those curses into the Arno.[6]

Soon after his Florence exhibition, Rauschenberg, welcomed Volpe's iconoclastic invitation, also because of the difficulty getting the works back to the United States. After choosing a few of the objects to take back with him on the plane, he threw the others into the river, writing to the critic: "I took your advice."[7] A gesture, almost a performance by the American artist that Duchamp himself would likely have appreciated. . . .
Leaving aside the more specialized and advanced cultural milieus, we might say that the general perception of American art in Italy definitively changed in 1964 when the Grand Prize for Painting at the 32nd Venice Biennale was awarded to Robert Rauschenberg himself. Although a part of the popular press and the usual critics continued to talk with some irony about a "Pop Biennale" (although it was actually for the most part New Dada), and despite the disagreements and ill-humor the award may have caused, the artistic preeminence of the United States was deemed to be "official" for the first time.
Consequently, things changed in Florence as well, which in the 1970s welcomed many American artists thanks to art/tapes/22, the "Videoarte" center founded by Maria Gloria Conti Bicocchi at 22 Via Ricasoli in 1972. The center was a place where people worked and experimented and was closely linked to the United States because of its collaboration with the major New York gallery owners Leo Castelli and Ileana Sonnabend.

← Vito Acconci and Maria Gloria Bicocchi at the Galleria Schema, fall 1973

↙ Nam June Paik at the art/tapes/22 studio, 1974

For art/tapes/22, in September 1973, Vito Acconci produced *Theme Song* [6.3], as well as four other works lasting 30 minutes each (*Home Movies*, *Full Circle*, *Come Back*, and *Indirect Approaches*). Acconci remained in Florence for three weeks, and *Ballroom*, his last public performance, took place at the Galleria Schema, 17 Via della Vigna Nuova. Acconci described his art/tapes/22 period as follows:

> It was much like a monastery—in a relatively short period of time I made, I think, four or five *tapes*. I worked at Maria Gloria's with [Alberto Pirelli and Raffaele Corazziari], two young first-rate technicians, but they were actually much more than that. I told them what I had in mind in vague terms; they suggested settings and frames, we always ate together, we spent the days together, we discussed and reasoned about things, and finally we developed an actual theory and practice of the video.[8]

In Florence that same year, through art/tapes/22, and in collaboration with the Galleria Multipla in Milan, Allan Kaprow produced the work *Then*, which was followed by *Third Routine* in 1974.[9] However, there was no need to cross the Atlantic and travel to the banks of the Arno to make Video Art; indeed, in 1974, for art/tapes/22, in collaboration with the Castelli-Sonnabend Videotape and Films, while in New York, John Baldessari made the video *The Italian Type*: "An almost stylized, Neapolitan marionette that danced and translated commonplaces, while attached to a blackboard by the nails in its joints." Nam June Paik arrived at art/tapes/22 in 1974 as well, but his utopian project—a video showing the destruction of the three video cameras in the studio—was never made.[10]

This short but intense tale of connections and exchanges between Florence and the American avant-garde toward the mid-1970s was already to a certain extent told at Palazzo Strozzi on the occasion of the 2017 *Bill Viola. Electronic Renaissance* exhibition. In September 1974, Viola came to Florence to work as first assistant and technical director of art/tapes/22, remaining there until February 1976. Viola's encounter with Florence was a game-changer: The awe of a young man from New York before the city's Renaissance art, which he was able to metabolize in the midst of the lively Florentine cultural scene, laid the foundations for the expressive language of one of the most important interpreters of images in movement in all of art history.[11]

The Florence of those years, with art/tapes/22, the Galleria Schema, and Zona art space, likewise allowed Dara Birnbaum to approach Video Art. In an interview she said:

> I came back from Florence, Italy, in 1975, after living there for a year and being exposed for the first time to "Video Art" through a small gallery by the name of Centro Diffusione Grafica, owned by Maria Gloria Bicocchi [before creating art/tapes/22 Maria Gloria Bicocchi had managed the Centro Diffusione Grafica]. Many artists whom I met through that gallery told me to return to New York, as they thought the city provided an invigorating workspace at that time—an exciting moment for the exchange of ideas in all genres of the arts. The artists, whom I remember as encouraging me, included Vito Acconci, Charlemagne Palestine, and Dickie Landry. I was trying to further the commencement of my own artmaking, mainly painting and drawing, through the Accademia di Belle Arti in Florence, and that just was not working out—too "academic" (conservative) for my taste and I didn't speak the language, which was also a great disadvantage.[12]

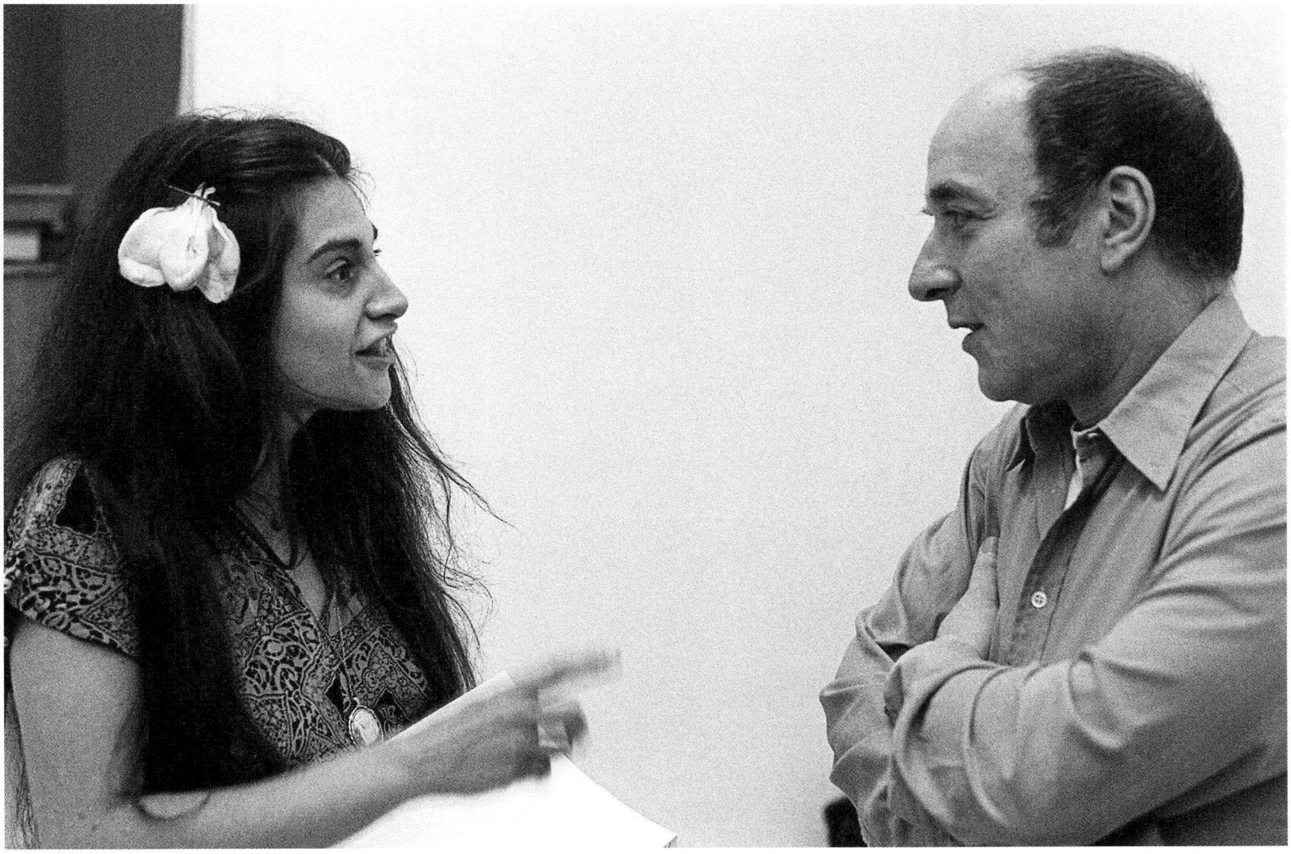

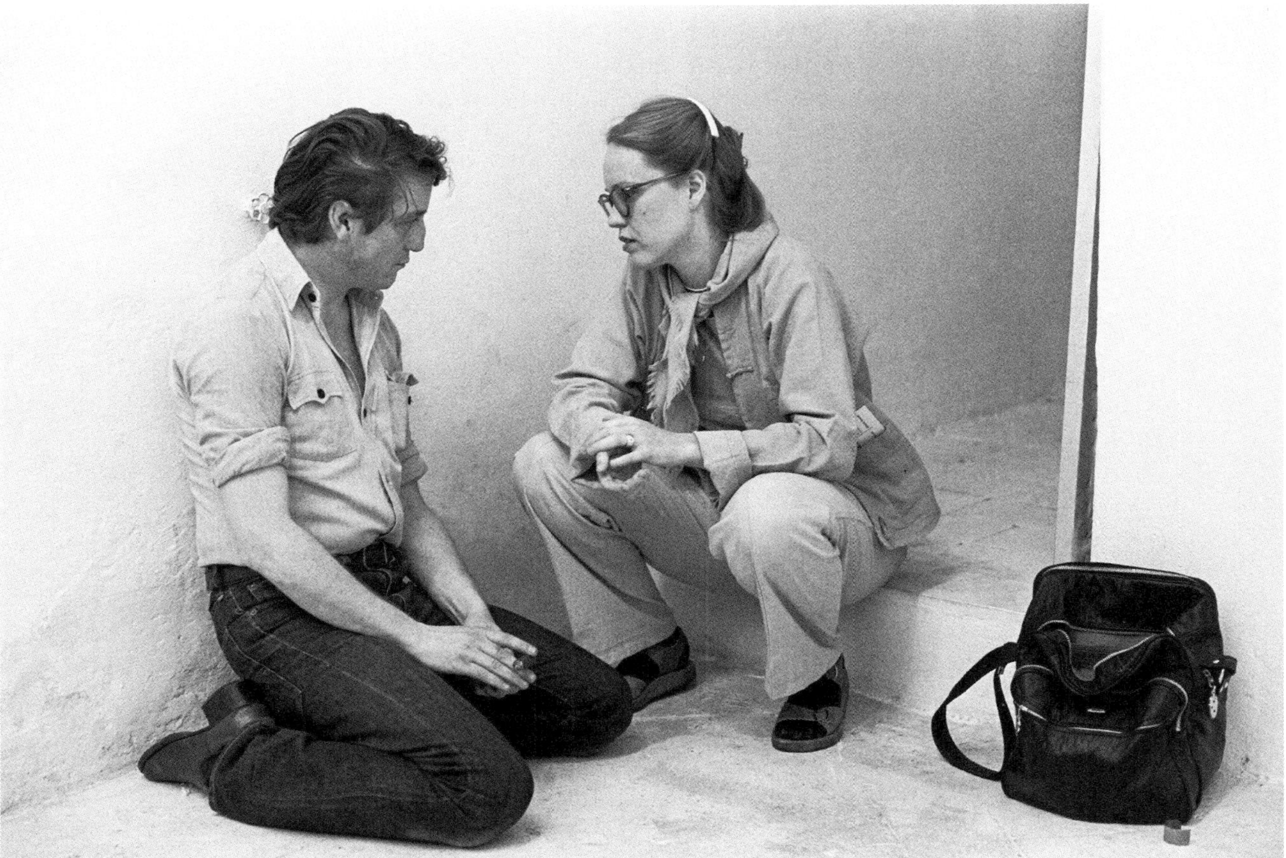

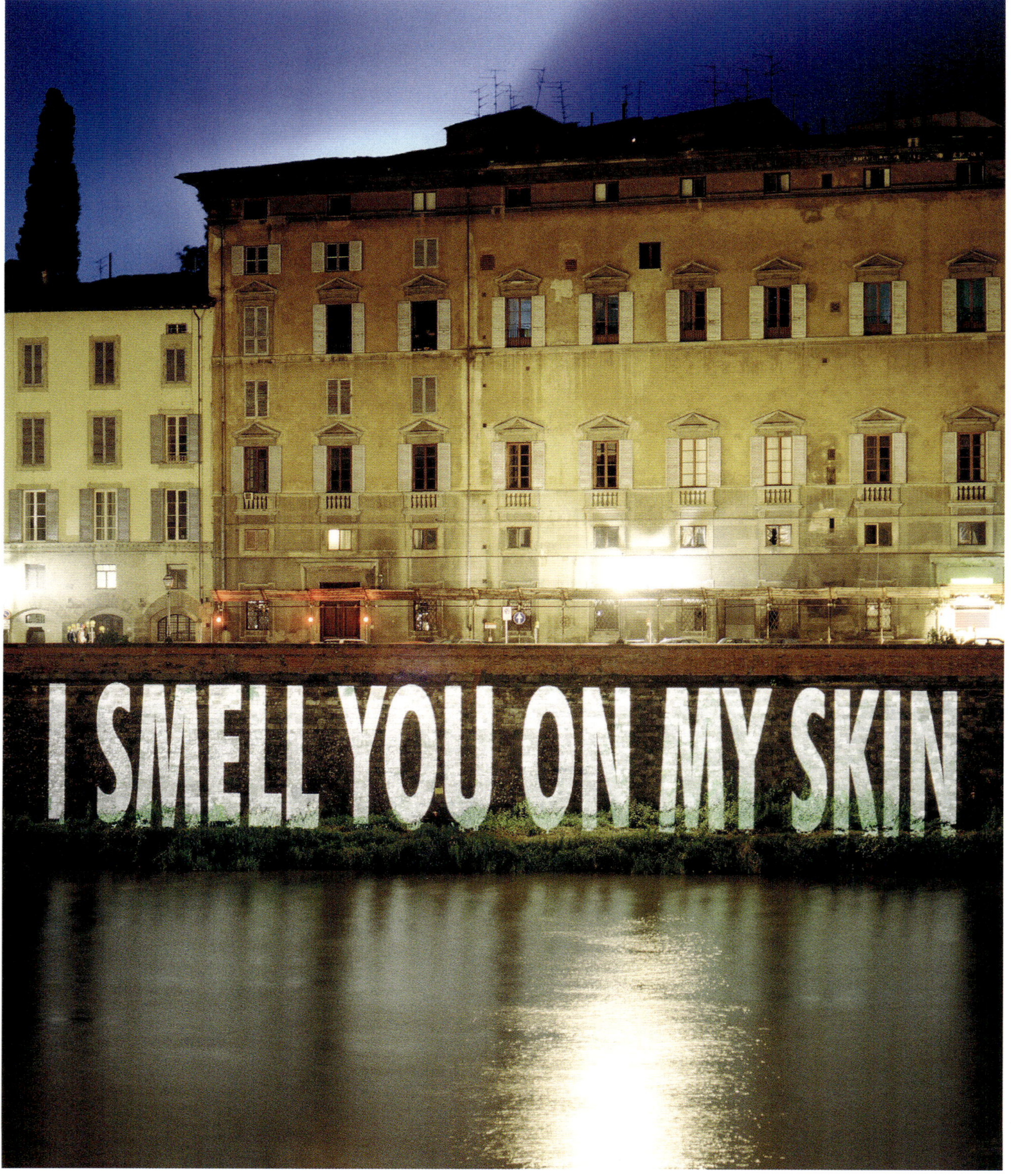
I SMELL YOU ON MY SKIN

It was again Zona art space, in April 1976, that presented *Zona Artists' Film*, a cycle curated by Andrea Granchi and Maurizio Nannucci, which showcased the works of Gordon Matta-Clark, Walter De Maria, Dan Graham, Vito Acconci, John Baldessari, and Bruce Nauman among others. And in September 1978, the Sarah Charlesworth exhibition *Second Reading (Lago Duchessa, 20 aprile 1978)*, part of the *Modern History (1977–1979)* series, opened there as well. The artist had photographed the front pages of all the newspapers of the world on the same day to show how one event could be afforded different amounts of space and visibility.[13] On display [7.1], as part of the same series, were the newspapers printed on April 21, 1978, with the news of Aldo Moro's kidnapping, one of the most tragic events in those terror-laden *Anni di Piombo* (Years of lead).

The 1970s in Florence were years of great vitality and openness toward the American art world. Proof of this new course was the celebration of Robert Rauschenberg—him again—in a major show at the Forte di Belvedere in the fall of 1976, with Leo Castelli and Ileana Sonnabend in attendance, more than two decades after his self-destructive gesture on the banks of the Arno.

The season was short-lived, however, and not until the second half of the 1990s would there be an occasional return of the most innovative American Visual Art, and mostly in events related to the world of fashion. In September 1996, as part of the first edition of the Biennale di Firenze, titled *Il Tempo e la Moda*, Jenny Holzer presents on the banks of the river her first xenon projection, with the toponymic title Arno. Words in capital letters projected on the embankments and the palazzi with which she explores sexual experience and the reasons for being naked or clothed. At the same time she created a line of perfumes which she called *I SMELL YOU ON MY SKIN*, a combination of alcohol, tobacco, starch, sweat, and sperm: "For every kind of love."[14]

In 1999, at the Teatro del Rondò di Bacco at Palazzo Pitti, thanks to the collaboration between Pitti Immagine and the Walker Art Center of Minneapolis, Matthew Barney's *Cremaster 2* [9.11] was screened in Europe for the first time. Attending the opening were the artist and Richard Flood, then-chief curator of the Walker Art Center: a collaboration between Florence and Minneapolis, more than twenty years before today's exhibition, under the sign of the new American avant-gardes.

Today's exhibition presents, for the first time ever in Italy, and extensively so, the collections of the Walker Art Center, one of the world's most important modern and contemporary art institutions. The uniqueness of the collections and the history of the Center are conveyed in the catalogue essay by Vincenzo de Bellis, who traces the connections between history and American art history, while the rich chronology curated by Ludovica Sebregondi clearly conveys the breadth of the historical horizon that this event refers to.

With *American Art 1961–2001*, Palazzo Strozzi once again puts modern art at the center of a broader cultural debate.

Focusing on these decades of artistic production in the United States, during forty years in which the United States was considered the undisputed world leader from the political, military, and economic standpoint, means looking back at the phenomena that have influenced and changed the entire world, from consumerism to lifestyle, from geopolitics to civil rights. A journey that begins with the hopes embodied by JFK's "new frontier"—an unlimited, moral, and imaginary frontier—and reaches, in Richard Prince's horse saddles or on his Harley-Davidsons, without ever really ending, a "West"

← The installation titled *Arno* by Jenny Holzer in Florence, 1996

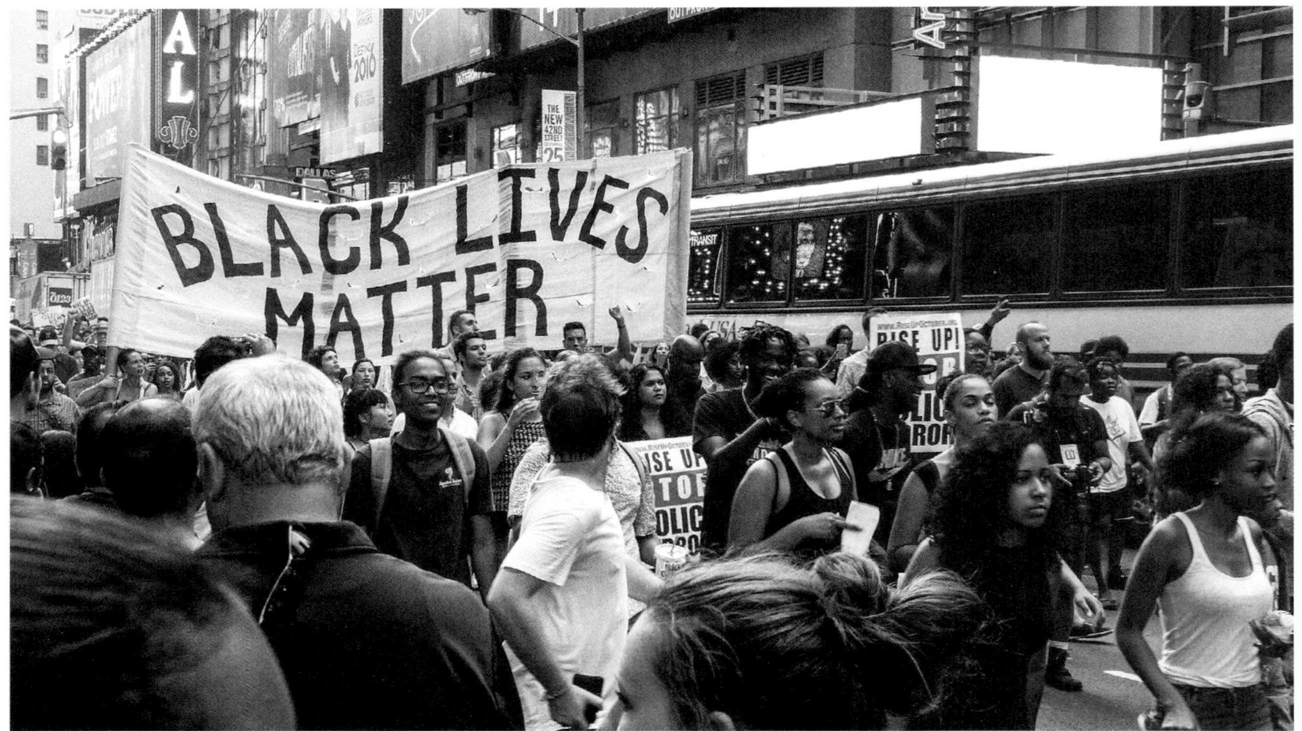
BLACK LIVES MATTER
RISE UP!

that evokes the epic story of a continent; from the Pop supermarket and Jackie's exhausted face estranged by Andy Warhol's colors, to Kara Walker's delicate yet violent silhouettes, projected against a background where voices that have been left out of the main story for too long can be heard at last.

The exhibition ends with the beginning of the new millennium, with the terrorist attack on the Twin Towers that changed the world, bringing into our lives the specter of global terrorism, preventive war, and a new phase of the *Pax Americana*. Two decades later, the Covid-19 pandemic has turned the planet upside down with unimagined speed and scope, precisely at a time when the United States has gradually been losing ground in its role as economic and political leader of the free world and the global economy. In light of the times we are living through, with all eyes on America as it begins its new democratic leadership while facing huge challenges both domestically and internationally, and with the new attempts at social renewal that have become more intense since the tragic death of George Floyd in Minneapolis, a reinterpretation of this trajectory is perhaps decidedly relevant today.

←    Black Lives Matter protest after the murder of George Floyd in Minneapolis, 2020


1    *Americani a Firenze. Sargent e gli impressionisti del Nuovo Mondo*, catalogue for the exhibition (Florence, Palazzo Strozzi, March 3–July 15, 2012), curated by Francesca Bardazzi and Carlo Sisi (Venice: Marsilio, 2012).

2    *La grande arte dei Guggenheim*, catalogue for the exhibition (Florence, Palazzo Strozzi March 19–July 24, 2016), curated by Luca Massimo Barbero (Venice: Marsilio, 2016).

3    See *La grande arte dei Guggenheim*, 182–183.

4    In Calvin Tomkins, *Off the Wall. A Portrait of Robert Rauschenberg* (New York: Picador, 2005), 12.

5    *La grande arte dei Guggenheim*, 115–125, 122–123.

6    [Carlo Volpe], "Vita culturale," in "Cronaca di Firenze", in *Il Nuovo Corriere* (March 20, 1953).

7    Tomkins, 73–74; Rossella Caruso, "Robert Rauschenberg alla Galleria L'Obelisco. Scatole e feticci personali," in *Irene Brin, Gaspero del Corso e la Galleria L'Obelisco*, curated by Vittoria Caterina Caratozzolo, Ilaria Schiaffini, and Claudio Zambianchi (Rome: Drago, 2018), 205–215, 213–214.

8    Maria Gloria Bicocchi, *art/tapes/22 tra firenze e santa teresa dietro le quinte dell'arte ('73–'87)* (Venice: Cavallino, 2003), 25.

9    Bicocchi, 37 and *sub verbo*.

10    Bicocchi, 38, 47.

11    See *Bill Viola. Rinascimento elettronico*, catalogue for the exhibition (Florence, Palazzo Strozzi March 10–July 23, 2017), curated by Arturo Galansino and Kira Perov (Florence: Giunti, 2017), 214–222.

12    https://www.ngv.vic.gov.au/ebooks/transmission/chapter/turning-the-television-on-itself-dara-birnbaum and Leonardo Bigazzi, "art/tapes/22: ricordi, riflessioni ed eredità. Conversazione con Maria Gloria Bicocchi," in *Arte a Firenze 1970–2015. Una città in prospettiva*, edited by Alessandra Acocella and Caterina Toschi (Macerata: Quodlibet, 2018), 121–131, and especially 123.

13    Caterina Toschi, "Lo spazio Zona e la scena internazionale degli artist-run space: l'orizzontalità nella gestione dell'arte e l'archiviazione delle effimero (1974–1985)," in *Arte a Firenze 1970-2015*, 39–62, and especially 53.

14    *Jenny Holzer* (London: Phaidon Press, 1998), 33.

VINCENZO DE BELLIS

# AMERICAN ART AT THE WALKER, 1961–2001

On January 20, 1961, President John Fitzgerald Kennedy took office at the White House, sworn in before the people of the United States and the world. Kennedy was the first president born in the twentieth century, and one who wanted to give his country a definitive change in direction. His inaugural address encouraged all Americans to be active citizens: "Ask not what your country can do for you; ask what you can do for your country."[1] Kennedy called on all nations of the world to come together to fight against what he described as the "common enemies of man: tyranny, poverty, disease, and war itself,"[2] continuing, "All this will not be finished in the first one hundred days. Nor will it be finished in the first one thousand days, nor in the life of this Administration, nor even perhaps in our lifetime on this planet. But let us begin."[3]

For many Americans, and also for young people around the world, President Kennedy would come to symbolize the spirit of hope for the nation and the world. When he was assassinated on November 22, 1963, it was a crushing blow, especially for a younger generation and for underrepresented communities. But history has shown us that his ideals of openness lingered on, contributing decisively to changes that ensued in politics, culture, and global society in the decades that followed.

Forty years after Kennedy's assassination, the world witnessed the events of September 11, 2001. It was a morning like many others, one of the last warm days before autumn winds start to blow. But the horrors that would unfold that day—as four coordinated suicide terrorist attacks were carried out against US civilian and military targets, including New York's World Trade Center—would change lives and the landscape of national security forever, causing the death of 2,977 people (including nineteen hijackers), with over 6,000 people injured. These pivotal events, forty years apart, belong to two different centuries and millennia, and bookend a period filled with what were until then unprecedented political, social, and cultural changes, which reverberated not only through American society at large, but through the art being made at the time.

With over eighty artworks by the major American artists from the 1960s to the first decade of the twenty-first century, *American Art 1961–2001* is an exhibition that attempts to tell the story of developments in art and American society that ensued over the course of those four decades. But acknowledging that no single exhibition can do this, we are here offering one possible version, as seen from the perspective of a singular American institution.

WHAT IS THE WALKER ART CENTER?
A mid-sized institution located in Minneapolis, Minnesota, the Walker Art Center is dedicated to presenting and preserving the art of our time. Its story, which begins with one individual, is ultimately one of connecting art and artists to a broad public. In 1874, the businessman Thomas Barlow (T. B.) Walker started an art collection comprising an eclectic group of works—ranging from Chinese jades to French and American landscape paintings— that became one of the most important collections in the Midwest. Just five years later, he decided to open the doors of his home to visitors who wished to view the collection. He named it the Walker Art Gallery, and the site became the first public gallery west of the Mississippi. By 1915, this fourteen-room museum would host a hundred thousand visitors a year, which prompted T. B. Walker to purchase a piece of land in 1916 in the part of the city known as Lowry Hill. Walker offered the site to the city of Minneapolis as a place where a public library and an art museum could be built, but after five years of futile negotiations, Walker decided to go it alone and build his museum. Construction work began in 1925 and ended in 1927, on the very site where it still stands today.

With the onset of the Great Depression, only three staff members remained. Walker's grandchildren Hudson Walker and Louise Walker McCannel helmed the museum from 1935 until 1939, when the Minnesota Arts Council offered a new model. The Council, which was funded by the Federal Art Project (FAP), by way of the program known as the Works Progress Administration (WPA), suggested turning T. B. Walker's personal museum of historical paintings into a model contemporary art center, a place destined to be a "venue for all the arts" that could house a distinct and varied art collection.

With this new mandate, the years 1939–1940 marked the birth of the Walker Art Center as we know it today. Daniel Defenbacher became the Walker's first director. To make its new cultural direction clear, the "Walker Art Gallery" was renamed the "Walker Art Center." As the economy improved, the FAP diminished its support, and in 1943 the involvement of the WPA came to an end.

The institution's mission was clear: to support the production of new art, and to preserve cultural artifacts deemed to be historically important. Over time, this made it possible to shape a collection that evolved well beyond the original vision of its founder.

The Walker distinguished itself from traditional museums, exhibiting contemporary art as early as 1940. And it further challenged artistic tradition with its first performance event, the Spring Dance Festival, which took place soon afterwards.

One of the key moments in the history of the Walker took place in 1961, the same year that Kennedy assumed the Presidency of the United States. The Walker's then-curator, Martin Friedman, was appointed as its Director. At just thirty-six, Friedman was one of the youngest museum directors in the United States, and under his leadership, the Walker became even more ambitious and contemporary. Recognizing the changing nature of at in the 1960s, where artists were making large-scale sculpture without pedestals, and introducing installation and media-based works, Friedman advocated for the creation of a new building that could accommodate expanding artistic practice. Inaugurated in 1971, and designed by Edward Larrabee Barnes, the

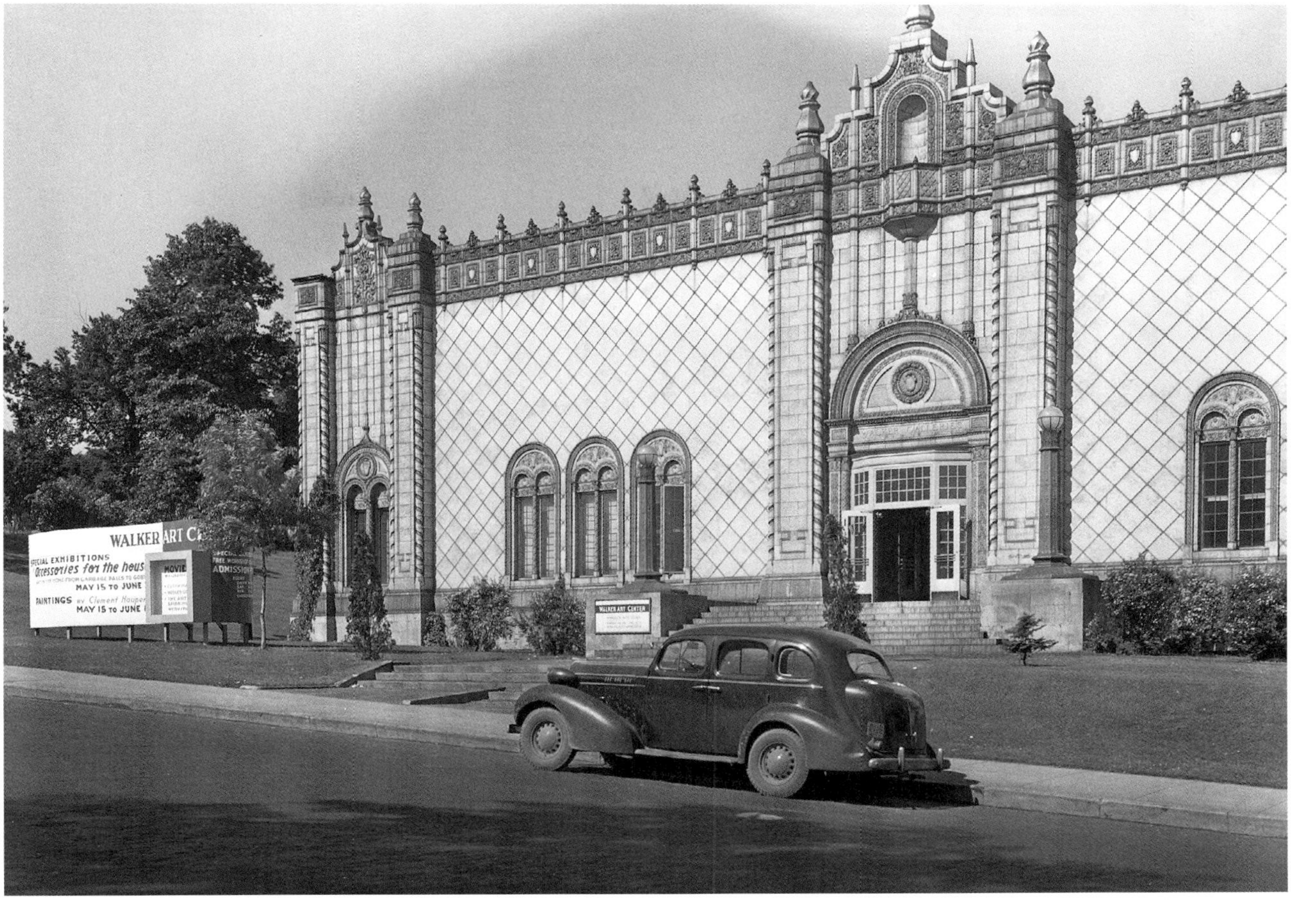

WALKER ART CENTER
SPECIAL EXHIBITIONS
Accessories for the house
MAY 15 TO JUNE
PAINTINGS by Clement Haupers
MAY 15 TO JUNE
MOVIE
ADMISSION
WALKER ART CENTER

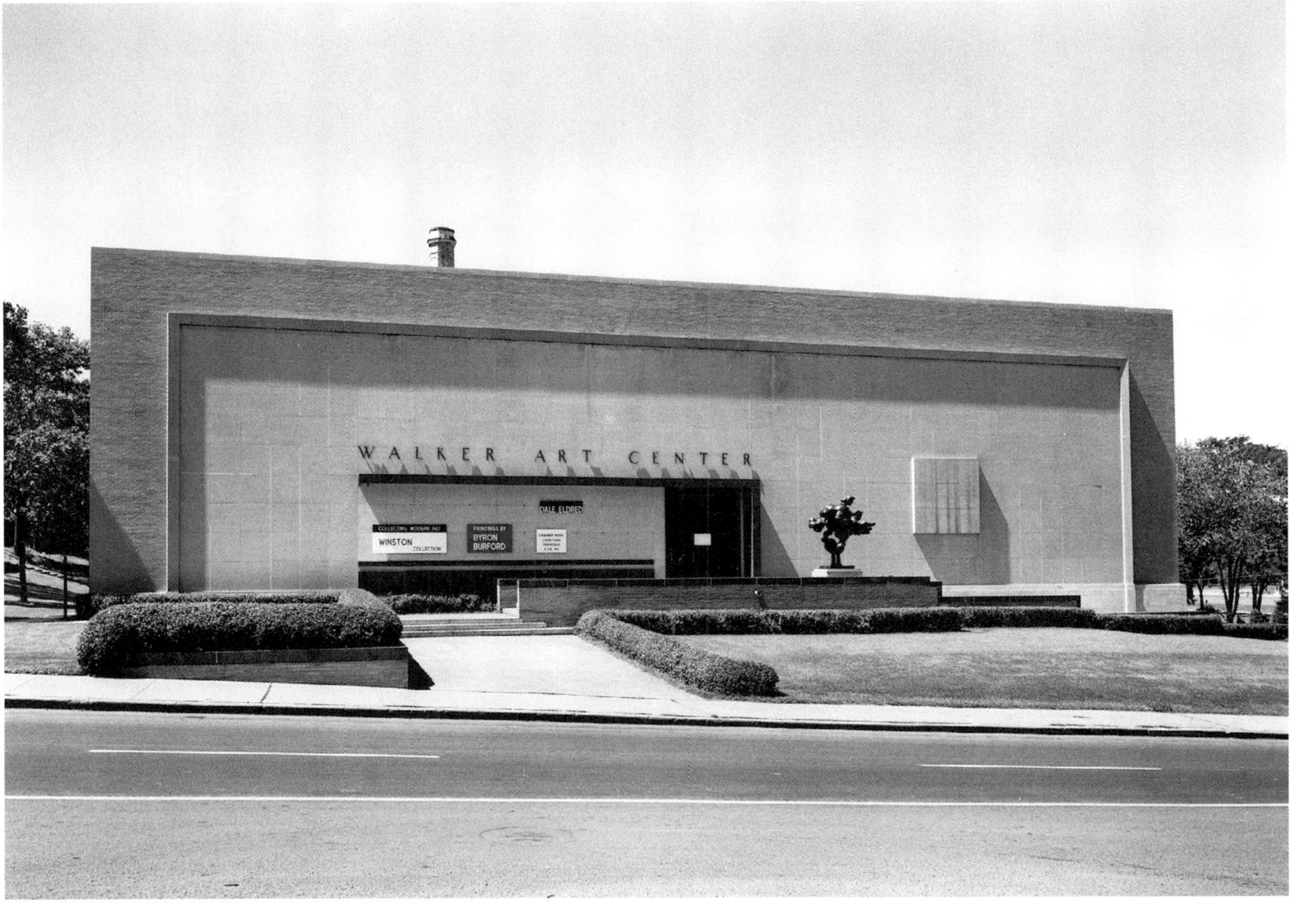

WALKER ART CENTER
DALE ELDRED
COLLECTING MODERN ART
WINSTON COLLECTION
PAINTINGS BY BYRON BURFORD

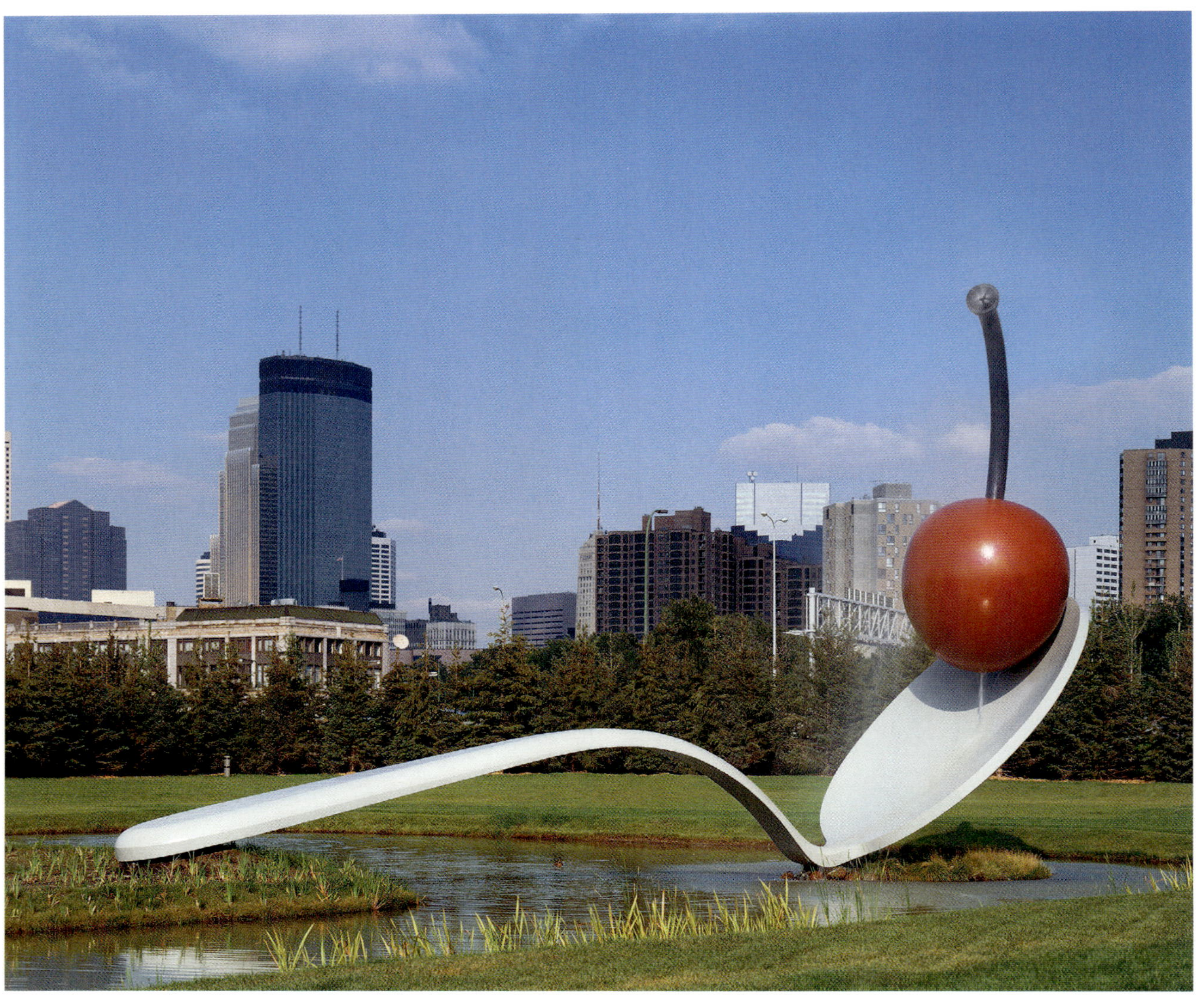

new Walker building was able to host increasingly impressive exhibitions, bringing it into the conversation with contemporary museums in the United States and abroad. The Walker collections grew apace at this time, reflecting the most important examples of developments in contemporary art. At the same time, the performing arts, film, and educational programs, which grew in proportion and achieved national importance, were among the art center's core activities. In 1988, the Walker and the Minneapolis Park and Recreation Board inaugurated the Minneapolis Sculpture Garden in an expansive park adjacent to the museum, which introduced new artists and brought broad audiences to the center.

In 1991, following Friedman's retirement after a thirty-year tenure, Kathy Halbreich became the Walker's fourth director. Under her leadership, the museum further deepened its international reputation, and its collections and exhibitions program became increasingly diverse. Halbreich oversaw an ambitious expansion of the museum that was completed in 2005 and designed by the architectural firm Herzog & de Meuron, which added a dedicated theater for the performing arts, new spaces for temporary exhibitions, and additional galleries for the collections.

In 2008, Olga Viso took charge of the museum, completing Halbreich's vision for an integrated campus both inside and outside the museum by culminating in a 2017 expansion and renovation of the Minneapolis Sculpture Garden, which included the addition of seventeen new outdoor works. Under Viso's guidance, the Walker acquired almost four thousand objects from the Merce Cunningham Dance Archive for its permanent collection, thus establishing a fundamental precedent in the acquisition of works representing the performing arts. The Walker is now known as a unique model of multidisciplinary artistic organization and as a national leader for its innovative approaches to the involvement of the public. The Walker's current director Mary Ceruti assumed her role in 2019.

THE 1960S, THE BEGINNINGS OF CHANGE

The exhibition *American Art 1961–2001* includes a selected group of works from the early 1960s to 2001 that chart aspects of the Walker's evolution as a collecting institution. Among these, works by such artists as Mark Rothko and Louise Nevelson represent the link between the formalism backed by the critic Clement Greenberg, one of the greatest champions of Abstract Expressionism, at the time considered a quintessentially American movement. Mark Rothko, one of mid-century America's most prominent artists, is included in the exhibition with an example of his best known paintings, made in sweeping fields of monochromatic tones that have now come to represent the artist's existential tragedy [1.3]. Another key work here is Nevelson's *Sky Cathedral Presence*, a sculpture made between 1951 and 1964 [1.4]. At the outset of her career, Nevelson mainly worked with painting and sculpture in the Cubist and Surrealist vein, but toward the late 1950s she began creating experimental assemblages made with wood and found objects. Both Rothko and Nevelson sought to create an intensive relationship with the viewer. Like Nevelson, Rothko held that the work must invite the viewer to a visual and emotional contemplation of an almost religious nature.

← Claes Oldenburg and Coosje van Bruggen, *Spoonbridge and Cherry*, 1985–88, Walker Art Center, Minneapolis Sculpture Garden

ABOVE AND BEYOND YOURSELF: MERCE CUNNINGHAM COLLABORATIONS WITH JOHN CAGE, ROBERT RAUSCHENBERG, AND JASPER JOHNS

Merce Cunningham revolutionized dance in the twentieth century, and today, ten years after his death, he continues to influence generations of artists, composers, and choreographers.

Cunningham's long relationship with the Walker Art Center had significant impact on the institution. In 1953, in the early days of their careers, Cunningham and the composer John Cage—both emerging artists—wrote to the then director of the center and offered to show their works there, but, as often happens in such cases, they were ignored. A decade later, the Woman's Club of Minneapolis Theatre, located across the street from the Walker, presented the city's first ever performance of Cunningham's work, with John Cage as musical director and Robert Rauschenberg as set designer.

Cunningham's first bona fide performance at the Walker was not until 1969, but from that point forward, the relationship would be rich and sustained— with over fifteen productions—that allowed for fruitful and unprecedented collaborations between a museum and an artist. This culminated in the posthumous acquisition of the more than four thousand scores, set designs, drawings, and costumes that now make up the Merce Cunningham Dance Company Archive, one of the Walker Art Center's most significant collections.

A key section of the exhibition emphasizes Cunningham not only as a choreographer, but as a trailblazing, interdisciplinary artist open to collaborations with other artists as a way to propel his own work forward. Cunningham's collaborations with Cage, Robert Rauschenberg, and Jasper Johns, elucidate one of the most successful models for what can be called multimedia art. Highlights from this part of the collection are stage props and other materials made to accompany Cunningham's choreographies, including Rauschenberg's scenography and costumes for *Minutiae* (1954–76) [2.2] and Johns's unique set—based on the works of Marcel Duchamp—for Cunningham's *Walkaround Time* (1968) [2.3].

From the outset of his career, Cunningham was interested in working with the artists, but his earliest efforts did not lead to the hoped-for results, as the decors were made by the artists *a posteriori* with respect to the dance, almost in response to it. With *Minutiae*, Cunningham tried a different approach, asking Rauschenberg, with whom he would continue to collaborate for over a decade, to intervene sculpturally with a set design before the choreography was completed. He gave no other indications except the need to create something around which the dancers could move. This process—to create the choreography independently from the projects of his collaborators for the decor and the music—became Cunningham's trademark and working method of choice. This allowed each element to maintain its artistic independence, while at the same time being part of a whole.

The same can be said for Cunningham's remarkable collaboration with Johns for *Walkaround Time* (1968). The stage elements created by Johns were inspired by Marcel Duchamp's seminal work *The Large Glass* (1915–23). Johns's design, in which he painted onto clear plastic, boxlike forms, is divided into seven sections that allowed viewers to gaze both *at* the objects and also *through* them to the viewers/performers on the other side, thereby imposing the temporal circularity under-scored in the title of the work itself.

THE AMERICAN DREAM: ANDY WARHOL AND AMERICAN POP ART
In American art, the era of the 1960s and early 1970s was marked by the emergence of Pop Art onto the international scene. The art and artists at its fore brought togeth-er various contemporary issues: the postwar "American dream" of consumerism, coupled with a critique of the growing predominance of media and mass culture in society. Pop advocated for an art for the masses, something to supplant the "high-brow" and tedious art of the intellectual elite.
This section of the exhibition showcases key examples of American Pop from the Walker's collection, including works by Andy Warhol, Roy Lichtenstein, Robert Indi-ana, and Claes Oldenburg.
In one of Warhol's most famous statements, in which the artist remarked on the re-petitiveness of his subjects, he noted, "The more you look at the same exact thing, the more the meaning goes away, and the better and emptier you feel."[4] Warhol's belief that reproducing images from popular culture could be a visual means for expressing detachment from emotions is evident in his painting *Sixteen Jackies* (1964) [3.10]. The painting is a composite of images of First Lady Jacqueline Kenne-dy—appropriated directly from magazine photographs—that Warhol silkscreened directly onto canvas panels. The work was made in response to the assassination of President John F. Kennedy in November 1963, an event for which mass media cover-age reached an unprecedented number of people.
The four images of Jacqueline Kennedy selected by Warhol were pulled from news photographs that appeared in issued of *Life* Magazine after the assassination, each are repeated four times. The images depict, from top to bottom: the First Lady step-ping off the plane upon arrival in Dallas; stunned during the swearing-in ceremony of Lyndon B. Johnson on board Air Force One after her husband's death; grieving at the nation's Capitol; and, lastly, smiling as she rode in the presidential motorcade through the streets of Dallas immediately before the assassination. *Sixteen Jack-ies* combines several important themes that engaged Warhol: his fascination with American icons and celebrities, his interest in the mass media and the dissemination of imagery, and his preoccupation with death.
Alongside Warhol, the most well-known practitioner during the 1960s Pop move-ment was Roy Lichtenstein [3.15]. Lichtenstein's characteristic use of enlarged Ben-Day dots from commercial printing, his embrace of the comic strip as subject matter, and his stylized renderings of works from art history have become such recognizable and signature images within mass culture that they have influenced the look of many consumer items themselves.
Robert Indiana, whose text-based works drew inspiration from the signs, symbols, and visual rhetoric of the images of trade brands [3.1], had a somewhat different stance than Lichtenstein's. Rather than embrace the consumerism seen in the work of his peers, Indiana's work is often openly critical of contemporary culture, espous-ing—as his famous LOVE sculptures would indicate—alternatives to war, and to America's political and social ills.

A highlight from the Pop era in the Walker's collection is Claes Oldenburg's *Shoe-string Potatoes Spilling from a Bag* (1966) [3.14]. This soft sculpture was originally conceived as part of a group of fast-food items—French fries, ketchup, and Coke—and like much of Warhol's work—was based on an ad the artist had seen in a 1965 issue of *Life* Magazine. Made with acrylic on canvas, this sculpture becomes a painting in three dimensions, evidence of Oldenburg's constant experimentation with the properties of scale when applied to common objects.

THE OTHER SIDE OF THE MOON: MINIMALISM AND PROCESS ART

Alongside Pop Art, the other trend that played an important role in the artistic changes that occurred in the 1960s was Minimalism, characterized by the removal of the artist's "hand" via a reliance on pure line, form, and color; a preference for industrial fabrication and materials; and a shift toward large scale work. The movement's principal exponents included Carl Andre, Dan Flavin, Donald Judd, Sol LeWitt, Fred Sandback, and Ann Truitt. Although not directly connected to Minimalism, Frank Stella also played an important role in its development. His *Black Paintings* [4.1], begun in 1958, feature parallel black bands of paint divided by thin white lines of exposed canvas. By using commercial house paint and applying paint with rollers, Stella's aim was to develop a new kind of painting, one that was impersonal and object-oriented. Unlike the gestural bravura of Abstract Expressionism, Minimalism's impact was direct and its process of realization was evident upon first sight.

Despite its apparent simplicity, however, Minimalism had great formal diversity, and its practitioners a wide range of approaches. In a text he wrote in 1965, considered by many to be the manifesto of Minimal art, Donald Judd spoke of a new genre of three-dimensional works, otherwise known as "specific objects," incorporating aspects of both painting and sculpture, while being neither one nor the other [4.7]. Judd often based his own works based modular sequences of elements similar in form, but different in color, material, quantity, and proportion: minimal sculptures (an attribute that the artist nonetheless rejected) produced to investigate and illustrate the properties of the actual space.

Judd did not embrace the work of all of his peers associated with Minimalism, however. He criticized the artist Dan Flavin, for example, for his focus on the phenomenological. In the summer of 1961, while working as a guard at New York's American Museum of Natural History, Flavin had started to make sketches for sculptures that incorporated electrical light fixtures. Later that year, he translated his sketches into assemblages he called "icons," which juxtaposed light onto monochromatic Masonite constructions. By 1963, he had removed the canvas altogether and began to work with his signature fluorescent tubes. Flavin's works were made with standard fluorescent lighting tubes, which, while rare now, were at the time available in any hardware store. In his work *Untitled (to dear, durable Sol from Stephen, Sonja, and Dan) two* (1966–69) [4.2], these luminous tubes are combined to create a square that creates an intervention into the gallery architecture, as it occupies a corner of a space with both light and form.

Fred Sandback took a similar approach to space in his work, but he used profoundly different means. Renouncing the weight of materials, he sculpted space with sim-

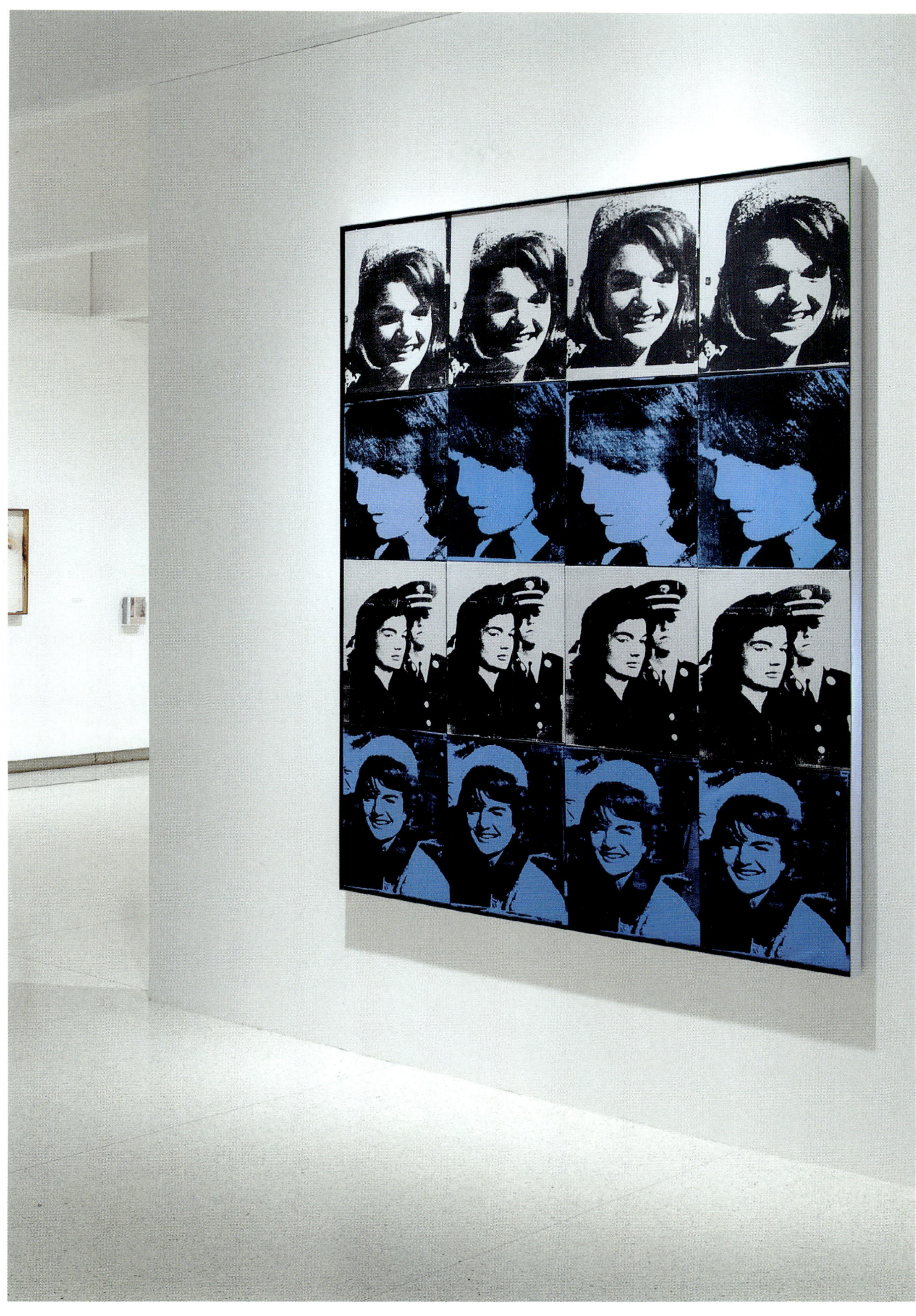

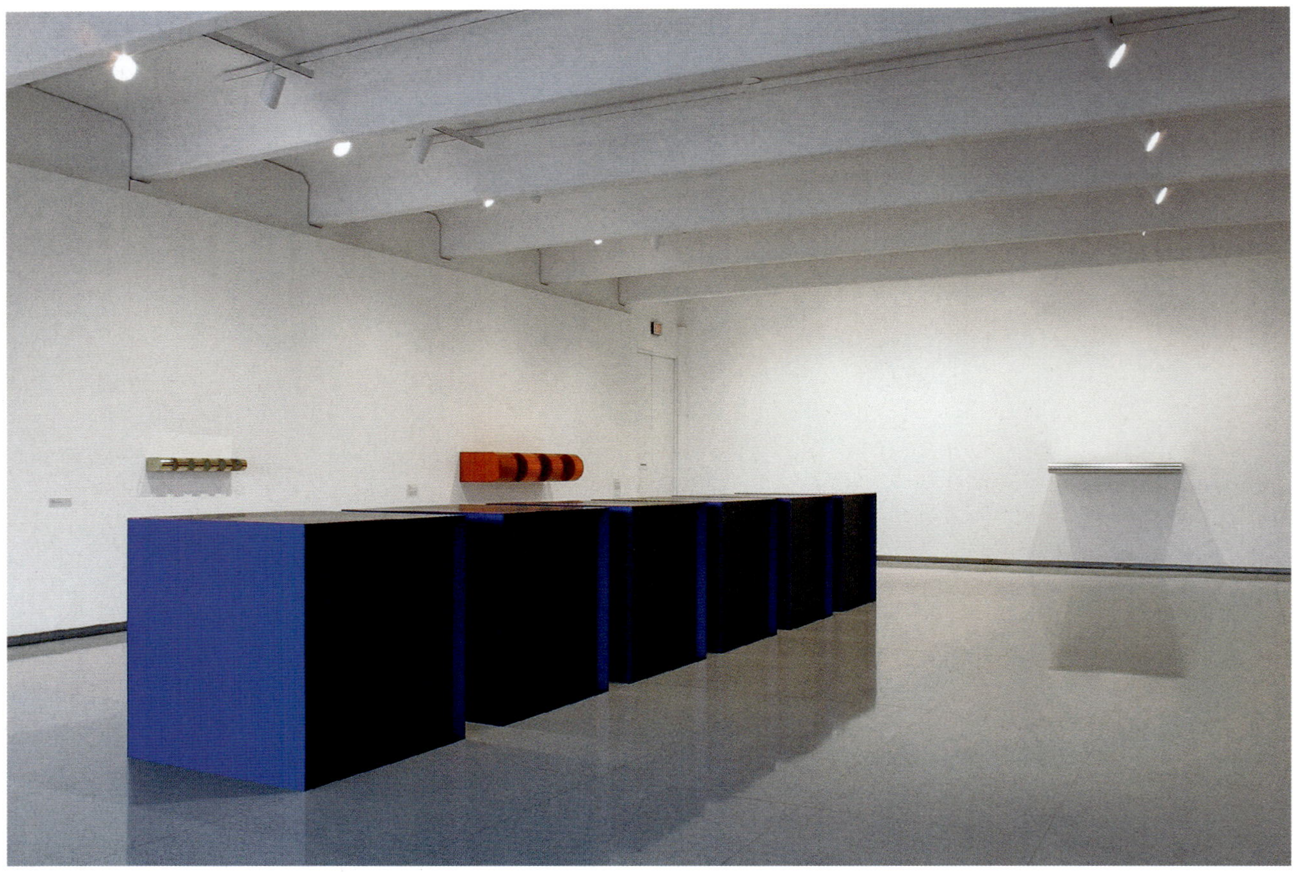

ple and economical lengths of acrylic yarn, which he stretched to create geometric figures. In doing so, Sandback created a merging of drawing and sculpture, as he formed nearly intangible planes and volumes [4.8] within the architectural space. The elemental geometry characterizing much of Minimalism, as seen in the work of these artists, also underlies the work of Sol LeWitt. LeWitt's was engaged in his work with mathematical theorems and sentiments of logic, but also with the power of linear language and simple poetry. Many of his works use the basic geometric shapes of the square and the cube as a point of departure, exploring possible configurations and combinations—open cubes and and closed cubes, for instance[4.3]. Often, his accumulations of repetitive geometries appear chaotic, while from other perspectives, they can assume perfect order.

The artists Ann Truitt and Agnes Martin were two female practitioners whose work also gained attention at this time, despite art world recognition being directed almost exclusively toward men. Unlike many of her male peers, who eschewed hand-painted surfaces in favor of more industrial methods, Truitt adhered to traditional in-studio production, painting and smoothing her sculptures by hand [4.9]. Although she is often associated with Minimalism, Agnes Martin never wanted her work to be defined as such, as she was interest in expressing ideas of the sublime through abstract means. Her square, often ethereal canvases are characterized by their monochrome surfaces or bands of subtle hues, against which she overlaid grids of delicate graphite lines that emanate from a central axis, creating a sense of order within which to experience her subtle meditations [4.10].

An artist who embraced the tenets of Minimalism while pushing it into new territory was Robert Morris. Until 1966, Morris produced canonic works of minimal art but, beginning the following year, he shifted to a style that was first called Postminimalism and later became known as Process Art or Anti-Form. Unlike the prescribed and repetitive forms often present in Minimalism, Morris began making works that embraced the principles of permutation and chance, allowing the process to be determined by the physical and mechanical properties of the material itself. Morris experimented with many materials, but is best known for his use of felt, such as in the emblematic work showcased in the exhibition, which assumes its draped form from the weight of the material as it hangs from two fixed points[4.6]. Artist Richard Serra followed a similar line of inquiry in his work, compiling in 1967 a list of verbs that might serve as directives for making sculpture: to roll, to crease, to fold, to store, to bend, to curve, to shave, to tear, to chip, to bond, to cut, to drop, and so on. He later subjected various flexible materials such as lead, latex, and vulcanized rubber to these same verbal actions, examining the results to see which of them had proven to be feasible [4.5].

BRUCE NAUMAN: THE ARTISTS' ARTIST
While Pop Art, Minimalism, Process Art, and Conceptual art were moving forward into the early 1970s, Bruce Nauman was emerging, becoming known as an artist able to nod to various movements and "isms," without allowing himself to align with any of them. Although he has spent much of his artistic career working away from art world centers, Nauman is nonetheless one of the most influential figures of the

← Exhibition, *The Essential Donald Judd*, Walker Art Center, 2001 past five decades, with an expansive practice that ranges from sculpture to photography to video. Nauman has had a long relationship with the Walker Art Center, which devoted a major survey exhibition to the artist under the tenure of director Kathy Halbreich, followed by a sequence of important acquisitions. Featured in the current exhibition is *Art Make-Up* (1967–68), one of Nauman's seminal video works in which the artist transforms himself for the camera with variously-colored stage make-up, a work that shows both his engagement with the body as subject, and his deep affinity for avant-garde performance [5.1].

THE GENERATION OF IMAGES
In 1977, the art critic Douglas Crimp (1944–2019) curated an exhibition at Artists Space, which was then a new venue in New York that would eventually become one the most influential alternative spaces in the city. The exhibition, simply titled *Pictures*, presented a roster of artists whose work examined the relationship between art, mass media, and society generated a shockwave in the world of American and international art. Now referred to as the Pictures Generation, the artists from that groundbreaking show—which included Sherrie Levine, Jack Goldstein, Philip Smith, Troy Brauntuch, and Robert Longo —had grown up in the 1960s during a decade when art and society were undergoing radical change, and the country was experiencing a concurrent rise in the reach of mass media outlets including television, cinema, newspapers, and magazines. As the tumult of the 1960s—from the struggle for social justice within the civil rights movement to the ongoing atrocities of the Vietnam War—continued into the 1970s, the everyday lives of Americans had become saturated with media images. Crimp followed the *Pictures* exhibition with a 1979 essay written in *October*, the journal of art criticism, in which he maintained that these artists were focused on "*re*-presentation, not representation," a distinction that foregrounded the appropriation of found images by these artists, who were then presenting them in a new context, encouraging viewers to reflect on other possible meanings.
In his essay, Crimp discussed the work of Cindy Sherman, an emerging artist at the time who was in the midst of her *Untitled Film Stills* series, in which the artist photographed herself in a range of poses taken from the characters in films of her own invention, highlighting stereotyped women's roles in 1950s and 1960s movies, from the heroine to the lonely housewife[7.3]. In his works from the series *Untitled (Cowboy)* [7.5–7.7], artist Richard Prince borrows an ad for Marlboro cigarettes and removes the logos and brand name, thus taking the image back to its photographic form, and inviting the viewer to contemplate the network of meanings associated with the image of the cowboy.
As Prince strips the advertisement of its commercial logos, he isolates an image with a generally recognizable association within American culture. A similar strategy used by artist Sarah Charlesworth can be seen in the series *The Modern History* [7.1]. Made between 1977 and 1979, Charlesworth worked with a series of newspapers—published on the same day—from around the world, removing all text on the front page except for the masthead. The remaining images thus become the only means by which the viewer is cued to what is happening in the world.

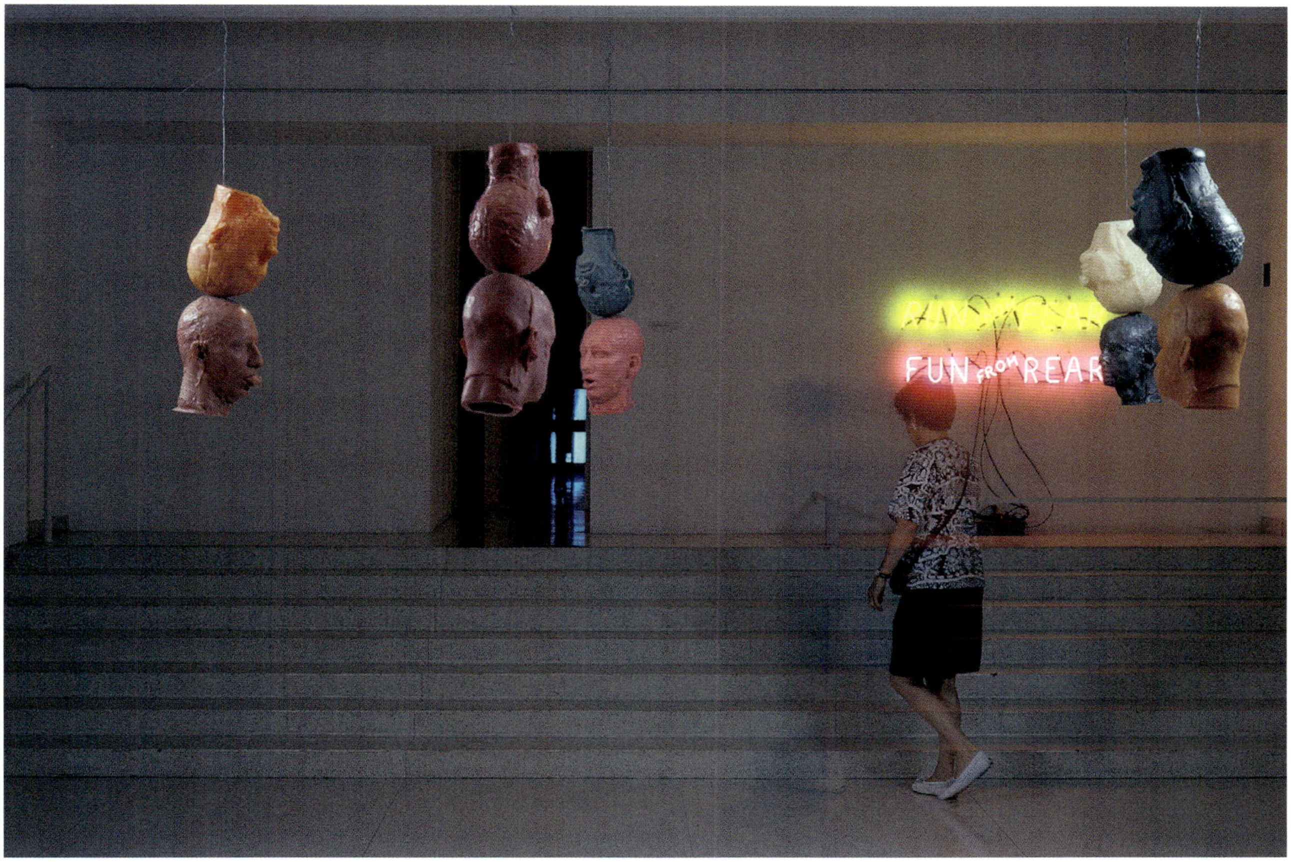

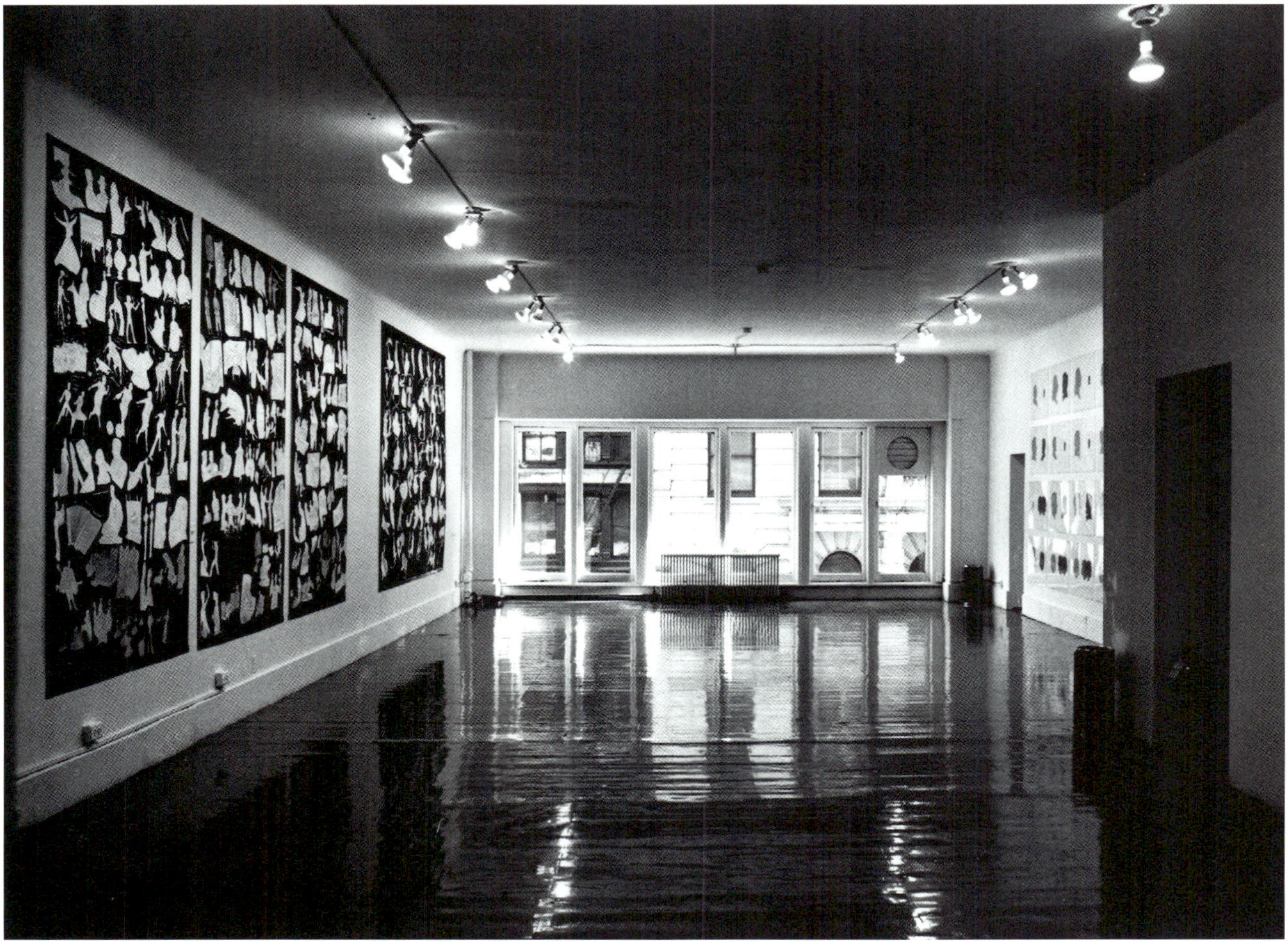

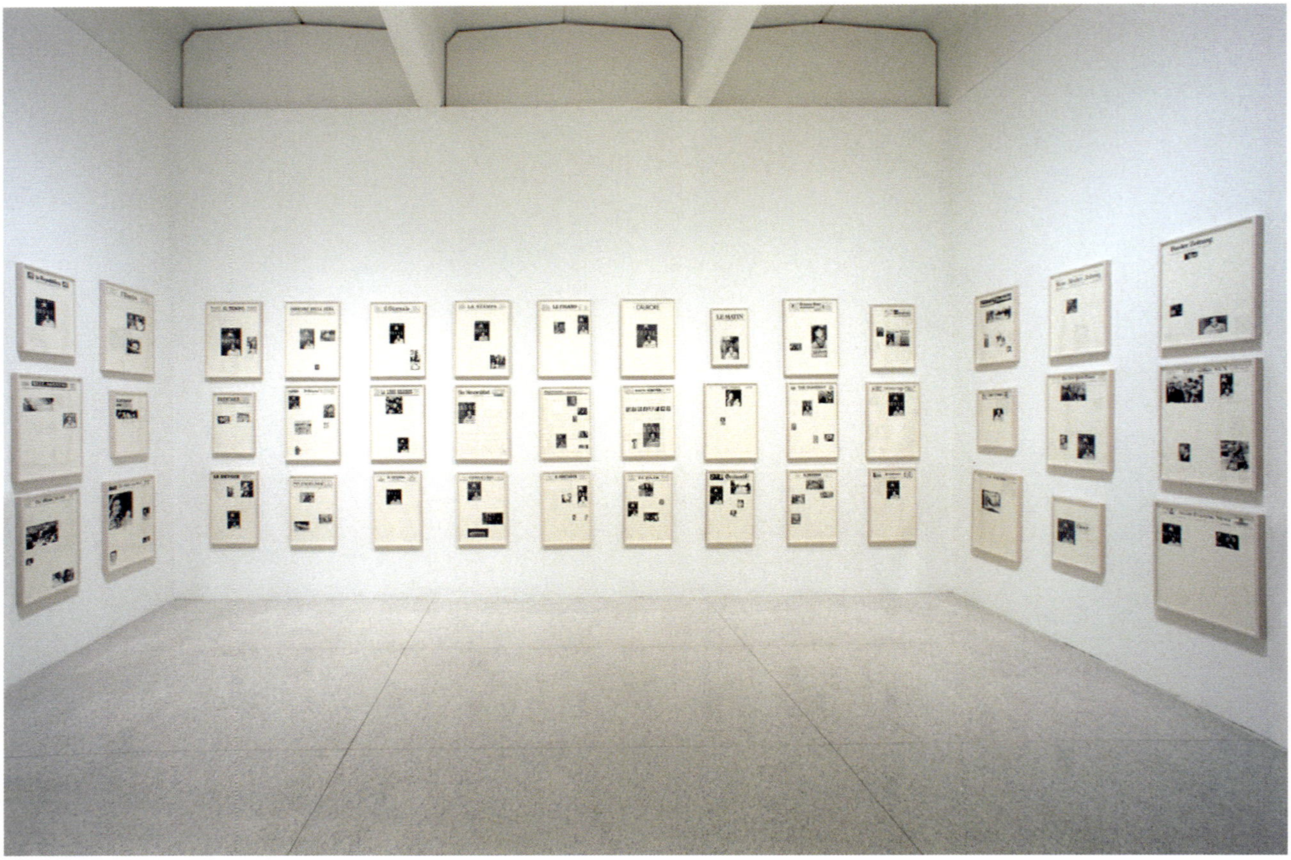

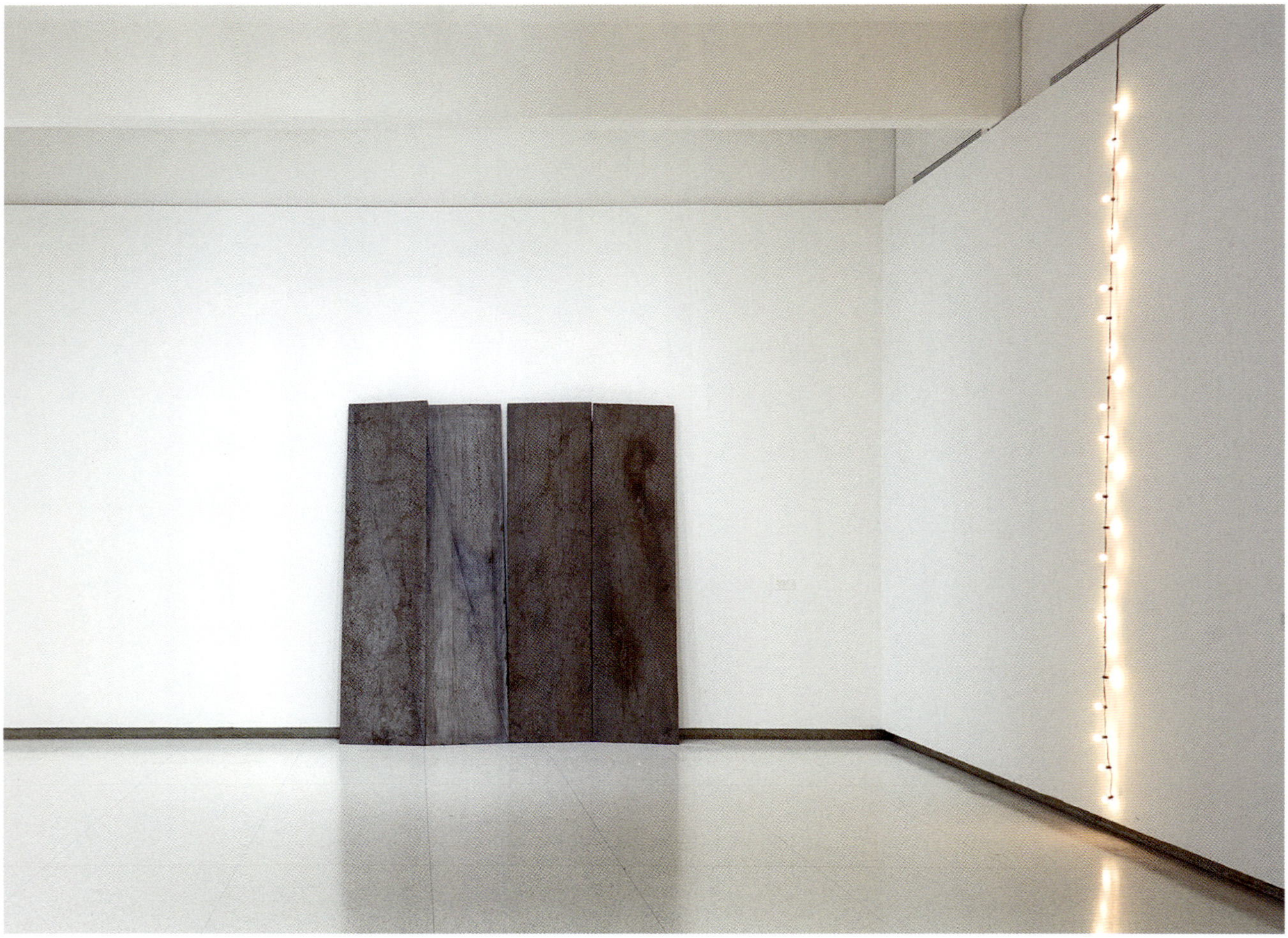

The use of text as imagery would also become the preferred means of communication of two other artists from the this generation, Barbara Kruger and Jenny Holzer. For Kruger, who first trained and worked as a graphic designer, the relationship between text and image was still crucial. Her best-known works are built on a black-and-white photograph with bold statements emblazoned in red across the surface of the image. Holzer, by contrast, isolates text from any association with imagery so that it remains the sole protagonist of her work, which can assume different forms and meanings depending on the context, which is often in public space: her works have appeared on posters and t-shirts; as LED signs; on stadium scoreboards; and on the screens of Times Square in New York.

ART AND THE AIDS CRISIS

Before the Covid-19 pandemic, perhaps no other event in recent US history impacted art and artists as much as did HIV/AIDS (human immunodeficiency virus infection and acquired immunodeficiency syndrome), when the virus became known in the 1980s. During a time when the country's administration under President Ronald Reagan would not acknowledge this epidemic that was having a devastating effect on the gay community, and a society still not discussing homosexuality openly, some in the artistic communities decimated by the disease responded with the production of protest art and activism, while other artists addressed it from a more personal perspective.

The latter approach was seen in the work of Robert Gober, who infused his works with language and imagery rooted in memory and the subconscious to express the horror, fear, and pain that accompanied coming of age as a gay man in New York during the AIDS crisis [8.4]. Felix Gonzalez-Torres's work, on the other hand, took an aesthetic approach more rooted in Minimalism, but this sparseness was a container for highly-charged emotional and melancholy content. His works used metaphor as a means by which to explore the various phases of the love relationship, from the initial discovery of the other, to the happy moments spent together, the progression of the disease, and untimely death.

One of Gonzalez-Torres's most iconic and delicate works is *"Untitled" (Last Light)*, made in 1993 [8.5]. Using a strand of lightbulbs, a fragile and temporary instrument, Gonzalez-Torres imbues this found object with deeper meaning, selecting lightbulbs as a material in remembrance of his long-time partner, who died of AIDS.

The fusion between life, personal experience, and artistic output is central to the work of Robert Mapplethorpe. Well-known for his black-and-white photographs depicting celebrities, male and female nudes, self-portraits, and still lifes, Mapplethorpe's work was at the core of the political debates between conservatives and liberals in the 1980s known as the "Culture Wars" due to the overtly homosexual nature of some of his works. [8.1–8.2] The power of Mapplethorpe's imagery often comes from his juxtaposition of explicit yet honest content with the formal elegance of his black-and-white photography; together these allowed the medium to become used in a new way, as an agent that could explores the human condition and human rights more broadly, and assert a politics of representation.

←  Installation of *April 21, 1978 from Modern History* (1978), Sarah Charlesworth, Walker Art Center, 2003

↙  Installation of *"Untitled" (Last Light)* (1993), Felix Gonzalez-Torres, Walker Art Center, 2017

IDENTITY POLITICS AND THE ART WORLD

Just as themes of the 1980s were foreshadowed by Crimp's *Pictures* exhibition, the beginning of the 1990s was marked by a bellwether presentation entitled *The Decade Show: Frameworks of Identity in the 1980s*, organized in New York by the New Museum of Contemporary Art, with the Studio Museum of Harlem and the Museum of Contemporary Hispanic Art in 1990. The exhibition, which showcased over two hundred works by ninety-four artists from diverse backgrounds, was based on the premise that the perspectives of historically marginalized people can have a major political impact. This exhibition was followed by the controversial 1993 Whitney Biennial—curated by Thelma Golden, John G. Hanhardt, Lisa Phillips, and Elisabeth Sussman—a groundbreaking exhibition in which white male artists were in the minority. Many of the featured works addressed key questions regarding gender identity and pressing issues facing the US, including racism, the AIDS crisis, women's rights, and economic inequality. Though its critical reception was mixed, this Biennial is now seen as a landmark in museum practice, and a turning point in identity politics. It helped to pave the way for an entire generation of artists exploring topics of sex, identity, race, culture, history, and memory in their work.

This exhibition from the Walker's collection features a group of artists, including Lorna Simpson, Jimmie Durham, and Glenn Ligon, who were included in the Biennial, alongside artists also emerging at the time. Lorna Simpson's 1994 work *Wigs (Portfolio)* [9.3], which presents images of an array of hairpieces printed on panels of felt, questions perceptions of sexuality, gender, and race as they relate to notions of beauty and disguise. This section of the exhibition includes the work of Jimmie Durham [9.1], whose work was also showcased in a large room at the 1993 Whitney Biennial, and Hock E Aye Vi/Edgar Heap of Birds. Both artists are members of Native American tribes, and took part together in projects and exhibitions in the early years of their careers. In 1990, Heap of Birds participated in a major project with the Walker Art Center. Entitled *Building Minnesota* [9.2a–9.2c], the work references the dark and tragic events of December, 1862, in which 38 Dakota men were hanged in Mankato, Minnesota at the order of President Abraham Lincoln, the largest one-day mass execution in the nation's history. Heap of Birds created an installation of public art comprised of 38 text-based signs installed along the Mississippi River, which runs through the city of Minneapolis, each sign memorializing an individual whose life was lost.

AT THE THRESHOLD OF A NEW MILLENNIUM

*Matthew Barney and* The Cremaster Cycle

While the 1990s marked a decade of social awareness following the Reagan-era hedonism of the 1980s, the decade also was a time of anticipation for the new millennium. During those years, many new figures came on the American artistic scene. Two emerging figures of this moment whose unique approaches to representation were noteworthy (and collected in depth by the Walker) are Matthew Barney, who had been invited to the 1993 Whitney Biennial at the age of twenty-six, and Kara Walker, who gained attention beginning in the late 1990s.

Barney's ambitious works are simultaneously engaged with performance art, the body as subject, and the narrative power of the moving image. Featured in the ex-

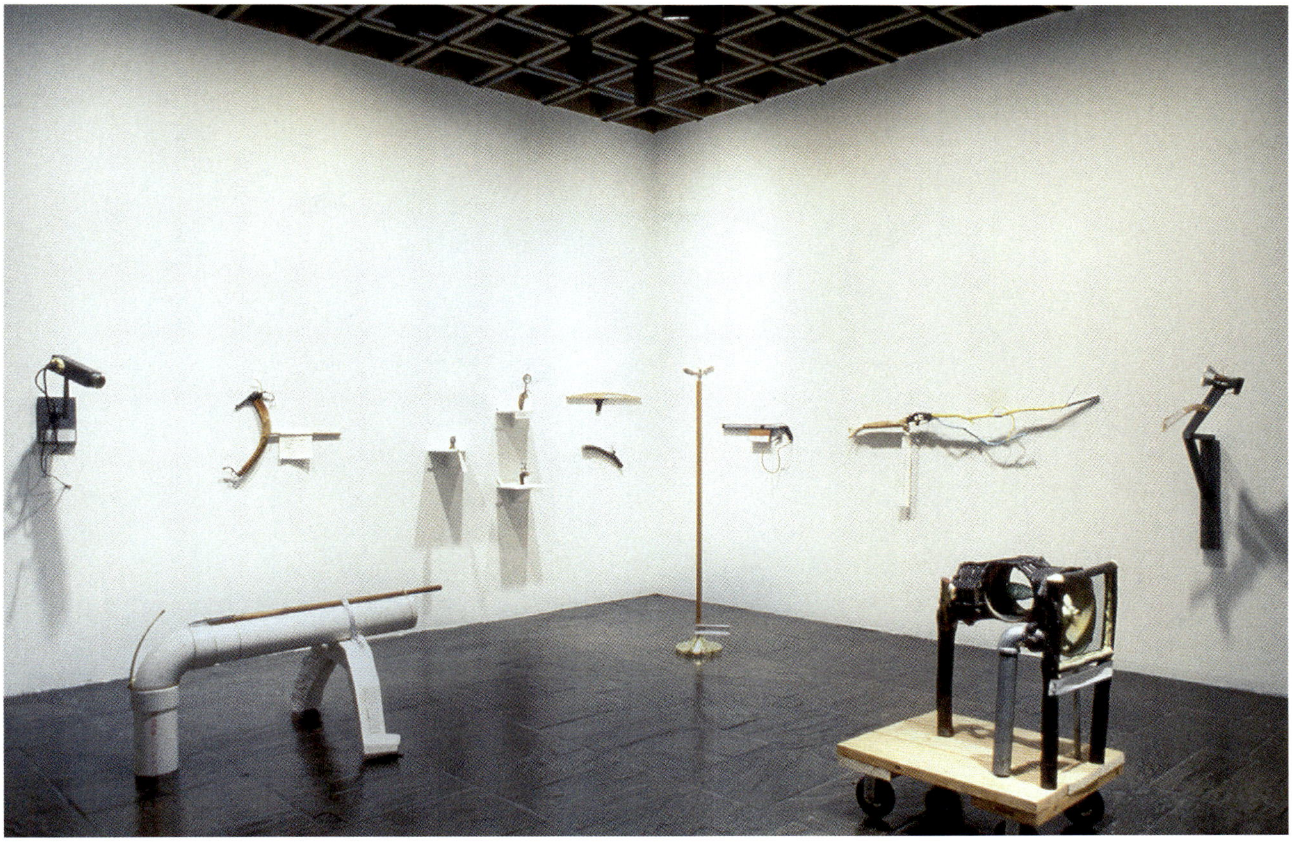

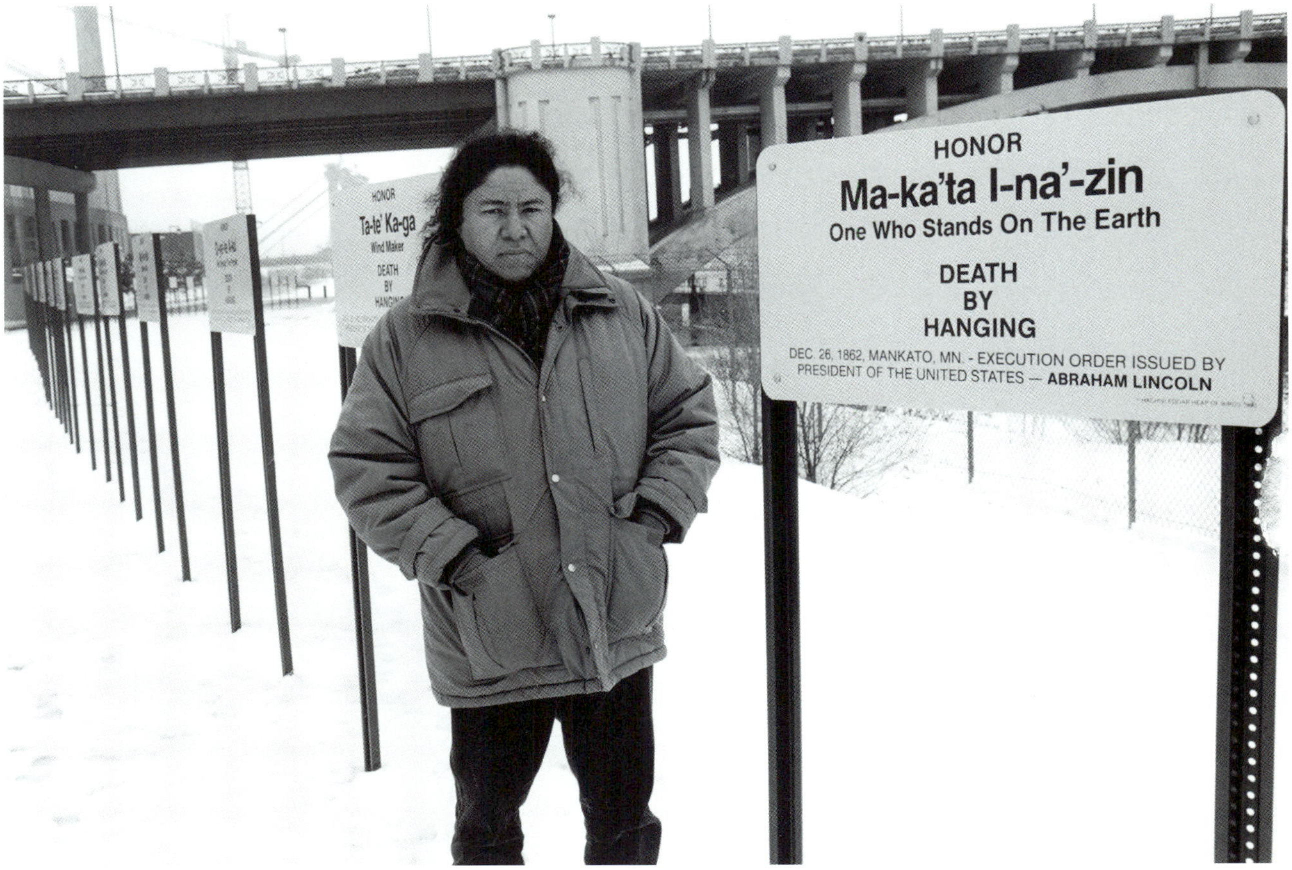

HONOR
Ma-ka'ta I-na'-zin
One Who Stands On The Earth

DEATH
BY
HANGING

DEC. 26, 1862, MANKATO, MN. - EXECUTION ORDER ISSUED BY
PRESIDENT OF THE UNITED STATES — ABRAHAM LINCOLN
HONOR
Ta-te' Ka-ga
Wind Maker

DEATH
BY
HANGING

→  Kara Walker at Walker
Art Center, 2007

hibition is *The Cremaster Cycle* (1994–2002) [9.11] an epic series of works that occupied the artist over the course of eight years, and resulted in five feature films accompanied by photographs, sculptures, and multi-element installations. The series is rife with thematic threads, including the biological process of sexual maturity as a metaphor for creation and artistic production. It is an understatement to say that all five episodes are visually extravagant, perhaps even baroque in their many layers. The films are feature length, which drew attention upon their release, as feature films had not had major presence in contemporary art to this point. They also eschew chronological order (*Cremaster 4* is the first in the cycle, followed by *Cremaster 1*, and then by *5*, *2* and *3*). Barney's explosive combination of history, autobiography, and mythology in the cycle delves into an intensely private world where symbols and metaphor are interconnected within a dreamlike visual experience.

*Kara Walker and the underbelly of history*
Another artist working with narrative at the turn of the millennium whose influence on contemporary art continues to be profound is Kara Walker. Walker, who is Black, gained early attention for her unflinching explorations of US history and the painful legacy of slavery, confronting issues of physical and sexual violence; white supremacy and oppression; and racial stereotypes that have been experienced by African American people for centuries.
Walker's career has had a fast ascent, beginning with her debut at the age of just twenty-five in a group show at the Drawing Center in New York, where she showed an installation of startling vignettes across a more than 22-foot-long wall. The work, entitled *Gone: An Historical Romance of a Civil War as It Occurred b'tween the Dusky Thighs of One Young Negress and Her Heart* (1994) was explosive for its brutal honesty and frank imagery slyly emerging from her use of a cut paper silhouette technique that had been highly popular in the US from the mid-eighteenth to the mid-nineteenth century.
In 1997, the same year the Walker Art Center included her work in her first museum exhibition, Walker became one of the youngest artists ever to receive a MacArthur Fellowship; in 2002, she represented the United States at the Bienal de São Paulo; and in 2012 she was elected to the American Academy of Arts and Letters. The Walker Art Center began collecting her work from the start, and now has deep and important holdings. In 2007, the Walker mounted a full retrospective of the artist's work entitled *Kara Walker: My Complement, My Enemy, My Oppressor, My Love* (2007), which traveled to the ARC/Musée d'art moderne de la ville de Paris, the Whitney Museum of American Art in New York, and the Hammer Museum in Los Angeles.
Within the museum's collection the artist's seminal work *Do You Like Creme in Your Coffee and Chocolate in Your Milk?* (1997) [9.12], which consists of sixty-six pages of drawings and texts the artist created as a response to criticism she had received from some other artists of color, who felt that her works reinforced cultural stereotypes, and that she was therefore not worthy of such recognition. In the silhouette work entitled *Cut* (1998) [9.13], Walker presents a female figure who at first seems to be dancing exuberantly, until we realize that her wrists are severed, blood spurting from them in plume-like gestures. Another important work in the exhibition is *Testimony: Narrative of a Negress Burdened by Good Intentions* (2004) [9.14], Walker's

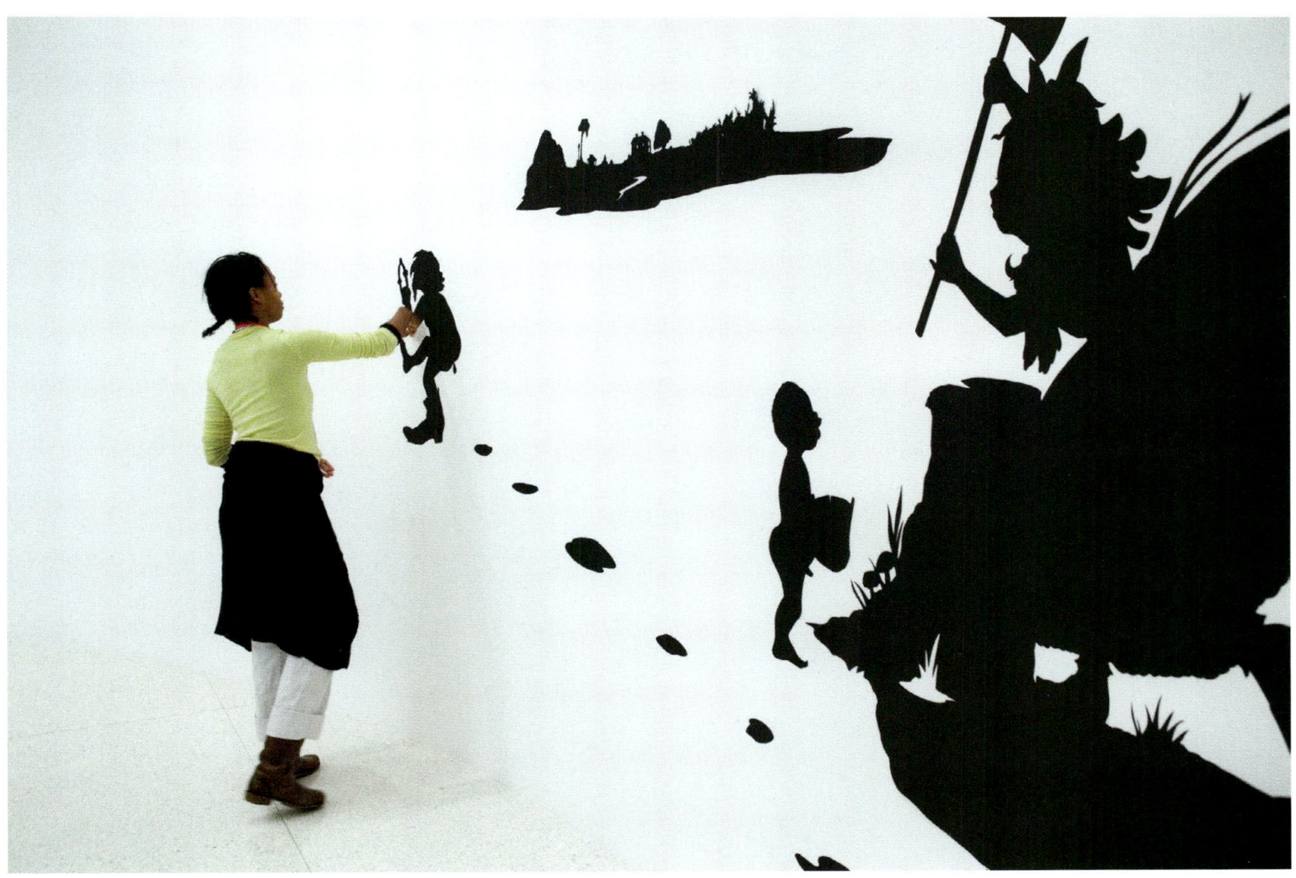

first moving image work, in which she uses the stylistic techniques of early silent films to tell a story of masters and slaves in the American South.

THE WEST: THIS COULD BE HEAVEN OR THIS COULD BE HELL
While New York remains a major artistic center in the US, beginning in the 1950s, other regions across the country began to assert themselves as viable artistic hubs. In particular, the California cities of Los Angeles and San Francisco became increasingly relevant at mid-century, in large part because of the growth of major cultural institutions, along with the rise of prominent art schools, which attracted prestigious faculty and talented students, becoming an important part of the arts ecosystem. After having been at the heart of the counterculture from the Beat Generation to the Summer of Love, California was attractive to many artists as a base. Los Angeles was famous worldwide for its dominance in the film and porn industries, its beach culture, and an important center for the rise of hip-hop.
In the years between the 1970s and 1990s, California became a center for a new wave of consciousness, with underrepresented minority and LGBTQ communities gaining increasing visibility and major events changing the social and political landscape, including the police brutality against the African American taxi driver Rodney King that sparked the Los Angeles riots of 1992.
Within this environment, two significant figures featured in the exhibition—Mike Kelley [10.3] and Paul McCarthy [10.2]—gained attention on the West Coast. Though born nearly a decade apart, both artists became known for complex and disturbing works that often criticize the constant reinforcement of power structures by the mass media, political entities, and educational institutions. In *Documents* (1995–99), Paul McCarthy photographed amusement parks and architectural elements, juxtaposing them with Nazi-era city plans and Nazi memorabilia actively collected but often hidden from public view. Using a very different visual language, and yet addressing similarly critic to oppression and violence, Mike Kelley's *Four Part Butter-Scene N'Ganga* features four galvanized washtubs filled with fake fruit, accompanied by a soundtrack gleaned from Bertolucci's sexually violent film *Last Tango in Paris*.
The impulse to surface issues of inequality and critique power structures is prevalent in the work of many artists in the Walker collection working since the 1990s, including Gary Simmons, who focuses on the stereotypes in popular American culture to explore issues of race, politics, and memory. His 1991 work *Us & Them* [10.1], a simple pair of embroidered bathrobes, is laden with cultural references, and speaks to the differences experienced between racial and social groups in the US. The work of Catherine Opie, one of the most influential photographers to emerge from Los Angeles in the 1990s, explores the landscape of America through the perspective of gender and class. Her photographs—which are often made in series or typologies, have portrayed Los Angeles freeways, same-sex couples in domestic environments, mini-malls and gated homes of Southern California, surfers, and other topics—each series of images exploring various notions of community [10.4–10.5].
Mark Bradford is another artist who explores community, gathering materials from the city for use in his large-scale works on canvas and in sculptural form. The artist uses wastepaper and debris produced by the city of Los Angeles: old newspapers, pictures,

flyers, receipts, and other cast-off items [10.6]. The materials he chooses can be seen as fragments of the life of a certain place at a specific time, which Bradford then combines to create large pictorial compositions hovering somewhere between the figurative and the abstract, in which the city enters the work and vice versa.

The work by Bradford, a strong voice in American art today, is emblematic of the change that is underway in American society. His work closes this exhibition and, on the other hand, represents a chapter that is still to be written in American art. *American Art 1961–2001* provides an opportunity for audiences to reexamine some key figures in art of the United States during a period of enormous change, as charted through the collection of one institution. The exhibition tells the story of a museum, its ideas, its successes, its weaknesses, its failures—all the result of the mission to unwaveringly support art, artists, and their visions.

Despite the limits of space that every exhibition must face, the exhibition aims to elucidate some of the themes, ideas, and passions that encouraged American artists to work against established conventions, whether inherent to the art system or related to political and social contexts. It is fitting that this exhibition is now being presented to an Italian public with a selection of works that appear to be more relevant now than ever.

1    Transcript of President John F. Kennedy's Inaugural Address (1961), https://www.ourdocuments.gov/doc.php?flash=-false&doc=91&page=transcrip.

2    *Ibid.*

3    *Ibid.*

4    Jason Kass, Beth Harland, and Nick Donnelly, "Warholian Repetition and the Viewer's Affective Response to Artworks from His *Death and Disaster* Series," in *Leonardo* 51, 2, 2018: 138–142: https://www.mitpressjournals.org/doi/pdf/10.1162/LEON_a_01191.

# CHANGES

1.

**JOSEPH CORNELL**
(Nyack, New York 1903–New York 1972)

[1.1]
### *Untitled (Canis Major Constellation)*
### *c. 1960*
wood, glass, cork, metal, sand, paper, paint
19.4 × 32.9 × 8.9 cm
Minneapolis, Walker Art Center
Gift of The Joseph and Robert Cornell Memorial Foundation, 1993

[1.2]
### *Eclipsing Binary, Algol, with Magnitude Changes*
### *c. 1965*
wood, glass, clay, rubber, steel, paper, paint
20.2 × 43.5 × 9.8 cm
Minneapolis, Walker Art Center
Gift of The Joseph and Robert Cornell Memorial Foundation, 1993

On first glance, Joseph Cornell's works of collage and assemblage (or "montage" as he is noted to have described them) may appear somewhat quaint, evoking nostalgic scrapbooks or historic toys or displays. However, his box constructions are carefully and deliberately assembled, and, with close consideration of their details, they reveal themselves gradually to the viewer. This careful balance between precision and charm was described by Cornell's friend, the artist Robert Motherwell, who wrote: "Why doesn't it end in something too precious? You mustn't forget the depth of his deliberateness nor the masculinity of his method. Who would have thought a puritan would have so much sensuousness and richness of images?" (Motherwell 1993, 15).

Cornell's works are difficult to date, as he created many pieces gradually over time, revisiting and amending earlier compositions. These two pieces are dated c. 1960 and c. 1965, the later years of Cornell's life, and both are shadow box pieces, the form that Cornell is most recognized for, although he also produced more straightforward collage works and films. *Untitled (Canis Major Constellation)* [1.1] and *Eclipsing Binary, Algol, with Magnitude Changes* [1.2] both make reference to astronomy, one of Cornell's many overlapping interests that featured in his artwork, which also included other natural phenomena, modes, and stories of travel, literature, ballet, taxonomy, Americana, and films.

*Eclipsing Binary, Algol, with Magnitude Changes* [1.2] references the star system Algol, in which two of its stars form an eclipsing binary where one star orbits the other, and viewed from Earth this is seen as a partial eclipse. Within Cornell's wooden box, a diagram of this phenomenon is placed with a cut-out that references red dwarf stars, and an orange ball set atop two metal rods that can be rolled along the length of the box. These are accompanied by a small block carved with the image of a rooster, and a Dutch white clay pipe that signifies his family heritage. The moving component points to the orbiting star and is a feature also employed in *Untitled (Canis Major Constella-*

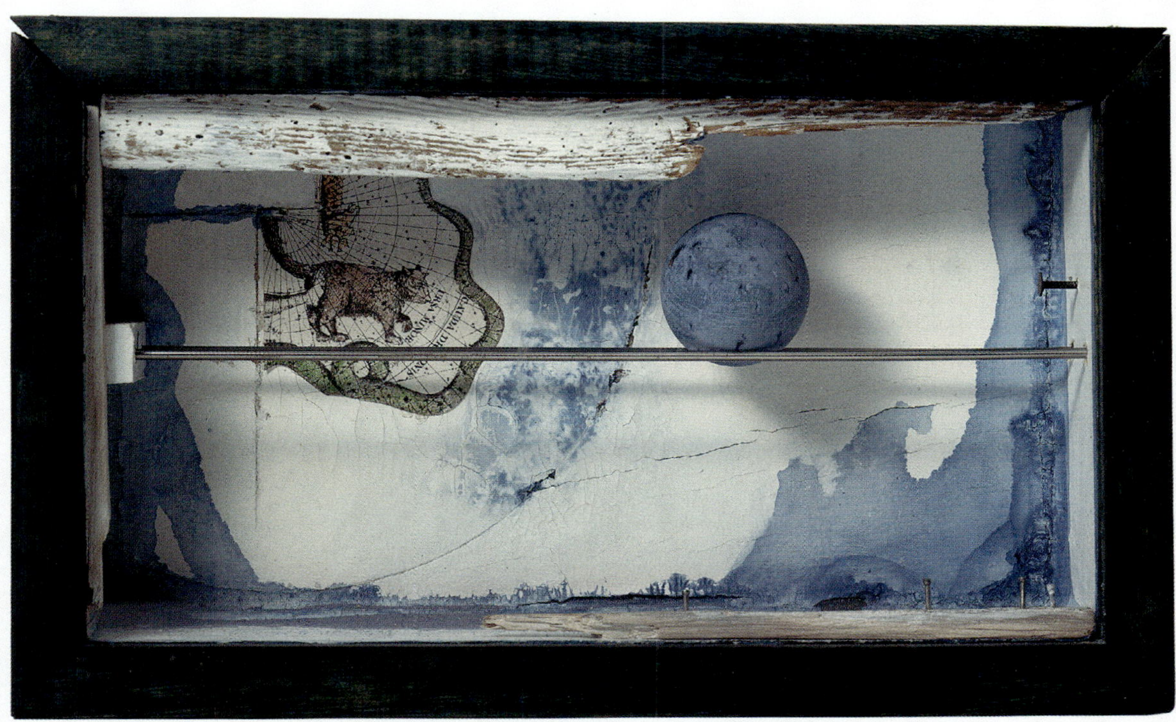



[1.1]

*tion)* [1.1] (the title of which refers to the Great Dog constellation) that includes an image of the Little Bear constellation.

Kinetic components in Cornell's works add further complications in defining his work, which touches on collage, sculpture, and assemblage, as well as on modes of collecting and displaying that reflect his interest in the *Wunderkammer* tradition. These moving elements also join up different aspects of his practice, pointing to his work in moving image and to pieces such as a collaged book that recalls a flipbook, or pieces with drawers or lids that are opened to reveal further details (Lea 2015, 26, 37).

These boxes hold multiple items of differing scales and types: painted surfaces, moving balls, cut and pasted images, carefully positioned objects. Together they form a composition and appear to capture a moment in time, but the individual objects remain just that; in assembly they create a world composed of parts, but not compounded into one (Lea 2015, 38).

Martin Friedman, the former director of the Walker Art Center, wrote an account of visiting Cornell in the development of an exhibition of his work and the eventual acquisition of pieces, including these two, and he describes the boxes as "miniature realms—reliquaries whose contents were viewed through glass windows" in which the "juxtaposition of their contents—fragments of the everyday world that alluded to fragments of imaginary ones—gave rise to free-associating on the part of viewers" (https://walkerart.org/magazine/martin-friedman-joseph-cornell). Such an approach reflects multiple points of inspiration for the boxes (such as diorama displays, theater sets, Victorian cabinets, shop windows, Dutch still life paintings, and arcade machines) and in turn their open-ended readings (Lea 2015, 37–8). Viewed in relation to time, these pieces speak to Cornell's contemporary world—for example in their reference to astronomy at a time of growing interest in space exploration—and to his historical interests in their form and the inclusion of heritage references (the ceramic pipe in *Eclipsing Binary, Algol, with Magnitude Changes*; the constellation names and illustrations that correspond to ancient myths in *Untitled [Canis Major Constellation]*. Driven by a sense of curiosity, romance, and longing, these pieces are examples of Cornell's sustained interest in the cosmos, but the same ethos is present in the many works he produced that referenced European culture and history, a place that he never visited but of which instead he "reconstructed the nineteenth-century 'grand tour' of Europe for his mind's eye more vividly than those who took it" (Motherwell 1993, 13).

During his life, Cornell developed correspondences and friendships with a number of other artists, including Marcel Duchamp, Robert Motherwell, Lee Miller, Roberto Matta, Dorothea Tanning, and Yayoi Kusama. His earliest work was presented in exhibitions dedicated to the medium of collage and in connection with surrealism, with his first solo exhibition taking place in 1932 at the Julian Levy Gallery in New York, where the movement had been introduced to America. He remained connected with avant-garde artistic movements and the professional world of galleries, but also maintained an independence from them. In the years since his death in 1972, the impact of his approach to art-making and the centrality of practices of collecting, archiving, and displaying in his work can be seen in artists from the twentieth century such as Andy Warhol and artists from the arte povera movement, to contemporary practitioners like Mark Dion, Michael Rakowitz, and Theaster Gates.

*NIKKI KANE*

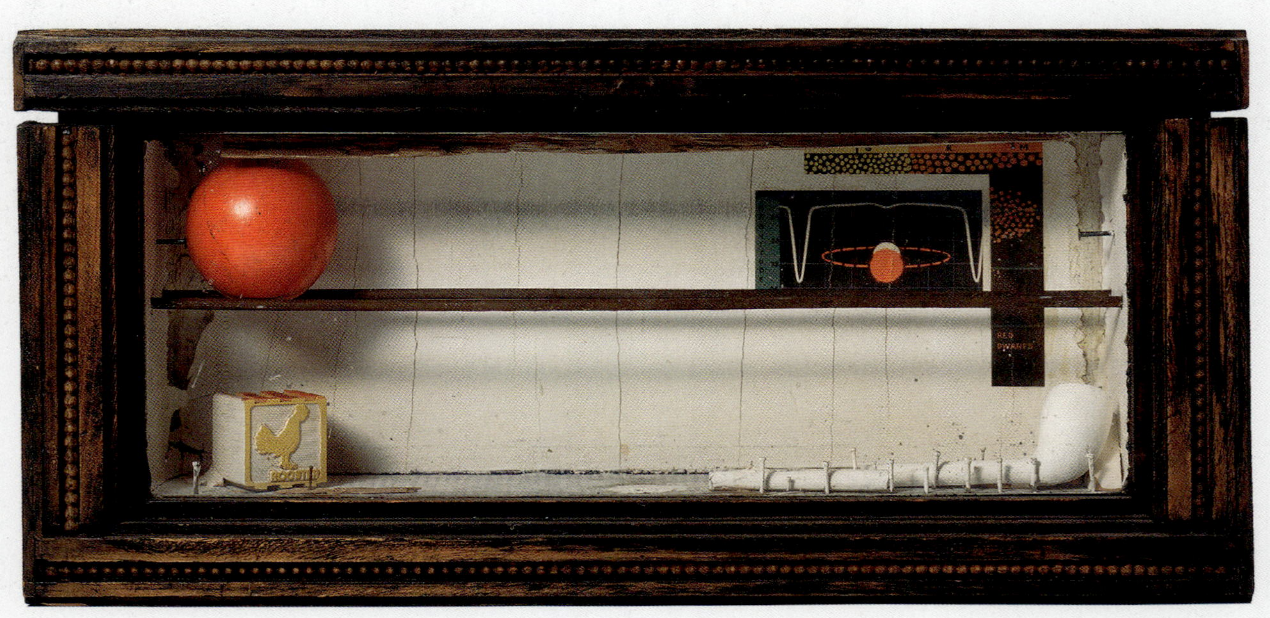




[1.2]

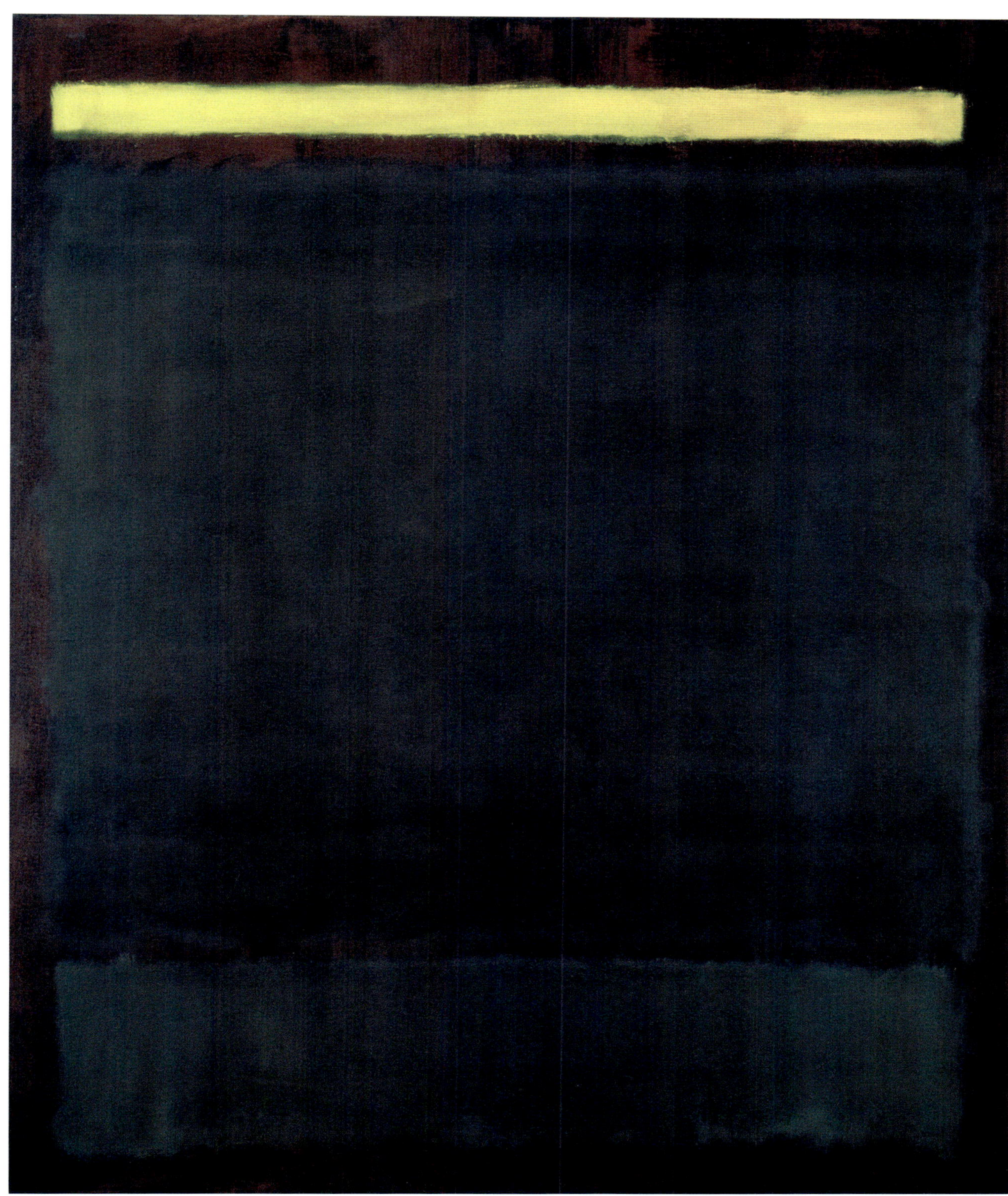

[1.3]

**MARK ROTHKO**
(Markus Rothkowitz; Dvinsk, Latvia 1903–New York 1970)

[1.3]
***No. 2***
**1963**
oil, acrylic, glue on canvas
203.8 × 175.6 cm
Minneapolis, Walker Art Center
Gift of the Mark Rothko Foundation, Inc., 1985

Mark Rothko's journey toward a signature style has been characterized as one of struggle and ambiguity that, after two decades of effort, resolved itself in the simplest possible way: luminous, pure abstractions that are now benchmarks in the history of postwar American art (Anfam 1998, 71). His earliest works, made during the 1930s, were muted, often melancholy urban scenes and landscapes. These were colored by his involvement in left-wing political committees and activist groups such as the Artists' Union in New York; equally important were his studies with Max Weber at the Art Students' League and his long friendship with Milton Avery. Both his

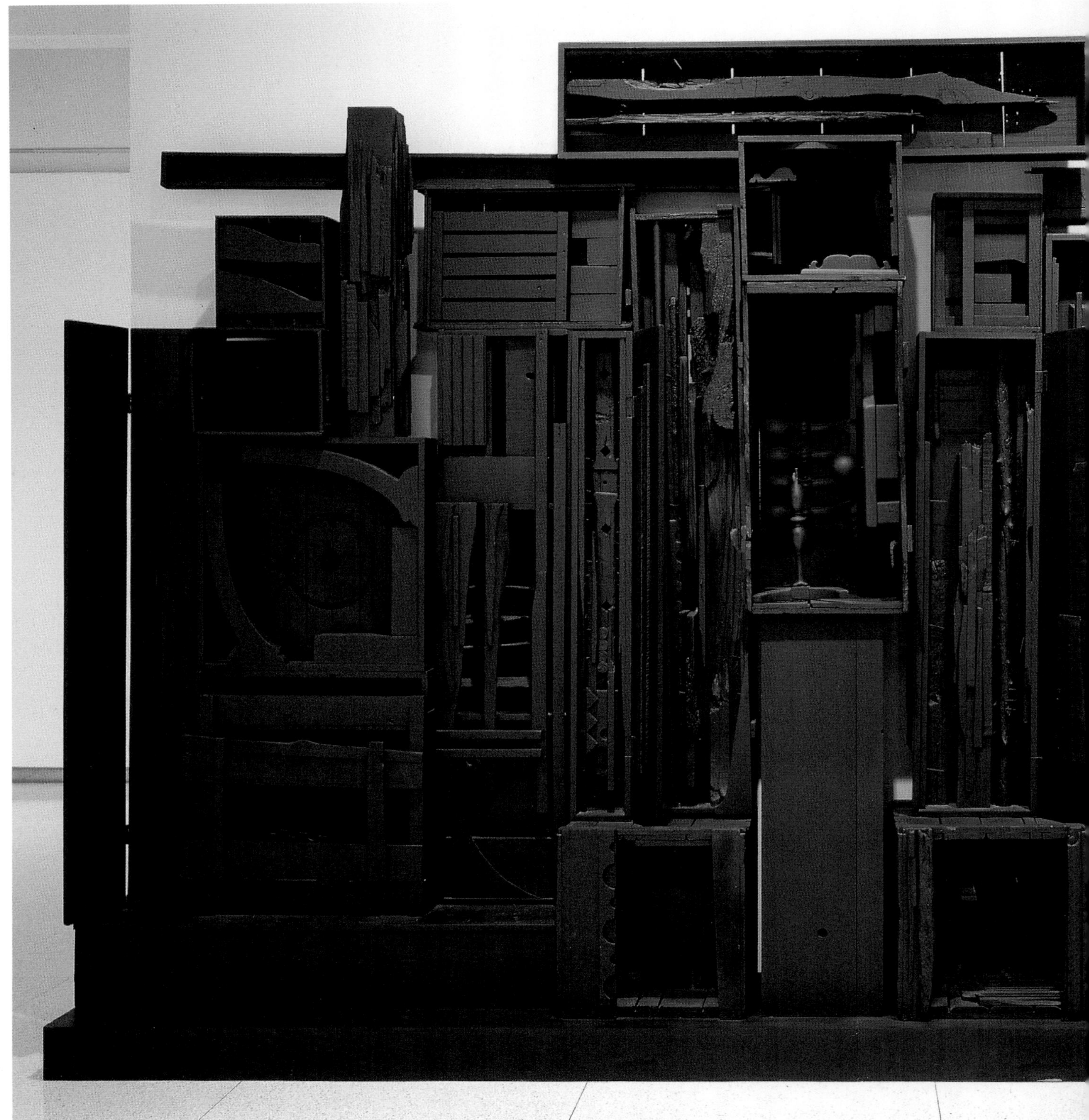



mentors painted in a figurative style heavily informed by the ideas of Pablo Picasso and Henri Matisse, but during the 1930s Rothko also encountered Surrealism, which was to prove the more salient influence for the next decade. He was especially captivated by the automatist abstractions of Joan Miró, and (along with fellow New York School artists Barnett Newman and Adolph Gottlieb) cultivated an interest in myth, Greek drama, tribal arts, and the art of children. For a time, Rothko attempted to bring all these interests together in canvases that communicated both the grim social reality of the day and the irrational, tragic nature of the human condition. But around 1938, as Hitler's troops began stirring in Europe and the Depression continued in the United States, Rothko turned away from current events and committed himself to "the forms of the archaic and the myths from which they have stemmed" (From Rothko's notes for a letter—cowritten with Adolph Gottlieb—to Edward Alden Jewell, quoted in Ashton 1983, 75). Believing fervently that "there is no such thing as good painting about nothing" (from the letter referenced in Ashton 1983, 75, reprinted in *Mark Rothko* 1987, 77–78), he set out to embed the messages of his own time within a new semiabstract idiom. His canvases were filled with amorphous shapes swirling in

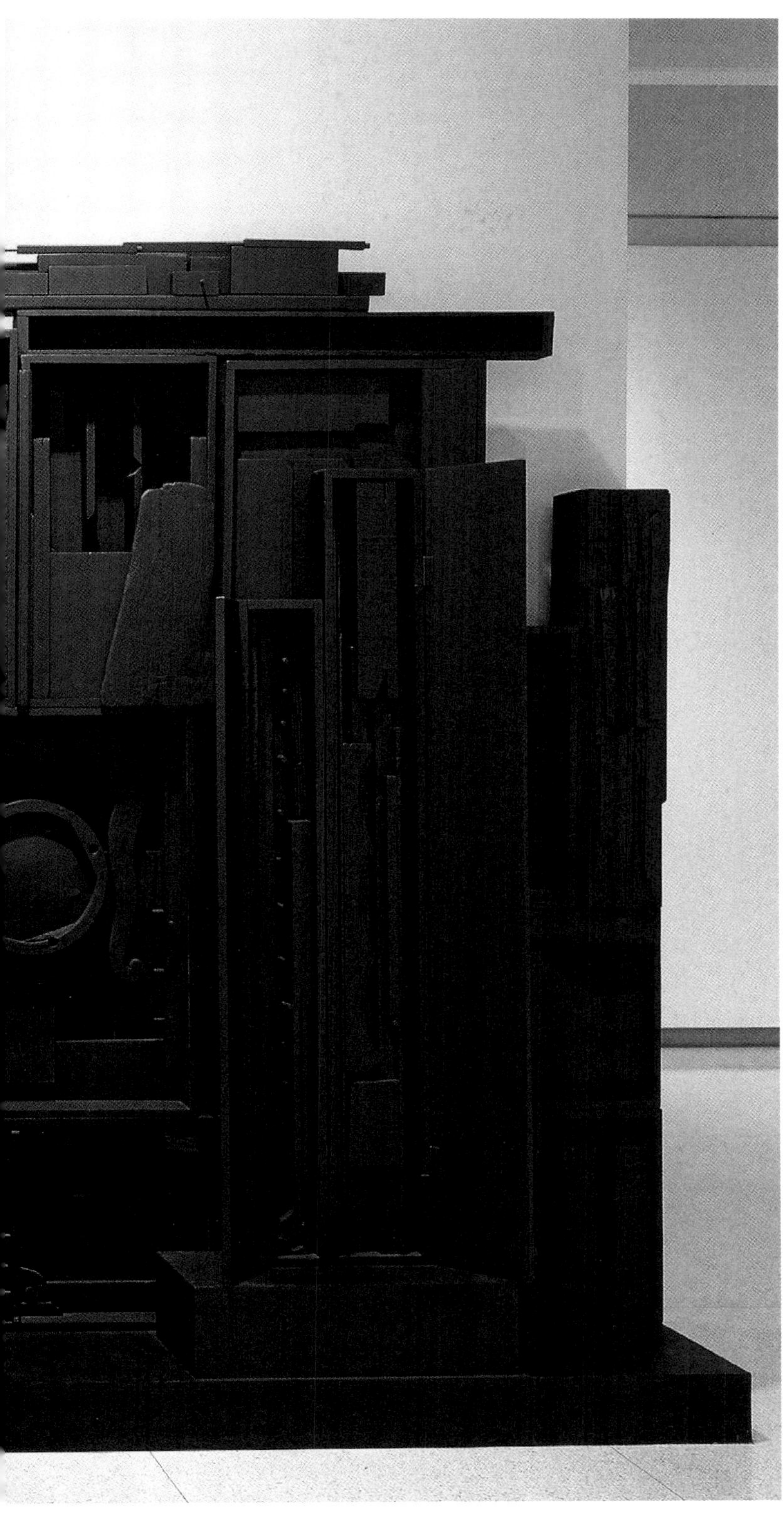

ry Gallery, which had opened in New York three years earlier with a mission to show work in difficult modern styles such as Surrealism). Rothko's fervent desire to make his art the vehicle for transcendent experience led him to systematically eliminate representation and even allusion from his images. He forced his Surrealist-inspired forms of the 1940s to gradually dematerialize until, by 1950, he had distilled them into soft blocks and bands of luminous color arranged in simple, flattened compositions. He abandoned evocative narrative titles and began simply numbering his works, letting the content reside completely within the visual information. After 1950, he also ceased publishing statements about his aims and ideas, confiding to Newman that he had "nothing to say in words" about what he was doing on canvas (quoted in Compton 1987, 50). But he made it known that he was not a formalist: His paintings were experiences and ideas in their own right, not illustrations of experiences and ideas, and certainly not mere experiments with color and space. What Rothko was after were visceral, emotional, intimate encounters with objects that offered no less than complete physical and emotional immersion.

In 1963, Mark Rothko, with his friend the painter Adolph Gottlieb, wrote several philosophical statements that would continue to guide their art for years to come. The two painters seemed to be interested in "simple expression of the complex thought." They also moved on larger scale arguing that would be impactful as well as worked more on flat forms, which would undermine the idea of illusion and aim to the truth.

The *No. 2* [1.3] painting reflects these ideas. Rothko abandoned traditional Renaissance three-point perspective, which conceives of the canvas as a window onto another world. Multiple glazes of dark pigments of varying opacity make the picture's surface feel flat, yet it quivers and vibrates, offering a sense of atmospheric depth. Rothko hoped that these compositional strategies would invite visual and emotional contemplation on the part of the viewer, creating the conditions for silence and reflection.

*JOAN ROTHFUSS* (revised version of text, published in *Bits and Pieces*, 2005, 491–492)


## LOUISE NEVELSON

(Leah Berliawsky; Pereyaslav, Russian Empire 1899–New York 1988)

[1.4]
### *Sky Cathedral Presence*
**1951–64**
wood, paint
310.5 × 508 × 60.6 cm
Minneapolis, Walker Art Center
Gift of Judy and Kenneth Dayton, 1969

Louis Nevelson was an American sculptor best known for her monochromatic wooden assemblages. Beginning in the 1950s, Nevelson began to experiment with arrangements of objects in wooden frames. These objects were most often woodcuts, bits of furniture, and joinery offcuts. They would be assembled and painted in a single color, typically black, gold, or white. Throughout her life, Nevelson also produced a series of drawings and etchings

shallow space, allusions to vast skies and oceans, musical notations, microscopic life, and fragmented human and animal forms. Typical of this period is the Walker Art Center's *Ritual* (1944), in which a figure—with truncated limbs and an oversized ear that doubles as a head—floats mysteriously in an undefined space. Delicately painted in thin washes of magenta, ochre, and black, this lilting composition suggests ancient rituals and myths involving music and its often-hypnotic power—the irresistible song of the Sirens, or Orpheus, who lulls the Furies with his lyre (*Ritual* was one of fifteen oils Rothko included in a 1945 solo exhibition at Peggy Guggenheim's Art of This Centuwhich drew on unconventional and recycled materials. Across her practice, she exhibited a clear talent for making her works more than the sum of their material parts.

Nevelson's career began in the early 1940s, when she received her first solo show at Nierendorf Gallery. After critical recognition, she began showing in prominent New York exhibitions. While at this stage of her career her work was mostly comprised of cubist and surrealist painting and sculpture, she also began the experiments with wood and found objects that would come to define her work beginning in the 1960s. These experiments culminated in the creation of large wall pieces like *Sky Cathedral Presence* [1.4]. While she received critical success for these large assemblages, she nevertheless faced serious financial hardship, which in time pushed her to accept a fellowship for lithography in California. While initially reluctant, this new exploration in lithography and printmaking became distinct yet important element of her artistic practice. Her major retrospective was curated by the Walker Art Center in 1973, and the latter half of her career was met with significantly more success. To this day her large monochrome assemblage sculptures are key parts of museum collections worldwide.

Louise Nevelson is highly regarded as a groundbreaking, key figure within the feminist art movement. Scholars have often framed her work as a challenge to what was traditionally perceived as masculine versus feminine styles of art making, and her sculptures were often mistaken to be made by a man. Her early work had faced significant resistance because of her gender, and so it was no surprise that by the 1970s when the feminist art movement was in full bloom that a new generation of artists saw her as a pioneering figure. Nevelson's opinion of her own experience was much less broad, instead turning to her resiliency and persistence in the face of the artworld as the reason for her success, deemphasizing the role gender may have played. Regardless, her work proved a critical contribution to not only feminist art history, but mid-century American Art.

Standing at a daunting 3 meters tall and 5 meters wide, *Sky Cathedral Presence* [1.4] lives up to its name. This imposing structure consists of wooden fragments and furniture components amassed over a decade. The pieces of furniture create fluid, almost musical forms that clash against splintered pieces of timber, hard-edged boards, and the knotted, untreated forms of natural wood. At some points the sculpture, on close look, appears as a cluttered closet of miscellaneous objects. At other points it looks like a carefully constructed three-dimensional puzzle. The result is an uncompromising optical tug-of-war that demands both reverence and attention. The scale and color of the piece is what viewers likely notice first. Not unlike some abstract expressionist painters working contemporaneously, Nevelson experiments with size in particular to explore ideas of the sublime, spiritual transcendence and the evaluated vertical presence of soaring cathedrals. By stacking the boxes that comprised the compartments of the work, she creates a physical presence that causes viewers to intuitively regard its size and perceive its presence. As for the color black, Nevelson fell in love with the color because "it contained all color. It wasn't a negation of color. It was an acceptance. Because black encompasses all colors. Black is the most aristocratic color of all. [...] You can be quiet

and it contains the whole thing." By juxtaposing this regal, subtle color with a grandiose and physically imposing structure, Nevelson creates a push and pull which on the one hand pushes the viewer away from the sculpture but on the other hand invites the viewer to puzzle over its material intricacies.

These material intricacies stem from the delicate and layered arrangement of the various components within the wooden compartments that comprise the sculpture. The push and pull of scale is, in some ways, echoed in the relationships between materials themselves, and the visual effect is one that draws the eye inward, like the careful reliefs on a cathedral portal. Appearing both informal yet meticulously assembled, the materials comprising *Sky Cathedral Presence* echo the tensions between color and scale.

With this unapologetic and uncompromising work, Nevelson presents the viewer with a unique visual experience, one that at times resembles sculpture, architecture, or even painting. She presents a proud structural façade that, on close inspection, enwraps the viewer in its tensions and dynamics without ever losing the deep satisfaction one feels in its presence.

*WILLIAM HERNANDEZ-LUEGE*

## BRUCE CONNER

(McPherson; Kansas 1933–San Francisco 2008)

[1.5]
### COSMIC RAY
**1961**
16mm color filmstrips encased in two ¼-inch plexiglass sheets
mounted film: 96 frames, 68 strips wide
129.5 x 167.3 x 1.3 cm
Minneapolis, Walker Art Center
Gift of the artist, 2001

Over the course of his fifty-year career, Bruce Conner was something of an artistic chameleon, working in sculpture, film, collage, painting, photography, printmaking, performance, and conceptual art. He courted diversity and unpredictability to the point where he seemingly made an art out of elusiveness, abandoning a given type or style of work whenever he felt he was becoming too closely identified with it.

In 1957, shortly after graduating from the University of Nebraska, he moved to San Francisco at the urging of his high-school friend Michael McClure, who had moved there earlier in the decade and become a key figure in the celebrated San Francisco Poetry Renaissance. There Conner quickly fell in with a vibrant group of artists that included Wallace Berman, Joan Brown, Jay DeFeo, Wally Hedrick, George Herms, and Jess, many of whom worked or experimented in a mixed-media style that came to be called "assemblage."

Although he had worked in collage prior to his move, it was in San Francisco that Conner began working in the assemblage style that first brought him to national and international attention. Conner's first true assemblage, RATBASTARD (1958), began as a thickly impastoed, vaguely flesh-toned painting, which, in a fit of frustration, the artist sliced and gouged. Intrigued by its injured condition, he then

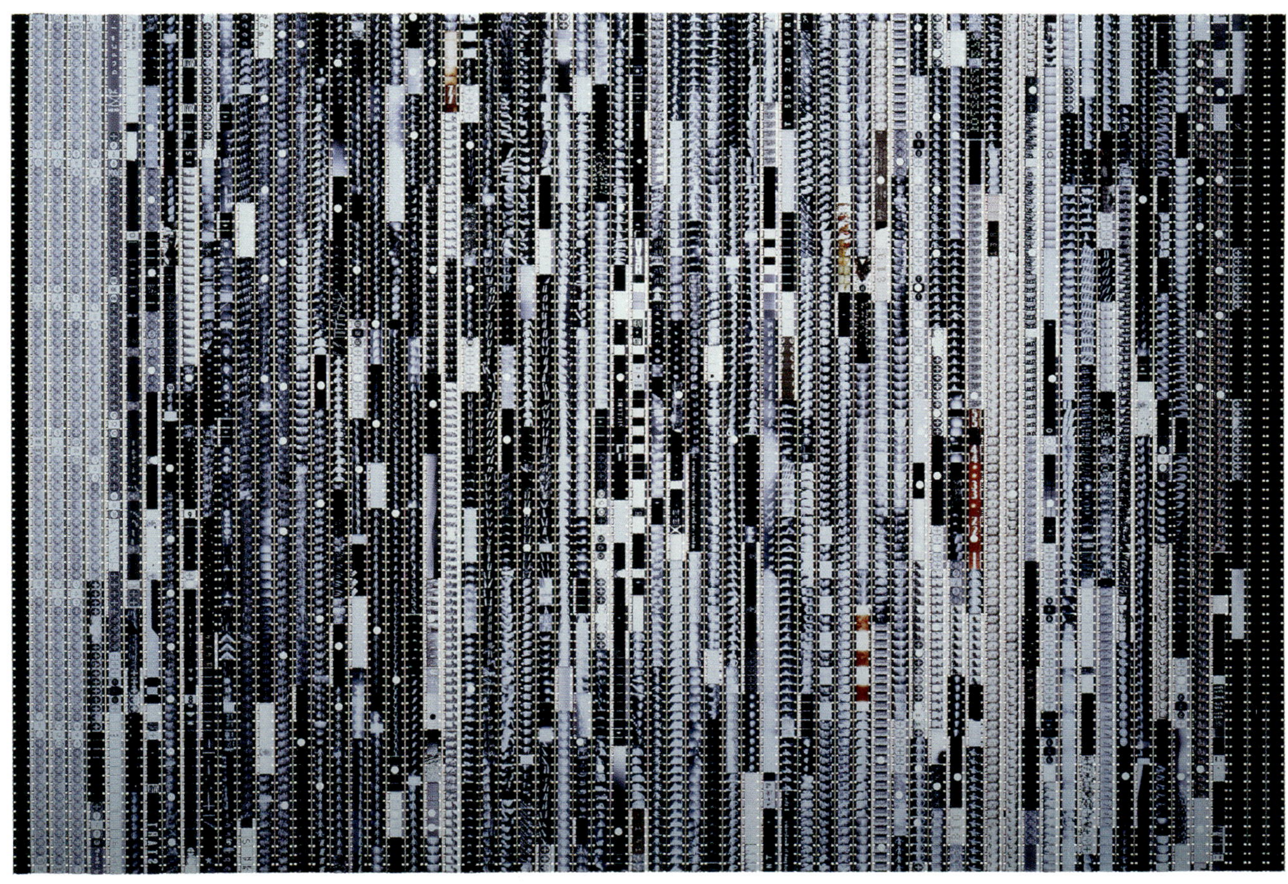

[1.5]

ran a thick steel wire through the various wounds, added collage elements—including a photo of people viewing a cadaver on a table and an illustration of a medieval torture scene—swathed the work in nylon (attractive because of its capacity to both reveal and conceal, nylon became a staple of many of his assemblages), and pierced it with nails. As a final touch, he added a cloth "handle," so that he could carry it as a portable emblem of psychic distress and alienation.

Other assemblages attest to Conner's lifelong love of movies. THE BRIDE (1960), one of his few freestanding sculptures, features a wooden armature swathed in white-painted nylon and topped with candles whose melted wax has dripped down over it. As Conner was making the piece, it reminded him of the figure of Miss Havisham, the aging spinster and jilted bride whose accidental self-immolation is the climax of David Lean's 1946 film version of Charles Dickens's *Great Expectations*.

Much of Conner's own reputation rests on the influence of his films of the late 1950s and 1960s, such as A MOVIE (1958), COSMIC RAY (1961), and REPORT (1963–67), which were made from scraps of found footage edited together to create dense, ambiguous narratives.

Conner's involvement with film, which he produced mostly in black and white, influenced much of his nonfilmic work from the mid-1960s to the present. Many of these later works—principally collages, drawings, and photographs—explore visual effects of black and white in terms of darkness and light.

For all its diversity, there are some consistent threads that run through much of Conner's work. The most important of these is the conception of the artwork as subject to renewal and redefinition each time it is viewed, almost as if it were a living being continually regenerating and metamorphosing. By and large, he achieves this through a kind of optical overload, a high-density presentation that results in a tug-of-war between the detail and the whole. No matter how many times one views a typical Conner work—be it an assemblage, drawing, movie, or collage—it typically resists full resolution. There is always something that changes—perhaps a detail never noticed before, perhaps a visual effect based on the optical phenomenon of "persistence of vision"—that keeps it uncertain and alive. In this sense, his individual artworks share something in common with his career as a whole.

COSMIC RAY [1.5], from 1961, was made from footage taken from cartoons and soft-core porn films paired with footage Conner had shot himself and graphic elements such as the countdown leader and logos (Smith 2005, 169; Jenkins 1999, 196). In COSMIC RAY, Conner works with the relationship between black and white, playing with their visual effects by contrasting dark and light footage and with the rhythms of editing (Boswell 1999, 54). This was set to a recording of a live performance by Ray Charles, edited to produce moments of correlation and contrast between the audio and visual elements. In 1999, Conner produced a "frozen film frame" form of COSMIC RAY for his retrospective exhibition at the Walker Art Center, in which the print of the film is encased in plexiglass. This creates another way for viewers to experience the film—silently, seeing all the frames together. In this form, the artist noted that the piece "represents both time and space" (Bruce Conner in correspondence with the Walker Art Center in 2000, Walker Art Center archives): the physical manifestation of the film emphasizes its material qualities, and the visibility of each frame conveys duration, movement, and the effects of light and dark, even within its static form. *PETER BOSWELL* (revised version of text, published in *Bits and Pieces*, 2005, 166–169)

## ELLSWORTH KELLY
(Newburgh, New York 1923–Spencertown, New York 2015)

[1.6]
***Black Curve***
**1962**
oil on canvas
107 × 87.9 cm
Minneapolis, Walker Art Center
Donated by Mr. and Mrs. Edmond R. Ruben, 1995

[1.7]
***Red Green Blue***
**1964**
oil on canvas
228.6 × 167.6 cm
Minneapolis, Walker Art Center
Gift of the T. B. Walker Foundation, 1966

[1.8]
***Yellow/Red***
**1968**
oil on canvas
187.3 × 258.4 cm
Minneapolis, Walker Art Center
Gift of Penny and Mike Winton, 1994

[1.9]
***White Curves I***
**1978**
Edition: A. P. from an edition of 4
aluminum, lacquer
182.2 × 131.4 × 27.3 cm
Minneapolis, Walker Art Center
Walker Art Center, Tyler Graphics Archive, 1984

[1.6]

For more than fifty years, Ellsworth Kelly worked to refine elements of the observed world into rigorous abstraction with a bold clarity and elegance. In doing so, he demonstrated remarkable versatility as a painter, sculptor, draftsman, photographer, and printmaker. "My work has always been about vision, the process of seeing," he notes. "Each work of art is a fragment of a larger context. [...] I've always been interested in things that I see that don't make sense out of context, that lead you into something else" (Kelly in conversation with Mark Rosenthal, January 1991, New York. Quoted in Rosenthal 1993, 83). His flat, immaculate compositions of pure line, simple forms, and saturated, unmodulated color are, in essence, found images, distillations of architectural details, shadows, plants, and other subtle forms that often might be overlooked. The contour of a leaf, the arch of a bridge and its reflection in water, and the soft curve of a hillside seen from the road have inspired paintings and sculptures alike.
Though Kelly's work has been aligned with Pop Art, Color Field Painting, and Minimalism, it is more aptly placed along the fringes of these movements. Because he worked in Paris, his development in the 1950s occurred independently of such artists as Jasper Johns and Robert Rauschenberg, whose art was a direct reaction to the then-dominant style of Abstract Expressionism. Kelly's first mature works made in France predated by more than a decade the paintings of Frank Stella, Brice Marden, and other Americans associated with Minimalist Art in the 1960s.

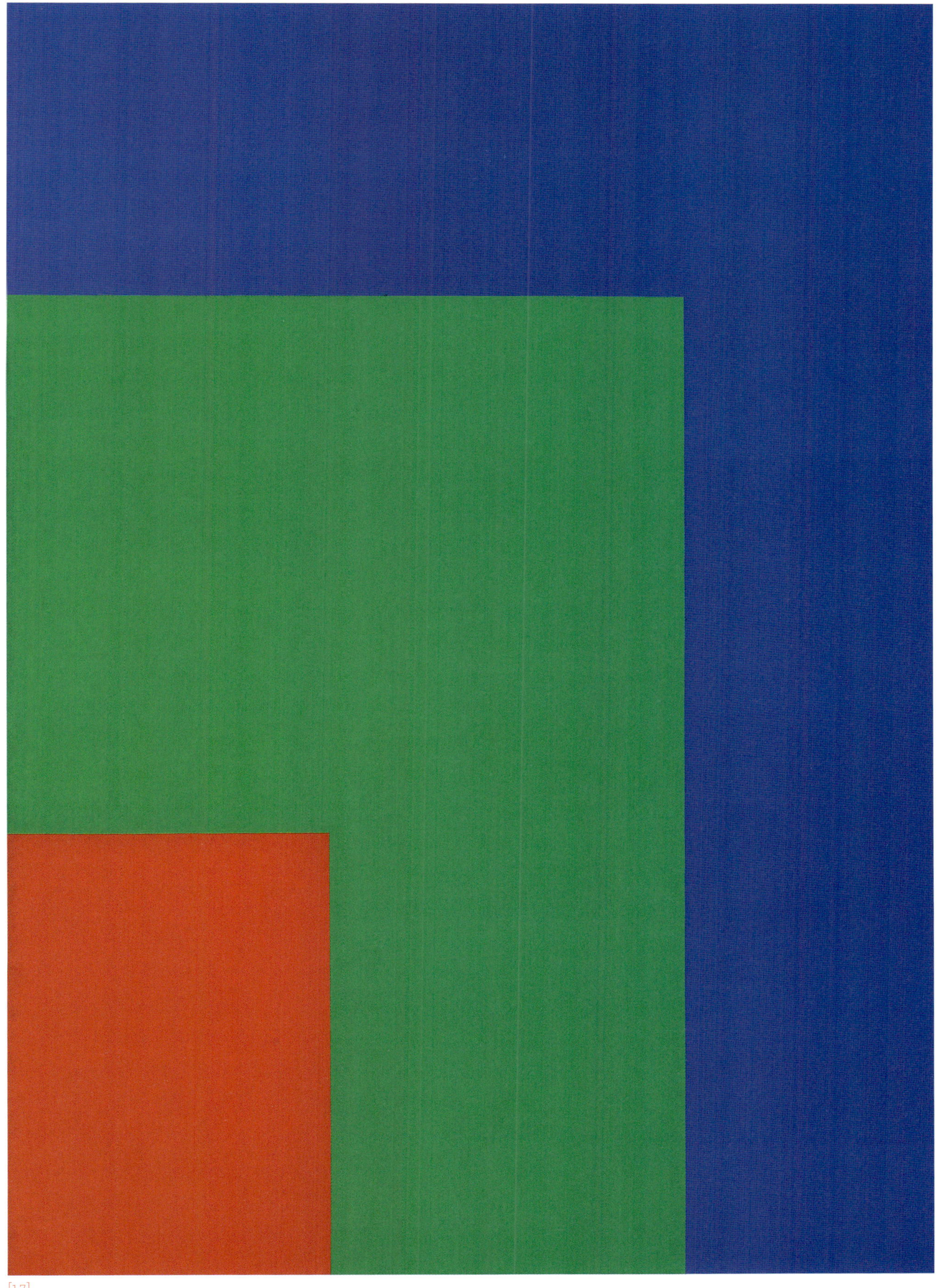

[1.7]

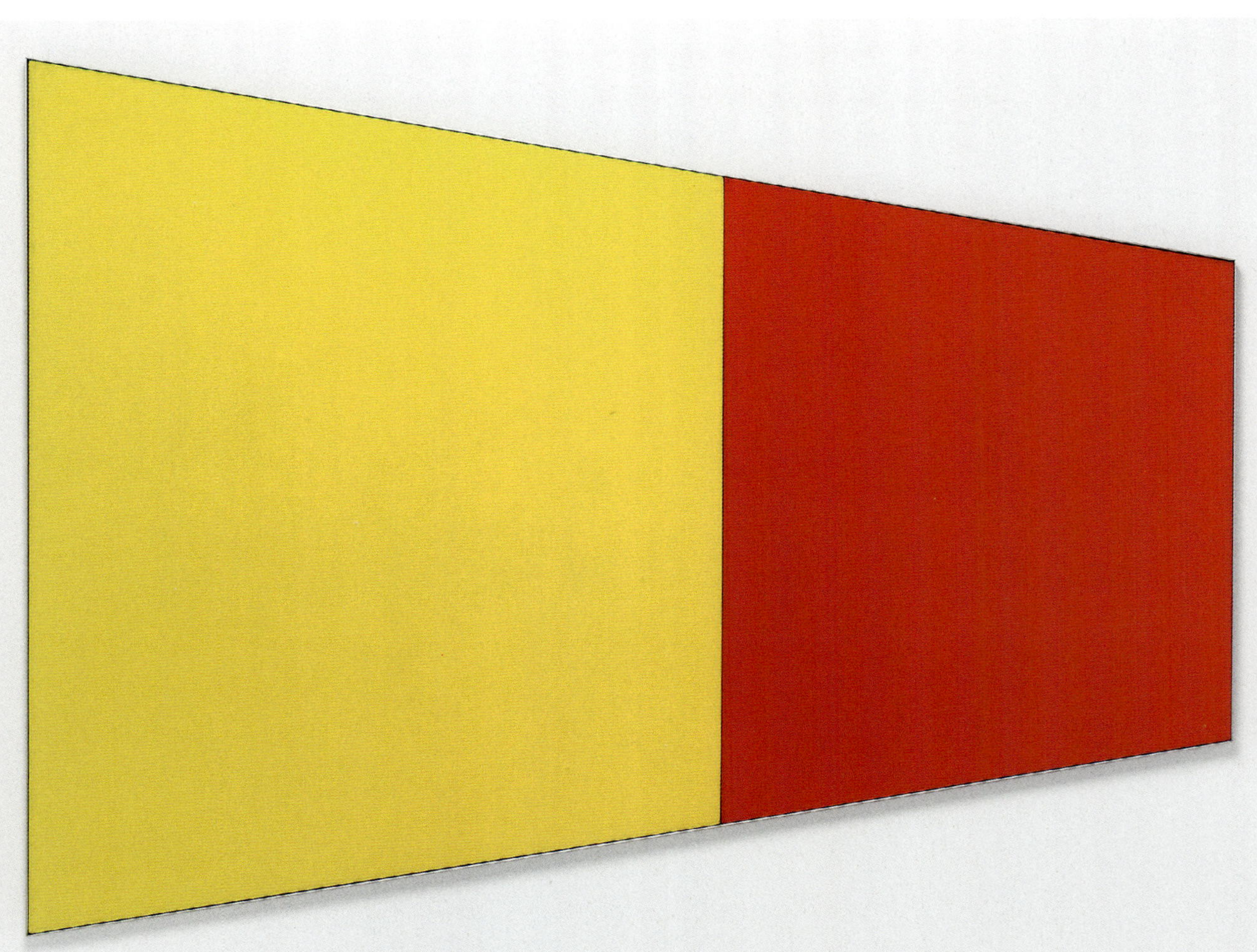

[1.8]

From his early collages made in Paris to his large, freestanding sculptures, Kelly has continually searched for ways whereby his art might compose itself through chance—his forms, he has stressed, are shapes that "have always been there" (Kelly, interview with Henry Geldzahler, in Geldzahler 1963, not paginated).

From his earliest paintings, Kelly has been interested in liberating color and form from content, asserting that the painting is an object and the white wall, essential to the perception of the piece, is its ground. Throughout his career, the artist used abstraction as a means for viewing the world with coherence and clarity. His works articulate his concerns about form, color, and their relationship to physical space, and present in themselves an opportunity to examine his process of seeing.

*Red Green Blue* (1964) [1.7] is one of the few canvases executed in the 1960s in which he chose not to separate the colors into individual panels, a practice he had begun during his years in Paris. Kelly's interest in flat, unmodulated color is evident in the painting. Though not interested in texture and gesture, he nonetheless avoids a mechanized look, and strives for his hand to be apparent in the finished surface.

In the double canvas *Yellow/Red* (1968) [1.8], the positioning of the joined, shaped panels on the white wall is key, as the work becomes a study in perspective. Though perceived as pure, hard-edged shapes, *Yellow/Red* can be traced to Kelly's observant eye, as these shapes recall the artist's photographs of shadows cast by open barn doors in the New York countryside (Bois 1999, 23).

Kelly returned to New York in 1954, and soon after moved to Coenties Slip, a former landing place for wooden ships in lower Manhattan that housed a community of artists, including Robert Indiana, Agnes Martin, and Jack Youngerman, in deserted sail-making lofts. It was here that he made the painted aluminum sculpture *Gate* in 1959. He once described the work as taking shape by chance from an × he outlined on an envelope: "I folded it and cut it and it stood. I did it almost without thinking, almost as if I didn't decide" (Kelly, interview with Henry Geldzahler, Geldzahler 1963, not paginated). The X-configuration used in the sculpture occurs frequently in Kelly's art of the late 1950s. Though it retains an element of flatness and frontality, *Gate* was a pioneering piece for the artist in that it marked the first time one of his forms moved fully off the wall, breaking ground for his sculptures in the round (which were initiated that same year) as well as for large-scale, freestanding indoor and outdoor pieces, which he executed in various metals and in wood.

It was also while living in Coenties Slip that Kelly painted *Black Curve* (1962) [1.6]. The painting is related to five canvases from the early 1960s that were composed of free-drawn curves executed in various colors. He has often worked in cycles, alternating between the curve, the rectangle, and other forms that interest him, moving freely between painting, sculpture, and works on paper. The curve in this painting was made during a period when the artist's shapes were often organic. After 1969, his curve paintings and wall reliefs were always "fragments of a circle," based on geometric figures rather than found contours (Artist's statement, March 21, 1996, Walker Art Center Archives).

*White Curve* (1978) [1.9] is a form cut out of aluminum, painted white and attached to the wall.

Kelly's work from the beginning has been an investigation of form and ground, which gradually led him to separate form from ground, a development that results in works that lie between painting and

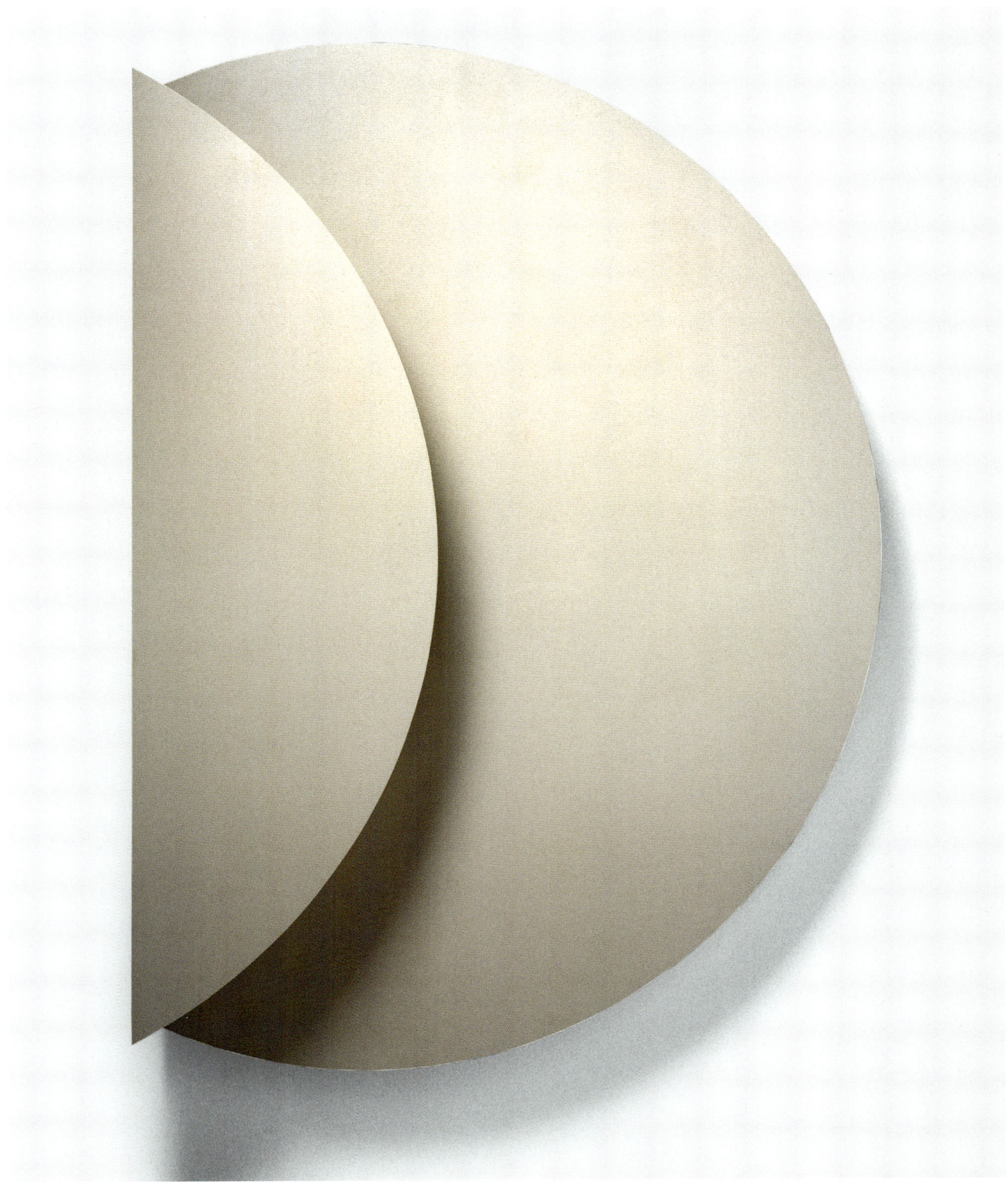



sculpture. The genesis of the idea for *White Curve* and other similar metal wall sculptures can be found in Kelly's paintings using segments of a circle. The use of metal, which is a thin but stable element, enabled him to space the object from the wall.
*SIRI ENGBERG* (revised version of text, published in *Bits and Pieces*, 2005, 315–316)

# CROSSING BOUNDARIES

2.

**Artistic collaborations: Merce Cunningham, John Cage, Robert Rauschenberg, Jasper Johns**

The shared work of Merce Cunningham, John Cage, Robert Rauschenberg, and Jasper Johns is key to understanding the nature of the cross-medium collaboration and innovation that took place from the mid-1900s on, and that has had lasting repercussions for artistic practice till the present day. Indeed, their work together even raises important questions about the meaning of collaboration itself; their works have also been described as "well-orchestrated noncollaboration" or "noncollaborative collaboration" (Paxton 1997, 261; Davis 2017, https://news.artnet.com/exhibitions/merce-cunningham-common-time-869543).

Such descriptions rest on the particular way of working that took place in the Merce Cunningham Dance Company (MCDC), whereby pioneering figures of music, dance, and visual art created independent works that, in the context of a performance, came together to coexist. That is to say, these collaborations were not centered on the artists working together to produce complementary elements for a single production, or that they were driven to create by a sense of shared content or thematic; their work tested the boundaries of each of their disciplines and their collaborations respected and emphasized "leaving space around each art" (John Cage in an interview with Merce Cunningham in 1981, https://walkerart.org/magazine/chance-conversations-an-interview-with-merce).

Cunningham and Cage first met at a dance class in which Cage was providing the musical accompaniment. They began working together and, in the summers of 1948, 1952, and 1953, they attended the experimental art school Black Mountain College where they first met Robert Rauschenberg. Rauschenberg had become a regular resident at Black Mountain College, and here had begun to test key artistic developments that would go on to punctuate his work, including his *White Paintings* (1951) that dealt with painting and surface but also drew in elements of movement and shadow in their presentation. The connections and experiments at Black Mountain College eventually led to an extended collaboration between Cunningham, Cage, and Rauschenberg, with Rauschenberg becoming the Artistic Advisor for MCDC. Through this connection, Johns became involved in the company, first helping his friend Rauschenberg with set elements and later taking on the Artistic Advisor role. In this position, Johns invited other artists to create designs for MCDC productions, taking on an almost curatorial approach to the role.

The work of Cunningham and Cage and their artistic collaborators continues to be hugely influential in the fields of visual art, music, dance, theater, and design. Their cross-discipline collaborations, use of elements of chance, and emphasis of pushing boundaries has paved the way for contemporary art practices that incorporate performance and installation, while also provoking challenges and innovations in the field of museum collecting and conservation, as seen in the Walker Art Center's acquisition of the MCDC archives in 2001.
*NIKKI KANE*

**JOHN CAGE**
(Los Angeles 1912–New York 1992)

[2.1a]
**Preliminary notations for *Williams Mix score***
**1952**
graphite on paper
27.9 × 21.6 cm
Minneapolis, Walker Art Center
T. B. Walker Acquisition Fund, 2012

[2.1b]
**Preliminary notations for *Williams Mix score***
**1952**
graphite on paper
27.9 × 21.6 cm
Minneapolis, Walker Art Center
T. B. Walker Acquisition Fund, 2012

[2.1c]
**Preliminary notations for *Williams Mix score***
**1952**
graphite on paper
27.9 × 21.6 cm
Minneapolis, Walker Art Center
T. B. Walker Acquisition Fund, 2012

**ROBERT RAUSCHENBERG**
(Milton Ernest Rauschenberg; Port Arthur, Texas 1925–Captiva Island, Florida 2008)

[2.2]
**Décor for *Minutiae***
**1954/76**
oil, paper, fabric, newsprint, wood, metal, and plastic with mirror and string, on wood
214.6 × 205.7 × 77.5 cm
Minneapolis, Walker Art Center
Walker Art Center, Merce Cunningham Dance Company Collection, Gift of Jay F. Ecklund, the Barnett and Annalee Newman Foundation, Agnes Gund, Russell Cowles and Josine Peters, the Hayes Fund of HRK Foundation, Dorothy Lichtenstein, MAHADH Fund of HRK Foundation, Goodale Family Foundation, Marion Stroud Swingle, David Teiger, Kathleen Fluegel, Barbara G. Pine, and the T. B. Walker Acquisition Fund, 2011

Robert Rauschenberg has been known especially for blurring the distinctions between painting and sculpture, but he also worked in several other media such as photography, printmaking, papermaking, and performance.
In 1959, Robert Rauschenberg included the following, now infamous statement in the catalogue for the landmark exhibition *Sixteen Americans*, organized by the Museum of Modern Art in New York: "Painting

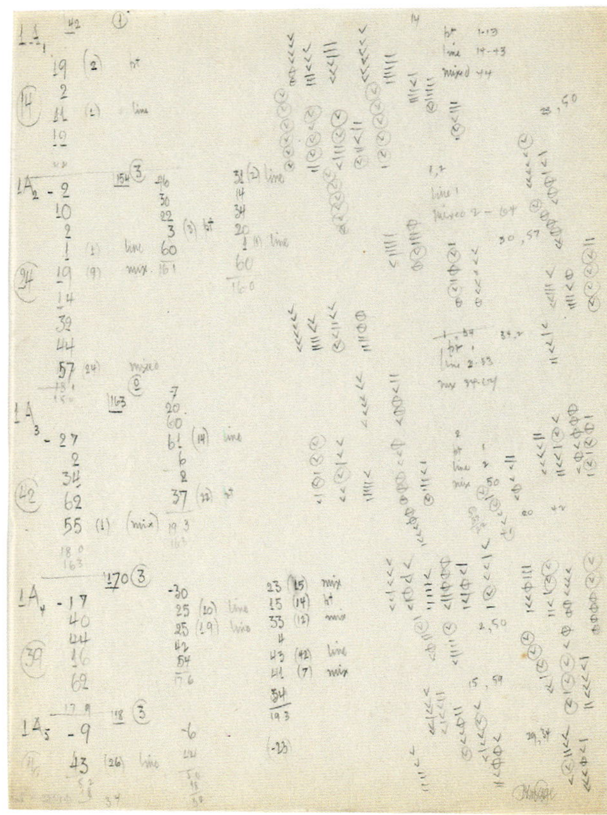

[2.1a]

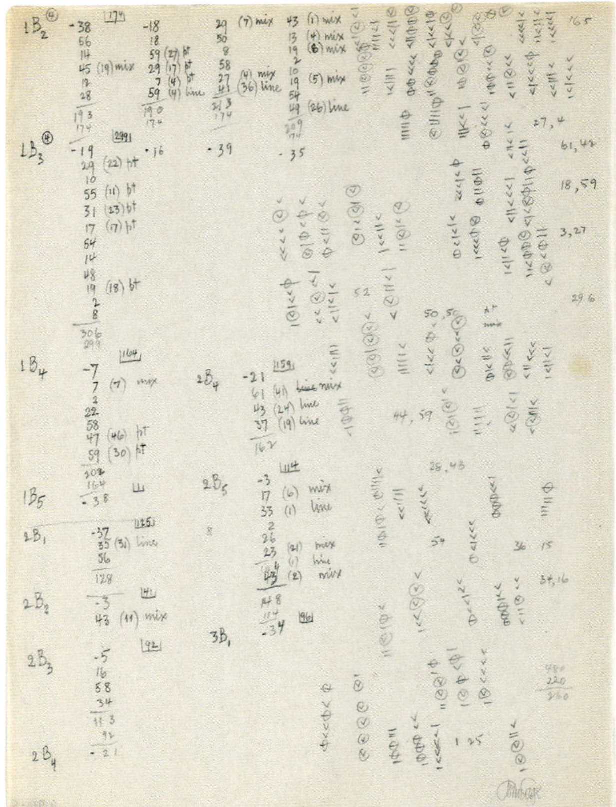

[2.1b]

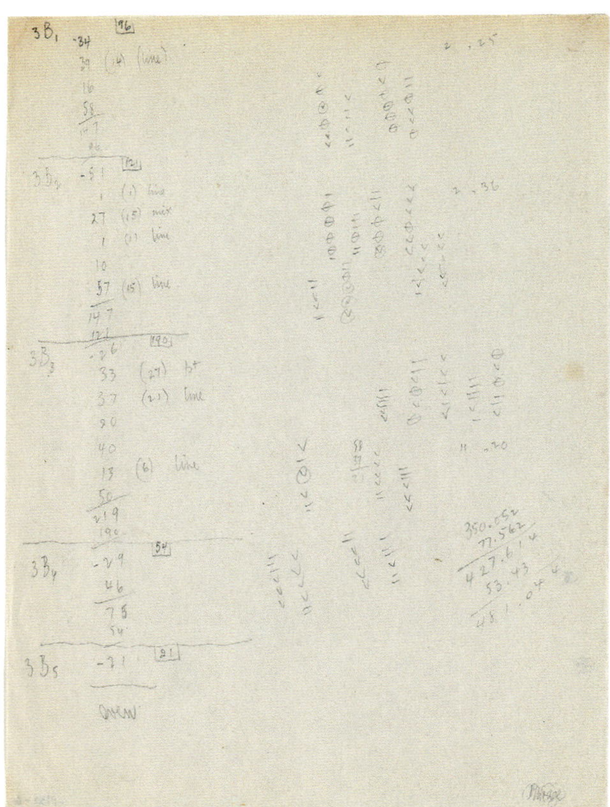

[2.1c]

relates to both art and life. Neither can be made. (I try to act in that gap between the two)" (Artist's statement in *Sixteen Americans* 1959, 58). The importance of this statement cannot be underestimated in terms of the intellectual floodgates that it would open in the art world of the 1950s, altering the discourse surrounding the age-old question of what art is.

In 1973, critic Brian O'Doherty coined the term "vernacular glance" to describe Rauschenberg's insatiable appetite for collecting and re-producing visual phenomena in the form of mass-produced images and his ability to translate sensory overload into nuanced juxtapositions within his works (O'Doherty 1973, 197–198). He was writing about Rauschenberg's "combines"—which the artist began producing in 1954—a body of work that straddled the lines long established between painting and sculpture.

Rauschenberg's work as a painter is inseparable from the story as set designer. Throughout his sixty-year-long career, Robert Rauschenberg sought out projects in which he could collaborate with others. "I've always been attracted to and tempted into nearly any situation where the final work was the result of more than one person's doing," he said (Rauschenberg quoted in *Robert Rauschenberg* 2016, 10).
*ELIZABETH CARPENTER*

Merce Cunningham and John Cage were invited to attend Black Mountain College, an experimental school, in the summers of 1948, 1952, and 1953. Here they connected with artist Robert Rauschenberg who was a regular and prominent resident there. Beginning in 1954, Rauschenberg began working with Cunningham's Dance Company (MCDC) and became its first Artistic Advisor.

Cunningham asked Rauschenberg to create a set in 1954 for *Minutiae* [2.2], the dance piece he was working on. Characteristic of Cunningham's approach to collaborating with other artists and art forms, Rauschenberg was given freedom in this process, with only the suggestion to make something that could be placed in the performance area, that the dancers might move around or through. Rauschenberg first designed a drop that was to be suspended from the ceiling in the performance area, with the dancers able to move beneath it;

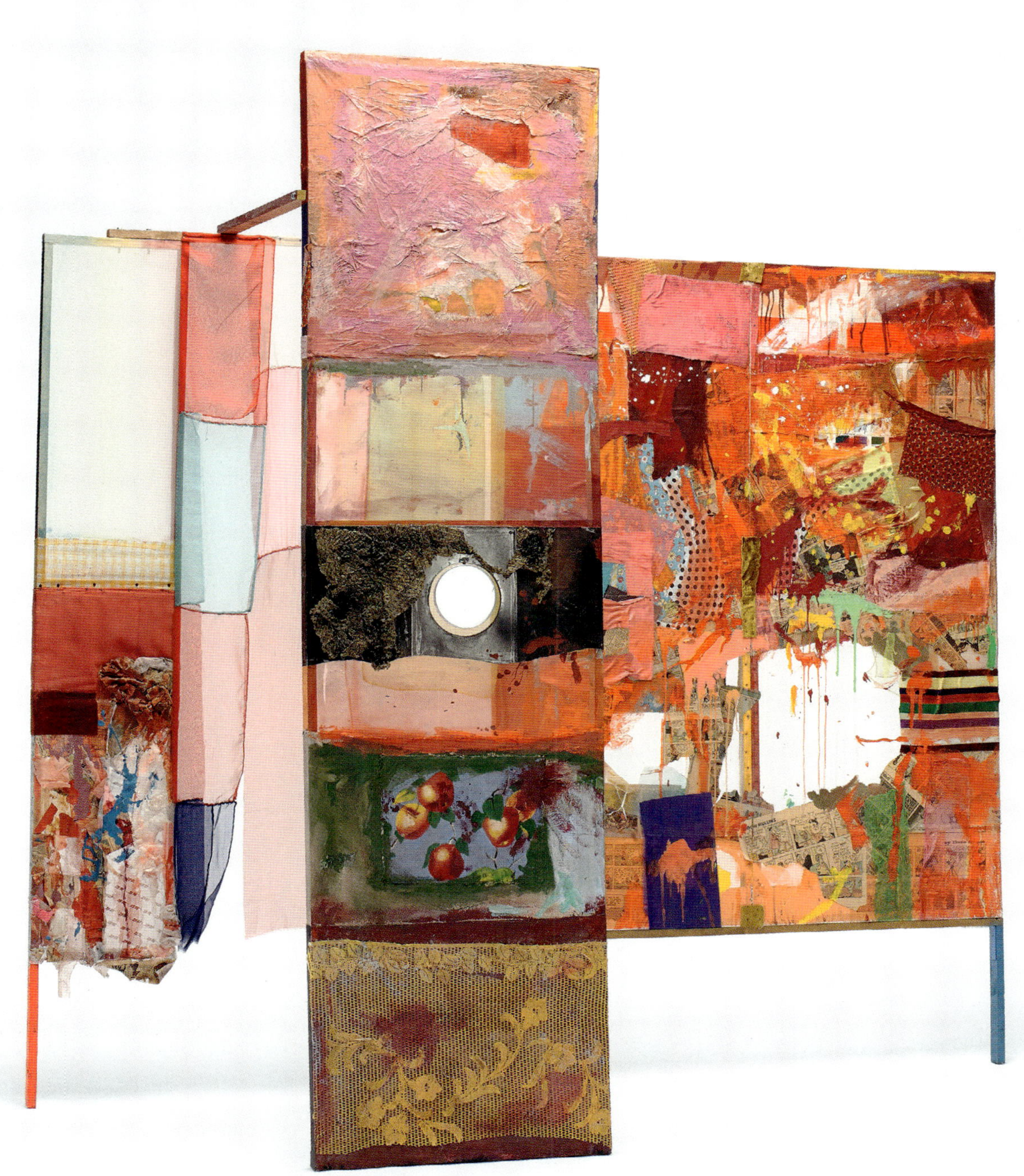



[2.2]

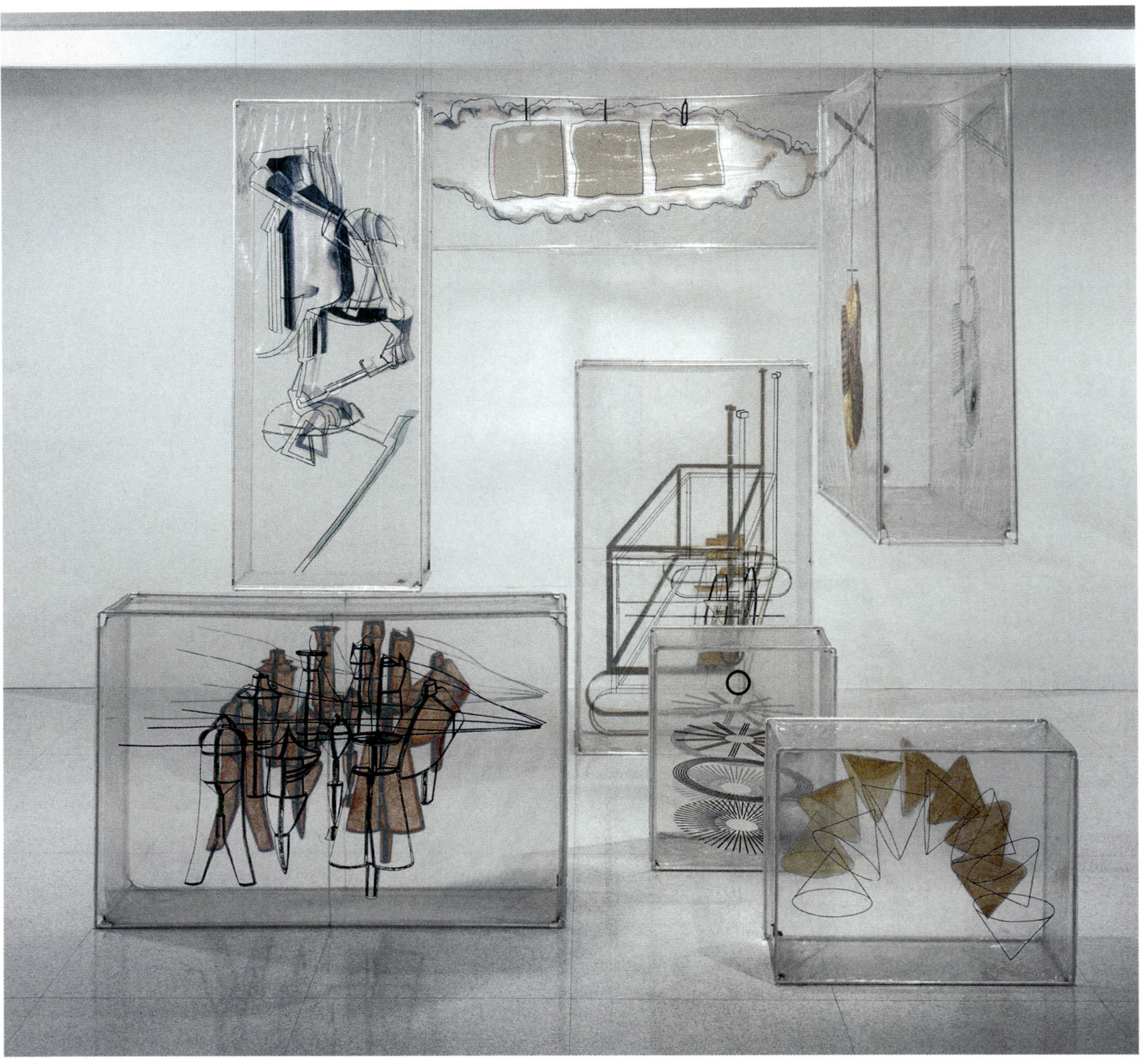

[2.3]

however, this rejected on practical grounds, as the stages the Company performed in at that time were often without fly areas and the means to install such a piece. Rauschenberg then revised the piece based on these practical considerations and made a free-standing work. Consisting of a wooden frame, covered in collaged cloth, paper, paint, and a mirror, it sits across two planes, creating space for the dancers to move through it.

The set for *Minutiae* is colorful, combining fabrics and other materials of various textures and shades; the overwhelming tones however are reds, pinks and oranges. Because of this, it has an affinity with Rauschenberg's *Red Paintings*, a series he produced around the same time. In this series Rauschenberg had included collaged elements such as fabric and newspaper, as seen in *Minutiae*. This was a pivotal period in Rauschenberg's practice, and in *Minutiae* he extended his experimentation with such materials as well as other objects into his work, into what is considered the first of his *Combines*. In these works, Rauschenberg blurred the definitions between painting and sculpture by incorporating three-dimensional objects into his wall-works, and in some free-standing structures.

*Minutiae* debuted at Brooklyn Academy of Music in December 1954.

Cunningham's choreography was comprised of small, abrupt movements that he had developed through a process of chance and after observing the everyday incidental movements of people on the street. Rauschenberg's set piece was placed on the stage while the dancers performed, and the music for the piece was from an existing work, *Music for Piano 1–20*, by Cage. While Rauschenberg's designs were shaped by some back-and-forth discussion with Cunningham about the practicalities of working in the theater, the set was not created as an after-the-fact decoration for the stage, or with a brief that tied it to the choreography, thematically or otherwise. Instead, the process of creating the set was in keeping with the nature of Cunningham and Cage's collaboration, in which each element was produced independently and then brought together to "coexist" in the performances. This process "[leaves] space around each art" and creates an experience for the audience in which they are asked to "place [their] attention in three different directions" (interview with Merce Cunningham and John Cage, 1981: https://walkerart.org/magazine/chance-conversations-an-interview-with-merce) rather than on a single whole made of parts. In doing so, MCDC and its collaborators also blurred the distinctions between art and design; indeed Rauschenberg's set was shaped by the pragmatics of its purpose but easily fits into his broader artistic practice that encapsulates the transitions in his practice at that time as his layered *Red Paintings* made way for his more three-dimensional *Combines*.
*NIKKI KANE*

## JASPER JOHNS

(Augusta, Georgia 1930)

[2.3]
**Set elements for *Walkaround Time***
**1968**
plastic, paint, 7 inflatable pillows
dimensions variable
Minneapolis, Walker Art Center
T. B. Walker Acquisition Fund, 2000

Jasper Johns and Robert Rauschenberg worked in the same studio building in New York City, and as well as working together as freelance display artists, Johns assisted Rauschenberg on almost all of his sets and costumes for the Merce Cunningham Dance Company, including helping him to get *Minutiae* "to stand up and not fall over" (Klosty 1975, 85).

Johns became the Artistic Adviser for MCDC in 1967, despite having some reservations: "I wasn't asked to be Artistic Adviser to the Company until 1967, and I was reluctant. In the theater, there is something about the setting up and taking down of things that I dislike. But when I thought of the people who might be available to do the work that I was being invited to do, I decided that I might do it in ways that would offend me less when I went to see the performance. It was a poor way to make a decision, an arrogant way, but that was my feeling." Instead of designing and making sets himself, Johns preferred to invite other artists "for whose work [he has] a high regard" and "who could understand a difference between theater and studio, or gallery scale and space" (Vaughn 1989, 55) to make work for the stage, beginning with Frank Stella and over the years including Robert Morris, Andy Warhol, and Bruce Nauman.

The design for *Walkaround Time* [2.3] was a collaboration with Marcel Duchamp, at a remove: While visiting Duchamp's home one evening, Johns suggested to Cunningham that they could have a set based on his *The Bride Stripped Bare by Her Bachelors, Even (The Large Glass)*, and when Cunningham agreed, Johns approached Duchamp who was supportive of the idea as long as someone else would actually do the work to produce it. The set was then designed and produced by Johns, after Duchamp.

Consisting of seven transparent rectangular boxes, or pillows, made of clear plastic, each was painted and screenprinted by Johns with a motif from *The Large Glass*: the Bride, the Chocolate Grinder, the Milky Way with Nets, the Watermill, the Nine Malic Molds, the Occult Witnesses, and the Sieves/Parasols. In the performances, these could be lifted and moved by the dancers as part of the choreography, with all seven elements coming together at the end of the piece, placed to correspond with their arrangement in Duchamp's work. The music for this piece was titled *For Nearly an Hour* and composed by David Bahrman, and while the performance itself lasted for nearly an hour at 50 minutes long, this title also refers to another work by Duchamp from 1918, *To be looked at (from the other side of the glass) with one eye, close to, for nearly an hour*. The choreography for *Walkaround Time* is unusual within Cunningham's oeuvre in that it was "in homage to Duchamp," too, as Cunningham's compositions usually reject direct thematic content, but Cunningham maintains distance here as well by referring to qualities of Duchamp and his work in the broad sense, rather than responding specifically to *The Large Glass*. The choreography includes a sequence in which Cunningham runs on the spot while changing from one pair of tights into another, which refers to Duchamp's *Nude Descending a Staircase* in both its sense of movement and its undressing. The piece also includes an intermission where the dancers do ordinary break-time things but on the stage, accompanied by popular music recordings—which are sort of "ready-mades in yet another sense." This intermission moment also recalls the film *Entr'acte* (which means "between the scenes") which was included in the Dadaist ballet *Relâche* (1924), with Duchamp appearing in both the film and the ballet (Basualdo 2017, 145–154; Vaughan 1998, 66–70).

The transparency of the boxes Johns produced, like the glass of Duchamp's *Large Glass*, allowed viewers to see beyond the surface of the work and through it. With the two parallel, painted planes of the boxes combined with the movement of both the boxes and the dancers in front or behind them, the piece played with senses of perception for the viewer, in a sense echoing Cunningham's usual modes of collaboration in which movement, sound, and visual elements coexist without necessarily corresponding.

John did not consider the set elements for *Walkaround Time* to be an artwork of his, but rather a design he made after Duchamp. However, his own artwork as a painter and a printmaker often included a sense of movement, for example in the gestural strokes and patterns of *Cicada* (1979) or *Dancers on a Plane* (1979); and

in the suggestion of moving paint across the canvas with items like brooms or squeegees in works such as *Fool's House* (1962), *Voice* (1964–67), and *Good Time Charley* (1972).
*NIKKI KANE*

**MERCE CUNNINGHAM**
(Centralia 1919–New York 2009)

[2.4]
CHARLES ATLAS, MERCE CUNNINGHAM
***Walkaround Time***
**1973**
16mm film (color, sound) transferred to HD video
51:06 min
Minneapolis, Walker Art Center
Butler Family Fund, 2018
Courtesy Electronic Arts Intermix (EAI), New York

[2.5]
***Story***
**1964**
digital video (black and white, sound)
20:10 min
Minneapolis, Walker Art Center
Butler Family Fund, 2019
Courtesy Electronic Arts Intermix (EAI), New York

Merce Cunningham's iconic work *Walkaround Time* (1973) [2.4] was filmed by Charles Atlas who was the Cunningham company's production stage manager and who collaborated with Cunningham on a number of video events in later years. *Walkaround Time* is composed of seven sections, each approximately seven minutes long.
The performance documentation was recorded in two parts. Part 1 was filmed in Zellerbach Auditorium at the University of California, Berkeley with only one hand held camera, and shot in a single day of start-and-stop rehearsal. Part II was filmed several years later at the Théâtre de la Ville in Paris (1972) with three cameras during a live performance. Atlas's concern was to capture the actual performance quality of the dancers and, in the last two sections, make a filmic approximation of the experience of the dance.
It was made to be shown in a two-screen presentation requiring two precisely synchronized projectors. The use of two screens was an attempt to approximate the viewing of the dance on stage.
The video *Story* (1963) [2.5] is the only recording of Merce Cunningham's *Story*. It was shot by film director Hakki Seppala and it documents a 1964 live telecast in Helsinki, Finland, during the world tour of the piece.
*Story* was, in fact, originally performed the first time on 24 July, 1963, at the University of California, Los Angeles. In the following year and half, it was performed forty-eight times in forty-one different venues around the world.
*Story* had an indeterminate structure. There were eighteen sections—solos, duets, trios, and larger group units—but the overall duration and the order of the sections all changed from one performance to the next.
The dancers could make choices about the space, time, and order of their movements. The music was composed by Toshi Ichiyanagi, who gave musicians similar flexibility for instrumentation and duration of sound. Robert Rauschenberg constructed a new set for each performance, using material he found in or near the theater. He also designed the costumes with a basic outfit of leotards and tights over which the dancers could wear an assortment of garments, changing as often as they wished.
All considered, this video represents only one iteration of the dance's indeterminate structure and does not capture the full spectrum of possible materials and options.
*VINCENZO DE BELLIS*

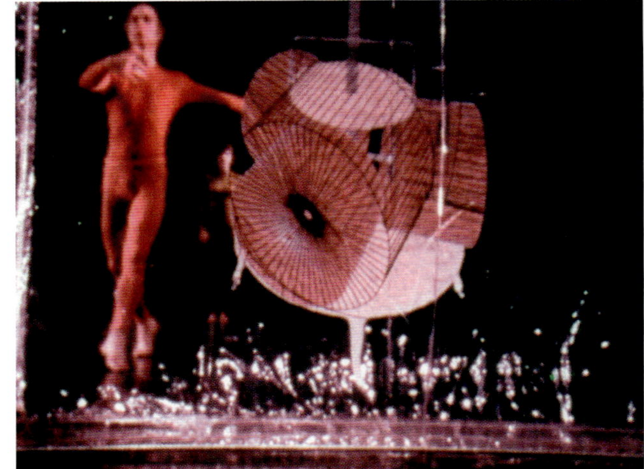

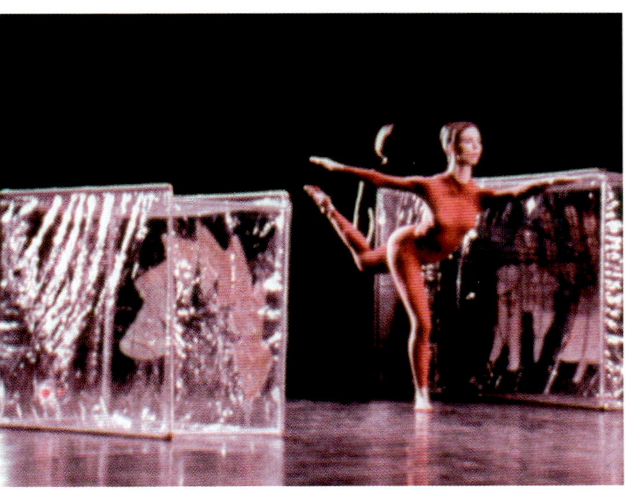

[2.4]

Merce
Cunningham

STORY
(1963)
MUSIIKKI
Toshi Ichiyangi
TANSSIT:
Merce Cunningham
Carolyn Brown   Viola Farber
Deborah May   Barbara Lloyd
William Davis   Steve Paxton
Sandra Neels
Albert Reid
SAESTYS:
John Cage ja David Tudor

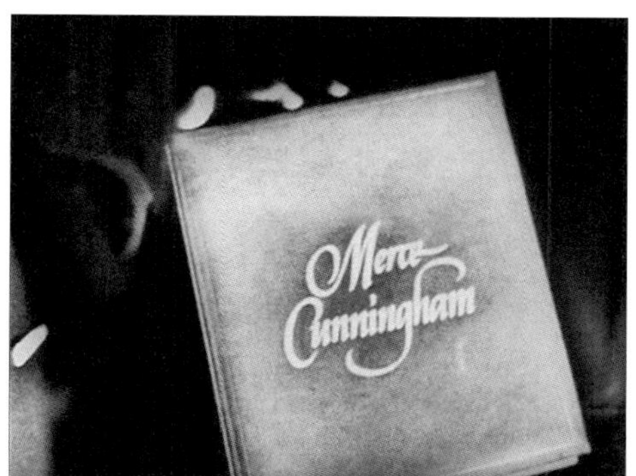

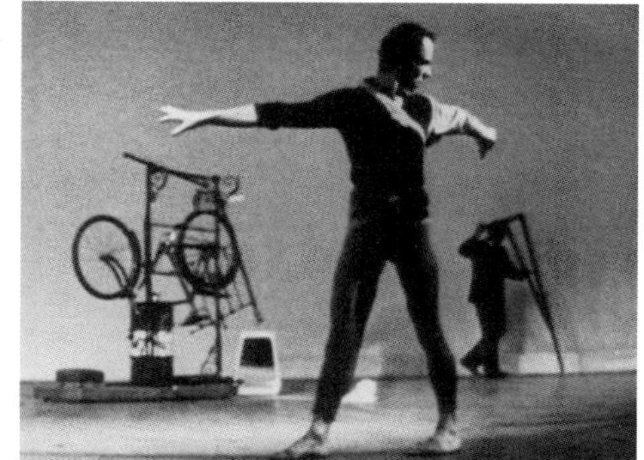

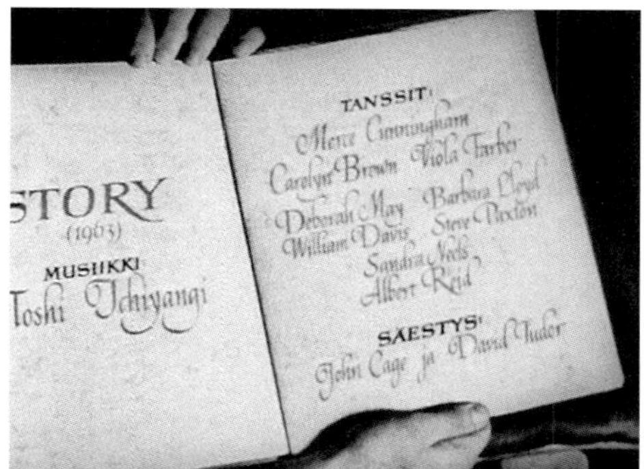

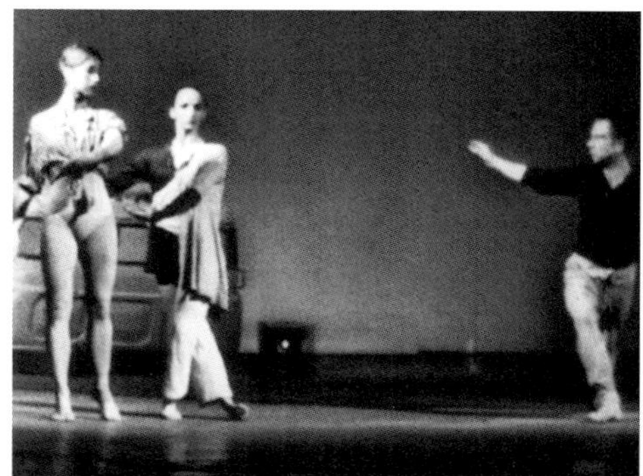

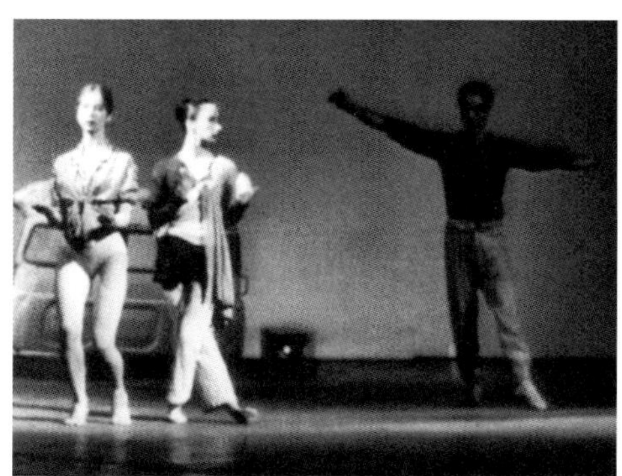

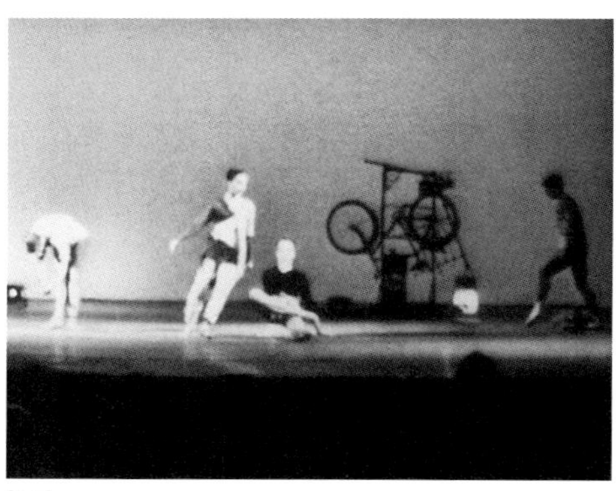

[2.5]

# POPS

3.

## ROBERT INDIANA

(Robert Clark; New Castle, Indiana 1928–Vinalhaven, Maine, 2018)

[3.1]
***The Green Diamond EAT The Red Diamond DIE***
**1962**
oil on canvas
215.9 × 215.9 cm each
Minneapolis, Walker Art Center
Gift of the T. B. Walker Foundation, 1963

Though always skeptical of the art movement that he helped pioneer, Robert Indiana is best known for his Pop Art paintings and sculptures. Indiana developed some of his earliest work alongside other artists living in Coenties Slip, a neighborhood in New York City, working alongside a group of artists that would ultimately include Ellsworth Kelly, Agnes Martin, Jack Youngerman, and James Rosenquist. His early years of experimentation settled into a fascination with color and language, establishing him as a Pop Art forerunner in the early 1960s.

Indiana began with abstract shapes, and in 1961 further introduced words like *Fun* into the paintings, as well as making wooden constructions. These first iterations were included in the two-person show with Peter Forakis at the David Anderson Gallery, where Alfred Baar, then director of MoMA, acquired one of the paintings for their collection. Over the next several decades, Indiana became best known for his sculpture *LOVE*, which he made in various languages and iterations throughout his career. The sculpture was referenced in the title of his 2013 retrospective at the Whitney Museum of American Art, *Robert Indiana: Beyond LOVE*. True to the title, Indiana's practice has been far more than a single, widely circulated work. While his four-letter sculptures made him famous, his practice was nevertheless varied.

Given his founding influences in Pop Art, it is only natural that he would turn to public art as a way for his works to gain greater visibility. Most of his sculptures, such as *LOVE* and his series *Numbers*, are all made to be outdoor monumental sculptures and can often be found in city centers, parks, and the outdoor lobbies of skyscrapers. A theatrical set and costume designer as well, Indiana turned his talents not only to the theater stage, but the hardwood floors of the basketball court, famously painting the unique design of the Milwaukee Buck's home court in that city's MECCA Arena. This engagement with public space only reinforces Indiana's interest in the visual material found every day.

Indiana drew his inspiration from the signs, symbols, and visual rhetoric of mid-twentieth-century corporate branding imagery. Rather than embracing the consumerist undertones found in other Pop Artists, his work often was overtly critical of contemporary culture. His style, over the course of his long career, developed a more poetic and contemplative tone compared to peers such as Andy Warhol. In all, Indiana's oeuvre demonstrates the power simple marketing overtures and their underlying ideologies have on our daily life.

Conceived of as a single painting, *The Green Diamond EAT The Red Diamond DIE* [3.1] contains two diamond shaped canvases presented next to each other, left to right. The leftmost canvas is green with a red circle occupying the center. The word *EAT* is placed in the middle of the circle in the same green color as the corners. On the right is a red square with a black circle. The word in the middle is *DIE*,

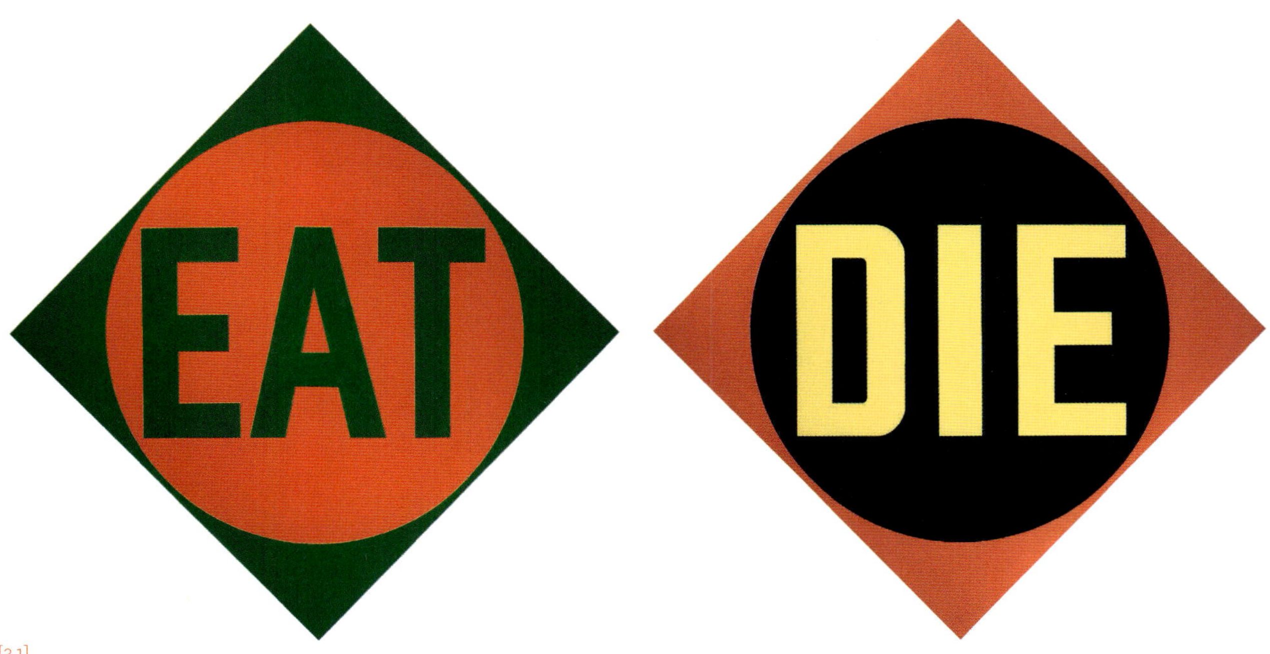



[3.1]

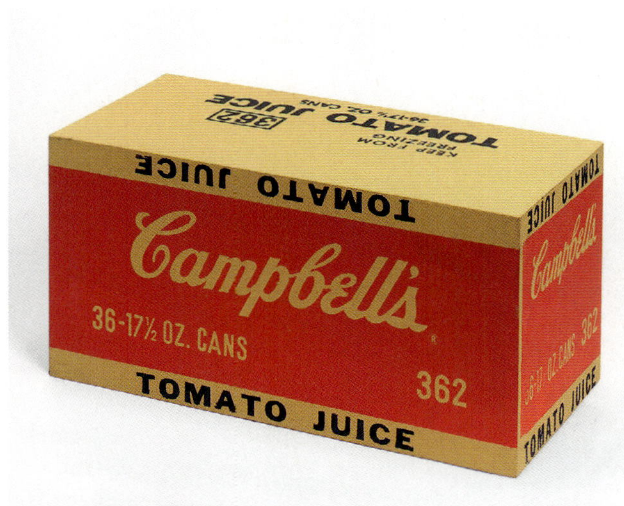

[3.2]

which breaks from *EAT* in that it avoids mirroring the same color pattern. The letters are in a bright gold. The resulting *DIE* is nearly as jarring a visual effect as the red/green color combination of *EAT*. The relationship of the colors between the two canvases is intense and sometimes even visually uneasy.

The artist attributes these colors to his childhood encounters with oil company Phillips 66, where this father worked. The stark color contrast between the red, green, and black was iconic of the company for decades until it changed to red and white in the middle of the century. The artist also attributes the word *EAT* to his childhood, noting that his mother owned a restaurant, and having been raised during the Great Depression, signs for "Eat" took on a deeply personal meaning. *DIE*, Indiana states in a 1963 interview, represented "the other side of the coin." He continues, "Everybody eats, and everybody enjoys life, and everybody consumes, and very few people ever think about what all this is really leading to. And after all that is where we are all going, and I find it provocative perhaps to think about it once in a while, and that's why the *DIE* is on the other side."
In a way, the two canvases of the diptych function like competing neon signs. They draw attention from one to another creating a cycle. Eat, die. Eat, die. The more one spends time with this cycle, the heavier the implication. What began as a nod to mid-twentieth-century consumer culture becomes a road sign for a distilled life under capitalism. The conflicting colors, at first kitschy and playfully clashing, become a jolting and uneasy pulse of contemporary life. These "signs" may be bright, clear, and eye-catching but there is something uneasy in them, a broken pattern, a discordant set of colors. They serve as a purposeful imbalance that reminds us to consider life from both sides, the beginning and the end.
*WILLIAM HERNANDEZ-LUEGE*

**ANDY WARHOL**
(Andrew Warhola Jr.; Pittsburgh, Pennsylvania, 1928–New York 1987)

[3.2]
### *Campbell's Tomato Juice Box*
**1964**
synthetic polymer paint, screenprint on wood
25.4 × 48.3 × 24.1 cm
Minneapolis, Walker Art Center
T. B. Walker Acquisition Fund, 2001

[3.3]
### *Campbell's Tomato Juice Box*
**1964**
synthetic polymer paint, screenprint on wood
25.1 × 48.3 × 24 cm
Minneapolis, Walker Art Center
Gift of Kate Butler Peterson, 2002

[3.4]
### *Del Monte Peach Halves Box*
**1964**
synthetic polymer paint, screenprint on wood
24.1 × 38.1 × 30.3 cm
Minneapolis, Walker Art Center
Gift of Kate Butler Peterson, 2002

[3.5]
### *Heinz Tomato Ketchup Box*
**1964**
synthetic polymer paint, screenprint on wood
21.6 × 26.7 × 39.4 cm
Minneapolis, Walker Art Center
Gift of Kate Butler Peterson, 2002

[3.6]
### *Kellogg's Corn Flakes Box*
**1964**
synthetic polymer paint, screenprint on wood
63.5 × 53.3 × 43.2 cm
Minneapolis, Walker Art Center
Gift of Kate Butler Peterson, 2002

[3.7]
### *Mott's Apple Juice Box*
**1964**
synthetic polymer paint, screenprint on wood
45.7 × 75.9 × 55.9 cm
Minneapolis, Walker Art Center
Gift of Kate Butler Peterson, 2002

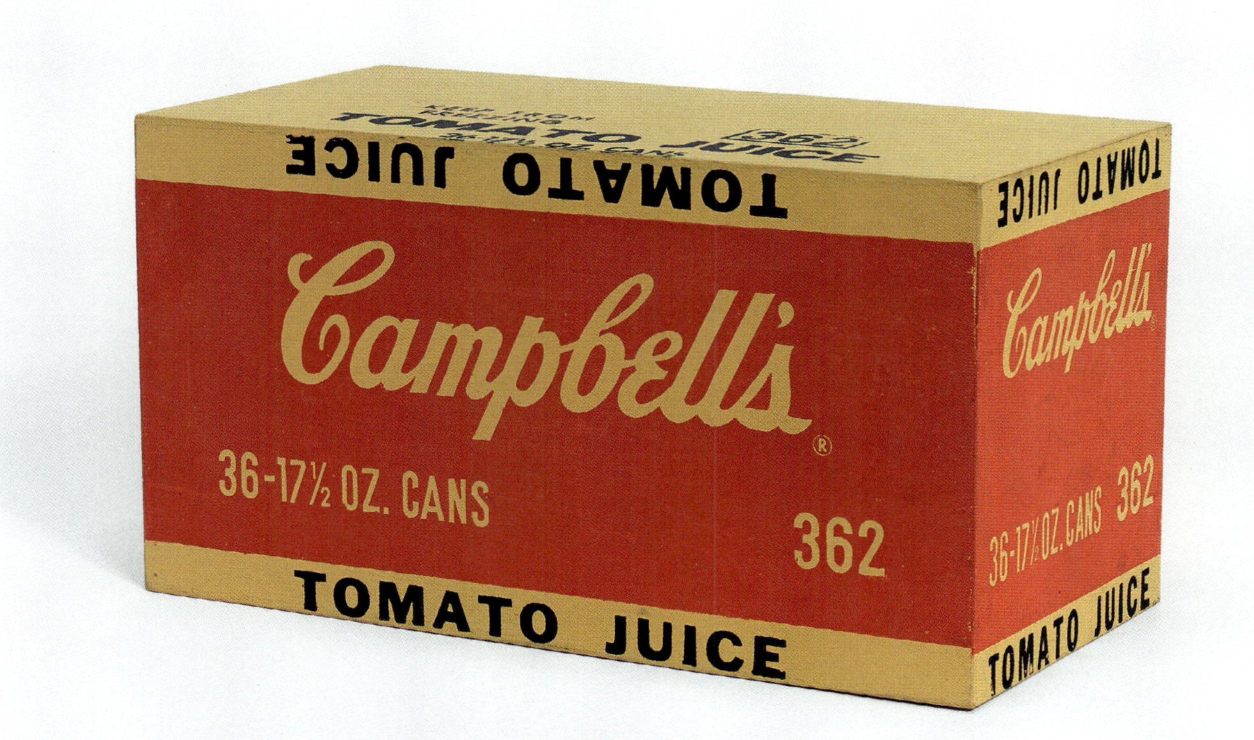

[3.3]

[3.8]
***White Brillo Box***
**1964**
synthetic polymer paint, screenprint on wood
43.2 × 42.9 × 35.6 cm
Minneapolis, Walker Art Center
Gift of Kate Butler Peterson, 2002

[3.9]
***Yellow Brillo Box***
**1964**
synthetic polymer paint, screenprint on wood
33 × 40.6 × 29.2 cm
Minneapolis, Walker Art Center
Gift of Kate Butler Peterson, 2002

[3.10]
***Sixteen Jackies***
**1964**
acrylic, enamel on canvas
204.2 × 165.9 cm
Minneapolis, Walker Art Center
Art Center Acquisition Fund, 1968

[3.11]
***Electric Chair***
**1971**
Edition: 138/250, screenprint on paper
90.2 × 121.9 cm each of 10
Minneapolis, Walker Art Center
McKnight Acquisition Fund, 1995

[3.12]
***Self-Portrait***
**1978**
acrylic, silkscreen ink on canvas
41 × 33.5 cm
Minneapolis, Walker Art Center
T. B. Walker Acquisition Fund, 1993

[3.13]
***Self-Portrait***
**1978**
acrylic, silkscreen ink on canvas
40.6 × 33 cm
Minneapolis, Walker Art Center
T. B. Walker Acquisition Fund, 1993

Andy Warhol is probably the most famous American artist, and the most famous artist of the twentieth century. He began working in New York as a commercial illustrator, but soon reinvented himself as an artist, gaining recognition for his work that reproduced the designs of consumer culture and mass media. As well as his extensive series of silkscreen works, Warhol also produced many films in his later career, and throughout his practice he pushed the boundaries of what art could be.

Andy Warhol's series of painted and screenprinted boxes are icons of Pop Art, eye-catching and instantly recognizable now as Warhol artworks just as much as the famous branded products and logos they are based on.

First exhibited at Warhol's second solo show at the Stable Gallery in 1964, they were displayed in stacked towers, echoing shop stockroom storage and were for sale for low prices at around $200–$400 each. Although they sold poorly at the exhibition, they were a critical success and have become iconic works of Warhol's artistic practice, emblematic of his preoccupation with reproduction and mass consumer culture and media (Rothfuss 2005, 573–574).

Warhol began his career as a commercial artist, producing illustrations for magazines and advertisements before he reinvented himself as a fine artist producing works that made use of repetition and the reproductive techniques of printmaking, and that used media imagery as source material. These boxes are made of wood, with their designs screenprinted and painted onto the surfaces. There is necessarily a tension in the placement of the consumer aesthetic into the fine art object, but this is somehow heightened by the materials of the work. Wood in place of disposable cardboard (although later versions were produced in different woods and cardboard), and the combination hand-painting and small-scale screenprinting of the boxes' designs (as opposed to factory-scale printing) points to the complicated nature of these artworks: They are simultaneously reproductions in multiple of disposable mass-produced objects, but have also been created to an extent by hand.

The question of the hand-of-production is also pertinent in Warhol's practice, as much of his output was created in his famous Factory, an old warehouse building occupied by a lively, rotating group of people who, as well as socializing, assisted in producing artworks (and even featured in some film works). The wooden boxes themselves were produced out-of-house, made-to-order from a woodwork shop and then painted in the Factory to match the base colors of the original cardboard packaging and screenprinted with the logos and designs (Danto 2009, 49–54). In some ways, this Factory set-up harks back to art historical traditions of artists' workshops but, when combined with Warhol's appropriated imagery and reproductive techniques, it raised many questions in the 1960s American art world about the figure of the artist as the author of their work. Similarly, outsourcing the production of certain aspects of an artwork is a practice that became increasingly common in the 1960s, perhaps most notably in the industrially fabricated works of Minimalism. Warhol's boxes, however, straddle these multiple modes of production: part-prefabricated, part-painted, part-printed; both standardized and handmade.

The nature of Warhol's boxes as facsimiles of standard, mass-produced objects places them in a lineage of appropriation in modern art, connecting to—but not entirely fitting in with—practices of re-

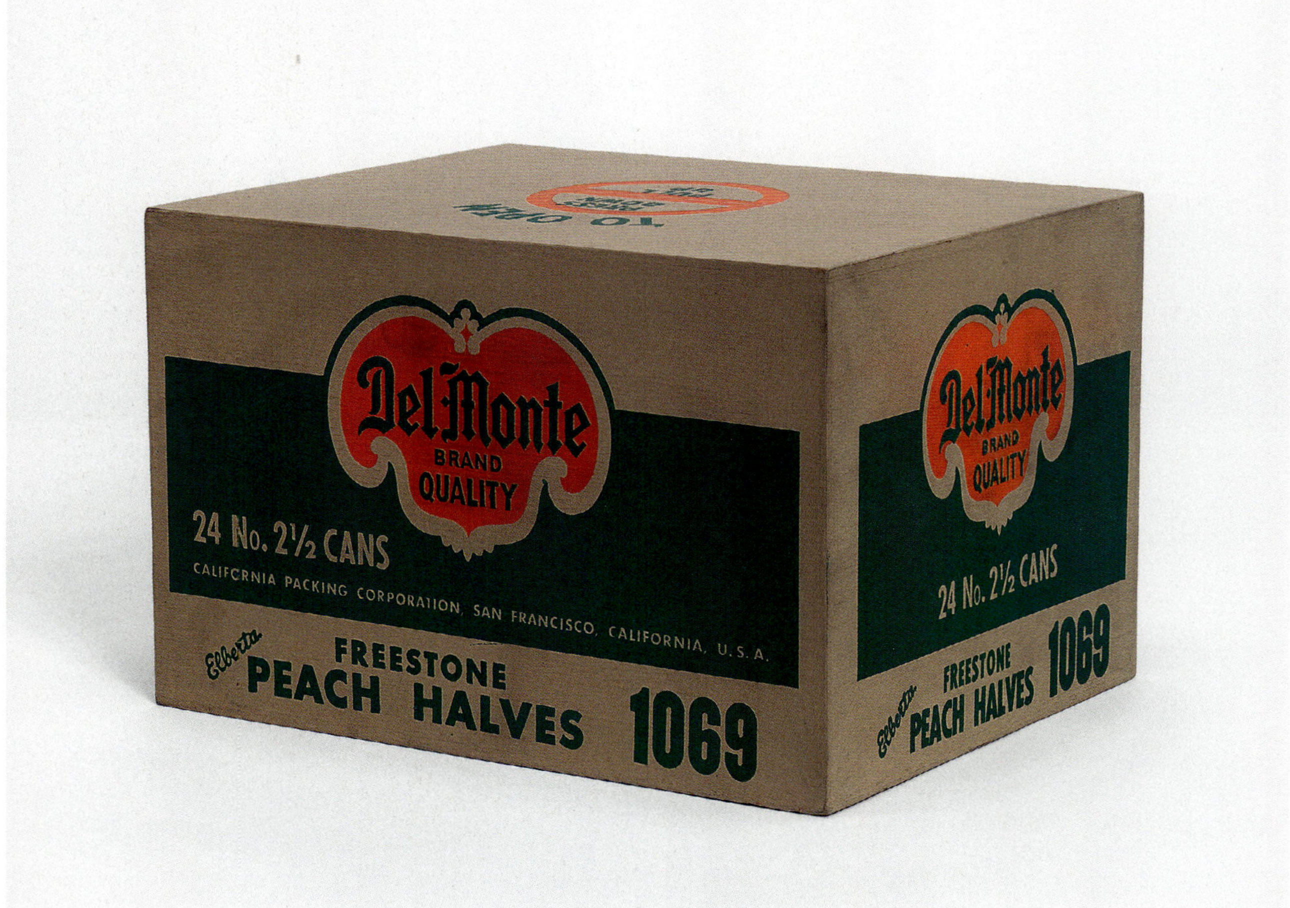

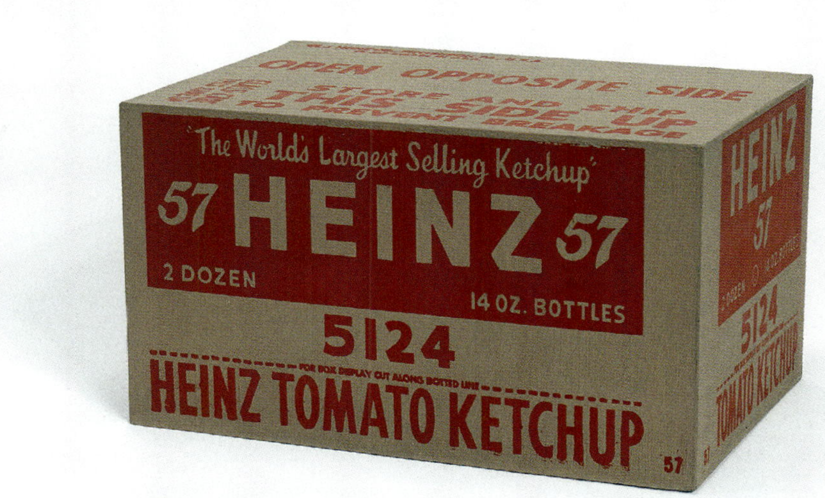

[3.5]

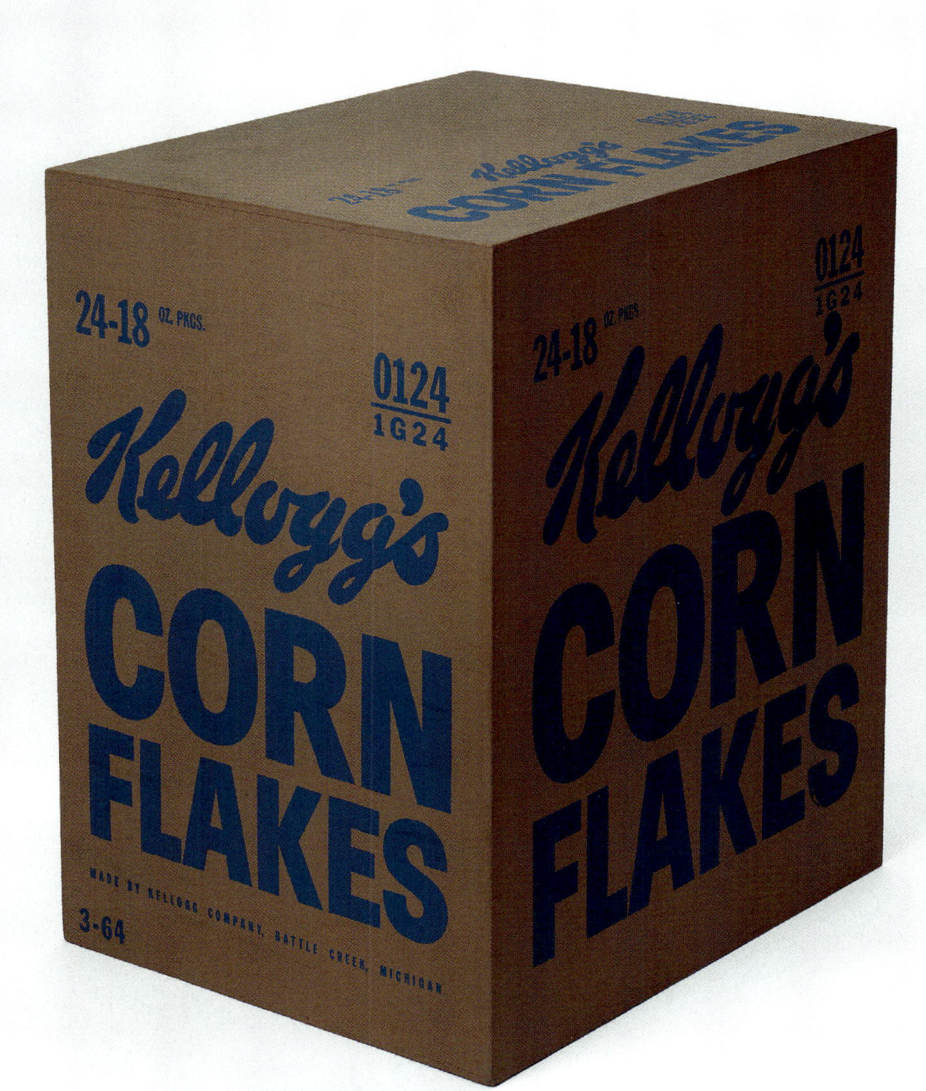

[3.6]

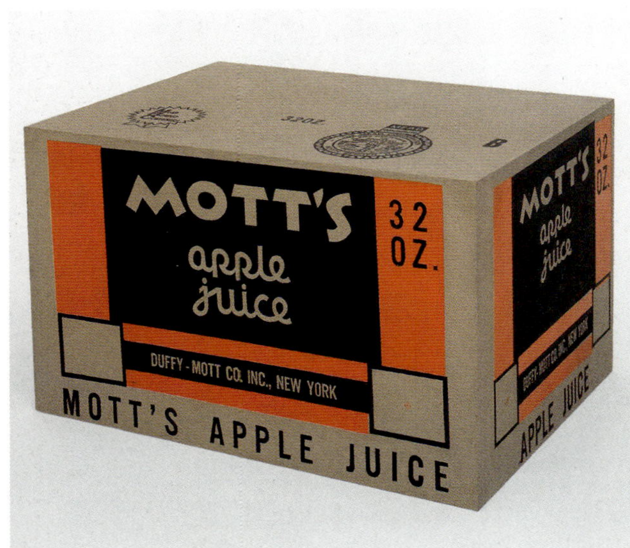

[3.7]

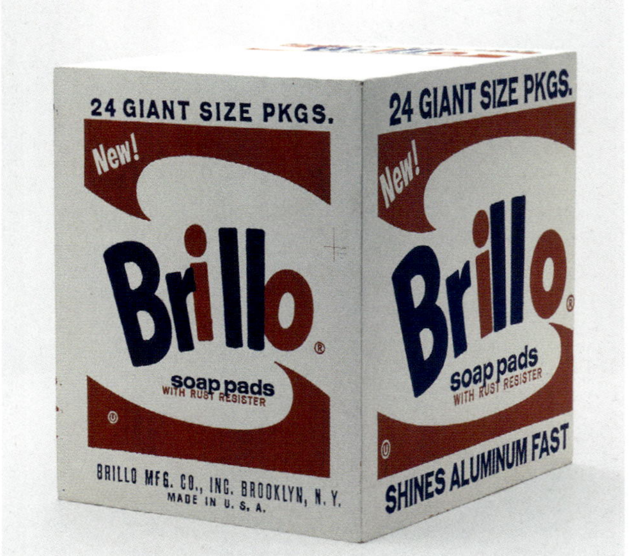

[3.8]

This work is occupied by a grid structure, creating a uniformity to the repeated images with each photo of Jackie repeated horizontally. This gridded format gives the canvas a sense of pace and is suggestive of film strips or contact sheets, pointing to the extensive and repeated news coverage of Jackie in the wake of the assassination. For Warhol, this was key. He was concerned not just with Jackie as an individual figure and celebrity, but with her image and its presentation in the media, and he made several works based on images of her repeated in various configurations.

The four different photographs that make up this work were sourced photographing, collage, assemblage, and the ready-made. These works are not preexisting objects themselves placed directly into the gallery, but instead are constructed in a studio by hand(s), using printing techniques similar to those used in industrial processes, resulting in an object that looks like the one it copies. Warhol, however, did not use reproductive mediums to fool the viewer. In his large-scale prints and paintings on paper, for example *Sixteen Jackies* [3.10] produced in the same year as these boxes, process marks such as ink smudges and misalignments are incorporated into the work, making the process of production visible to the viewer. Here, this can be seen by looking closely at the materials used: The texture of the paint and wood is visible, and the edges of some of the lettering is uneven. Unlike the "real" boxes where each one is identical, in Warhol's each reproduction slightly differs.

These works from the Walker's broad Warhol collection shows a range of box designs, including those from iconic brands Campbell's, Brillo, Heinz, Kellogg's, Del Monte, and Mott's [3.2-3.9]. Displaying these works today, they appear to capture a specific moment in time and so bring with them a sense of nostalgia. When first exhibited in 1964, these designs were modern and familiar, present in supermarkets and homes across the United States, and they captured the boom of American consumer culture.

With this series of sculptures, Warhol raised important and lasting questions about what counts as art—as art critic and philosopher Arthur C. Danto notes, "It would have been impossible for Andy's boxes to have *been* art before 1964" (Danto 2009, 61).

Four repetitions of four images of Jackie Kennedy make up *Sixteen Jackies* [3.10], perhaps one of Warhol's most iconic works and based on media images of Kennedy from before and after the assassination of her husband President John F. Kennedy. This moment of violent tragedy that punctured the image of all-American glamour and success sets the scene for this work, and provoked Warhol's interest in the pervasive image of the widowed First Lady.

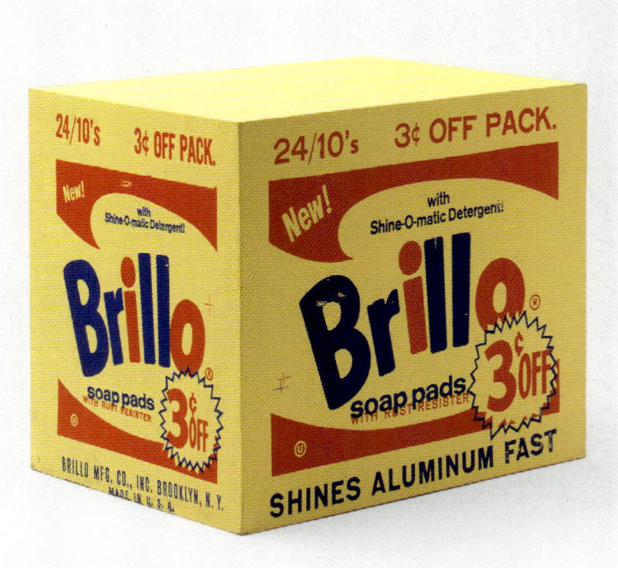

[3.9]

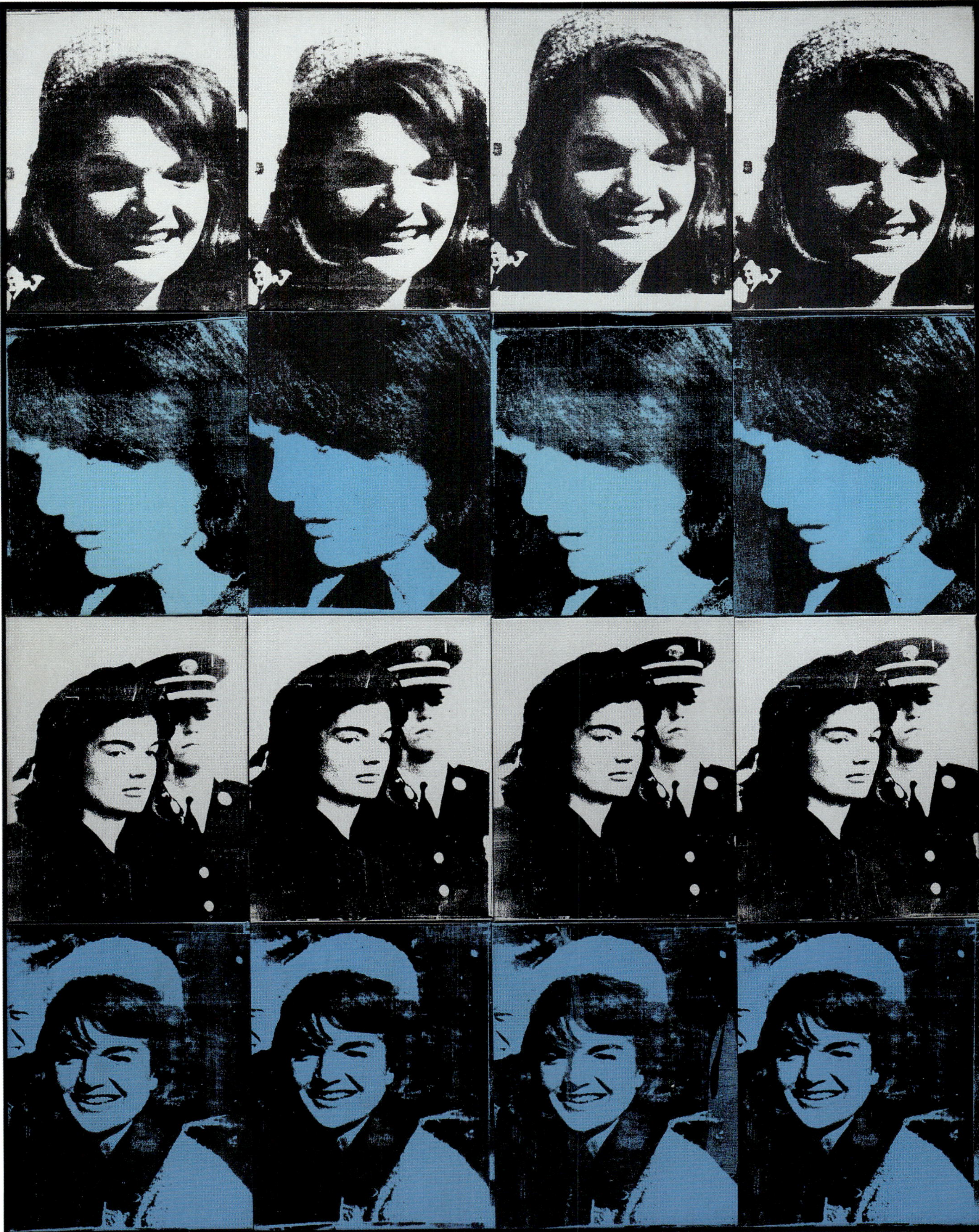

[3.10]

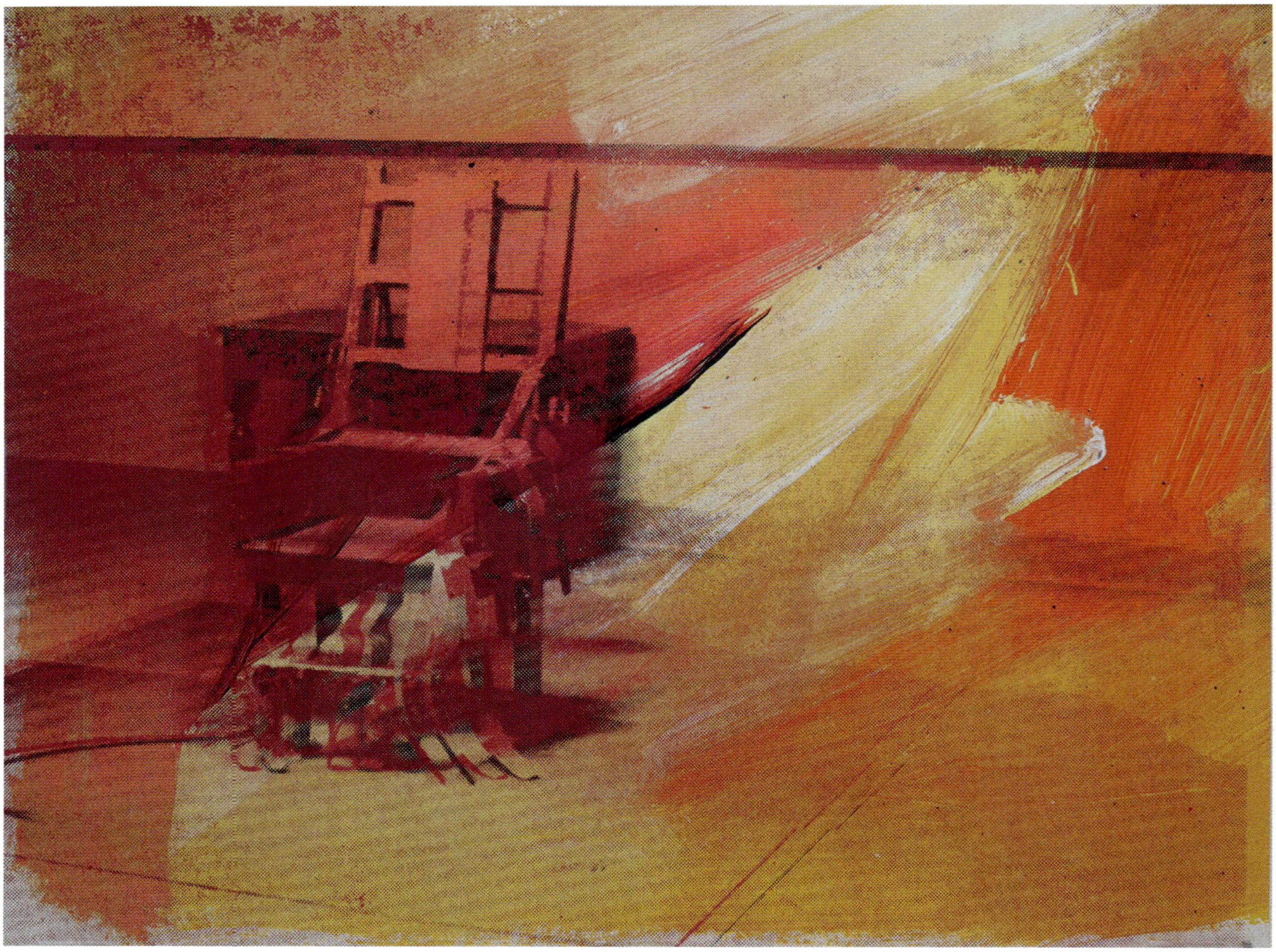

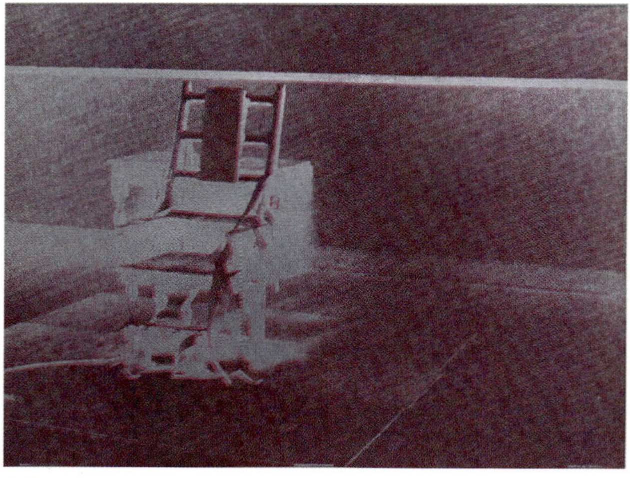

[3.11]

from print media and show Kennedy in different emotional states, smiling before the shooting and somber in moments afterwards. These different states are included nonchronologically, and with the close-cropping of each image to center on Jackie's face they heighten the sense of repetition in the work and in the barrage of news coverage of her key moments. The repetition in this work operates in multiple ways: All sixteen images are of the same figure, each individual photograph is repeated four times, Jackie wears a hat in both the top and bottom rows, each row alternates between black on white to black on shades of blue. The images in each repetition are the same but different—there are misalignments across the rows, smudges and process marks from the process of printing, and dif-

ferent shades and intensities of color—again pointing to the volume of repeated media coverage, like television flickers or newspaper prints. The repetition here neutralizes the impact of the individual image, but overwhelms through scale and multiplicity, much like the mass-media.

Warhol produced a number of Jackie portraits of different scales and compositions, and throughout his career created portraits of many figures from the worlds of entertainment, politics, and art. These, as is typical of the genre of portraiture, represent their subjects as recognizable, somewhat simplified and heightened versions of themselves. Warhol's portraits, however, are not wholly concerned with the figures they represent, but rather make their very representation part

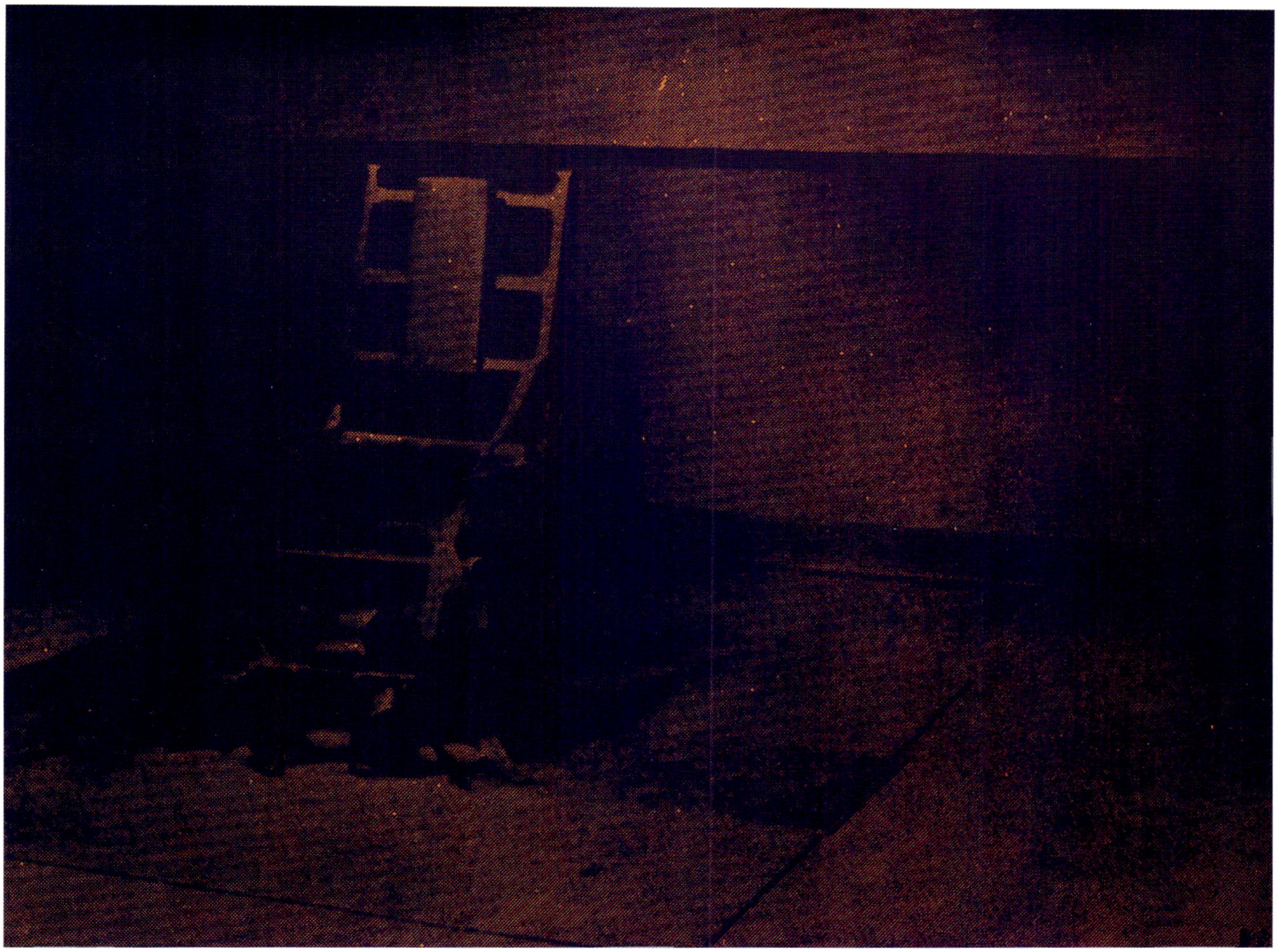

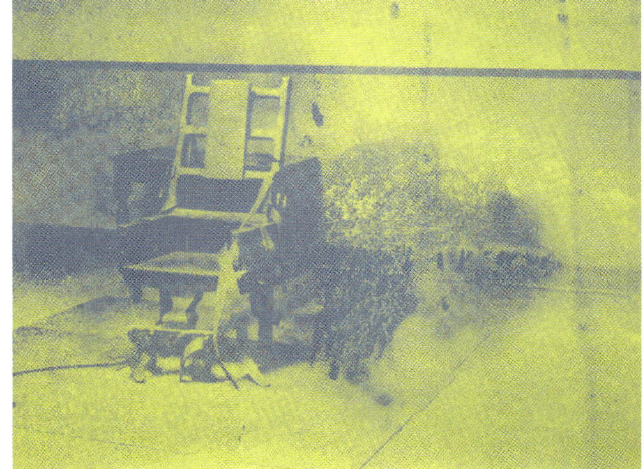

[3.11]

of the subject. This is emphasized through the repetition in his panel portraits, but also conveyed through his choices of cropped-in source imagery from mass-media sources, his use of color, and the medium of screenprinting that echoes media representation and necessarily condenses the figure's features, removing detail. Frcm the late 1960s, he took on portrait commissions as a way to help finance his film projects, which had become his primary artistic interest.

At this time, Warhol was also producing "death and disaster" works with car crashes, electric chairs, riots, and other events as subjects, and this piece can be read as part of this body of work too. As well as the portraits of Jackie, five years after the assassination of President Kennedy in November 1963, Warhol produced an artist's book titled *Flash—November 22, 1963* in which he commemorates the event with images of JFK, Jackie, and Lee Harvey Oswald as well as other imagery and text (*Andy Warhol* 1988, 114–121).

While Warhol is most famous for his works depicting celebrity figures and consumer items, he produced works throughout his career that dealt with darker subjects in his extensive *Death and Disaster* series. The *Electric Chair* [3.11] is considered the "most iconic" (Printz 1988, 16) of this series, which also features images such as car crashes, riots, suicide, poisoned food, and wanted criminals. Some of these explicitly show the moments of disaster in the imagery while others, like the *Electric Chair*, reference violence and death without actually depicting it, instead calling to mind their place in broader narratives.

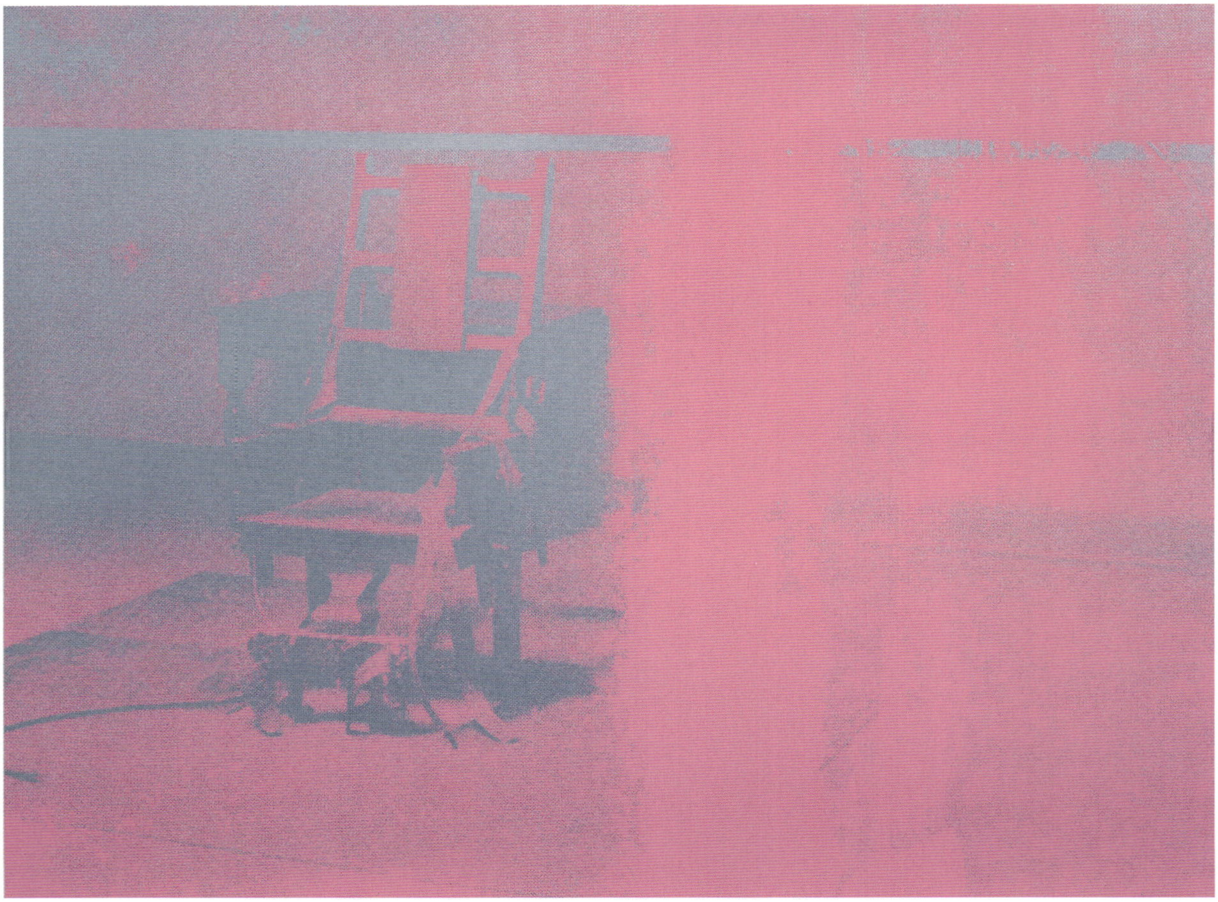

[3.11]

[3.11]

For his first show with gallerist Ileana Sonnabend in Paris in January 1964, Warhol wanted to produce an exhibition titled *Death in America* that centered on these *Death and Disaster* images, including electric chair works, but Sonnabend was reluctant about this presentation. In the end, the title of the show was changed to simply *Warhol*, but the content went ahead. The exhibition was respected by local European audiences, something that may not have been possible with an exhibition like this in America at the time (Danto 2009, XI).

Warhol produced works based on the image of the electric chair over a number of years, beginning in 1963, working with various sizes, colors, repetitions, and crops of the original image. In this example from 1971, the image is closely cropped, bringing the chair itself into the foreground so that it occupies most of the composition. Somewhat unusually in Warhol's broader work, this piece is fairly restrained in composition, with no figures present, no repetition, and no allusions to the pace or products of mass-culture. The screenprinting technique, however, highlights the graininess of the image, sourced from a newspaper, and emphasizes both the immediacy and distance of disaster within media images. As a representation of death, the sparse image conveys it as absence, emptiness, void (Printz 1988, 16).

While Warhol often repeated images within a piece, there is also repetition in his seriality: Many works were produced in editions and images were revisited and reconfigured over and over again, as with the *Electric Chair*. Interview accounts from Warhol point to two layers of meaning here. Firstly, there is the element of neutralizing the content of the images through their repetition, corresponding to the effect of ongoing mass-media coverage, as he said: "When you see a gruesome picture over and over again, it doesn't really have any effect" (Interview with G. R. Swenson: Swenson 1963, 142). However, his assertion in the same interview about the regularity of violent accidents and incidents in society—"It's sick, but I'm sure it happens all the time"—points to another way to consider the serial repetition of these images, as references to the repeating of such events, as well as their images (Printz 1988, 17).

It is also worth considering the "American-ness" of *Electric Chair* and other works in the *Death and Disaster* series within Warhol's broader work that depicted clear icons and items of American mass culture. While death, accidents, and violence are of course universal, Warhol's treatment of them through replications of mass-media images works to "Americanize" them and contextualize them alongside his more obviously Pop subject matter. Similarly, his selection of subjects to include tragic celebrity figures like Jackie Kennedy and Marilyn Monroe, as well as vehicle crashes and poisoned canned food, punctured the comfort and security of idealized American glamour and consumerism (Printz 1988, 16–21). The electric chair is a specifically American example of death, a mechanized mode of administering it, and so for the non-American viewer its connotations with the United States are clear, making it another (far darker, more muted and violent) symbol of twentieth-century America.

During his life as an artist, Warhol became a celebrity in his own right, joining the status of the figures he depicted in his work. These two paintings from 1978 are *Self-portraits* [3.12–3.13] by an artist whose practice was defined by portraits of iconic people and objects, and they allow us to capture a sense of how he regarded himself.

These canvases are small in scale, and each shows the artist's head, screenprinted in black, amidst textured, colored paint. In one, Warhol is seen in high contrast, his features somewhat reduced, with a skull placed on top of his head. The canvas is dark orange, which both intensifies the slightly ominous quality of the image and dampens the intensity of the black ink, so that Warhol appears to be emerging from, or receding into, the frame.

In the other portrait, Warhol appears startled and with hands—detached from any body—around his neck. He is framed by a bright, apricot-orange background and light green brushstrokes, and the coloring on his face is lighter, emphasizing his frightened or ghostly appearance. While both of these self-portraits have an eerie quality and directly allude to death, the collage-like compositions add an element of artifice or theater.

Warhol was clearly fascinated with the subject of death, depicting many fatal scenarios and incidents across his *Death and Disaster*

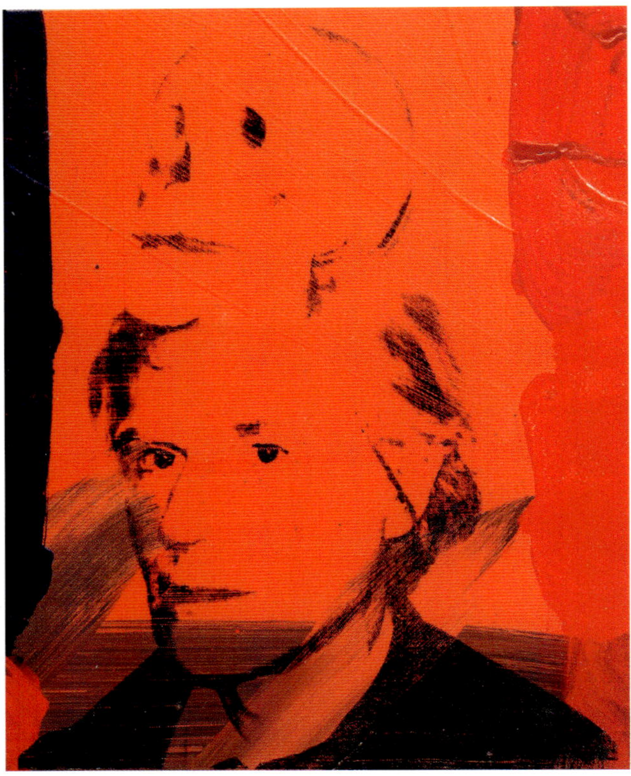

[3.12]

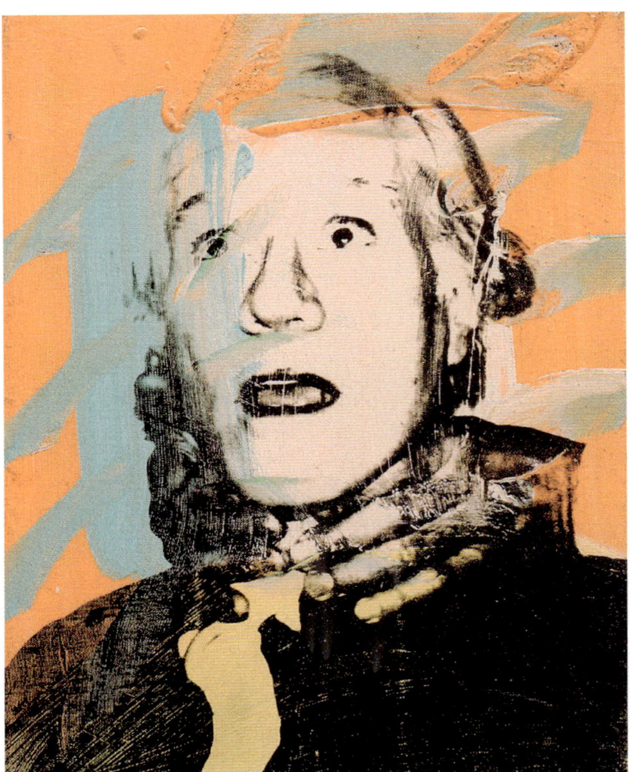

[3.13]

series. He faced his own encounter with death in June 1968 when his acquaintance and previous film extra Valerie Solanas shot him. While this incident is considered to have affected his art practice, these developments were also shaped by broader changes between the 1960s and 1970s, and his reconfiguring of the relationships between the art, film, and business elements of his work (Danto 2009, 120–125).
*NIKKI KANE*

## CLAES OLDENBURG
(Stockholm 1929)

[3.14]
### *Shoestring Potatoes Spilling from a Bag*
**1966**
canvas filled with kapok, stiffened with glue, and painted with acrylic
274.3 × 116.8 × 106.7 cm
Minneapolis, Walker Art Center
Gift of the T. B. Walker Foundation, 1966
Copyright 1966 Claes Oldenburg

An artist who believes in the interpretation and interrelation of art and life, Claes Oldenburg makes multimedia performances and artistic projects rooted in popular culture that have mirrored the human experience in surprising and sometimes unsettling ways.
Continuing traditions begun by such movements as Surrealism and Art Brut, which emphasized the role of the unconscious, the unrefined, and the uncivilized in art, Oldenburg uncovers the mystery and power of commonplace objects by morphing their scale, shape, and texture, embracing what he calls "the poetry of everywhere" (Oldenburg 1966, 33). The artist's inventive working process is cumulative. He orders his impressions of the world through sketches and writings in his ever-present notebooks; models and drawings form another layer of thinking. Some ideas are realized as

sculptures, ranging from the intimately scaled to the monumental, while others undergo a years-long period of study and change.
Born in Stockholm and raised in Chicago by diplomat parents, Oldenburg moved to New York in 1956. In 1960, he staged his first major project, entitled *The Street*, at the Judson Gallery. Responding both to the urban environment where he lived and worked and the flattened perspective of cartoon illustrations, Oldenburg covered the walls of the gallery with torn and crudely painted collages made from gritty, cast-off materials such as cardboard and burlap. The cutouts depicted inhabitants of New York's Bowery slums, including a Street Chick and an entity known as Ray Gun (also the artist's alter ego), characters that exemplified the seamy side of the city.
In 1961, Oldenburg presented *The Store*, an enterprise combining sculpture and performance, on Manhattan's Lower East Side. He filled a vacant storefront, which he called the Ray Gun Manufacturing Co., with hundreds of plaster and papier-mâché replicas of common products such as shirts, shoes, slices of pie, and baked potatoes—all made in the back of the shop.
These items were often larger than life, lumpy, misshapen, and garishly painted, and were sold as regular merchandise. *The Store* marked the first sounding of a main theme in Oldenburg's art—the exclusive use of inanimate objects to convey meaning. As he wrote in his now-famous manifesto of 1961, "I am for an art that takes its form from the lines of life itself. I am for US Government Inspected art, Grade A art, Regular Price art, Yellow Ripe art, Extra Fancy art, ready-to-eat art. . . an art that is political–erotical–mystical, that does something other than sit on its ass in a museum" (Oldenburg, artist's statement for the exhibition catalogue for *Environments, Situations, Spaces* at the Martha Jackson Gallery, 1961; published in definitive form in Oldenburg 1967).
Resembling hanging laundry, odd reptiles, or invented letterforms, the constructions of painted newspaper-stuffed fabric were key for Oldenburg in that they marked the beginnings of his work with "soft" sculpture, which would become an abiding interest and which he would explore with then-new materials (vinyl, fake fur, foam rubber) as well as traditional "painting" fabrics (canvas, and muslin).

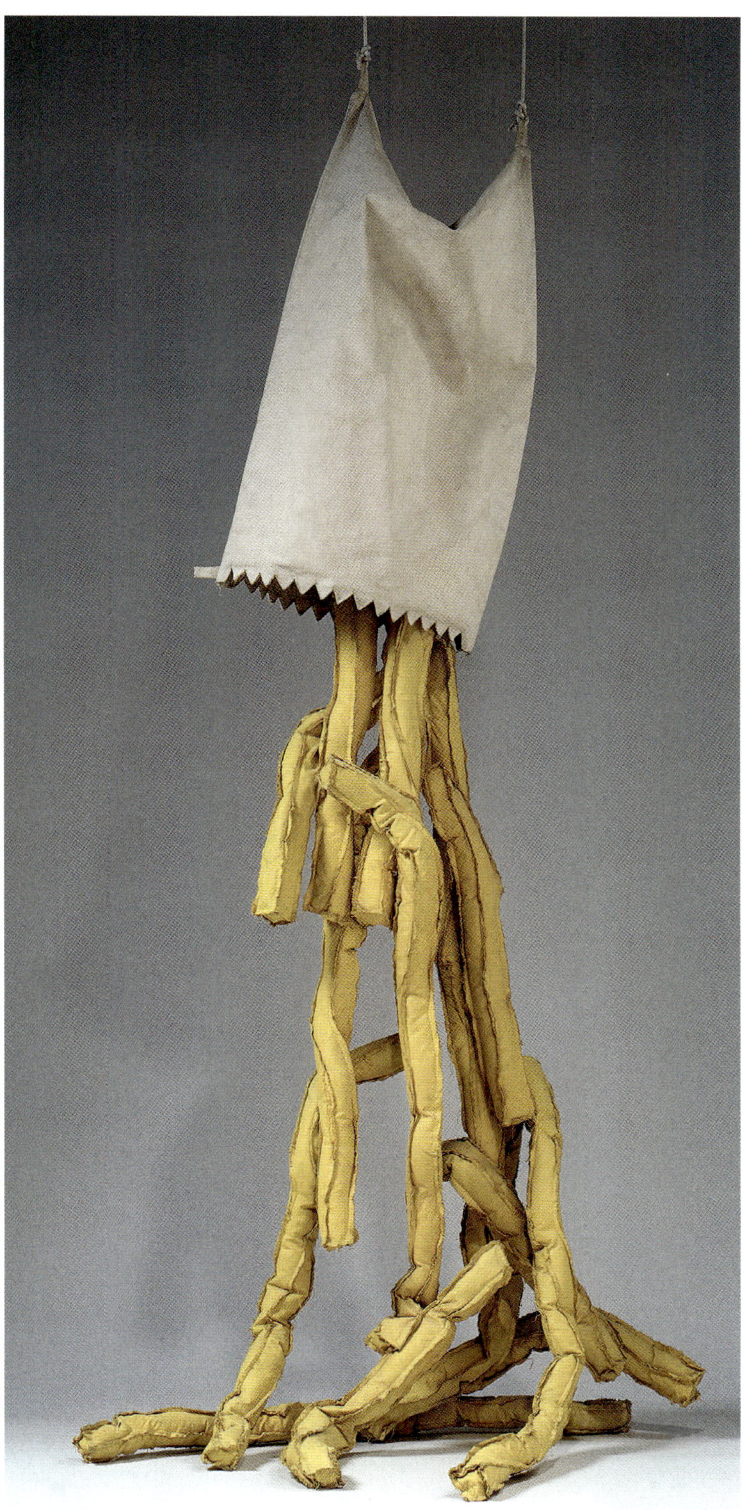

[3.14]

Beginning in the mid-1960s, Oldenburg began to conceive of works that he termed "colossal monuments," familiar objects enlarged to Brobdingnagian proportions that could be seen as alternatives to traditional public sculpture. Often, the ideas arose from the artist superimposing an image of an object on a landscape, either in the form of a collaged study.

The objects chosen for the proposed monuments are afforded the grand scale traditionally reserved for memorial architecture, though at the same time the vast scale denies their reality. By proposing, for example, a museum building formed from a tobacco can and cigarette package or a hybrid "vehicle" made from a giant lipstick poised on the treads of a bulldozer, Oldenburg heightens his subject's abstract qualities to inspire a sense of wonder in forms usually overlooked.

Since the mid-1970s, Oldenburg has made sculpture in collaboration with his wife, Coosje van Bruggen. The process behind the couple's proposals for what they term "large-scale projects" is integral to the work, regardless of whether a piece is realized. Over a period that may last years, an idea based on their impressions of a site is developed through drawings and models.

*Shoestring Potatoes Spilling from a Bag* [3.14], a soft sculpture from 1966, was originally conceived as part of a grouping of soft fast-food items—french fries, ketchup, and cola—and was based on an advertisement the artist had seen in a 1965 issue of Life magazine. By inverting the shoestring potatoes and applying gravity, his "favorite form creator" (Oldenburg 1966, 33), Oldenburg produced a new entity that took on a life of its own and, as he had done with other works previously, he further challenged convention by creating sculpture from painted canvas.

Various relationships to the potatoes are examined in the pages of Oldenburg's notebooks, through drawings, clippings, and notations. In one drawing, the artist compares the french fries, ketchup bottle, and cola glass to a cathedral, a chapel, and the Leaning Tower of Pisa, respectively. Another page relates the potato forms to female legs, with a fan of miniskirts forming the edge of the bag. *SIRI ENGBERG* (revised version of text, published in *Bits and Pieces*, 2005, 435–438)

### ROY LICHTENSTEIN
(New York 1923–97)

[3.15]
**_Artist's Studio No. 1 (Look Mickey)_**
**1973**
oil, Magna, sand on canvas
244.2 × 325.4 cm
Minneapolis, Walker Art Center
Gift of Judy and Kenneth Dayton and the T. B. Walker
Foundation, 1981

After working through several experimental idioms, Roy Lichtenstein started scrapbooking advertising and comic art. Overnight, he turned fuzzy pulp illustrations into Pop icons, becoming one of that movement's leading lights. It was 1961, and he was thirty-eight. Abstract Expressionism had founded New York School One; Pop Art and Minimalism initiated New York School Two.

The leap from One to Two took most collectors and curators by surprise. They failed to recognize that American innovation is not a conquering Cyclops but a Hydra whose several heads fight it out amongst themselves; there were, of course, winners and losers in the battle to be named most influential. Pollock's clotted tangles of puddles and drips, Rothko's sweeping fields of open color and unfocused form—these defined the extremes of Abstract Expressionism, and their utter eccentricity made a new American art but proposed no next step. Willem de Kooning's *Women* and *Abstract Landscape* canvases, though, were important to Rauschenberg, Johns, Oldenburg, and Lichtenstein—all of whom saw that de Kooning offered a way of working that did not exclude the possibility of linear structure. This is what we might call drawing, and what Lichtenstein called design.

*Artist's Studio No. 1 (Look Mickey)* [3.15], an ambitious canvas from 1973, revisits several of Lichtenstein's earlier motifs: from 1961, a stretch sofa, Donald Duck painting, rotary telephone, and paneled door; a 1970 Mirror painting, which defines the side wall; a meager dentil molding from the 1971 Entablature paintings running along the ceiling. Quotes from his 1972 *Still Life* paintings litter the floor—a Matisse pewter jug, a gaggle of grapefruit and bananas, a sculptor's modeling stand, a wall-to-wall carpet of diagonal stripes. In a 1973 interview, the artist said he took on two-tone stripes as nothing more than an alternative to benday dots (interview in Larson 1974, 16–8). Both were mechanical devices for spreading a percentage of broken color on a white ground. Here, the carpet is fifty percent black, as is the verso of a painting leaning against the door (a take on the artist's 1968 *Stretcher Frame*).

The disorder of the composition is disconcerting. Objects are spread rather evenly but seem not to relate to one another. This reflects the painting's point of departure, Matisse's 1911 classic *Red Studio*. The central irony is that *Artist's Studio No. 1 (Look Mickey)* is both an homage to Matisse and a retrospective look at Lichtenstein's own career. This is an original but not difficult idea: Lichtenstein is not as philosophical as his fans think he is, and he never intended to redefine Western painting. Like Flemish masters of domestic interiors and still lifes, he paints what is familiar and what he likes. For Lichtenstein, as for Matisse and Picasso, using devices such as dislocation of scale, short-circuit of memory, or even the effete dogmas of abstraction does not diminish an obsession with the ordinary, the knowable, the comfortable. Like most artists of the 1960s, he assumes you already know this is a rogue's gallery of previous work. Matisse's assumptions were similarly solipsistic.

PHILIP LARSON (revised version of text, published in *Bits and Pieces*, 2005, 350–351)

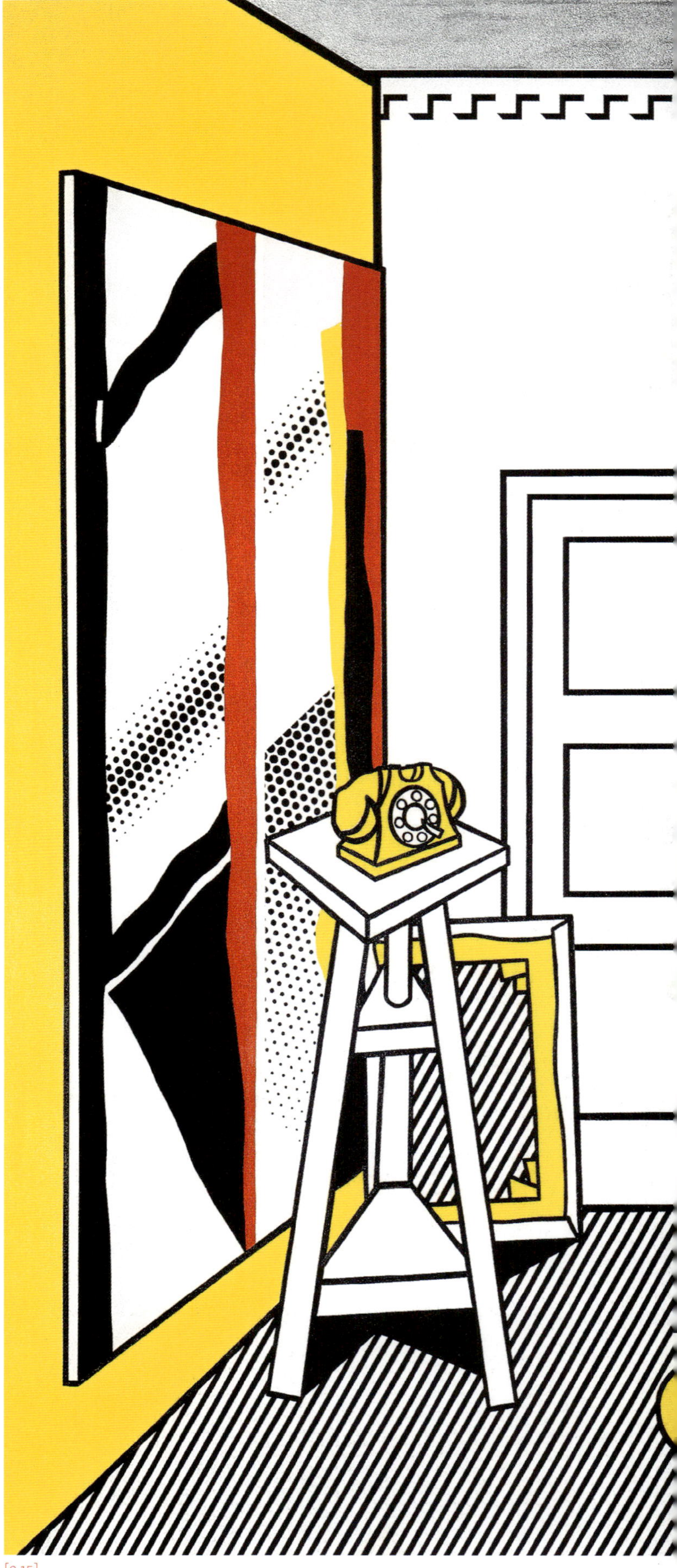

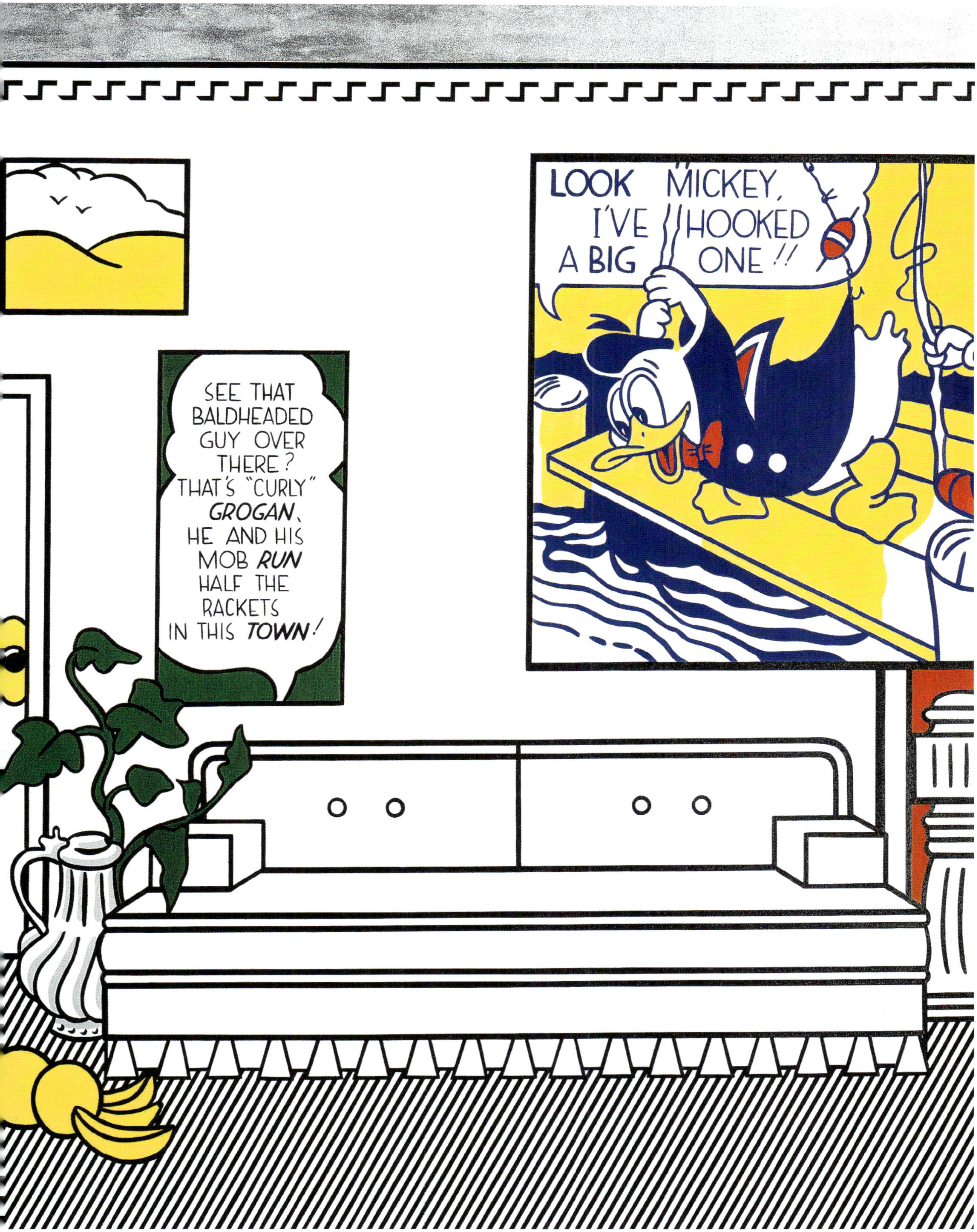

SEE THAT BALDHEADED GUY OVER THERE? THAT'S "CURLY" GROGAN, HE AND HIS MOB RUN HALF THE RACKETS IN THIS TOWN!
LOOK MICKEY, I'VE HOOKED A BIG ONE!!

# LESS IS MORE

4.

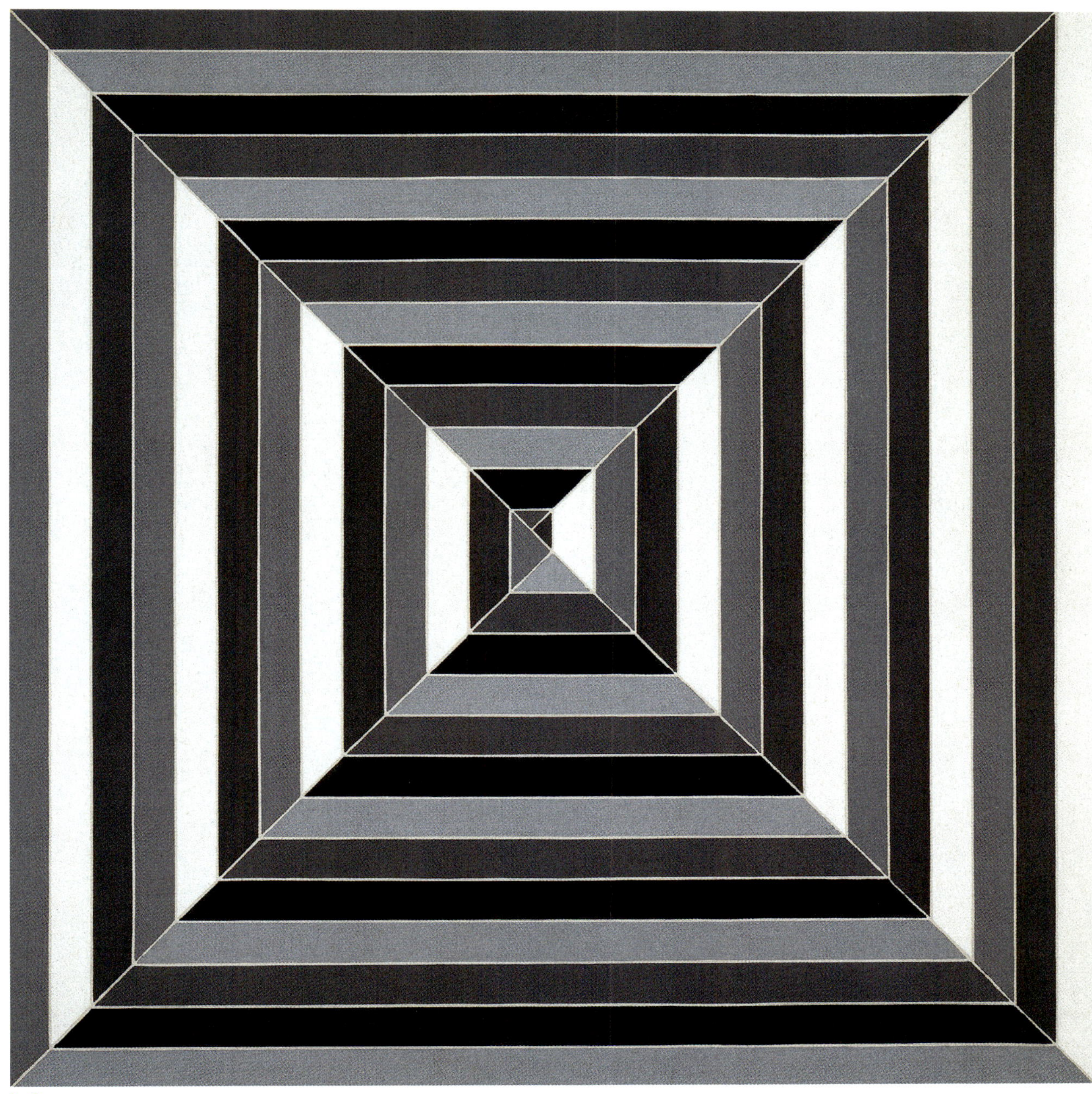



## FRANK STELLA

(Malden, Massachusetts 1936)

[4.1]
***Sketch Les Indes Galantes***
**1962**
oil on canvas
181.9 × 181.9 cm
Minneapolis, Walker Art Center
Gift of the T. B. Walker Foundation, 1964

Frank Stella's *Black Paintings*, which he began in 1958 at the age of twenty-two, are now widely considered to have led the way for the Minimalist movement of the 1960s. Stella produced these iconic paintings after moving to New York City, following his studies in history at Princeton University. While the art world at this time was still centered on Abstract Expressionism, Stella's deliberate approach to painting and his focus on the materials and forms of painting itself were the starting point for a nonexpressive and orderly art. In an interview with the artist, critic Saul Ostrow notes the lasting "mythology" around Stella and his impact on painting and Minimalist sculpture: "The mythology of you is almost like a cowboy movie. You rode into town and you transformed abstract painting and brought it into line with what Johns and Rauschenberg were doing in terms of pictorial stuff: You made it real" (Ostrow 2000, 28–35).

Throughout the 1960s, Stella expanded on the experiments with regular bands of paint that informed the *Black Paintings*, focusing on the surface and shape of the canvas by painting in regular, geometric forms, and even working with nonrectangular canvases. In 1967, on the invitation of Jasper Johns, Stella designed the set and costumes for Merce Cunningham's *Scramble*, with the set consisting of a number of movable stands of different sizes, each holding a stretched band of colored canvas. Throughout his career he continued to explore and extend the possibilities of abstraction, in painting and later in sculpture too.

*Sketch Les Indes Galantes* (1962) [4.1] is one of a number of paintings Stella produced in his *Concentric Squares and Mitered Mazes*

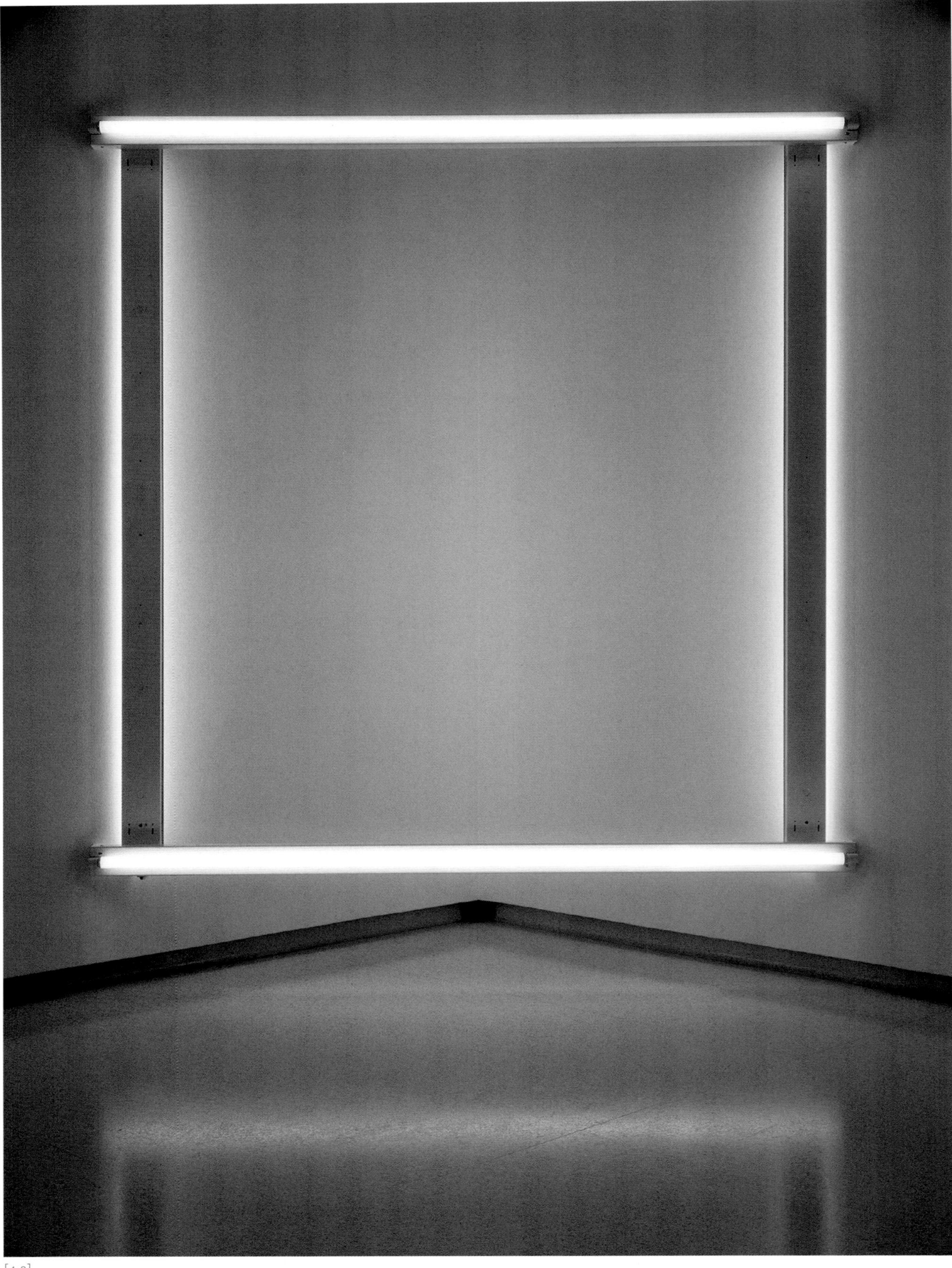

[4.2]

series. Diagonal lines split the canvas into four quadrants. The top right diagonal is slightly displaced and this, along with precise bands of black, gray, and white paint creates the impression of a gradual clockwise movement towards the center of the canvas where the bands do not quite line up. This disruption to the form "creates a twisting, pinwheel-like movement" (Auping 2015, 25) and when viewed at a distance the bands of color have a sense of solidity to them. Originally planned as one part of a diptych, paired with a version in color, it was instead completed as a standalone piece in grisaille. Other paintings in this series did, however, include primary and secondary colors, making this Stella's first series to include paintings with a multicolored palette (Engberg 2005, 530–532). The title of this piece refers to an opera–ballet by composer Jean-Philippe Rameau, that featured "orderly" harpsichord music in which Stella was particularly interested (Engberg 2005, 38, citing from an interview between Stella and Martin Friedman 1982, Walker Art Center Archives). Such references aside, Stella's paintings were notably "not records of inner psychological states" and "their meaning lay in the material surface of the painting." As such, there was nothing for the viewer to decode; their meaning was, theoretically, available to anyone (Haskell 1984, 92). This lack of pictorial concerns, and his use of solid color, meant that Stella's work straddled the boundary between painting and object; with his shaped canvases and later three-dimensional works he experimented with these demarcations even further.

*NIKKI KANE*

## DAN FLAVIN

(Jamaica, New York 1933–Riverhead, New York 1996)

[4.2]
### *Untitled (to Dear, Durable Sol from Stephen, Sonja, and Dan) Two*
### 1966/69
cool white, daylight fluorescent tubes, fixtures
243.8 × 243.8 × 20.3 cm
Minneapolis, Walker Art Center
Gift of the Northern States Power Company, 1969

As one of the key artists of the Minimalist movement, Dan Flavin produced many significant works throughout his career that both exemplified and expanded our understandings of the movement. In the early 1960s, he began make "icon" works that incorporated lighting, soon switching to produce works from commercially available fluorescent lighting tubes in various configurations. Such works were included in the seminal exhibition *Primary Structures* in New York in 1966, and he went on to exhibit widely across the US and internationally.

In reflecting on the avant-garde art and exhibitions of the twentieth century, curator and art historian Bruce Altshuler acknowledges that although with hindsight "it seems strange to ally Pop with the reductive sculpture of the mid-sixties, at the time the connection was a natural one" (Altshuler 1994, 220). A close consideration of Dan Flavin's work helps us to understand the overlaps—and distinctions—between the artistic developments taking place in the middle of the twentieth century, and in themselves his artworks represent a rea. artistic depth despite (or perhaps due to) their minimal forms.

Flavin's works are comprised of standard, commercially available fluorescent lighting tubes, and in *Untitled (to Dear, Durable Sol from Stephen, Sonja, and Dan) Two* (1966–69) [4.2] these are combined to create a square that occupies the corner of the gallery. The top and bottom tubes face outwards, into the gallery the space, while each vertical side includes two lighting tubes that face the walls. With this positioning of the vertical lights, Flavin both illuminates the corner—a typically unused and incidental space—and presents the functional reverse of the tube, normally unseen, to the viewer.

In his use of the ubiquitous, mass-produced fluorescent light fixtures, Flavin recalls some of the approach of Pop (these lighting tubes are familiar and banal, found in homes and in places of work and commerce), as well as ultimately aligning with the "new three-dimensional" (Judd 1999, 809–813; Haskell 1984, 83; Ragheb 2005, 214) work of the mid-1960s that came to be known as Minimalism. For while the fixtures he uses as material are pervasive in modern life, they also point to the sleek, industrial, standard-issue materials used by other artists such as Carl Andre, Donald Judd, and Robert Morris. Flavin's light tubes are "untransformed"; they bear no trace of the artist's hand except in their arrangement and placement within the context of art, and so call into question the ideas of art as distinct from life and the rarefied identity of the artist (Haskell 1984, 83).

In using unaltered commercial components, Flavin was restrained by their standardized sizing and colors. While in some of his work he made use of colored tubes and combinations of different sizes, this piece uses equally sized tubes in shades of white. The simple geometric composition is in keeping with the structured forms of other Minimalist artists, while Flavin's use of light as a medium extends the work beyond its parts, indicating a concern with space itself that was shared by the likes of Judd and Andre. The square form of the piece and its positioning elevated from the floor recall a framed painting, and the illuminated corner behind might remind us of the illusionary perspectival "space" of a painting, but here made real (Ragheb 2005, 214). Alternately, the horizontal tubes light the wider room space. Their glow reaches beyond the position of the work itself, to "penetrate, contain and define space," and, through the possibilities of shadow and reflection and the immediate impact of the bright light on the viewer, it adds a sensation to the experience that is unlike the traditional distanced contemplation or artworks (*Primary Structures* 1966, not paginated).

In his titling of this piece, he dedicates or addresses it to artist Sol LeWitt, which is in keeping with his practice of using his titles to dedicate the work to friends, family, or other figures he found meaningful. This practice also situates Flavin's work within its contemporary social and artistic context (as in this case of the friend and artistic contemporary LeWitt), and broader art historical contexts (as in his well-known work that references the Russian Constructivist Vladimir Tatlin, *"monument" for V. Tatlin* [1969]). Flavin also carefully considered the labels he used when referring to his work more broad-

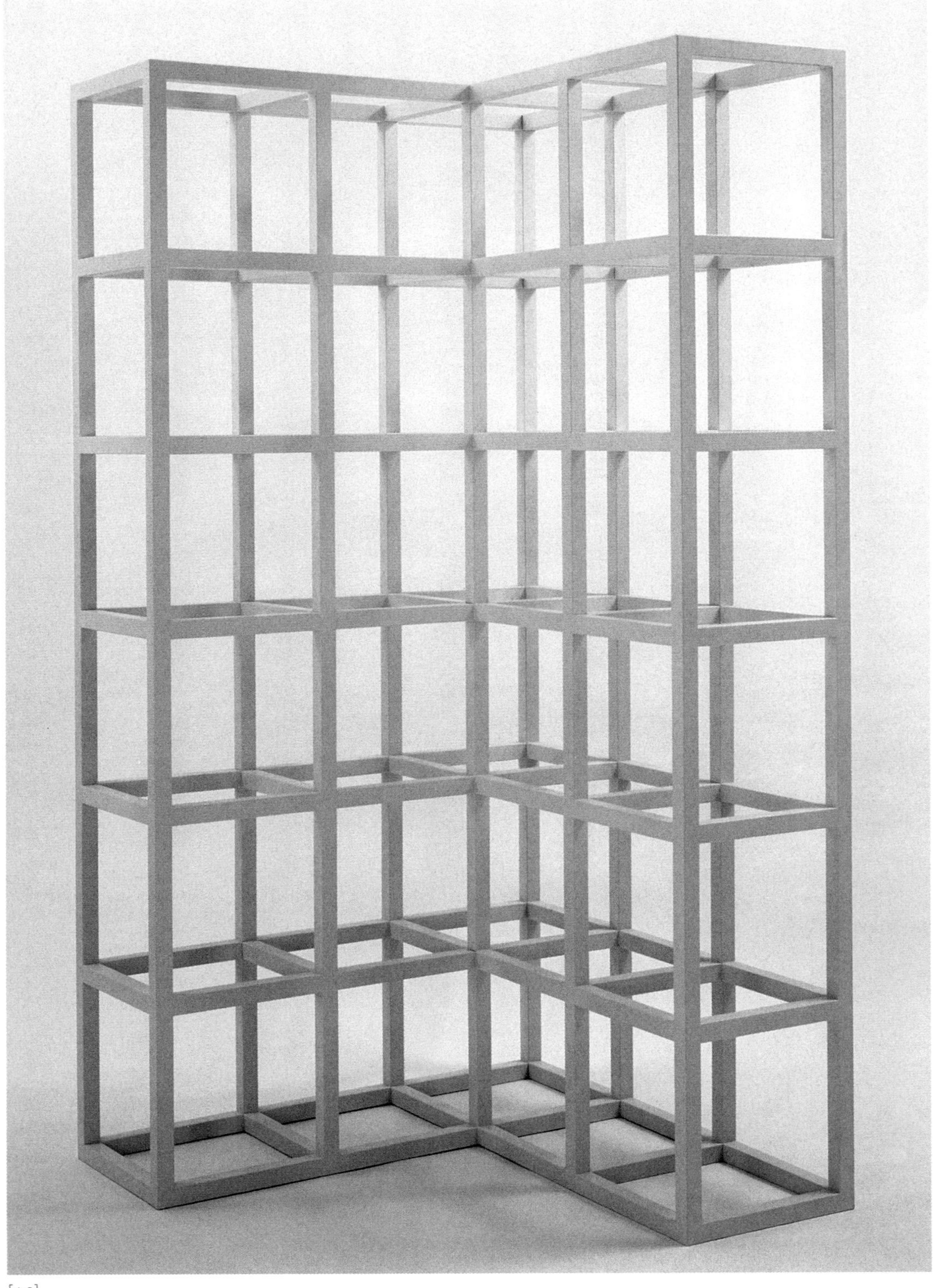

[4.3]

ly, describing his pieces as "proposals" or "situations" rather than "sculptures," and this can be viewed as a precursor to similar approaches in contemporary art practice, for example in Tino Seghal's "constructed situations" (https://walkerart.org/calendar/2008/statements-beuys-flavin-judd).
*NIKKI KANE*


## SOL LEWITT

(Hartford, Connecticut 1928–New York 2007)

[4.3]
### *Cubic Modular Piece No. 2 (L-Shaped Modular Piece)*
**1966**
baked enamel on steel
277.2 × 140.8 × 141 cm
Minneapolis, Walker Art Center
Purchased with a grant from Museum Purchase Plan, the National Endowment for the Arts, and Art Center Acquisition Fund, 1974


Considered one of the founders of Conceptual art and bridging both this movement and Minimalism, Sol LeWitt's work represents possibilities within limitations. He worked in a range of artistic mediums including installations and three-dimensional works, prints, drawings, and artist books, and across these he explores notions of seriality and variation, making use of self-imposed methods of chance, restrictions of form, and numerical processes. Working in New York in the 1960s, his work was included in seminal exhibitions including *Primary Structures* at the Jewish Museum in 1966, alongside other key artists of the period such as Donald Judd, Dan Flavin, Robert Morris, and Carl Andre.
*Cubic Modular Piece No. 2 (L-Shaped Modular Piece)* (1966) [4.3] is a large steel structure, coated in white colored enamel, which is composed of a series of cubes stacked six high arranged in five columns in an L-shape. Despite its taller-than-human height at over 2.7 meters, the "skeletal" nature of the piece whereby the structure articulates the edges of each cube leaving the surfaces open, prevents it from becoming overly monumental. This pared-down aesthetic and rejection of expressive, hidden meanings aligns LeWitt's work with the Minimalism of the 1960s, but his work also represents a bridging of this "movement" and the Conceptual Art that emerged in the same decade. Indeed, in 1967 he wrote an influential piece published in *Artforum* that was titled "Paragraphs on Conceptual Art" and that pointed to art's move from a focus on objects to emphasis on ideas and an intention to "engage the mind of the viewer rather than his eye or emotions" (LeWitt 1967, 80).
In this text, LeWitt notes the use of a "multiple modular method" in artistic work, whereby a "simple and readily available form [. . .] itself is of very limited importance [. . .] becomes the grammar for the total work" (LeWitt 1967, 80). In his own work, the cube became this foundational element that he could "manipulate," due to its "pretty uninteresting form" that "doesn't have any action involved in it" (Sol LeWitt interview with Patsy Norvell, see Norvell 2001, 113). With this form, LeWitt is able to work with "permutations," using the form as a

component part in assemblies of varying scales and arrangements, a practice that he says draws from the work of one his favorite artists, the photographer Eadweard Muybridge (Sol LeWitt interview with Patsy Norvell, see Norvell 2001, 119. Eadweard Muybridge, 1830–1904, was a photographer who pioneered the photographic study of movement, famously producing multiple series of stop-motion photographs of humans and animals in motion). In *Cubic Modular Piece No. 2*, the cubes have a uniform arrangement, yet as the viewer moves around the piece the cubes may overlap, and their views *through* them, to the surroundings, shift.
*NIKKI KANE*


## CARL ANDRE

(Quincy, Massachusetts 1935)

[4.4]
### *2004 Slope*
**1968**
steel
1.3 × 518.2 × 96.5 cm
Minneapolis, Walker Art Center
Art Center Acquisition Fund, 1969


Carl Andre was one of the leading artists of Minimalism. His first sculptures were made after he settled in New York in the 1950s and were influenced by the work of Constatin Brancusi and the early paintings of Frank Stella. He is best known for sculptural pieces composed of standardized materials, often aligned horizontally and drawing attention to the floor and architectural space of the gallery. Carl Andre's work is, according to art critic Kenneth Baker, Minimalist in the sense that it "refers to the tendency [. . .] to present as art things that are, or were when first exhibited—indistinguishable (or all but) from raw materials or found objects, that is, minimally differentiated from mere non-art stuff." This is distinguished from the second "current" of Minimalism that centers on industrial production, geometry, and the avoidance of expressive detail, as in the work of artists such as Donald Judd (Baker 1988, 9). Between these two strands, Minimalism examined philosophical and intellectual dilemmas about the boundaries of artistic medium, art itself, and its relations of production and presentation.
*2004 Slope* [4.4], from 1968, is characteristic of Andre's technique of "aligning," which along with "stacking" and "dispersing" can be seen to define his approaches to sculpture (Vergne 2005, 102). It consists of six thin hot-rolled steel plates on the floor that are placed in a line at a diagonal to the wall. With this placement on the floor of the gallery, Andre creates work that viewers can stand and walk on, in turn challenging the typical relationship between artwork and audience: sculpture here is no longer only visual, to be viewed at some remove, but rather now includes a tactile engagement (Vergne 2005, 102). The viewer, then, is "prompted to explore the perceptual consequences of a particular intervention in a given site" through the removal of expected formal modes of display such as the pedestal or frame, and of representation (Foster 1996, 38).

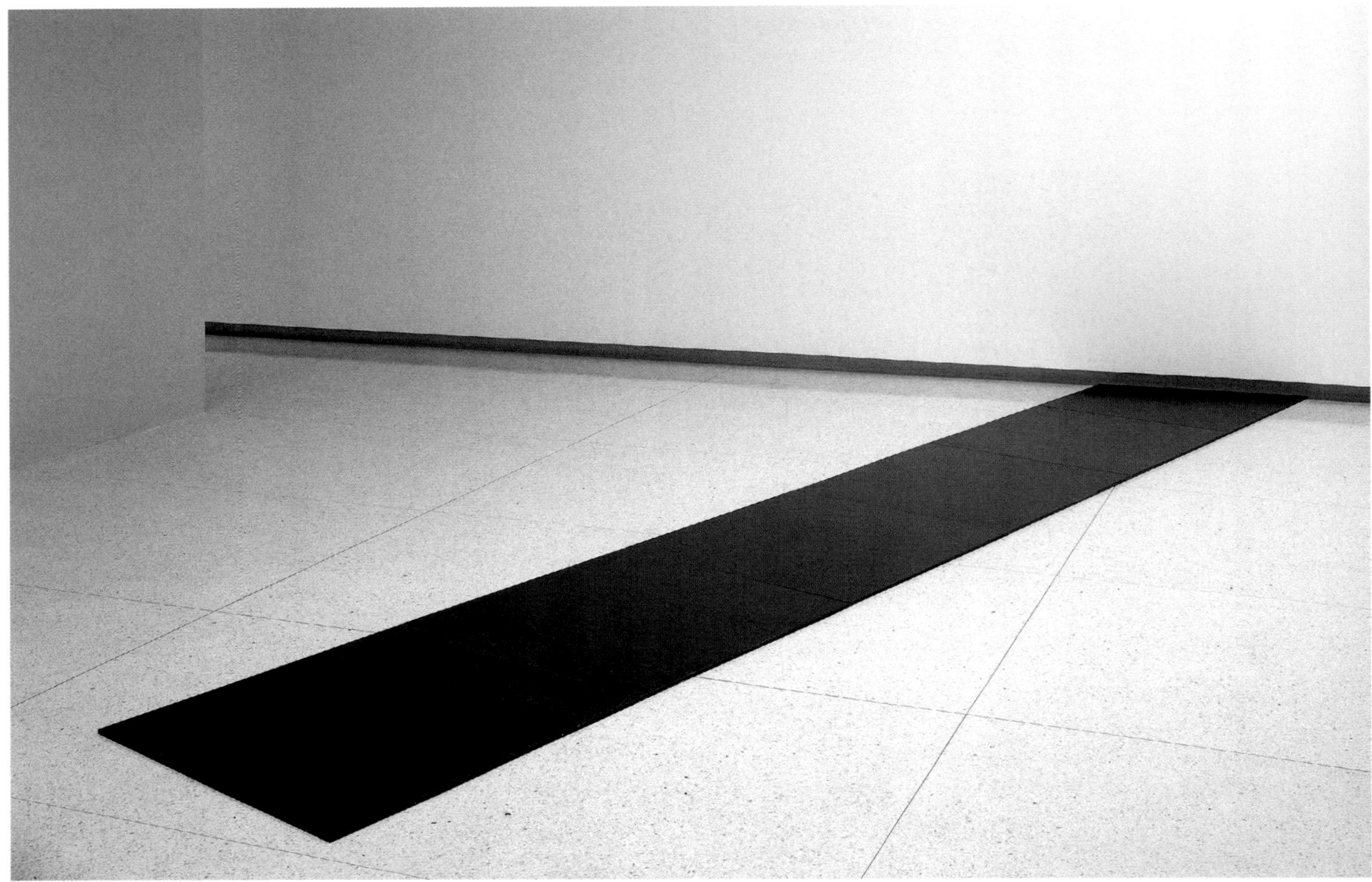

[4.4]

While earlier sculptures more clearly show his influences—notably the work of Constantin Brancusi whose forms and handling of material can be seen in Andre's early wooden pieces such as *Last Ladder* (1959) or *Timber Spindle Exercise* (1964), and of Frank Stella, with whom Andre was close friends, even working in his studio in the early 1960s, and whose linear compositions and "notched" canvases visually informed Andre's work—pieces such as this one, which make use of standard components without evidence of artistic handling, demonstrate his move from "a focus on the shapes and objects to the structure of space" (Vergne 2005, 102).

Similarly, Andre's floor sculptures (which also include works in brick etc.) emphasize the spatial elements of the gallery by articulating the floor and operating on a vertical plane in contrast to the notions of sculpture as vertical or monumental. While most of Andre's floor pieces are symmetrical, *2004 Slope* [4.8] is not entirely so, with one panel cut at an angle to sit against the wall and create the diagonal across the room floor. In this piece, the angled connection with the wall can also be read as a way of making the boundaries of the gallery explicit. Similar to the way painters are bound by the edges and shape of the canvas or frame, and throughout history have absorbed this into their compositions, Andre turns the floor into the picture plane and emphasizes the limits of the architecture.

The use of symmetry or near-symmetry and compositions made up of multiple regular-sized pieces removes the need for compositional decision-making on the part of the artist and in turn the overreading of hidden meanings in the work. With such arrangements, Andre also challenges our expectations of "creative" artistic work: "His limiting constructive effort to simple operations such as stacking and aligning objects signifies a refusal to heroize 'creative' activity on the one hand and, on the other, an insistence that physical labor is the least important determinant of 'art'" (Baker

1988, 55). These questions were echoed in the work of other Minimalist artists who made use of professional fabrication, industrial materials, and orderly aesthetics, such as Donald Judd and Dan Flavin, but have continued to be a point of discourse and debate in artistic practice throughout the twentieth and twenty-first centuries.

*NIKKI KANE*

## RICHARD SERRA

(San Francisco 1939)

[4.5]
***Prop***
**1968**
lead antimony
152.4 × 152.4 cm: lead sheet
242.6 × 10.2 × 10.2 cm: lead rod
Minneapolis, Walker Art Center
Gift of Penny and Mike Winton, 1977

Richard Serra was born in San Francisco on November 2, 1939. After completing his studies at the University of California at Santa Barbara, which he had supported by working as a worker in a steel mill, he attended Yale University (1961–64), where, in contact in particular with J. Albers, he became interested in research on chromatic interactions. He spent two years in Europe (from 1964 to 1966) thanks to a scholarship. At the time he lived mainly between Paris and Rome, approaching the contemporary experiences of pop art and Arte Povera.

Between 1967 and 1969, he came back to the US and settled in New York. As a young artist eking out a living and trying to find his niche in the fertile and frenetic New York art world of the mid-1960s, Richard

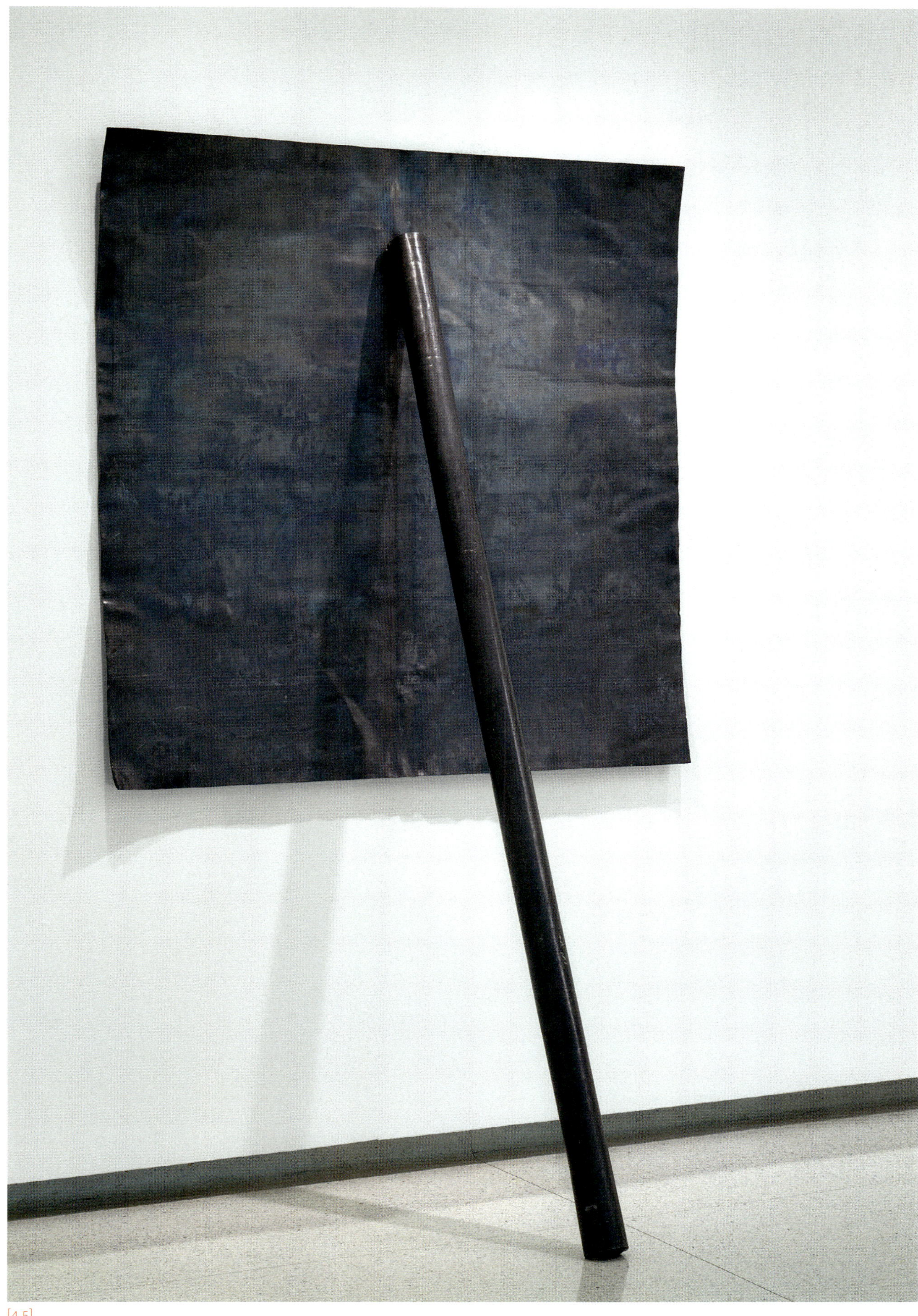



[4.5]

Serra composed a list of transitive verbs—"to roll, to crease, to fold [...] to bend [...] to splash," which he interspersed with phrases such as "of tension, of gravity, of entropy, of inertia, of equilibrium"—describing various forces acting on matter (this list was first published in Müller 1972, 94). This concrete poem of sorts became a lifelong "to do" list for Serra that would lay the conceptual groundwork for his sculptural practice, one shared by artists such as Robert Morris and Eva Hesse, who privileged the physical over the metaphysical, process over product, the literal over the abstract. According to Serra, "I was very involved with the physical activity of making. It struck me that instead of thinking about what a sculpture is going to be and how you're going to do it compositionally, what if you just enacted those verbs in relation to the materials, and didn't worry about the result? So I started tearing and cutting and folding lead" (quoted in Tomkins 2002, 57). In 1968, he began exploring the formal possibilities of this previously non-art material, which he favored over other metals for its weight and malleability. With composer Philip Glass, who for a time had become Serra's studio assistant, he began splashing molten lead with a large ladle into and against the angle of intersection between his studio wall and the floor. The risk and sheer muscle involved in this performative process were captured in a series of photographs by Gianfranco Gorgoni, which for their theatricality and the machismo they reveal might be compared to Hans Namuth's well-known pictures of Jackson Pollock hurling paint from a stick onto a canvas on the floor of his East Hampton studio (one of Gorgoni's photos serves as the cover image for Müller's *The New Avant-Garde*, 1972.) It was at this moment of discovery that he began to create his first "props," works of raw psychological power based on the fear of collapse. These cantilevered, completely self-supporting sculptures were created in perfect balance and counterbalance based on the artist's calculations, testing the laws of physics without recourse to clipping, gluing, or welding (their fully interdependent parts were assembled by art handlers, and not by industrial aids such as forklifts or cranes). In addition to Philip Glass, Serra turned to his friends and fellow Yale art students, including painter Chuck Close, musician Steve Reich, writer Rudy Wurlitzer, and monologuist Spalding Gray, to help assemble the early prop works.

Each element was integral to the integrity of the form, as is the case with a house of cards, the subtitle of the artist's *One Ton Prop (House of Cards)* (1969). In this piece, four lead plates were placed in an upright position and inclined toward each other, overlapping by two and one half inches to form an irregular cube. When discussing this body of work produced in the wake of Minimalism, a movement by which he is often co-opted, Serra explained, "The perception of the work in its state of suspended animation, arrested motion, does not give one calculable truths like geometry, but a sense of presence, an isolated time" (Serra 1970, 25).

The previous year, the artist had begun to create "wall props," for which he hand-rolled massive sheets of lead into poles and leaned them up against flat sheets. The Walker Art Center's *Prop* (1968) [4.5] is one such work. In a 1980 interview, Serra recalled the genesis of this and other pieces like it: "I realized that I was making one form, the lead roll, and I wanted to combine it with the other form, which was the sheet. It occurred to me that the roll could be used as a pole and the sheets could be propped from and off the wall without utilizing a joint. These pieces utilizing the floor and the wall retained a memory of pictorial concerns even though their content was predicated on their axiomatic building principles" (Lamarche-Vadel 1980, 142).
*ELIZABETH CARPENTER* (revised version of a text, published in *Bits and Pieces*, 2005, 506-7)

## ROBERT MORRIS

(Kansas City, Missouri 1931–Kingston, New York 2018)

[4.6]
### *Untitled*
### 1968
felt, metal
365.8 × 289.6 cm
Minneapolis, Walker Art Center
Gift of the T. B. Walker Foundation, 1969

In the mid-1960s, Robert Morris was producing work closely aligned with the work of artists such as Donald Judd and their "specific objects." However, towards the end of the decade Morris's interests and positions on the art object began to diverge from the geometric, industrial forms of Minimalism. This untitled piece dates from 1968, the same year in which Morris wrote a piece for *Artforum* titled "Anti Form" that articulated his growing concerns with chance, gravity, and nonrigid materials in his work and wider artistic practices (Morris 1968, 33-5). In keeping with the increasing practice of artists theorizing about their own work and contemporary practices during this period, in "Anti Form" Morris discusses these developments in artistic work with reference to broader art history (noting traces of process or unfinished work in both High Renaissance and nineteenth-century work), as well as to the recent work of the Abstract Expressionists and more contemporaneous artists to himself (singling out Claes Oldenburg's use of soft materials as particularly notable).

These shifts from the rigidity of Minimalism to a "softer" art has been referred to as Process Art due to the emphasis on the making itself, where the processes of production are incorporated as content of the work and are somehow present in the finished piece. This untitled piece is a key example of Morris's experiments with these ideas and is one of several works he made using felt. With this nontraditional material, Morris used the process of cutting and hanging, and allowed the effects of gravity to influence the form of the piece. The piece is comprised of several sheets of felt in various colors layered on top of one another, the cuts across their length and their hanging position making the colors of the lower layers visible in places, but in no formal order or arrangement. In other related pieces, strips of felt are dropped on the floor, leaving chance and gravity in control of the composition, or they hang from a point falling into a tangle, drawing attention to the intrinsic malleability of the material.

Throughout his career, Morris experimented with materials, forms, and modes of working. His work has been described as representing the interconnections between Minimalism, dance, and Fluxus, as well as the Process work we see here (Haskell 1984, 98). As well as discrete pieces such as this one, he also created performance

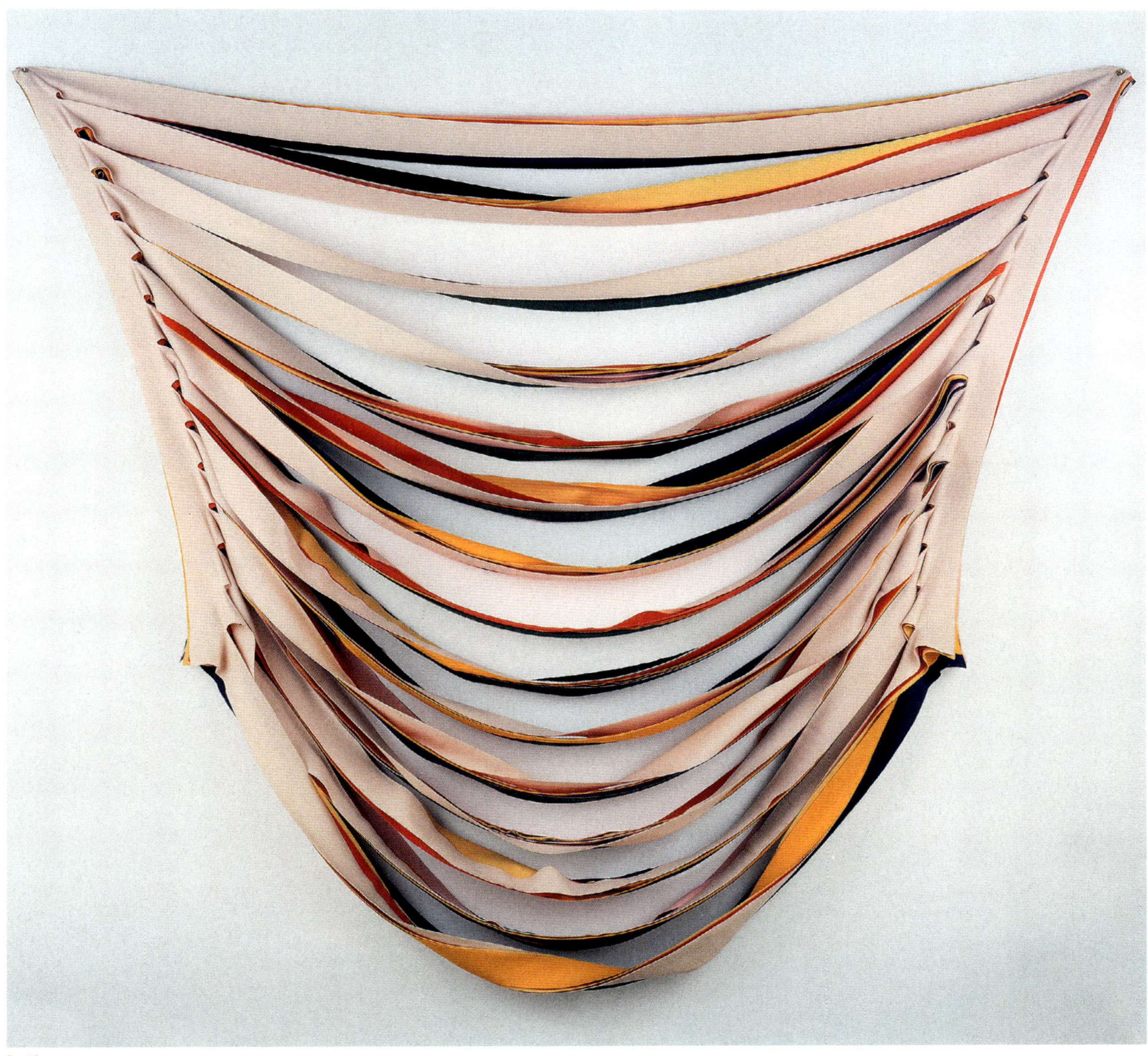

[4.6]

works, produced prop pieces for dancer Simone Forti (to whom he was married), designed for the Merce Cunningham Dance Company, worked with sound, and produced installations and works on large scale. Contemporaneous to his felt pieces, Morris produced a solo exhibition for the Whitney that art historian Julia Bryan-Wilson has carefully analyzed, describing its incredibly massive forms, use of construction materials, and scale of labor required for the installation (Bryan-Wilson 2007, 333–359). In considering this 1968 felt piece within the context of Morris's broader practice of the period and the 1970 exhibition, at first these two examples seem at odds. However, the *Robert Morris: Recent Works* exhibition at the Whitney also employed some of the techniques of dropping or "spilling," and the primary importance placed on gravity and chance that is seen in the felt works—albeit on a much, much larger scale. Bryan-Wilson notes that Morris "aligned chance and automation because they both deemphasize the artist's hand" in this exhibition, by using a system of metal rods to drop concrete blocks onto the gallery floor and "topple" large timber cuts (Bryan-Wilson 2007, 338). In these techniques, we see the parallels between these seemingly opposing art works, and how Morris explored his artistic and theoretical interests across materials and forms, as well as in writing in pieces such as "Anti Form."
*NIKKI KANE*

## DONALD JUDD

(Excelsior Springs, Missouri 1928–New York 1994)

[4.7]
***Untitled***
**1969/82**
anodized aluminum
304.8 × 68.6 × 61 cm
Minneapolis, Walker Art Center
Gift of Mr. and Mrs. Edmond R. Ruben, 1981

Donald Judd produced some of the most iconic sculpture of the twentieth century and is known as a key Minimalist artist. As well as his artistic practice, Judd was involved in writing about art for various publications, having studied art history at Columbia University in New York. His work is notable for its use of industrially manufactured materials and fabrication and geometric forms. In 1986, the Chinati Foundation opened in Marfa, Texas, which was founded by Judd, and preserves and presents his work, as well as that of several other artists.

*Untitled* (1971) [4.7] is made up of a row of ten identically sized metal boxes attached to the wall and placed about twelve inches from each other. Their blue color is the result of an industrial anodizing process. The recessed sides of each box show the thickness of the surface of each metal sheet, and also show how the color, an integral part of the material itself, is present on all surfaces and was not simply applied after the work was constructed. Their blue color is product of an industrial anodizing process in which the aluminum was dyed, and recessed sides on each box, as well as demonstrating the thickness of the metal sheeting, show that this hue is part of the material, present on all surfaces, and not applied retrospectively after construction.

Donald Judd is considered a primary—if not *the* primary—figure of Minimalism, despite his own distaste for the label. In this untitled piece from 1971, key characteristics of his practice are present from an aesthetic point of view, but also, inextricable from this, conceptually. Judd, along with other artists working around the same time, wrote about art as well as making it, and published his reflections on the theoretical concerns of his art works, something that has been attributed to these artists, unlike most of those of the previous education, having received college education (Haskell 1984, 102; *Primary Structures* 1966, not paginated). Judd's seminal piece, *Specific Objects*, was first published in 1965, and in it he articulated a conception of the developing three-dimensional art work of the time as "neither painting nor sculpture" but rather as "specific objects" in which "the form of a work and its materials as closely related" (Judd 1999, 809–813).

The "new three-dimensional work" of the period—that is the art of Judd and artists such as Dan Flavin, Carl Andre, and Robert Morris that came to be known as Minimalist—was "new" precisely in this concern with material and form, and its conception as three-dimensional but not sculpture as such. While "obviously resembl[ing] sculpture more than it does painting," this distinction was made as a rejection of the representational, vertical, monumental and hand-

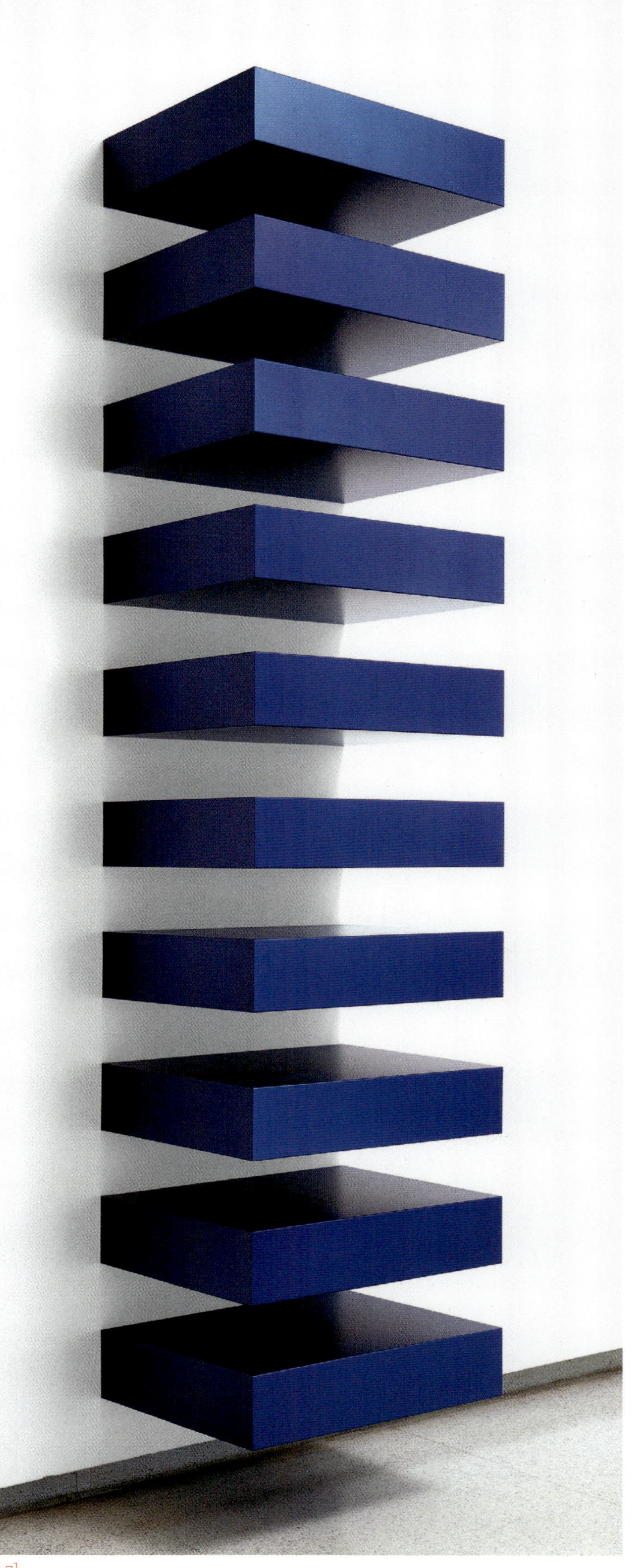

[4.7]

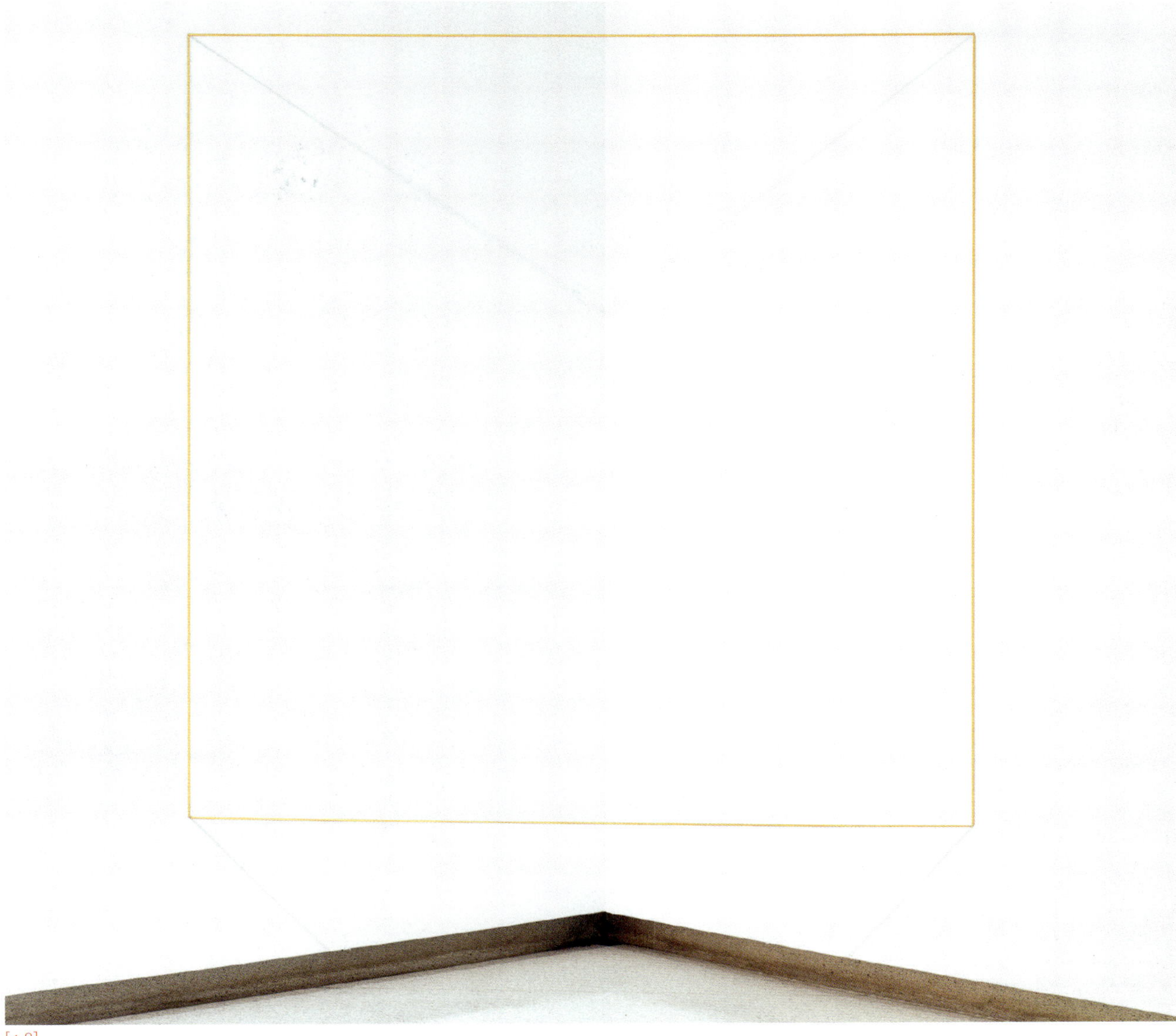



**FRED SANDBACK**
(Bronxville, New York 1943–New York 2003)

[4.8]
***Yellow Corner Piece***
**1970**
elastic cord
182.9 × 182.9 cm
Minneapolis, Walker Art Center
Donation of Virginia Dwan, 1986

crafted nature of sculpture, and a concern with space and place-ment over the individual object (Judd 1999, 809–813).

In *Untitled* [4.7] we see this in the regular spacing of the individual boxes and their contact with the floor rather than a plinth. The se-riality of spaced, repeated parts produces a "nonspecific composi-tion" that complicates the understanding of Judd's work as specific objects, and this has been read (perhaps reductively) as a represen-tation of industrial production, or as speaking more generally to the "alienating experience of modernity" through its rejection of person-ality or representation (Foster 1996, 36; Chong 2005, 306).

Such placing also serves to emphasize their industrial material and fabrication. For Judd, materials "are simply materials," with their own intrinsic qualities of mass, texture, weight, translucency, shine and so on (Judd 1999, 809–813). He made use of industrial materials including aluminum as in this piece, as well as other metals, ply-wood, and plexiglass, and had his works professionally fabricated. This commercial production eliminated traces of making—as well as the limitations posed by skill and technique—taking the repro-ductive processes of Pop a stage further to employ mechanical pro-duction fully. The implications of this have been lasting, with use of outsourced fabrication and materials not traditionally associated with art now common within artistic practice.

*NIKKI KANE*

Fred Sandback presented his first mature works while still a stu-dent, studying Sculpture at the Yale School of Art and Architec-ture where Donald Judd and Robert Morris were visiting teachers. Around this time, in 1967, he developed an artistic vocabulary that remained his mode of working throughout his career, in which he used lines of wire, elastic cord or, later, acrylic yarn, to create lin-ear compositions within exhibition spaces. Sandback grew up in New York, New Hampshire, and Connecticut, and studied philos-ophy at Yale before beginning his MFA. His practice can be read in connection with the various artistic movements that emerged in the United States in the 1960s, with clear visual connections to Minimalism, but also material links to Post-Minimalist works, and even ideological associations with Abstract Expressionism, which still dominated the decade's early years. Despite these connections, Sandback did not regard his work as belonging to a particular "school."

*Yellow Corner Piece* (1970) [4.8] consists of yellow elastic cord, which is precisely stretched between the gallery walls to create a square form in the corner. This sculpture is therefore an outline, with no internal volume and no surfaces as such. The cord is carefully affixed to the walls at each corner, articulating these walls as simultaneously boundaries and supports. This relationship to the space it occupies is a crucial factor across Sandback's work; the space "makes his sculptures possible [...] for it is only through the relationship between surfaces and corners—the boundaries of space—that the sculpture becomes intangible" (Meyer-Stoll 2005, 14). This is a somewhat modest relationship to space: in contrast to some Minimalist artists, such as Carl Andre's interest in "seizing" space through the expansive use of serial materials, Sandback's art "doesn't take over a space, but rather coexists with it" (Tuchman 1970, 55–56; Sandback 2005, 90). In doing so, he "avoids the arrogance of the artist who makes work, and exhibits in such a way as to overpower or cover the site itself" (McEvilley 2005, 59). Indeed, Sandback's work clearly makes its conditions of existing visible, even central in the work. Despite their configuration to the space in which they are situated, Sandback resisted description of his works as "site-specific"; his pieces are not about their locations and they deal more with space that site (Bois 2005, 30).

The placement of *Yellow Corner Piece* echoes Dan Flavin's *Untitled (to Dear, Durable Sol from Stephen, Sonja, and Dan) Two* [4.2], which is also situated in the corner of the gallery. However, while Flavin's piece draws attention to itself and its position through its use of fluorescent lighting tubes, and appears as a discrete artwork, Sandback's work is less contained, less visible, and less *object*. This is one of the key distinctions to be made between his work and that of what came to be known as Minimalism. While artists like Judd and Flavin were concerned with rigid materials and forms, Sandback's line pieces "add hardly any mass, or materiality to the space they occupy," with the spaces "reconceived" rather than occupied by the artworks (McEvilley 2005, 61).

While Sandback described his works as sculptures, their form overlaps the boundaries between sculpture, installation, and drawing. In this piece, he uses the yellow elastic cord to "draw" lines in the spaces between the gallery's walls, and while three-dimensional, the work's lack of volume is in contrast with traditional sculpture. The yellow colored "lines" here heighten the subtlety of the work, whereby it is not instantly visible to the viewer upon entering the gallery, however in other pieces Sandback did make use of brightly colored cords depending on the effect he wished to develop.

Viewing *Yellow Corner Piece* alongside other contemporaneous works, its relationships to the artistic experiments of the period are visible, and the breadth of experimentation of the period is emphasized.

*NIKKI KANE*

**ANNE TRUITT**
(Anne Dean; Baltimore, Maryland 1921–Washington DC 2004)

[4.9]
***Australian Spring***
**1972**
wood, paint
184.2 × 60.3 × 60.6 cm
Minneapolis, Walker Art Center
Gift of Mrs. Helen B. Stern, 1973

Anne Truitt has often been associated with Minimalism, although it is a label the artist consistently refuted. The term, for better or worse, continues to shape the reception of Truitt's oeuvre. The blame partially rests on the critic Clement Greenberg, an early champion of Truitt, who claimed that the artist "anticipated" the practices of the other minimalists such as Robert Morris and Donald Judd. While Truitt's human-scaled, geometric forms certainly bear formal resemblance to her minimalist contemporaries, the works draw on allusive personal references culled from childhood memories, personal experiences, historical events, and literary sources. Additionally, Truitt's investigation into the expressive capacities of color shared more affinities with non-gestural color field painters such as Mark Rothko, Ad Reinhardt, and Barnett Newman.

During the 1950s, Truitt worked primarily in drawing. However, the artist was profoundly influenced by a visit to the Guggenheim, New York, in 1961, during which she viewed the exhibition *American Abstract Expressionists and Imagists*, curated by H. H. Arnason. As Truitt would later recall, an encounter with Newman's zip painting *Onement VI* would alter the course of her artistic career: "'Enough' was my radiant feeling—for once in my life enough space, enough color. It seemed to me that I had never before been free [...] Such openness wiped out with one swoop all my puny ideas" (Truitt 1984, 150–151). The episode seems to have led Truitt to expand into three dimensions, allowing her to explore color as a spatial phenomenon. Truitt's early sculptures from the 1960s remained largely figurative. Representations of a picket fence, a gravestone, or a piece of shiplap called up memories of the stark coastal architecture in the artist's childhood town of Easton, Maryland. Over time, Truitt gravitated towards more abstract geometries, arriving at the column form for which she is best known.

*Australian Spring* [4.9] is an extraordinary example of Truitt's early columns. This simple, rectilinear shape proved to be fertile ground for Truitt's intuitive explorations of color. As the artist explained, "What I want is color in three dimensions, color set free, to a point where, theoretically, the support should dissolve into pure color" (Munro 1979, 324). For Truitt, color unfolds over time, perception is a durational affair. The artist achieved subtle tonal shifts through a laborious process of applying numerous coats of paint and sanding down each layer to create a smooth, luminous surface. The color of *Australian Spring* is unstable and elusive. At first glance the sculpture appears white, and only once one's eyes adjust to the light does the color radiate to the surface. In fact, the wooden plinth is wrapped in a

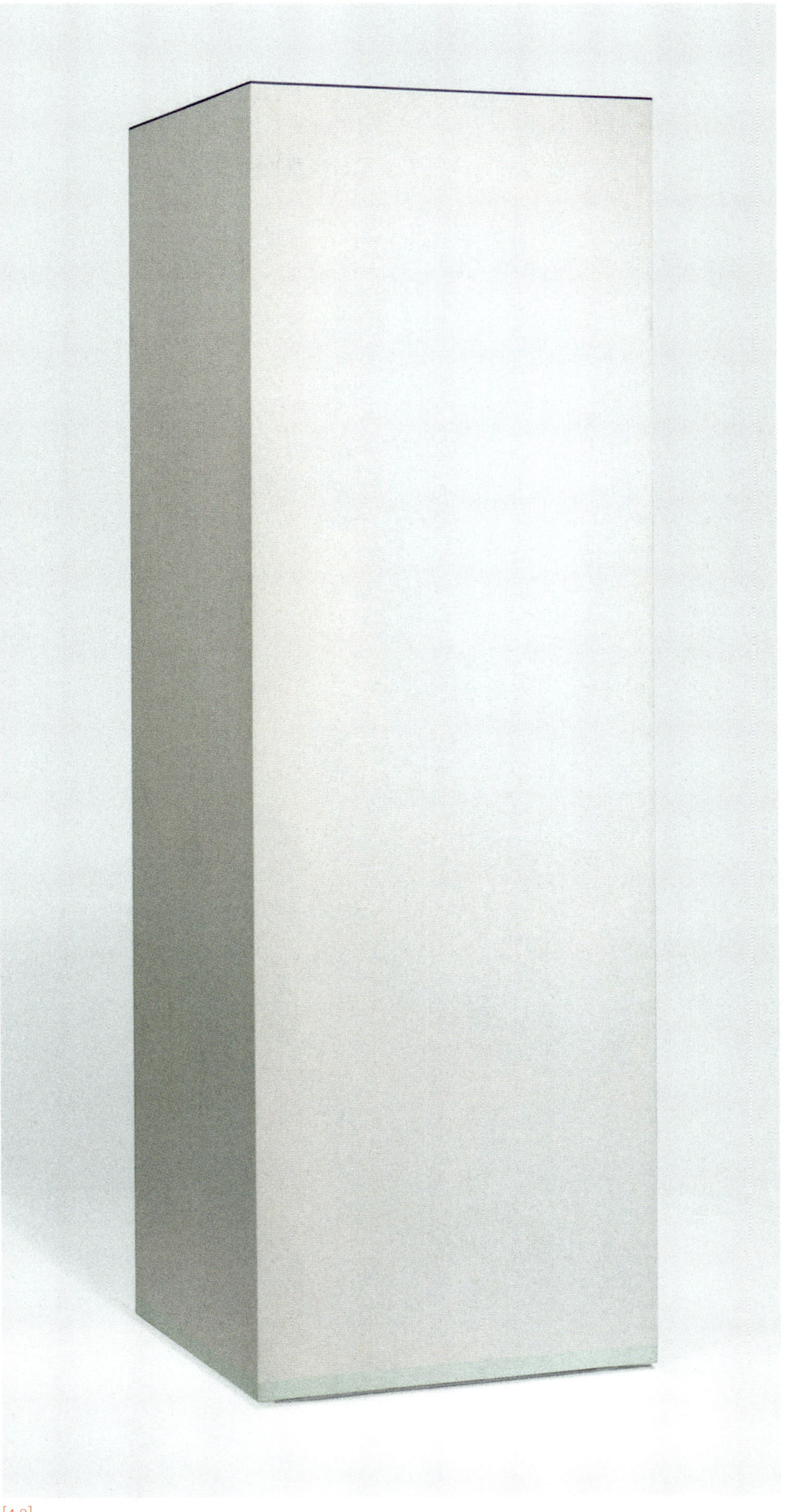

[4.9]

[4.10]

barely perceptible pale pink hue, thrown into relief against a narrow, bold band of cobalt blue. Below, a thin swath of light green dissolves the sculpture's base, making the solid monolithic form appear to be floating. To look at *Australian Spring* is to participate in a perceptual dance, flickering between lightness and darkness, heaviness and weightlessness.
*JADINE COLLINGWOOD*

**AGNES MARTIN**

(Maklin, Saskatchewan 1912–Taos, New Mexico 2004)

[4.10]
**Untitled #1**
**1980**
gesso, acrylic, graphite on canvas
184.8 × 184.8 cm
Minneapolis, Walker Art Center
Gift of Judy and Kenneth Dayton, 1999

Agnes Martin was born in Saskatchewan, Canada, in 1912 to a farming, Scottish Presbyterian family, and moved to the United States in the early 1930s, becoming an American citizen in 1952. Before becoming an artist, Martin was a teacher in schools and universities. She was living in New Mexico when gallerist Betty Parsons offered to represent her if she moved to New York. She did so in 1957, moving to a seaport area of downtown Manhattan occupied by many other artists, including Ellsworth Kelly, Robert Indiana, Jasper Johns, Robert Rauschenberg, and James Rosenquist.

At this point, her work centered on "biomorphic abstractions" but she gradually moved toward further abstraction, working extensively with grid formats in her paintings. This aligned her with the growing Minimalist movement in the city, and her work was shown alongside the likes of Carl Andre, Donald Judd, Frank Stella, and Sol LeWitt. However, despite the seeming correlations between her work and that of these artists (particularly LeWittt, who also made work based around grids and cubes), her concerns were not with conceptualism, exactitude, and material; rather she sought to express emotional experience and expansiveness through her spare, linear canvases.

In 1967, she left New York due to pressures of life there, difficulties with housing, and struggles with mental illness. She traveled across North America and then settled again in New Mexico, building herself a house in a remote area. She gave up painting and did not return to it again until 1974. When she did begin painting again, she made what she considered to be her first completely abstract work, subtly shifting from her early gridded work to bolder geometric compositions characterized by horizontal bands of colored washes.

In *Untitled #1* (1980) [4.10] Martin has filled the six-by-six foot canvas with horizontal stretches of whites and gray-blues, each bordered with graphite lines. She prepped her canvases with layers of gesso before painting and worked with watered-down acrylic paints that allowed her to create almost translucent washes of color (she gave up working with oils in 1964 as they took so long to dry). Her lines were marked out using a measuring tape (Cotter 1998, 77–80).

These faint lines and the distinctions between colors gradually fade as the viewer steps back from the painting, and reveal themselves again with proximity. This quality of changing experience has prompted viewers to spend time with Martin's work in order to fully appreciate and experience its depth.

Although the orderly and linear qualities of Martin's painting connected her with the formal, methodical work of Minimalists, her own affinities were with Color Field Painting, particularly the work of Barnett Newman and Mark Rothko with their expansive fields of color that encompass the entire canvases. Other precedents to her painting can also be seen in the work of Ad Reinhardt, Piet Mondrian, and Josef Albers. While artists such as Judd, Andre, and LeWitt emphasized precision and even turned to industrial materials or fabrication to eradicate traces of the artist's hand, Martin's lines and grids are inexact. Her pencil lines emphasize the contact with the canvas and draw attention to the texture of the gesso beneath, while brushstrokes are visible in her horizontal washes of color and their edges are not sharp, often extending into the neighboring bands. In *Untitled #1*, her lines of color do follow a subtle pattern of sorts, but one that does not present itself obviously, instead working to create a sense of rhythm and luminosity in the painting, described by critic Dore Ashton as "vitality achieved with an economy of means that defies words" (Ashton 1977, 13). This understated, nuanced handling of color came to define her later work.

Similarly, while so-called "Minimalist" artists worked in opposition to notions of expression, and intellectual and rational ideas were emphasized with the development of Conceptual Art (articulated by LeWitt in writing as well as through his artworks), Martin's limited forms and color palette were employed in the pursuit of expressing "impersonal emotion" and "abstract truths" (Haskell 1992, 106).
*NIKKI KANE*

# NO MORE BORING ART

5.

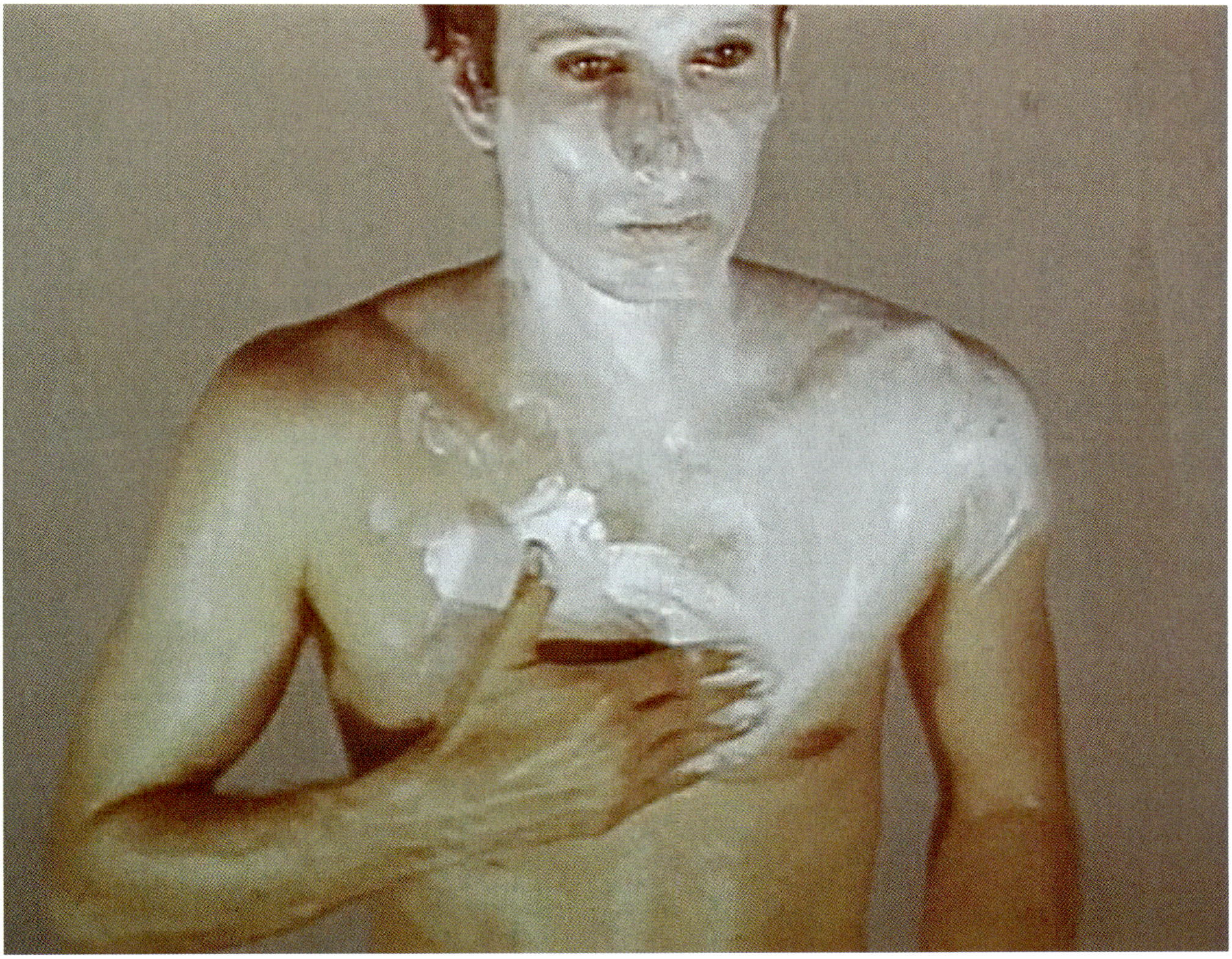

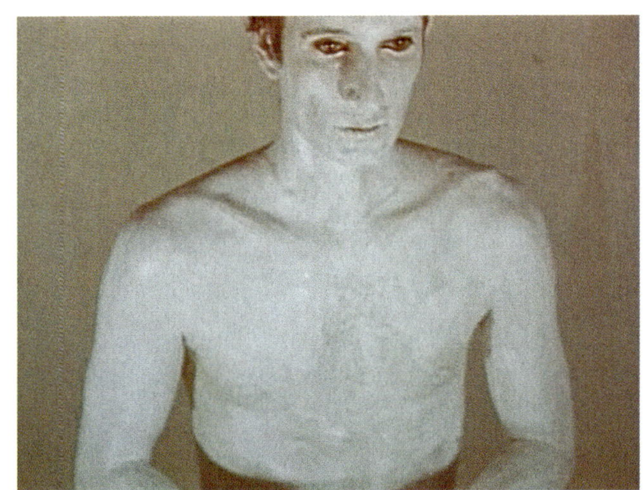

**BRUCE NAUMAN**
(Fort Wayne, Indiana 1941)

[5.1]
***Art Make-Up***
**1967–68**
16mm film (color, silent, sound) projection transferred to video
40:00 min
Minneapolis, Walker Art Center
T. B. Walker Acquisition Fund, 2002
Courtesy Electronic Arts Intermix (EAI), New York

If one wanted to argue that the major artistic innovations and break-
throughs in the second half of the twentieth century happened
through sculpture, Bruce Nauman would be one of a small handful of
artists on which to base the argument. Confronted with the question
of what to do in the studio after he graduated from the University of

[5.1]

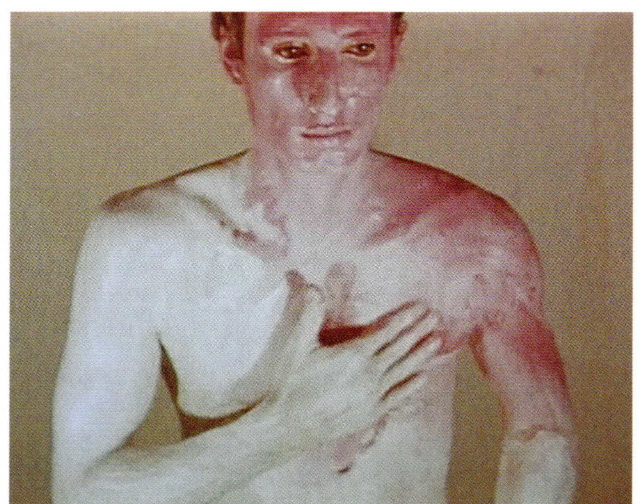

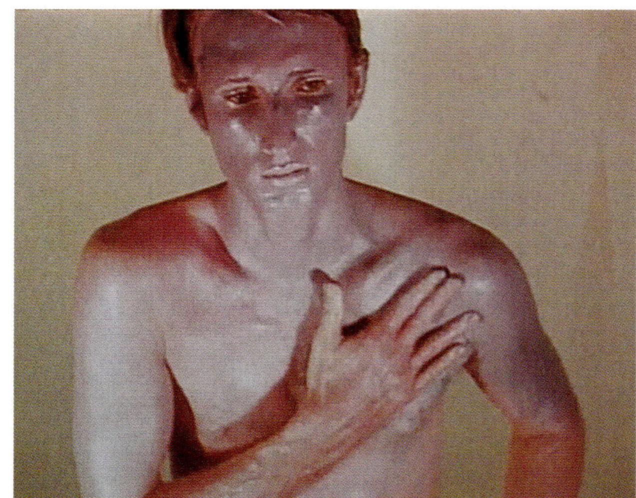

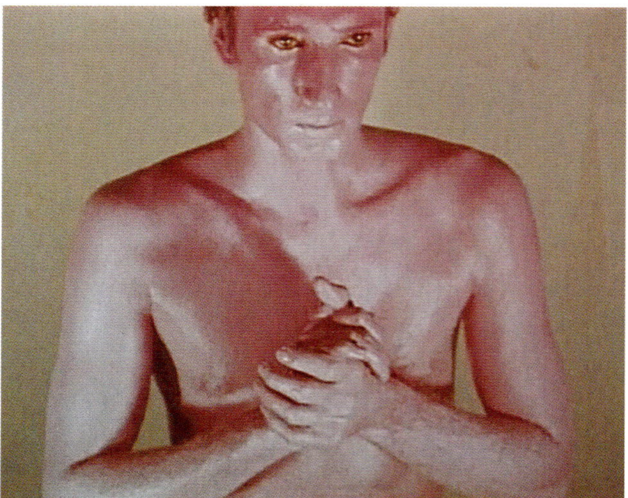

[5.1]

California at Davis in 1966, Nauman made the following assumption: "If I was an artist and I was in the studio, then whatever I was doing in the studio must be art" (quoted in Wallace, Keziere 1979, 18). From this premise he has expanded the field of sculptural practice through confrontations with language (spoken, shouted, or written), with dance and performance, with film and video, with photography, and with architectural environments. Because his work resists categorization, it might be more convenient to define where Nauman does not stand, rather than where he does. Defying canonical definitions, he encompasses and overcomes all of them, showing less interest in what art is than in what art could be.

Since his earliest experimentation with painting and sculpture in the mid-1960s, Nauman has developed a complex body of work built on the assimilation and the digestion of models coming from a diversity of fields and disciplines. Though Marcel Duchamp and Jasper Johns found their rightful places in his genealogy, Nauman claims Man Ray as the artist who—through the versatility of his activities and his radical denigration of style—freed him to open the practice of sculpture to a wide range of media across the disciplines.

The artist's early videos provide a broad understanding of Nauman's experimentation with the potential of moving images. The fifteen or so films and videos that he produced in the late 1960s testify to both his recurring interest in representation of the body and his awareness of the avant-garde dance and music scenes. In front of a stationary camera set in the studio, he performed mundane and often obsessive activities, such as walking (*Walking in an Exaggerated Manner Around the Perimeter of a Square*, 1967–68), bouncing (*Bouncing in a Corner No. 1*, 1968), pinching himself (*Pinchneck*, 1968), torturing himself (*Pulling Mouth*, 1969), or frantically playing an instrument he was unfamiliar with (*Violin Tuned D.E.A.D.*, 1970). Exploring physical awareness and limitation, these performances, during which the camera is the audience's proxy, use redundancy and duration to exhaust and then liberate the body. His research, based on repetition and ev-

eryday gestures and behaviors, paralleled the work developed in the early 1960s in New York by the Judson Dance Theater (its movement research performances) and choreographer Meredith Monk, whom he met in 1968. Through his friendship with Monk, his collaboration with Merce Cunningham, and his acquaintance with musicians Steve Reich, Terry Riley, and La Monte Young, Nauman became aligned with a generation of artists who attempted to apply to their own practices the methodology of chance, the consideration of everyday sounds and gestures that John Cage employed in his own art and way of life.

By the 1980s, Nauman's setups were more elaborate and the tone of the work more caustic. Anxiety courses through a series of sculptures that evoke absent bodies. In recent years, the tenor of Nauman's work has become more meditative and its appearance more refined even though he often circles back to his earlier concerns with new urgency, citing and reappropriating early pieces,

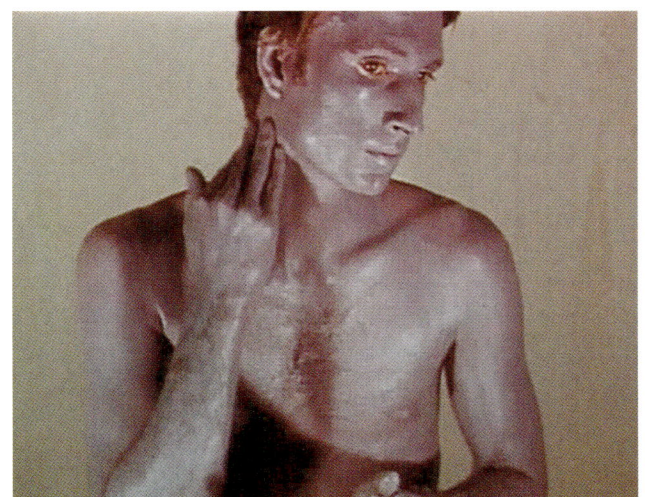
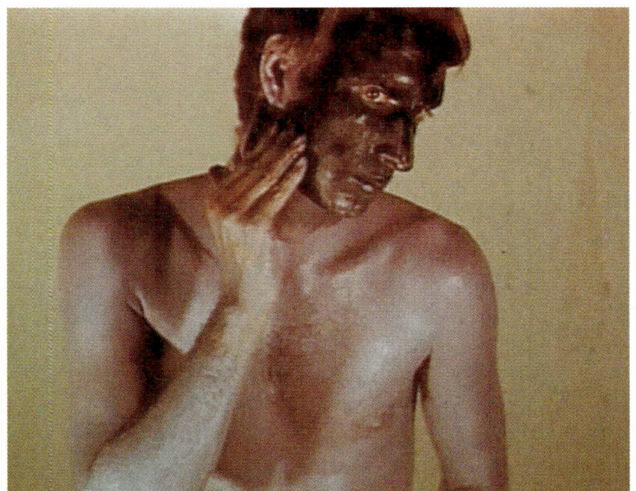



[5.1]

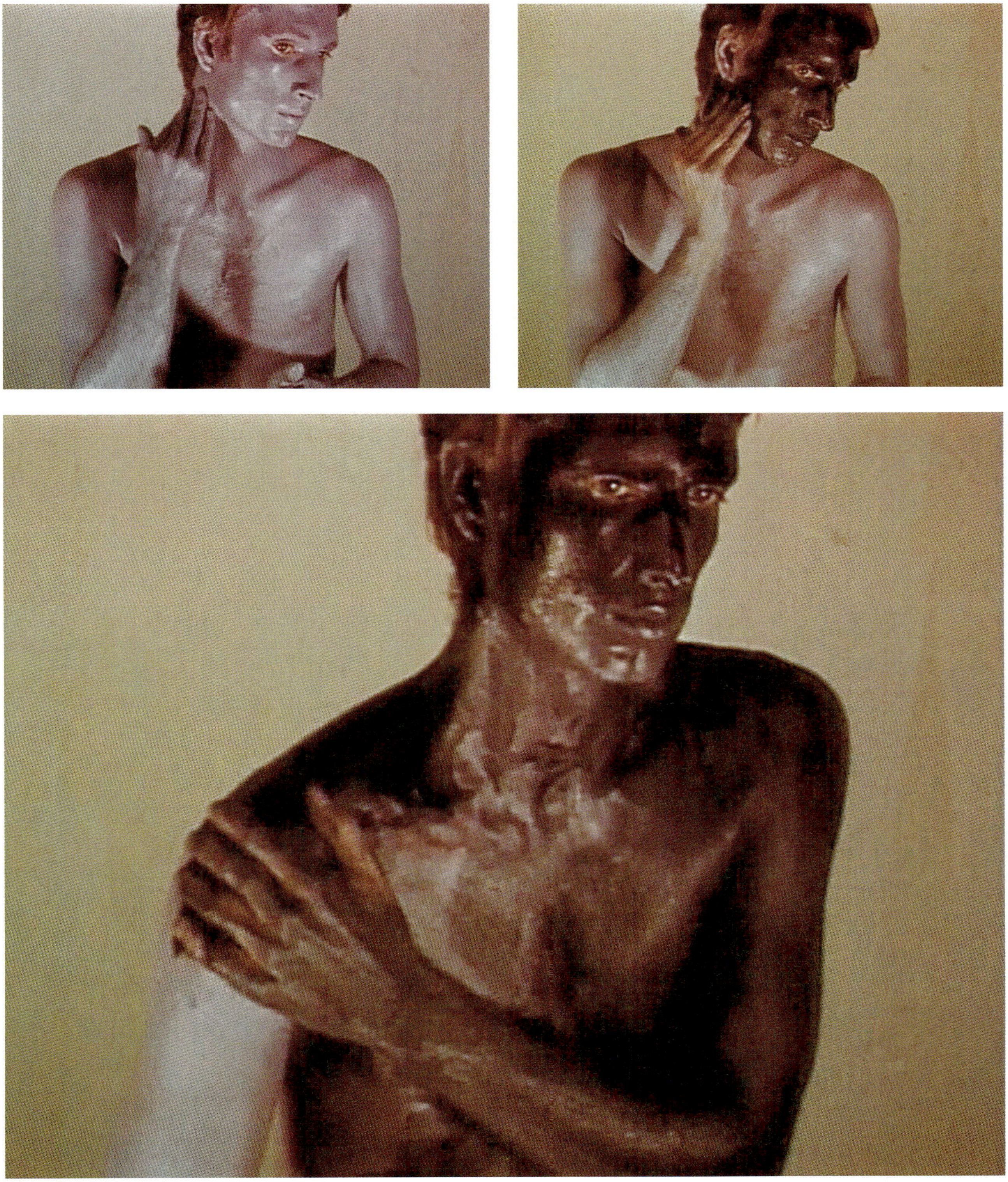

[5.2]

which, modified, become something new and unexpected.
*Art Make-Up* (1967–68) [5.1] is composed of four related films in which the artist applies a successive layer of colored makeup (white, pink, green, and finally black) to his face and upper torso. While he masks himself literally, the title implies that in so doing he also creates himself, "makes himself up." Initially, the films were intended to be projected simultaneously on the four walls of a room. Although this form of installation was never realized for this piece, Nauman employed the method for subsequent film and video installations.
PHILIPPE VERGNE (revised version of text, published in *Bits and Pieces*, 2005, 412-415)

**JOHN BALDESSARI**
(National City, California 1931–Los Angeles 2020)

[5.2]
***I Will Not Make Any More Boring Art***
wallpaper
original: lithograph on paper, 1971, 57.2 × 76.2 cm
Minneapolis, Walker Art Center
T. B. Walker Acquisition Fund and the Butler Family Fund, 2015

[5.3]
***Four Short Films***
**1972–73**
Super 8mm film (color, silent) transferred to video
5:42 min
T. B. Walker Acquisition Fund, 1999
Courtesy Electronic Arts Intermix (EAI), New York

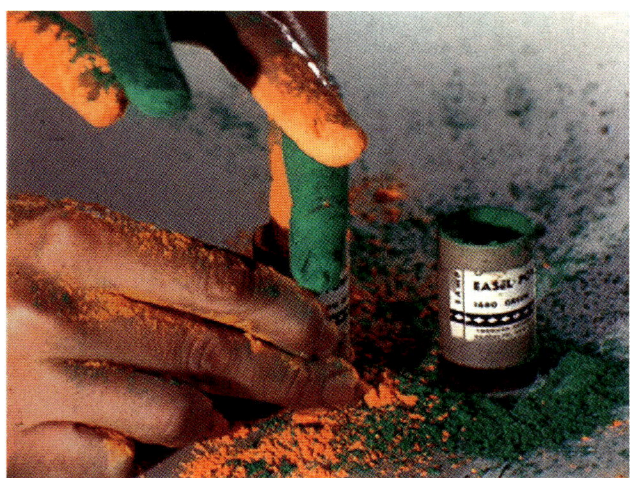

[5.3]

John Baldessari has been defined by *Los Angeles Times* art critic Christopher Knight as "probably the most influential conceptual artist in America." Baldessari has worked with a wide range of media including books, painting, text, installations, photography, video, sculpture, billboards, and public works. He is best known for his conceptual works, centered on the processes of choice and selection made with multiple techniques—photography, words, texts— whose rules are revealed and subverted, involving the viewer in a sort of ironic deconstructive game. In 1970, a pivotal year in his career, he decided to burn all the works he had crated from 1953–66— a true funeral his early work called *The Cremation Project*. The ash was then used in the dough for biscuits that he exhibited at MoMA on the occasion of the *Information* exhibition dedicated to conceptual art. Thus began his "real career" of witty attitudes combined with continuous experimentation, with tireless irony as the cornerstone of his art. And this is precisely the essence of Baldessari's art: conceptual, but irreverent, different from the cold and somewhat "boring" Conceptual Art so popular in those years.

Between the 1970s and 1980s, Baldessari created a variegated body of works but with the common denominator of the narrative power of words and images: from the video *Baldessari Sings Lewitt*, in which he sang Sol LeWitt's manifesto "Sentences on Conceptual Art," to photographic works decontextualized and modified to acquire new concepts, to performances—among which stand out *Unrealized Proposal for Cadaver Piece* inspired by Andrea Mantegna's *Dead Christ* and by *Police Drawing Project*, an experiment in which students created the identikit of the artist, all taken from a hidden camera.

From the 1990s onwards though, Baldessari returned to a certain pictorial sensitivity characterized by bright colors, isolating some parts of the images with acrylic, creating a link between "the parts" and "the whole," he never stopped combining words, texts, photographs, and images. In parallel with his artistic activity, Baldessari developed an extraordinary career as a teacher, which led him to professorships at major Californian universities where he was an appreciated professor and a key figure in the evolution of west coast art.

In 1971, the Nova Scotia College of Art and Design, Halifax, invited John Baldessari to exhibit his work. However, the college did not have the funds for Baldessari to travel to Halifax, so the artist proposed that the art students in Halifax act as his surrogates. The students were instructed by Baldessari to write "I will not make any more boring art" on the gallery walls for the duration of the exhibition (April 1–10, 1971). By enlisting the art students to slavishly write the phrase over and over, Baldessari poked fun at the entire system of art education, which he felt encouraged students to imitate rather than experiment and innovate. The artist also sent along a handwritten page of the phrase, from which the students produced prints.

In both cases, Baldessari gave scant instructions to the students from thousands of miles away, and he was not present to supervise, raising questions of authorship and the role of the artist.

After the work's completion, Baldessari committed his own version of the piece to videotape. The subversive, graffiti-like action of drawing directly on the gallery walls reflected the artist's dissatisfaction with the limitations of traditional painting in the early 1970s. His interest in language-based performative actions that could be realized by others became a hallmark of early conceptual art. Baldessari described his conceptual works as "what I thought art should be, not what somebody else would think art would be. You know, received wisdom, what you would get in school. And so a lot of my work was about questioning this received wisdom."

Realized during the early 1970s, when the artist engaged with the film as a main medium, the *Four Short Films* [5.3], Super 8mm, represent Baldessari's interest in intimate scale (only the artist's hands are visible as he manipulates a range of objects) and daily activities to be recorded as instructions almost like some form of chemical or physics experiments.

In *Time Temperature* he stages an inversely proportionate dynamic between two instruments. As the sands of the egg timer run out (well exceeding the anticipated three minutes), the thermometer registers a transition from freezing point to boiling point.

In *The Hollywood Film* a number of flat discs are tilted in the artist's hands, each revealing a mirrored surface and the face of a beautiful woman. Here, Baldessari reduces movie magic to its barest elements: actresses and lighting.

*Water to Wine to Water* features the artist performing an amateur magician's rendition of the holy miracle while *Easel Painting* shows him composing a picture through the action of thrusting his fingers into jars of pigment powder.

*VINCENZO DE BELLIS*

# VIDEO

6.

## CAROLEE SCHNEEMANN
(Fox Chase, Pennsylvania 1939–New Paltz, New York 2019)

[6.1]
***Meat Joy***
**1964/2010**
16mm film (color, sound) transferred to video
10:35 min
T. B. Walker Acquisition Fund, 2010
Courtesy Electronic Arts Intermix (EAI), New York

Carolee Schneemann was a visual artist and performer whose practice engaged with the politics of the female body. Emerging in the late 1950s, Schneemann's work mixed different styles, drawing from experimental cinema, music, poetry, dance, and Happenings. Among the most interesting pioneers of performance and body art, Schneemann has used her nude body for subversive and provocative means, rewriting a history of art through the renegotiation of values and symbolisms.

In the early 1960s, Schneemann started to be involved in the program of the Judson Memorial Church. There, she participated in works like Claes Oldenburg's *Store Days* (1962) and Robert Morris's *Site* (1964) where she played a living version of Édouard Manet's *Olympia*. That same year she realized *Meat Joy* (1964) [6.1], a work that can be considered a turning point in her production.

These themes continued to be explored in *Fuses* (1967), a profoundly lyrical film-collage that portrays the artist during a sexual relationship with her partner. The body as energy and as a primordial instrument is also powerfully reaffirmed in *Interior Scroll* (1975). The action took place in East Hampton, New York, and at the Telluride Festival, Colorado. During the performance, the artist lay down naked on a table and began to paint her body with mud. She then completely removed a roll of paper from her vagina, which she read aloud.

*Meat Joy* was first performed as part of the First Festival of Free Expression at the American Center in Paris, and later at the Judson Memorial Church in New York. The piece consisted of nude men and women dancing and playing with substances such as raw chicken, fish, sausages, scraps of paper, and wet paint. This Dionysian-inspired ritualistic rite was a "celebration of the flesh as material" and is similar to Kaprow's Happenings in that it used improvisation but focused on the concept behind the work rather than its execution. Rooted in erotic sensuality, *Meat Joy* is an early manifestation of Schneemann's concern for women's control over their bodies and their sexuality, as it emphasizes that women can be as openly sexual or sensual as men. Schneemann wanted to challenge social taboos against open and public sensuality, as well as female sexuality, and used this performance to begin breaking down existing barriers.

Up until her recent death, Schneemann continued to work in various media, including writings and installations, investigating the body and sexuality, as well as the complexity of the physical relationships between individuals, everyday life, and historical events.
*VINCENZO DE BELLIS*



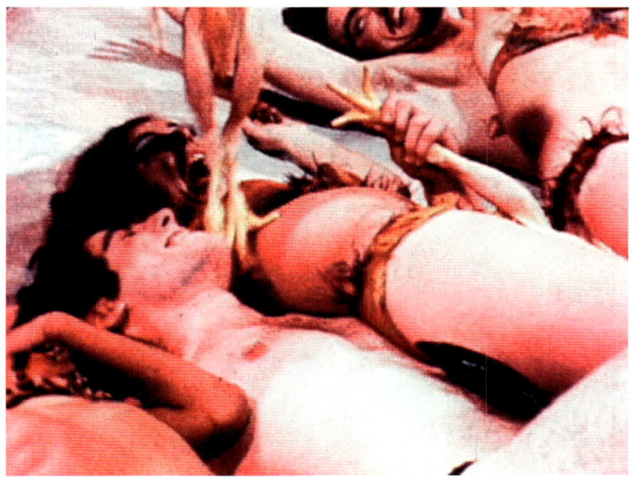
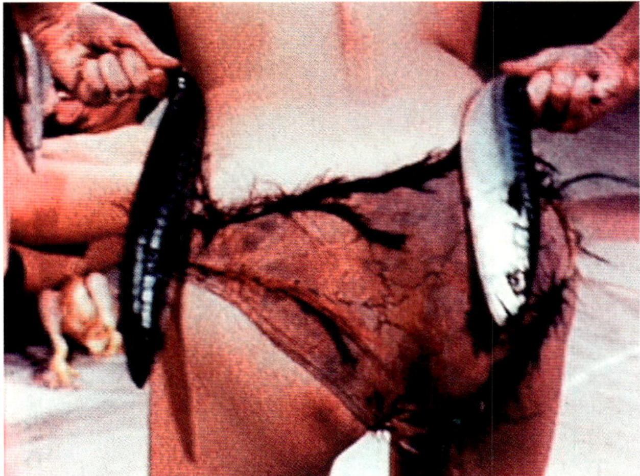
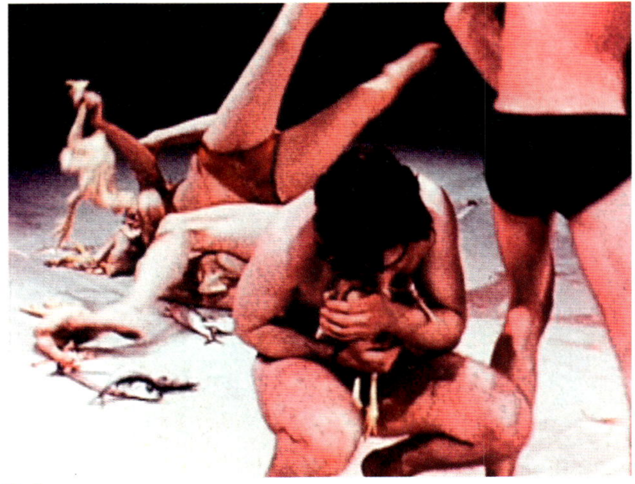

[6.1]

## NAM JUNE PAIK
(Seoul, South Korea 1932–Miami, Florida 2006)

[6.2]
### *TV Cello Premiere*
**1970**
16mm film (color, silent) transferred to video
7:25 min
Julie and Babe Davis Acquisition Fund, 2019
Courtesy Electronic Arts Intermix (EAI), New York

Nam June Paik, composer, performer, video artist, and great media experimenter, was one of the leading protagonists of the Fluxus movement. Paik was an artist aware of his time, able to use the television object and the camera both as elements with which to produce video–sculptures and video installations and as real performance components.

Nam June Paik's first use of television as an artistic material, in 1963, is a benchmark moment in the history of art. Since then, he has explored every corner of the vast aesthetic potential of television and video technology, an odyssey that has earned him the nickname "the Father of Video Art." But his first love—and the subject of his academic training during the 1950s—was musical composition. Paik wrote a thesis on Arnold Schoenberg and later studied with Karlheinz Stockhausen, who was experimenting with electronic sound at his studio in Darmstadt, Germany. His most important encounter was with John Cage, whose Zen-influenced, antimaterialist approach profoundly changed Paik's thinking as well as his art. His performances of this period were intensely physical, visual, often shocking, and sometimes violent.

Years later, Cage recalled that "His work is fascinating, and often rather frightening. Now I would think twice about attending one of his performances. He generates a real sense of danger, and sometimes goes further than we are willing to accept" (excerpted from promotional materials sent to Martin Friedman, Walker Art Center Archives). Paik doused himself with water, banged his head on the piano keyboard, leapt, yelled, and drank water from his own shoe. This "action music," he explained, was an attempt to renew the ontological, or essential, nature of music rather than just its form.

He was in great demand on the avant-garde circuit, performing throughout Europe with the nascent Fluxus group. During these years he also made his first altered televisions by manipulating the horizontal and vertical hold controls to obtain distorted images, or by hooking televisions to interactive radio controls to make sound "visible" on-screen.

Performance, music, video, and sculpture come together seamlessly in the objects Paik made for Charlotte Moorman, the cellist who became his chief collaborator after 1964. Paik and Moorman worked together for almost thirty years, sharing a common interest in avant-garde music and staging energetic live performances. Both artists believed that sexuality was unjustly excluded from classical music, and many of their performances involved Moorman playing the cello in various states of undress. Known as the "topless cellist," Moorman was arrested for indecent exposure during a 1967 perfor-

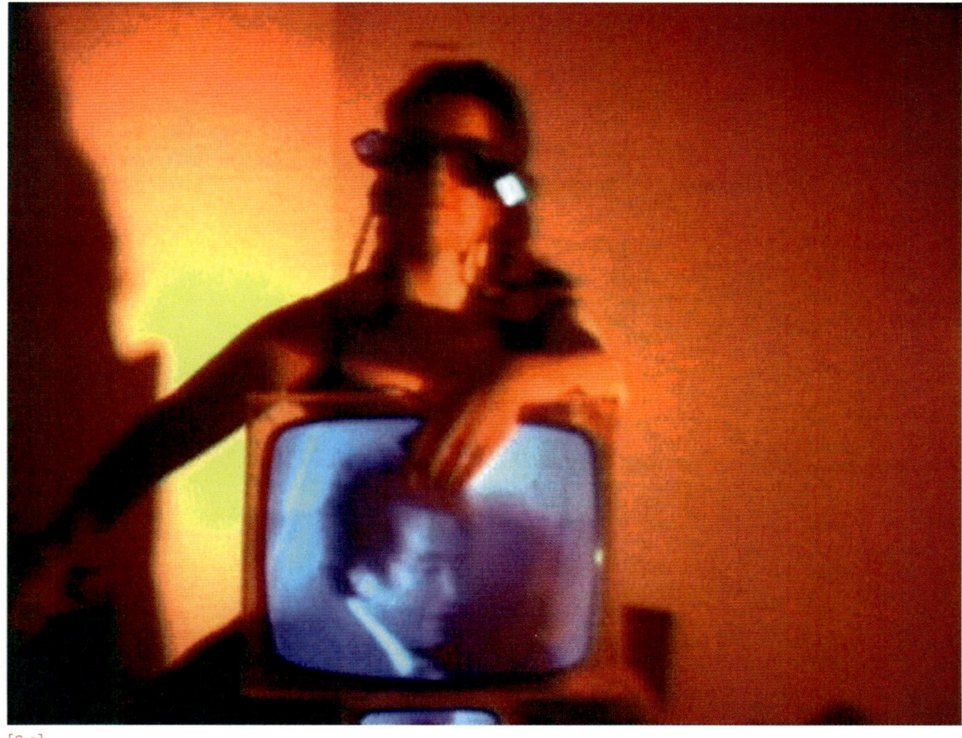

[6.2]

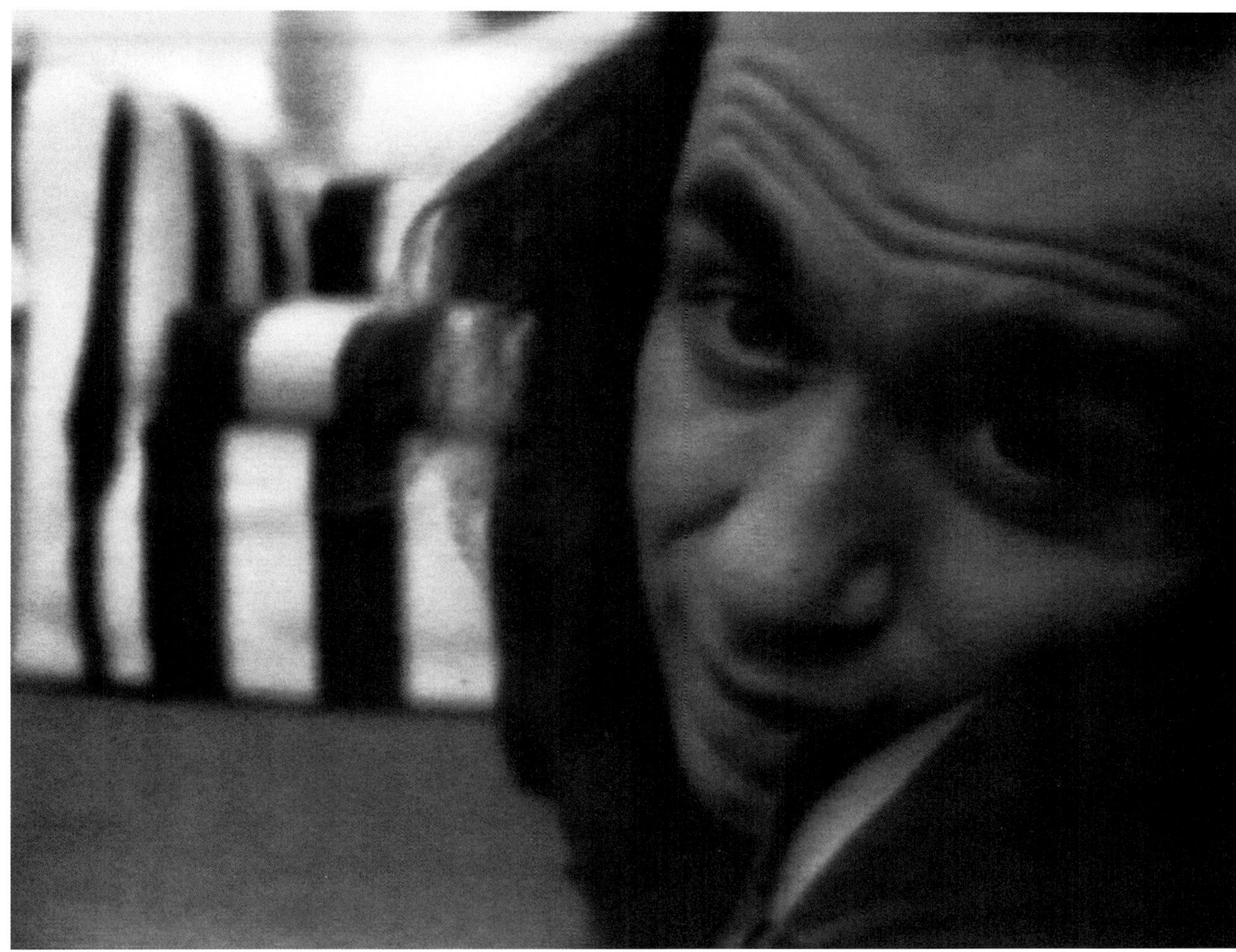

[6.3]

mance in New York. Paik responded by building a series of television sculptures, such as *TV Bra for Living Sculpture* (1969), *TV Cello* (1971), and *TV Eyeglasses* (1971), which she could use as costumes and props. Paik saw this as another opportunity to show that humanity could coexist and even partially merge with technology.

*TV Cello Premiere* (1971) [6.2] is a silent film documentation of Moorman in her first performance on Paik's eponymous *TV Cello* at the Bonino Gallery in New York in 1971. *TV Cello* is sculptural musical instrument constructed from television picture tubes encased in Plexiglas boxes, and its screens were meant to show broadcast TV, prerecorded tape, or live, closed-circuit images, all of which could be manipulated by Moorman. But *TV Cello*, a proxy for Moorman's traditional cello, was also a functioning musical instrument. According to Moorman, it was "the first advance in cello design since 1600" (Moorman makes this observation while performing on *TV Cello* in Paik's videotape *Global Groove*, 1973). It had strings, tuning pegs, a bridge and tailpiece, and even a rudimentary peg, just like a standard cello. The strings, however, were amplified and produced crashing electronic sounds when she played it.

This is also a singular work in the history of interdisciplinary art: unprecedented fusions of sculpture, moving image, live performance, sound, and popular culture that blurred the lines between Moorman's body and Paik's artwork. During the 1970s, Moorman performed with *TV Cello* dozens of times, in venues ranging from museums and galleries to shopping malls and community centers. Both objects perfectly melded her brilliance as a performer with Paik's artistic goal to "humanize technology."

*JOAN ROTHFUSS* (revised version of text, published in *Bits and Pieces*, 2005, 446)

**VITO ACCONCI**
(New York 1940–2017)

[6.3]
***Theme Song***
**1973**
video (black and white, sound)
33:15 min
T. B. Walker Acquisition Fund, 1999
Produced by art/tapes/22
Courtesy Electronic Arts Intermix (EAI), New York

Vito Acconci was a pioneer of video and performance art. As well as an innovator and visionary figure in the field of architecture and public art. Acconci began his career as a poet in the early 1960s. The written word was his primary way to reflect on space, movement, conceptual perimeters of the page, and the linguistic weight of the sign. By the end of the decade, he transitioned to images, with the body becoming an essential reference and fulcrum. His art could be classified as Body Art that denies romantic rhetoric or psychoanalytic approaches. For Acconci, it was a "purely political fact." His actions, in which flesh and screen, gaze and sexuality, self-awareness and relationship with the other were scandalously intertwined, remain true milestones for the history of contemporary art.

In the 1970s, Acconci produced a body of conceptual, performance-based video works that retain an astonishing originality and force more than thirty years later. The emblematic work of this period is *Seedbed* (January 15–29, 1971) presented at the Sonnabend Gallery. The audience walked in an empty room with a wooden floor. Hidden under

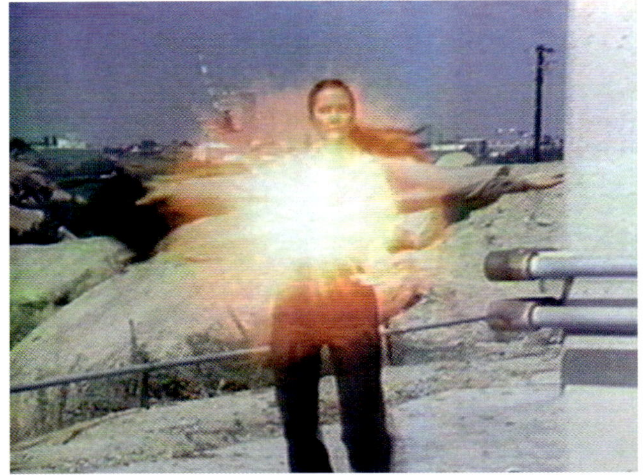 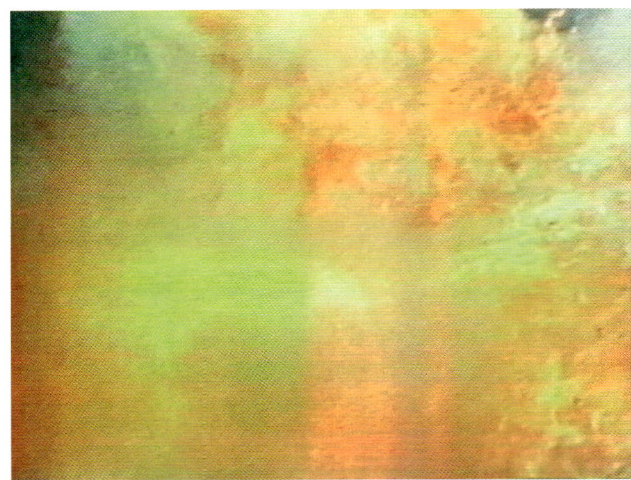

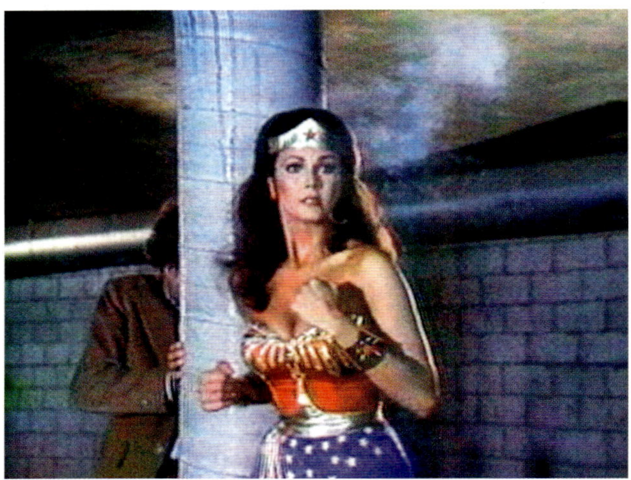 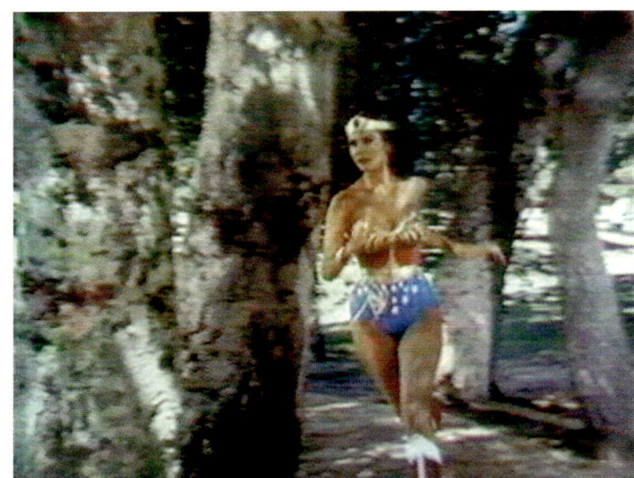



the boards was the artist lying down, masturbating and loudly expressing his erotic fantasies that resonate, through loudspeakers, throughout the gallery. This performance revolves around the idea of involvement of the public in the production of the artists work, creating a situation of mutual interchange between artist and visitor.

Most of the subsequent art actions were recorded on video. Acconci's stream-of-consciousness monologues and performative acts, documented in real time by a fixed camera, chronicle the insertion of the private self into the public sphere. Raw and crudely executed, Acconci's videos enforce an intensive dialogue between the artist and viewer, the body and the self, public and private, subject and object, absence and presence. Acconci used video as a vehicle for an intimate expression of self through the other, exploiting both the inherent immediacy and mediation of the technology.

Acconci's interest in the body and its relationship to space ultimately led to an interest in design. In 1988, he formed the Acconci Studio, a group of architects whose projects incorporate sculpture, furniture, public art, and architecture. The studio functioned as a thinktank, in which he worked with a team of researchers and designers. "One person works alone," he explained, "two form a couple or an image in the mirror, but three people together start the meeting, the discussion, inaugurate a public space."

In *Theme Song* (1973) [6.3], Acconci establishes an uncomfortably close relationship with the viewer, pushing his image into the personal space of the spectator. The artist lies on the floor, his head pressed against the television screen, as he talks directly to his viewer. Drawing on a cigarette, Acconci begins a monologue as he plays songs by famous rockers such as The Doors, Bob Dylan, Van Morris, and Kris Kristofferson, among others. Mimicking the erotic undertones of the

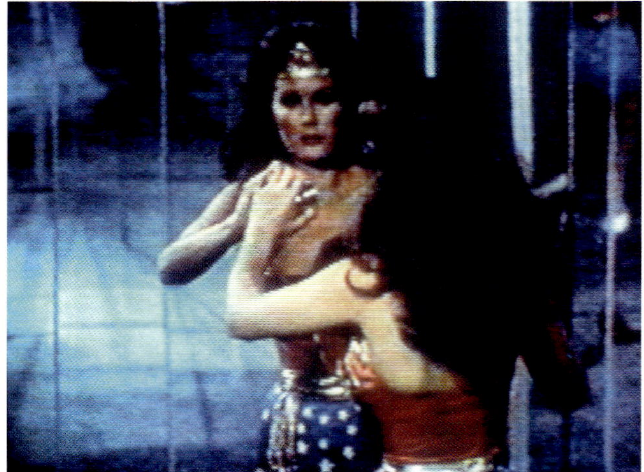

[6.4]

music, Acconci attempts to seduce his audience, while highlighting the absurdity of attempting to forge intimacy through the TV screen. "Of course I can't see your face. I have no idea what your face looks like. You could be anybody out there, but there's gotta be somebody watching me. Somebody who wants to come in close to me [...] Come on, I'm all alone [...] I'll be honest with you, O.K. I mean you'll have to believe me if I'm really honest..." The result is an unsettling reflection on the thorny matrix of desire and manipulation embedded in mass media.
*VINCENZO DE BELLIS*

**DARA BIRNBAUM**
(New York 1946)

[6.4]
***Technology/Transformation: Wonder Woman***
**1978–79**
video (color, sound)
5:50 min
Minneapolis, Walker Art Center
T.B. Walker Acquisition Fund, 1999
Courtesy Electronic Arts Intermix (EAI), New York

Dara Birnbaum is known throughout the world as major figure among artists who have experimented with the use of video, new media and installations. Over the last fifty years she has focused on the aesthetic and ideological facets of mass media images and her work is considered by many to be fundamental to our understanding of the history of media art. Birnbaum was one of the first artists to design complex and innovative installations that juxtapose images from multiple sources, also integrating physical objects—large photographs, sculptures, or architectural elements.

In her videos and multimedia installations, Birnbaum applies both low-end and high-end video technology to subvert, critique, or deconstruct the power of mass media, using images and gestures to uncover mythologies of culture, history, and memory. Through the superimposition of images, music, and text, the artist incorporates a dynamic televisual language, exposing the embedded ideological meanings of the media and using video to give voice to the individual. In her radical works of the late 1970s, Birnbaum used tactics of film deconstruction and image appropriation with the idea of dismantling the hitherto traditional codes of televisual representation. Analyzing the idiomatic grammar of TV (reverse shot, crosscut, inserts) and genres (game show, sitcom, crime drama), she recontextualized pop culture icons—*Kojak, General Hospital*—through fragmentation and repetition. She writes: "By dislocating the visuals and altering the syntax, these images were cut from the narrative flow and countered with musical texts, plunging the viewer headlong into the very experience of TV—unveiling TV's stereotypical gestures of power and submission, of self-presentation and concealment, of male and female egos" (https://www.eai.org/artists/dara-birnbaum/biography). Many of these works often focus on the representation of women. In the mid-1980s, Birnbaum began to explore other themes including the metaphorical and expressive potential of video technologies. Drawing on her background in architecture and painting, she invented new pictorial devices to extend the content of the works from a narrative but also an evocative point of view.

*Technology/Transformation: Wonder Woman* [6.4] has as its underlying subject the representation of women, power, and sexuality in the mainstream media. The artist achieves this by appropriating footage from the 1970s television series *Wonder Woman*. By isolating and repeating moments in which the ordinary woman Diana Prince transforms into the superhero, Birnbaum uses the language of television to deconstruct and reinvent it. Trapping the protagonist in the repetition of this metamorphosis, Birnbaum's montage seems to almost make fun of the heroine. This female pop icon is manipulated and at the same time the message of the television series is subverted. The artist stops the normal flow of the narrative, fragments it, repeats it.

The video also repeats over and over the same phrases from the song "Wonder Woman in Discoland." The lyrics' double entendres ("Get us out from under [. . .] Wonder Woman") reveal the sexual source of the superwoman's supposed empowerment: "Shake thy Wonder Maker." Writing about the "stutter-step progression of 'extended moments' of transformation from Wonder Woman," Birnbaum states, "The abbreviated narrative—running, spinning, saving a man—allows the underlying theme to surface: psychological transformation versus television product. Real becomes Wonder in order to 'do good' (be moral) in an (a) or (im)moral society" (https://www.eai.org/titles/technology-transformation-wonder-woman).
*VINCENZO DE BELLIS*

**DAN GRAHAM**
(Urbana, Illinois 1942)

[6.5]
***Rock My Religion***
**1982–84**
video (black and white, color, sound)
55:27 min
T. B. Walker Acquisition Fund, 1999
Courtesy Electronic Arts Intermix (EAI), New York

Dan Graham is one of the most important American artists of his generation. He first emerged in the 1960s, alongside artists such as Dan Flavin and Sol LeWitt, as an influential pioneer of Conceptual Art and performance-related Video Art. His multidisciplinary practice—which incorporates installation, pavilions, sculpture, photography, conceptual projects, architectural models, video, and performance—has proven groundbreaking for the development of conceptual art over the last forty years. During this period, Graham has developed a diverse practice that refuses to be defined as contemporary art and instead aligns itself with popular culture. Deeply influenced by the writings of anthropologist Margaret Mead and by psychoanalysis and ideological criticism inherited from the Frankfurt School via Herbert Marcuse, he has over the years produced a body of work that can be seen as an essay on the condition of human life in a postmodern, postindustrial era.

Whether his artistic interventions take place in a gallery, between the pages of a magazine, on a stage, in a movie theater, on television, or on the streets, Graham continues to deconstruct, clarify, and expose the nature and condition of an individual's status and behavior within a public sphere dominated by the logic and integrated spectacle of corporate capital and politics.

In 1964, Graham opened the John Daniels Gallery in Manhattan with friends (the gallery's other partners were John Van Esen and Robert Tera). He organized exhibitions of work by artists with whom he

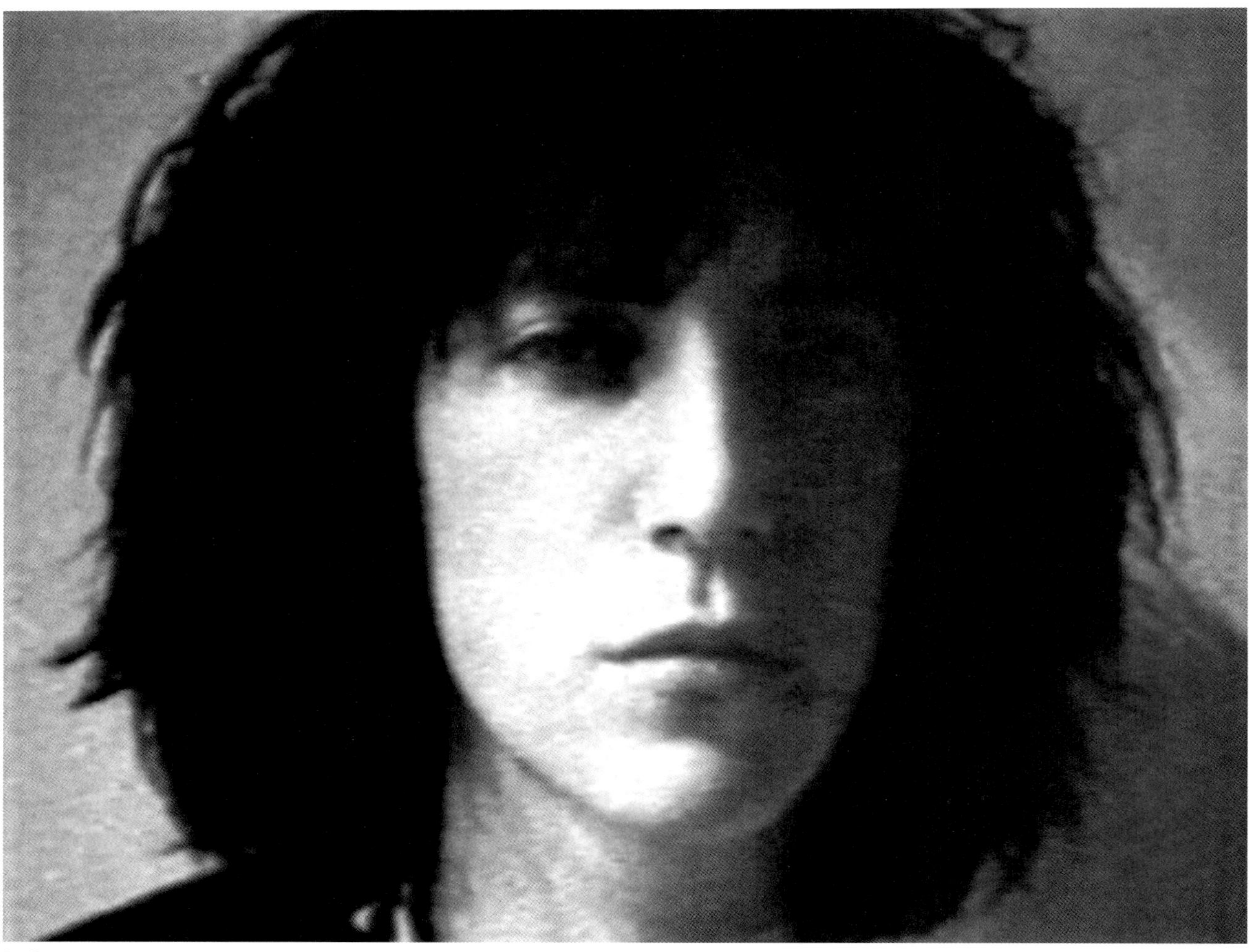

[6.5]

shared intellectual and aesthetic affinities, such as the already cited Sol LeWitt and Dan Flavin but also Donald Judd and Robert Smithson. Financial challenges overshadowed the artistic program, and the gallery closed in 1965. Graham escaped his creditors by moving to New Jersey. There he began a photographic series that is still developing as a matrix of his concerns and his oeuvre. Using a cheap Kodak camera, he photographed the housing environment of New Jersey.

His goal was to create images that anyone could produce. First shown as a slide projection, the work *Homes for America* is a series of images outlining a typology of all possible variations on decorative motifs or materials (as a slide show, *Homes for America* was shown in 1966 in the exhibition *Projected Art* at the Finch College Museum of Art, New York). Through the photographs, Graham draws a critical parallel between the housing industry and the seriality inherited from the aesthetic of Minimal Art. In December 1966, *Homes for America* was published in *Arts Magazine*, accompanied by an article written by the artist (unfortunately, the article was inadvertently il-lustrated with an image of a wooden house in Boston taken by photographer Walker Evans. Graham's intended illustrations appear in a lithographed edition of the original design for *Homes for America* realized between February 19 and May 20, 1971, at the Nova Scotia College of Art and Design in Halifax).

*Homes for America* was not a mere reproduction of an artwork; it was an artwork informed and distributed by the means of information itself, by the medium of the magazine as a public space. It was not art about the media (like Pop Art) but art as media, art as information. Graham used information as an aesthetic and the media as a vernacular form appropriate to the nature of his discourse.

From the late 1960s to the late 1970s, Graham shifted toward a largely performance-based practice, incorporating film and the new medium of video in his systematic investigations of cybernetics, phenomenology, and embodiment.

Media and popular culture have been other systems of signs and ritual ripe for scrutiny within Graham's own "comparative anthropology." The video documentary *Rock My Religion* (1982–84) [6.5] applies to rock music what curator Jean-François Chevrier has called a "montage of dissimilar historical moments" to define Graham's practices (Chevrier 1992, 16). In *Rock My Religion*, the artist drafts a history that begins with the Shakers and their practices of self-denial and ecstatic communal trances and ends with the emergence of rock music as the religion of the teenage consumer in the isolated suburban context of the 1950s. He identifies rock's sexual and ideological context in post-war America as a form of cathartic and secular religion.

Pedagogical, spectacular, and playful all at once, Graham's work has always attempted to expose the mechanism of alienation by analyzing the impact of social codes—propagated by the media or architecture—on the individuation process. Less a dogmatic criticism than an incitement to remain alert, his practice is, as critic Thierry de Duve wrote, a "stocking of utopia" (de Duve 2001, 49–67).

*PHILIPPE VERGNE* (revised version of text, published in *Bits and Pieces*, 2005, 244–245)

## MARTHA ROSLER

(New York 1943)

[6.6]

**If it's Too Bad to Be True, it Could Be DISINFORMATION**
**1985**
video (color, sound)
16:26 min
T. B. Walker Acquisition Fund, 2004
Courtesy Electronic Arts Intermix (EAI), New York

Martha Rosler is one of the most important figures in the recent history of art. In her pioneering and experimental work, she has used various media: from video to photography, installation, performance, text-photography, and even critical writings.

After an initial production of large-format paintings influenced by Abstract Expressionism, Rosler dedicated herself to assemblages, building small rooms with everyday objects. Rejecting a privileged medium such as painting coincided with her transfer from New York to San Diego in 1968. Here, within the university environment, she found favorable conditions for the development of her artistic interests in parallel with her political and social commitments. In particular, the contemporary development of the feminist movement constituted an ideal context for the development and formation of the practices and themes present in Rosler's artistic research.

In contrast to the canons of Modernism, in the course of her career Rosler has rejected the myth of stylistic unity and instead practiced many varied artistic expressions. Her writings are of particular importance, showing a strong critical attitude towards traditional modes of artistic expression.

In her video works, Rosler often places herself and her body in front of the camera, lending herself to impersonating different types of women in order to analyze broad social issues. By shunning metaphor, Rosler in fact maintains close adherence to reality, with an attitude that is sometimes ironic or intentionally didactic.

A similar intention is present in the photographic works that have

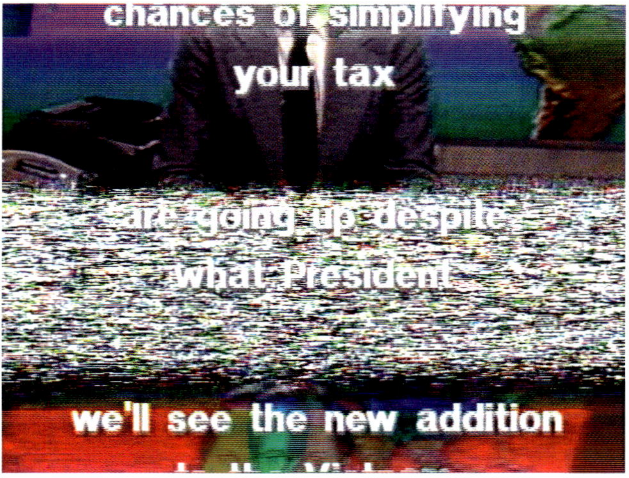


[6.6]

contributed to the revision of the concept of documentary photography, questioning the methods of production, presentation, and reception.

Rosler manipulates images, cuts them, glues them, and transforms them to create a different scenario, which is completely destabilizing for the viewer, highly emotional, and decidedly immediate. Looking at these images together affords us a sense of estrangement yet great familiarity—a dystonia that captures our attention within an all-too-familiar repertoire.

The 17-minute video *If it's Too Bad to Be True, it Could Be DISINFORMATION* (1985) [6.6] was part of an installation with the same title, taken from an article in *The New York Times* accusing the US Government of spreading false information on Nicaragua. According to the US Government, Nicaragua had bought MIG planes to attack the United States. By incorporating press material, Rosler creates a collusion of text and image that questions the authority and objectivity of the media. As in some of her other works, the formal structure is inseparable from her political analysis.

The artist re-presents the *NBC Nightly News* and other broadcast reports to analyze their deceptive syntax and capture the confusion intentionally inserted into the news script. The artist addresses the fallibility of electronic transmission by emphasizing the distortion and absurdities that occur as a result of technical interference. Stressing the fact that there is never a straight story, Rosler asserts her presence in a character-generated text that rolls over the randomly erased images, isolating excerpts from the broadcast sources. The work then reverts to intact excerpts, which we view with a new perspective.

*VINCENZO DE BELLIS*

# FROM PICTURES TO PICTURES

7.

**SARAH CHARLESWORTH**

(East Orange, New Jersey 1947–Falls Village, Canaan, Connecticut 2013)

[7.1]
***April 19, 20, 21, 1978*** from ***Modern History***
**1978**
3 black and white prints reproduced same size as original newspaper
46.3 × 30.4 cm; 58.4 × 46.3 cm; 45.4 × 31.7 cm
Image Courtesy the Estate of Sarah Charlesworth
and Paula Cooper Gallery, NY

Sarah Charlesworth was part of an influential group of artists working in New York in the late 1970s and 1980s who came to be known as the Pictures Generation. This name stemmed from their use, and analysis of, photographic imagery to produce artworks. Charlesworth was one of the key artists in this group, whose work "created a vital link between her generation and the next," and who explored and expanded the possibilities of photography in art (Respini 2016, 106–7: 107). She studied at Barnard College, New York, with the Conceptual artist Douglas Huebler and her use of series formats and modes of appropriations and editing situate her work in a pivotal point in American art that draws on the experiments of the early 1960s and turns a critical look towards practices of image-making and story-telling.

*April 19, 20, 21, 1978* (1978) [7.1] consists of three photographic prints of the front pages of newspapers which shows the front pages of three newspapers tracking the same main story: the kidnapping of former Italian prime minister Aldo Moro.

The artist deconstructs time in print: the first element is the April 19 edition of the Roman newspaper *la Repubblica*, announcing Moro's supposed assassination; in the next day's other Roman newspaper *Il Messaggero*, Charlesworth redacts the print text and leaves only the picture of Moro holding the first day's paper to prove he is still alive. The final element features the April 21 edition of the Geneva newspaper *Tribune de Genève*. Here the artist again redacts the text, which recounts the disproving of the rumor with an image of newspapers from both the previous days.

This work challenges photography's reputation as the embodiment of truth. Words are unnecessary. Charlesworth demonstrates the magnitude of the mass media's reliance on pictures. The blankness on the page is unsettling, but here the image recounts the entire narrative. In addition, the papers are reproduced in original scale and placement, revealing a newspaper within a newspaper within a newspaper.

The use of the "public imagery of newspapers" (Sussler 1989, 30) in Charlesworth's artwork points to connections with other artistic practices throughout the twentieth century. Print mass media has long been a site for artistic experimentation: from the critical collage works of Raoul Hausmann and John Heartfield through Robert Rauschenberg, Jasper Johns, and Robert Morris' incorporation of newspaper as a material to the appropriation of news content by Andy Warhol, and the more contemporaneous use of the news-paper or magazine as a format, source of material, and means of dissemination by Conceptual artists such as Douglas Huebler, Joseph Kosuth, and Martha Rosler. This has also continued in the decades that followed, for example in the work of Robert Gober in the 1990s, and remains a source for contemporary artists (*Shock of the News 2012*, 132; Ekland 2009, 145).

While Conceptual artists were using news media often as a means of presenting their artwork outside of the gallery or museum system, Charlesworth (as well as other artists of the Pictures Generation such as Laurie Simmons) was comfortable employing mass-media as a material within "discrete" art pieces. The seriality of Charlesworth's work also alludes to the repeated forms of Minimalism and is an approach also seen in the likes of Cindy Sherman's *Untitled Film Stills* (1977–80). While they used photographic images in their work, this generation of artists critically reflected on the medium, using techniques of rephotographing and editing to examine the functions of photography, making its hidden structures visible (Ekland 2009, 145).
*NIKKI KANE*

**ROBERT LONGO**

(Brooklyn, New York 1953)

[7.2]
***National Trust***
**1981**
charcoal, graphite on paper, fiberglass, aluminum
160 × 594.4 × 12.7 cm
Minneapolis, Walker Art Center
Art Center Acquisition Fund, 1981

Robert Longo was one of five artists included in the 1977 *Pictures* exhibition, organized by Douglas Crimp at Artists Space in New York, which has come to be regarded as a key moment in American art. Before this exhibition, Longo was one of the founders of Hallwalls, an exhibition space in the hallway of a studio building, sited in an old ice factory in Buffalo, NY. Through Hallwalls, he gained his first professional connections with the New York art world, hosting artists, curators, and critics such as Robert Irwin, Vito Acconci, Dan Graham, and Lucy Lippard (Evans 2009, 101–102). Longo's practice has included drawing, sculpture, performance, and video, and has frequently referred to the cinematic and the media: "I was raised on movies, television, and *Life* magazine. I wasn't interested in images that were based on reality; my concerns were more for representations of representations. I was interested in what art could be, not what art was" (Robert Longo talks to Mary Haus: Haus 2003, 238–239).

With this 1981 work *National Trust* [7.2], Robert Longo "killed off" his three-year series *Men in the Cities*, tying up its imagery of black and white drawings of contorted bodies with this triptych of man, woman, and skyscraper (Fox 1989, 26). The left and right panels respectively depict a man and woman in formal attire, lying down as if unconscious or dead. They are surrounded only by

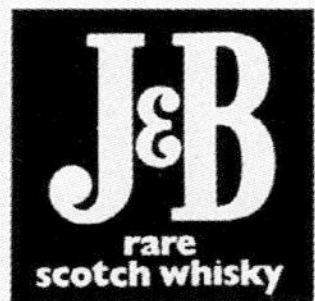



# la Repubblica

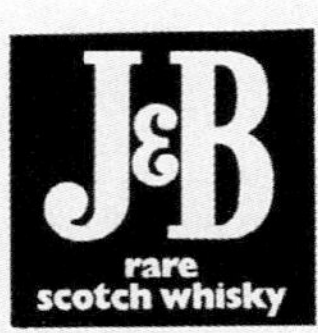



Direttore Eugenio Scalfari


Anno 3 - Numero 93 - L. 200

Redazione, Amministrazione: 00185 ROMA, Piazza Indipendenza, 11-b, tel. 497941 telex 68180-64005 (cas. post. 2412 Roma AD Sped. In abb. post. gr. 1/70 — Abbonamenti: ITALIA (c.c.p. n. 11200003 - Roma) anno L. 46.000, semestre 25.000, trimestre 15.000 - ESTERO: anno 80.500, semestre 41.500, trimestre 21.500 (posta ordinaria) — Copia arretrata? L. 400 — Redazione di Milano, via Turati 3, tel. 636525 - 6571717 - telex 25283. Concessionaria per la pubblicità: A. MANZONI & C. S.p.A., 20121 MILANO - via Agnello 12

mercoledì 19 aprile 1978


*Un messaggio delle Br annuncia che il cadavere si trova in un lago del Reatino*

# Moro assassinato?

## *Vane le ricerche di elicotteri e sommozzatori*
## *Non si esclude l'ipotesi di una falsa pista*

### Il paese è compatto

**N**ON CI POTEVA essere un 18 aprile più tremendamente fosco di quello che abbiamo passato: l'annuncio dell'assassinio, il pensiero di quel corpo affondato in un lago ghiacciato come la morte, il sadismo di quel comunicato, l'affanno delle ricerche, l'irruzione nel covo dei brigatisti al decimo chilometro della Cassia, carabinieri e polizia agli sbocchi delle strade del centro di Roma, Zaccagnini terreo, La Malfa in lacrime, la famiglia di Moro impietrita nel dolore.

Nel momento in cui scriviamo, ancora s'ignora se l'ultimo messaggio delle Br sia autentico, sebbene l'opinione degli inquirenti propenda per il sì. Ma autentico non vuol dire necessariamente veridico. Le ipotesi che attualmente s'intrecciano — fino a quando il piccolo lago della Duchessa non sarà stato interamente esplorato e dragato — sono dunque le seguenti:

1) Il volantino delle Br è un falso materiale, compiuto da un gruppo di macabri ignoti, desiderosi di "punire" la Dc nel giorno anniversario della sua vittoria politica di trent'anni fa. Quest'ipotesi non sembra credibile.

2) Il volantino è autentico e veritiero: il corpo di Moro è là, sotto quell'acqua gelata, sulla cima del Velino! Oggi o al massimo domani dovremo averne conferma.

3) Il volantino è autentico ma non veritiero. E' servito cioè a distrarre per alcune ore l'attenzione degli inquirenti, a "depistarli" verso un obbiettivo falso per consentire nel frattempo ai brigatisti di cambiare zona, rompere la stretta delle indagini e proseguire più al sicuro l'azione intrapresa il 16 marzo.

**SEGUE A PAGINA 2**

Il luogo indicato è inaccessibile per la grande quantità di neve. Solo con gli elicotteri è stato possibile raggiungerlo. Se il comunicato dei terroristi è veritiero il presidente della Dc sarebbe stato ucciso da diversi giorni e il suo corpo affondato

#### Oggi si ricomincia tra neve e ghiaccio

di PAOLO GUZZANTI

RIETI — Prima delle 19 le ricerche del corpo di Aldo Moro al lago della Duchessa sono state sospese. Le prime ricognizioni non hanno dato alcun risultato. E' forte il sospetto che il contenuto del settimo messaggio delle brigate rosse sia falso. Se fosse invece vero, e il corpo del presidente della Democrazia cristiana si trovasse realmente sepolto nelle gelide acque del laghetto, si dovrebbe accettare una delle seguenti ipotesi: Aldo Moro è morto da diversi giorni ed il suo corpo è stato affondato nel lago durante la scorsa settimana. Oppure, ipotesi: Aldo Moro è morto da diversi giorni con un elicottero e gettato giù. Ciò che spinge a queste conclusioni è l'assoluta mancanza di tracce sulla neve che circonda lo specchio d'acqua.

**SEGUE A PAGINA 2**

#### Tragico 18 aprile a Piazza del Gesù

di GIAMPAOLO PANSA

ROMA — *Doveva arrivare, questo 18 aprile a piazza del Gesù, ma nessuno lo immaginava così carico d'angoscia, così straziato fra notizie vere e notizie incerte, così crudele nell'alternarsi dei messaggi di morte e dei lampi di speranza. La prima telefonata, alle 10,30, è di Lettieri, sottosegretario all'Interno: c'è l'ultimo comunicato delle Brigate Rosse, Moro è stato assassinato, Zaccagnini ascolta, con lui c'è soltanto Pisanu, il capo della sua segreteria politica. E noi, adesso, siamo tutti qui col taccuino in mano, a torchiare Pisanu, per sapere le solite cose inutili e un po' feroci. Com'era Zac? Che cosa ha fatto Zac? Che cosa ha mormorato Zac? Pisanu ci fissa senza vederci, poi replica: «Zaccagnini non ha detto niente».*

**SEGUE A PAGINA 4**

### Annuncia l'esecuzione

#### Questo il testo del comunicato n. 7

ROMA — Ecco il testo del comunicato n. 7 inviato dalle Brigate rosse al « Messaggero ».

« Il processo ad Aldo Moro « Oggi 18 aprile 1978, si conclude il periodo "dittatoriale" della Dc che per ben trent'anni ha tristemente dominato con la logica del sopruso. In concomitanza con questa data comunichiamo l'avvenuta esecuzione del presidente della Dc Aldo Moro, mediante "suicidio". Consentiamo il recupero della salma, fornendo l'esatto luogo ove egli giace. La salma di Aldo Moro è immersa nei fondali lirancciosi (ecco perché si dichiarava impantanato) del lago Duchessa, alt. mt. 1800 circa località Car-

-tore (RI) zona confinante tra Abruzzo e Lazio.

« E' soltanto l'inizio di una lunga serie di "suicidi": il "suicidio" non deve essere soltanto una "prerogativa" del gruppo Baader Meinhof.

« Inizino a tremare per le loro malefatte i vari Cossiga, Andreotti, Taviani e tutti coloro i quali sostengono il regime.

« P.S. - Rammentiamo ai vari Sossi, Barbaro, Corsi, posti a libertà "vigilata".

« Comunicato n. 7  19-4-1978 « Per il comunismo

Brigate rosse »

---

*La polizia arriva per caso al covo terrorista nella periferia di Roma*

# Scoperta la base delle Br
## *Armi, esplosivi, divise, documenti*

### Berlinguer da Zaccagnini

ROMA — Il comitato centrale comunista che discuteva sulla lotta contro il terrorismo è stato sospeso, tutti i dirigenti sono partiti per raggiungere le sedi di partito. Berlinguer e Chiaromonte, dopo una riunione straordinaria della Direzione, sono andati a piazza del Gesù per esprimere a Zaccagnini la solidarietà del Pci. Sospeso anche il congresso della Fgci che doveva cominciare a Firenze. Bufalini ha letto una dichiarazione che impegna il Pci ad un'azione di massa per isolare i terroristi. Cossutta dichiara: « E' un atto di guerra ».

**IL SERVIZIO A PAGINA 4**

ROMA — Una base terroristica di estrema importanza è stata scoperta — quasi casualmente — nella mattinata di ieri in via Gradoli, a tre chilometri in linea d'aria da via Fani, dove fu rapito Moro. Ad accorgersi del « covo » sono stati i vigili del fuoco, chiamati da un inquilino del suo appartamento invaso dall'acqua proveniente dall'alloggio soprastante. Quest'ultimo s'è rivelato come un vero arsenale-magazzino dei terroristi: oltre a

pistole, bombe a mano, mitra, ordigni fumogeni e lacrimogeni della polizia, sono state trovate divise dell'Alitalia, da operai della Sip, camici bianchi, divise di poliziotto, targhe rubate, carte d'identità, tessere ferroviarie di sconto.

L'alloggio era abitato da un trentacinquenne, non tanto alto, robusto, che diceva di chiamarsi Borghi. All'arrivo della polizia è stata vista una ragazza bionda allontanarsi su una moto di grossa

cilindrata, invertendo la direzione di marcia; anche un uomo sarebbe fuggito dalla parte opposta. Secondo alcuni testimoni nel minuscolo appartamento di via Gradoli, nella notte fra lunedì e martedì, qualcuno ha battuto a macchina a lungo. Forse un nuovo messaggio delle Br? Pare accertato infine che sempre la notte scorsa, insieme al misterioso signor Borghi, si trovasse anche una ragazza.

I SERVIZI A PAGG. 2-3

---

## Antonio Ghirelli
## Intervista sul
## Calcio Napoli
a cura di Maurizio Barendson

pp. IV-160, lire 2.000

la storia come una grande squadra di calcio che riflette, forse meglio di qualsiasi altra, l'evoluzione tumultuosa di una città e la passione delle masse che la domenica, sugli spalti dello stadio San Paolo, portano tutta la carica di una passione di vivere che non trova sbocchi nei lunghi giorni della settimana

# Editori Laterza

---

*I due massimi scrittori italiani condannano i terroristi*

# "Le loro azioni ci fanno orrore"

di ALBERTO MORAVIA

COMUNQUE vada a finire, siamo arrivati all'ultimo atto di questa losca vicenda. In un momento come questo accetto volentieri l'invito a ripetere la mia opinione.

Sono stato in Unione Sovietica e in Cina e ho profonda ammirazione per le due rivoluzioni che ci sono state in quei paesi. Credo anche però che a quelle rivoluzioni non siano seguiti dei modelli di società accettabili nell'Europa occidentale e in particolare in Italia.

Perché dico questo? Lo dico perché le Brigate rosse di-

mostrano, sia attraverso la loro ideologia che il loro comportamento pratico, di essere un gruppo di tipo staliniano in ritardo. Il loro ricorso ad una sentenza di condanna a morte dimostra da solo la completa estraneità di questo gruppo alla cultura europea e italiana. A chi obietta che qualunque rivoluzione e qualunque gruppo di rivoluzionari ha in qualche modo praticato la pena di morte, rispondo che questo comportamento si valuta non in sé, bensì sullo sfon-

**SEGUE A PAGINA 2**

### Sciascia: è la fine delle Br

ROMA — Leonardo Sciascia ci ha rilasciato la seguente dichiarazione:

« Ripristinando nel nostro paese la pena di morte le Brigate rosse non solo si sono poste al di fuori di quella legittimità o legalità rivoluzionaria che follemente dicono di rappresentare ma hanno reso più difficile e angosciosa la difesa della libertà a coloro che per tutti la difendono. L'abolizione della pena di morte è stato un fatto rivoluzionario in Italia e io speravo che al di là della pietà per le Brigate rosse si ricordassero almeno nel loro dirsi rivoluzionari. Non è stato così. Si apre per tutti noi un duro avvenire. Ma per loro è il principio della fine ».

LEONARDO SCIASCIA

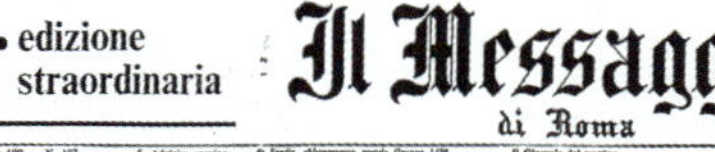

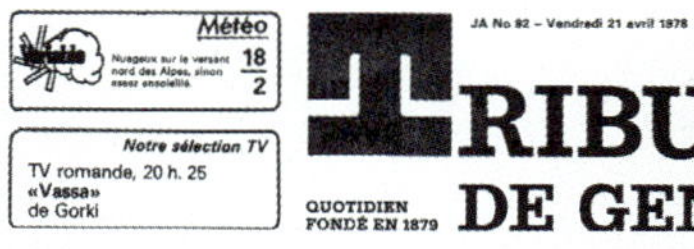

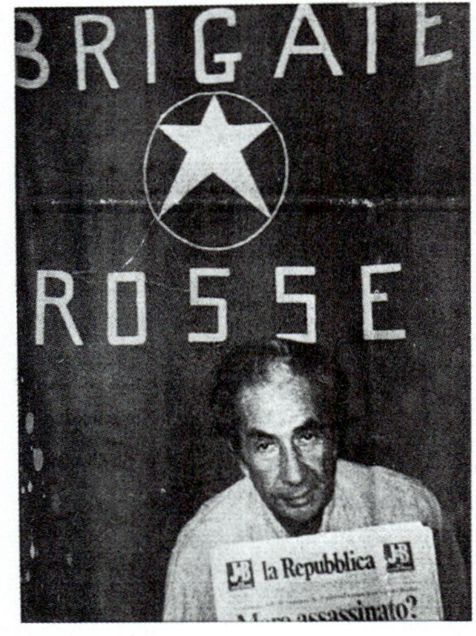


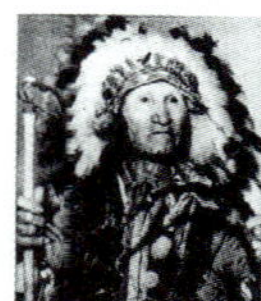

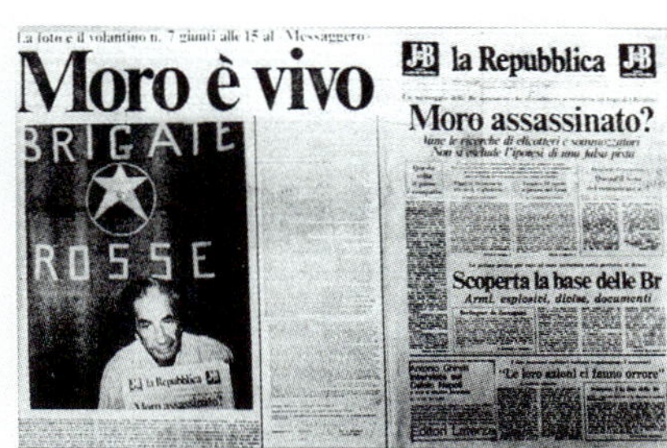


[7.1]

empty white space, giving the impression that they are somehow suspended. Between them, and slightly above, sits an aluminum relief of city rooftops, which separates, or unites, the figures, and appears as a sort of authority.

Longo created his figure drawings by first photographing friends on his roof, often throwing small objects at them to provoke twisted poses. He then projected these photographs onto large paper and traced them out, making adjustments to the expressions, clothes, or hairstyles. He worked with a professional illustrator to complete the drawings, to give them a polished finish. This approach is similar to, but distinct from, other artists' practices of appropriation at the time: his works are "pictures of other pictures; however, they are not appropriated from sources in the mass media but rather from the artist's own photographs" (Fox 1989, 23–24). The contorted poses that Longo favors in his works have their origins in cinematic depictions of conflict; his first work to incorporate such poses directly referenced a scene from the movie *The American Soldier* (1976). However, Longo's treatment of these figures, void of any clear narrative and depicted in isolation, makes their poses ambiguous; in some of

the series the figures could be interpreted as either dancing or in pain (Fox 1989, 17–18).

While the figures' lying-down positions in *National Trust* are perhaps less ambiguous, the lack of narrative or additional information remains: they are "subject to control by forces that they and we cannot see" (Fox 1989, 12). This is compounded by the "confusion of temporalities" in his work (Crimp 1979, 83). Each panel of the piece points to a moment frozen in time, bodies in motion rendered still, and the triptych form collapses these together into one. These might be read as film storyboards, or as pointing to the "chronic discontinuity and disjunction of television" with its "uncanny juxtapositions of the most incompatible images" and is a characteristic that was in keeping with the artistic developments of the time that embraced montage, artificiality, and contingency (Fox 1989, 31; Foster 1989, 52).

*NIKKI KANE*

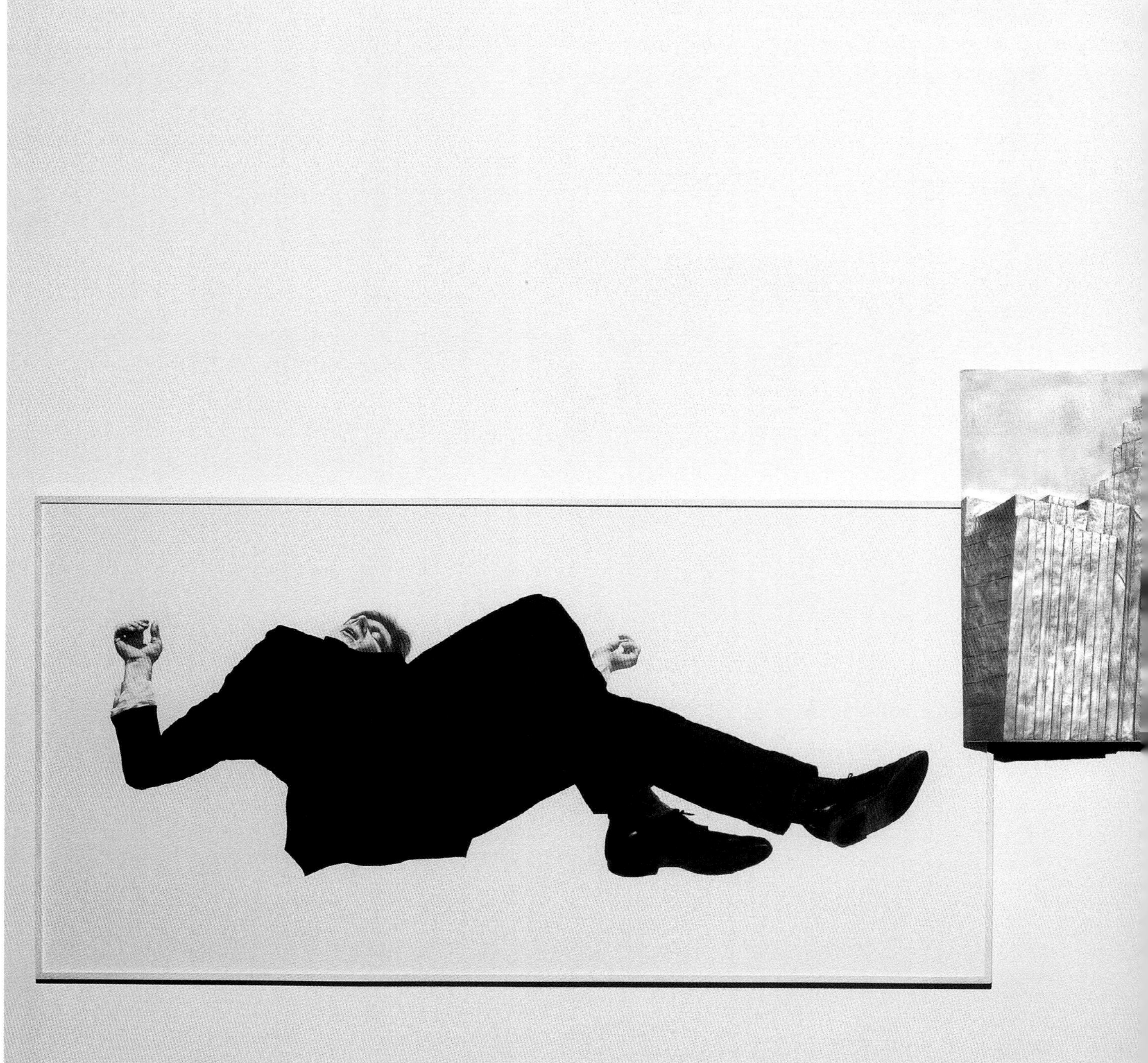

[7.2]

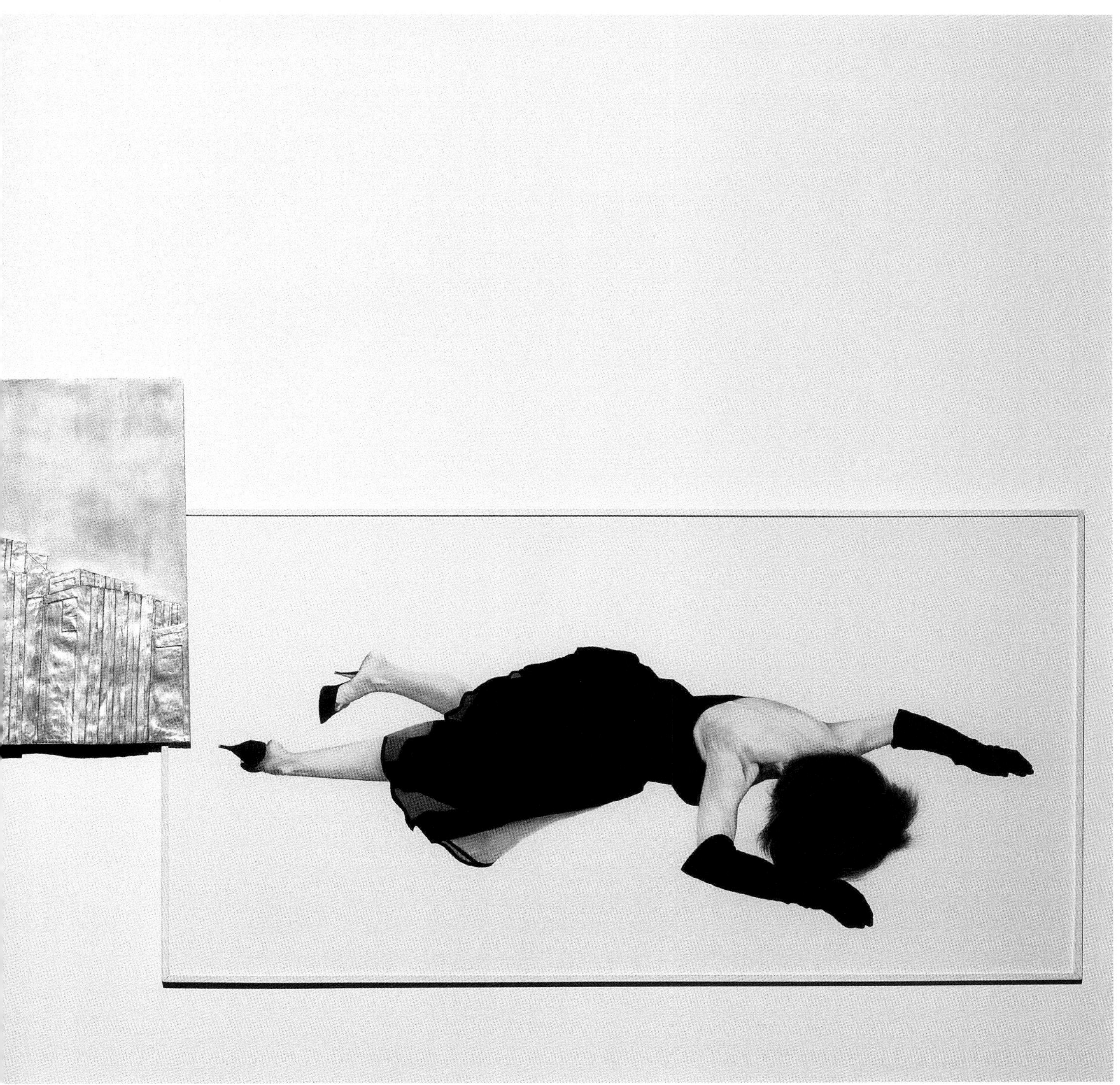

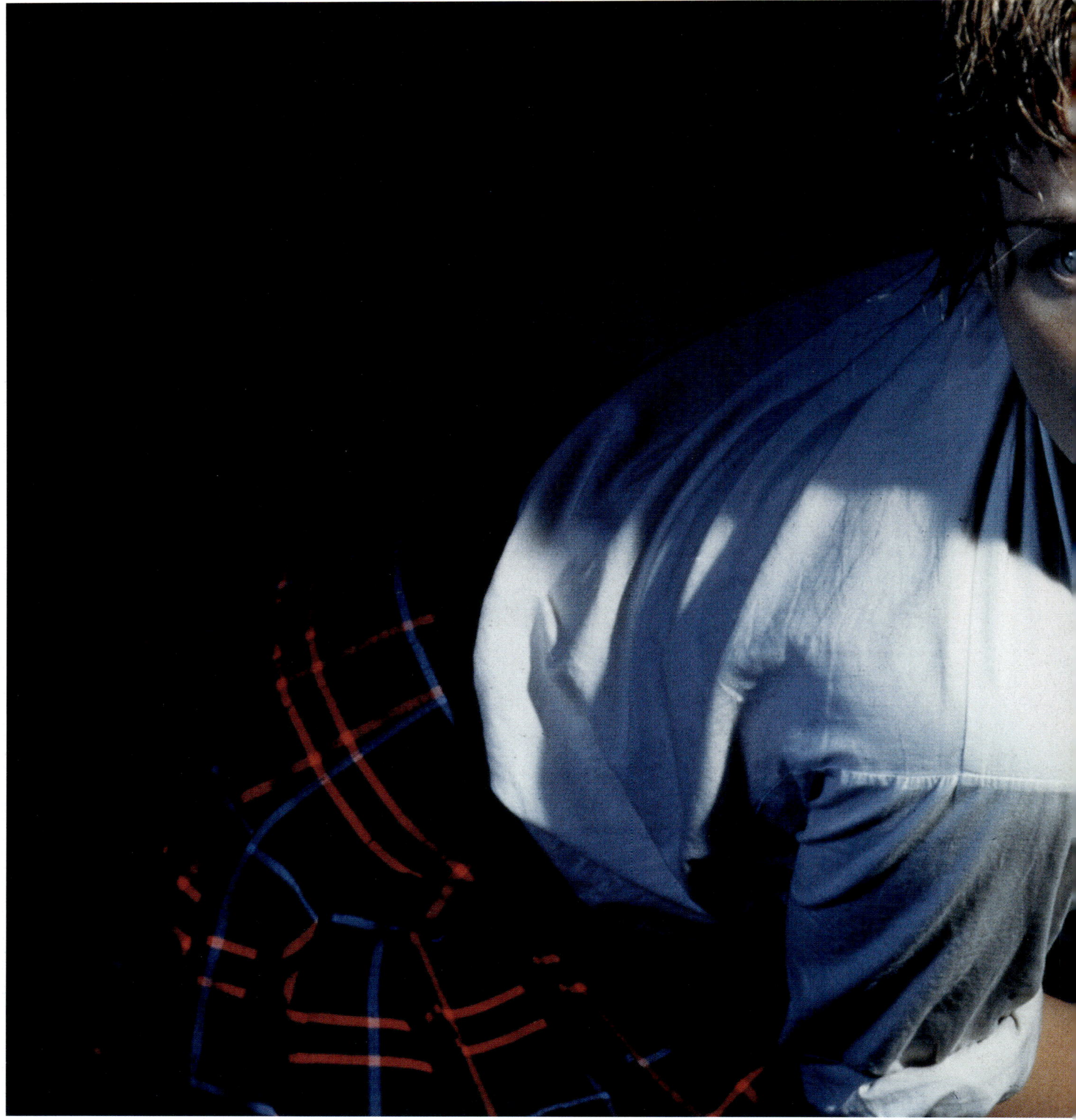



**CINDY SHERMAN**
(Glen Ridge, New Jersey 1954)

[7.3]
***Untitled #92***
**1981**
Edition: A.P. 1/2 from an edition of 10; color chromogenic print
61 × 121.9 cm
Minneapolis, Walker Art Center
Art Center Acquisition Fund, 1982

As one of the most prolific and influential artists of our time, Cindy Sherman has come to represent a generation of artists who, emerging in the late 1970s and early 1980s, worked with the techniques and tropes of photography to make art works that examined the function of the image itself in society. Sherman first gained critical attention with her *Untitled Films Stills* (1977–80), a series of sixty-nine black-and-white photographs in which the artist herself poses in various locations and as various characters. Across the photographs she transforms herself using wigs, makeup, props, and vintage clothing, and each image appears to capture the charac-

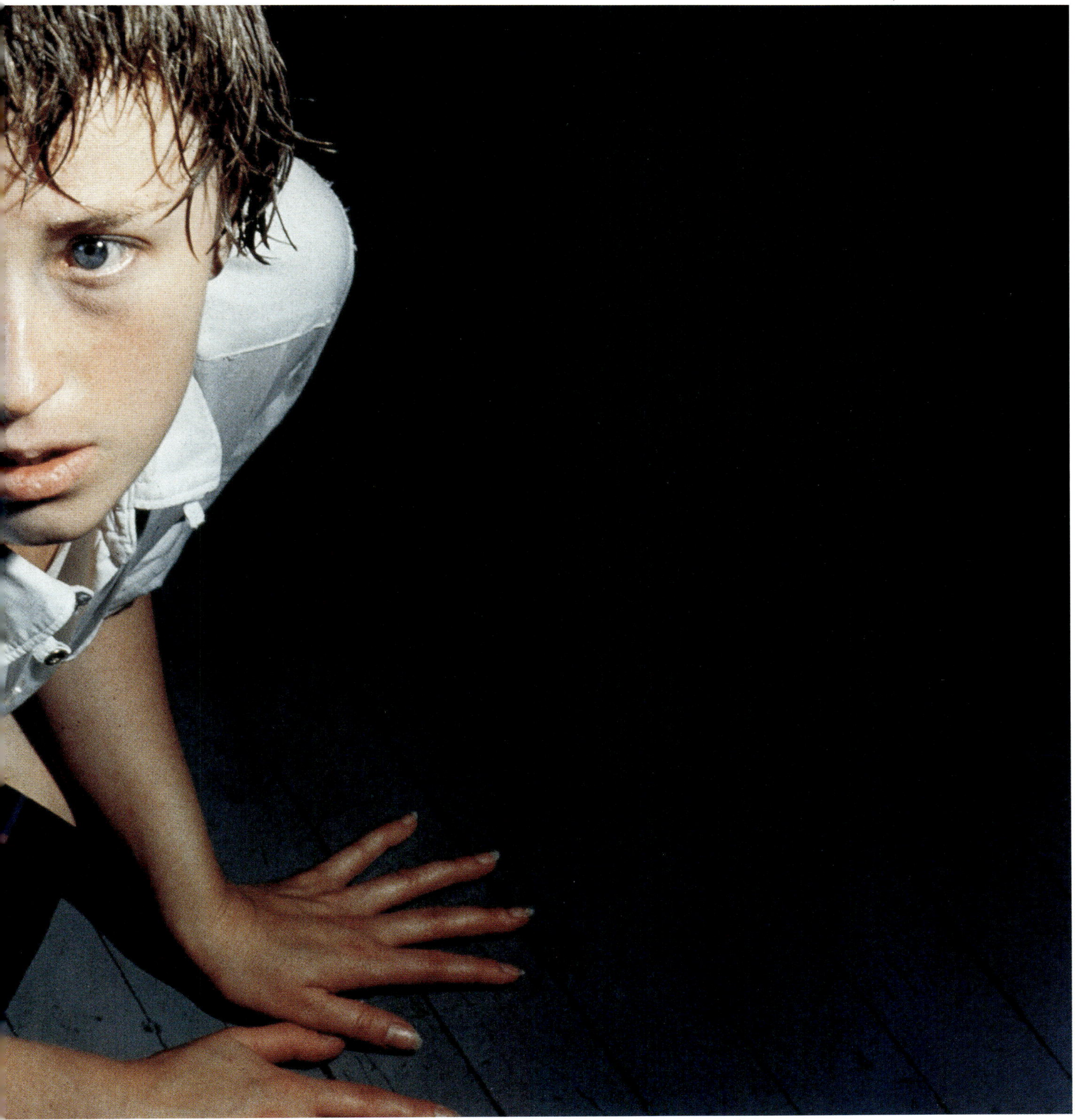



ter in the midst of some unrevealed and ambiguous narrative. This practice came to define Sherman's work and, throughout her career, she has continued to cast herself as characters ranging from historical figures and film stars to clowns and high-society socialites, incorporating changing technologies from her first analogue works to more recent digital and green screen processes (Respini 2012, 53).

*Untitled #92* [7.3] is from Cindy Sherman's "centerfolds" series (sometimes also referred to as "horizontals"), which was originally commissioned for *Artforum* but never published in the magazine due to worries that the images would be "misunderstood" (Phillips 2003, 5–7). In this series, first exhibited at Metro Pictures in November 1981, Sherman departed from the format of her *Untitled Film Stills* (1977–80) to work in color and on a much larger scale, with each photograph measuring 2 × 4 feet. The horizontal format is key to this work: it references the format of a magazine centerfold, which is usually occupied by suggestive imagery aimed at a male viewer, and its proportions also suggest the cinematic.

Sherman's centerfolds do represent female figures, but with their emotional states taking prominence. In *Untitled #92*, Sherman casts herself as a young woman in a white shirt and plaid skirt, crouching on the floor and looking fearful. The camera looks from above, downwards toward the girl on the floor. She looks beyond the frame and her angled, crouched body occupies most of the composition with her face central and only floorboards and dark corners visible beyond. While Sherman's earlier work had carefully constructed whole scenarios through their locations, props, and clothing, the centerfolds photographs are closely cropped into the character's expressions and bodies, resulting in "psychological studies" rather than the more "situational constructions" of her earlier work (Metro Pictures 1981, https://www.metropictures.com/exhibitions/cindy-sherman2/press-release).

Sherman's work has provoked much art historical and theoretical debate, and the centerfolds heightened this, particularly in relation to feminist discourse. The seminal essay "Visual Pleasure in Narrative Cinema" by Laura Mulvey (written in 1973 and published in 1975) was influential in these debates and on readings of Sherman's work—and although Sherman herself has noted that such feminist readings have not necessarily been her intention (specifically in relation to her *Untitled Film Stills*), she has not negated them (Respini 2012, 27–32). In her essay, Mulvey posited that cinema invariably embodies a "determining male gaze" that "projects its fantasy onto the female figure" and that women on screen function "on two levels: as erotic object for the characters within the screen story, and as erotic object for the spectator within the auditorium" (Mulvey 1975, 11). In Sherman's centerfolds, we can read this "male gaze" in the viewpoint of the images and the references to magazine pages, but Sherman has subverted the expectations of the viewer, by presenting images of vulnerability and emotion within the format.
*NIKKI KANE*


## BARBARA KRUGER
(Newark, New Jersey 1945)

[7.4]
***Untitled (We Will no Longer be Seen and Not Heard)***
**1985**
Edition: 10/50; lithograph, photolithograph, screenprint on paper
52.1 × 52.1 cm each of 9
Minneapolis, Walker Art Center
Walker Special Purchase Fund, 1985


Barbara Kruger's practice centers on combinations and juxtapositions of image and text, resulting in graphic works that implicate the viewer in the complexity and imbalance of our mass-media fueled world. Kruger began her career working in graphic design, art direction, and picture editing in magazines, working in the early 1970s for Condé Nast on publications including *Mademoiselle* and *Home and Garden*. Her early art pieces involved textile materials and painting before, following a break from producing art to teach and to read, she began working with the artistic methodologies and techniques that have now become characteristic of her practice: appropriating, cropping, repositioning, and enlarging imagery from a range of consumer sources, overlaying these with blocks of text in in bold, oblique Futura type. In the early 1980s, she gained visibility as an artist through participating in high profile exhibitions such as the Whitney Biennial (1983), documenta 7, and the 1982 Venice Biennale, and also began to exhibit and sell work through commercial art galleries. As well as producing artworks, Kruger is also involved in a broad range of activity that includes teaching, writing, and curating (Goldstein 1999, 32–34).

Her background in graphic design has shaped her artistic practice, in which she makes use of a fluency in combining and shifting words and images to produce works that are recognizable and that play on our familiarity and comfort with media messaging. In her own words, she states that "I think I've tried to appropriate the means and instrumentality of design practices on a formal level, but to alter the concerns of the enterprise, to some degree" (from an interview with Lynne Tillman: Tillman 1999, 190).

This untitled work [7.4] from 1985 encapsulates many of the key aspects of Kruger's practice, with its close-cropped images of faces and hands, and collage-like placements of text on top, which, read together, direct a message to the reader: "We will no longer be seen and not heard."

"We" appears frequently in Kruger's works, along with "you" and "I"—pronouns that are not fixed or specifically tied to individuals, but that produce what Kruger calls "direct address." So who is the "we" in this case? This is really only part of the question (Indiana 1999, 10: "and people writing about this work have frequently gotten entangled and tripped all over themselves puzzling out who 'I' am and who 'we' are and who 'you' is, as if the work were 'embodied' in the artist and the spectator [. . .] but something almost opposite is at work in Kruger's activity, which resists the idea of the self-heroizing gesture, but more importantly repudiates the fixing of the subject in the conventional artist/spectator relation."); the way in which Kruger's methods of direct address operate extends and complicates her statements, by directly implicating the viewer and requiring them, through the process of reading, to take a position—to identify here with the "we" or outside of it. The sentence in this work recalls the old sayings that "women and girls should be seen and not heard," or that "children should be seen and not heard" and so it can be read as a call of resistance and a clear example of Kruger's feminist works. In works such as this one, or those more explicitly related to feminist debates and the female body, the "position of women [. . .] is the ideal subject-position that the artwork constructs" and so for it to make sense to men they must empathize and attempt to place themselves in the experience of women (Alberro 2010, 198). Here, this might be extended from women, to all those who are without power or a voice.

Kruger's "concerns of the enterprise" in working in such a way are to challenge the power structures and stereotypes embedded within mass visual culture, through using its very own vernacular. In doing so, she has also developed her own recognizable style, which is adaptable to many media and forms of presentation—from transport cards and merchandise to discreet printed artworks, outdoor posters to whole gallery installations, and architectural designs to digital text and film installations. While her diversified output may

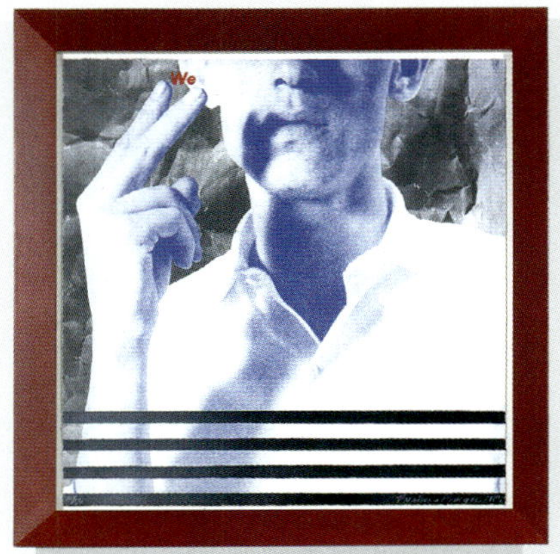


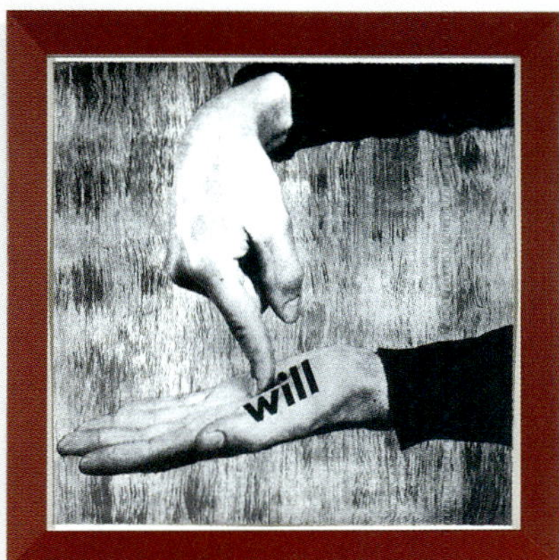


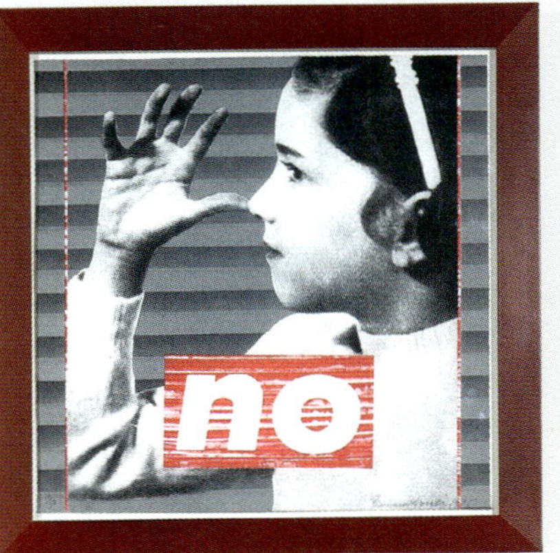


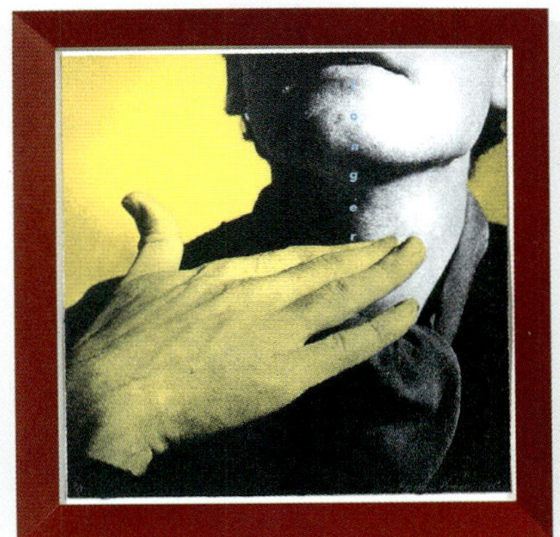

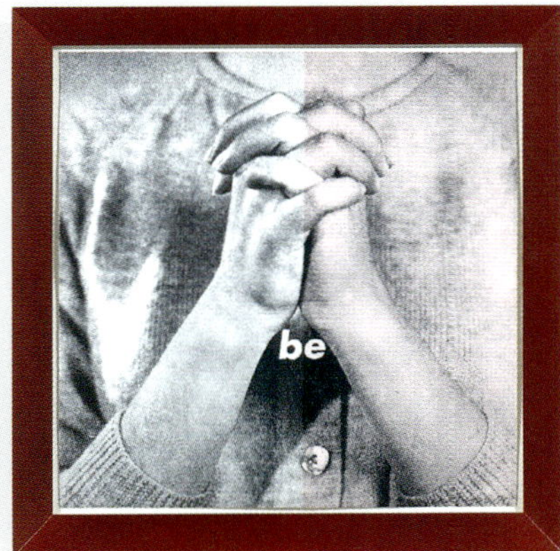


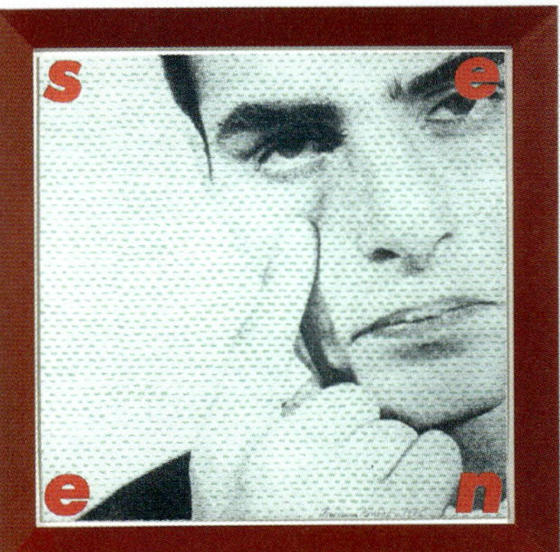


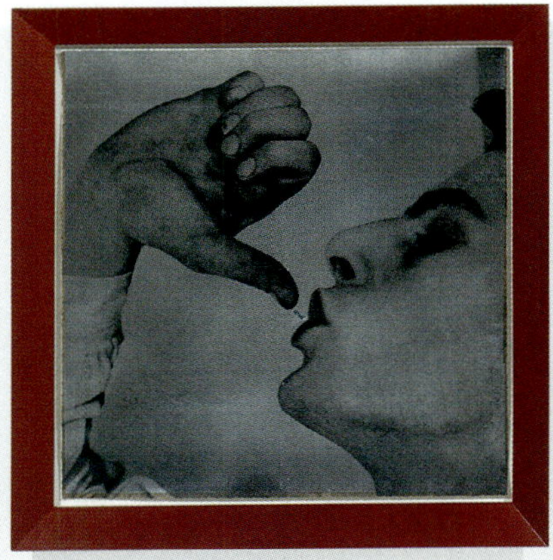

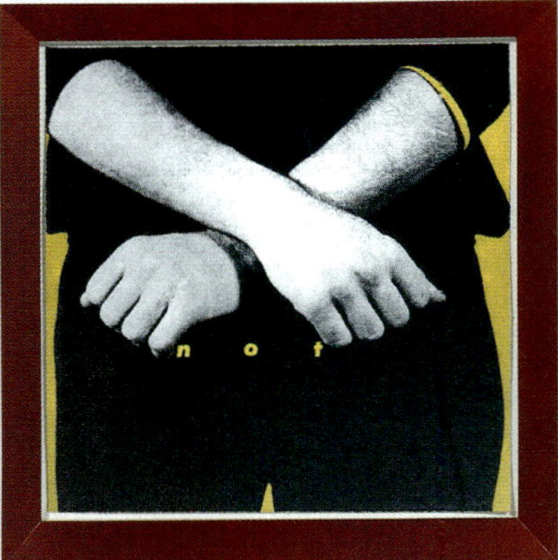


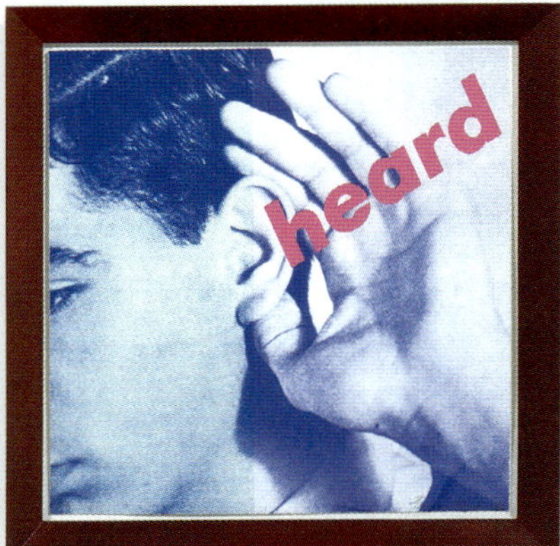


[7.4]

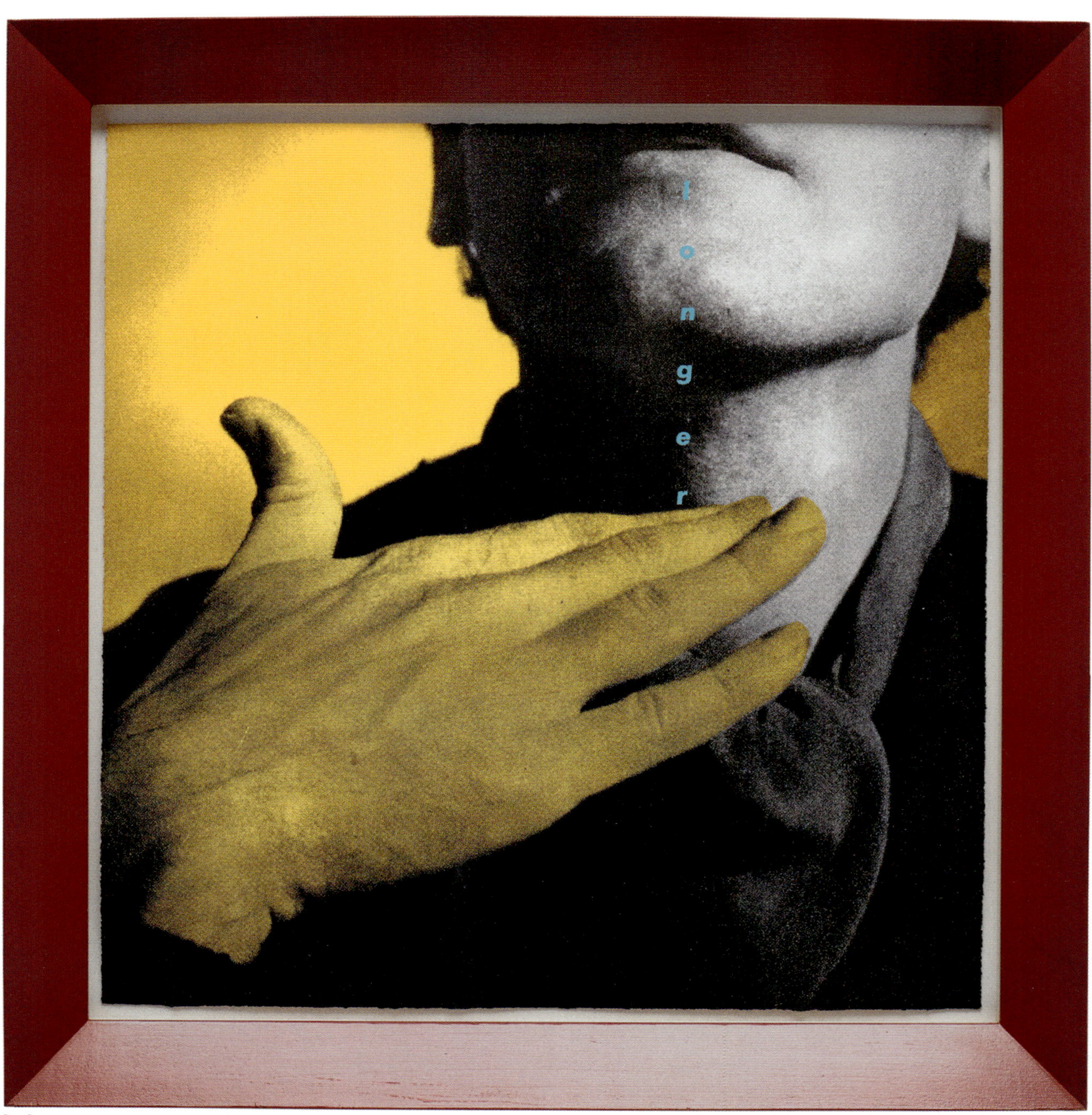




[7.4]

call to mind artists such as Andy Warhol and her use of found media imagery recalls the work of Richard Prince's "cowboy" series (Goldstein 1999, 34; Alberro 2010, 195), her concern with *how* (not simply what) we see—as informed by feminist ideas about vision and gaze in the 1970s–80s—relates her work to that of artists such as Cindy Sherman, Sherrie Levine, and Laurie Simmons, and to wider critiques of the art institution as a politically neutral site.

Spread across nine prints, the words in this work are inserted, at varying scales, into close-up images of hand gestures—suggesting, but not wholly representing, sign language. This combination of textual language with implied physical language here emphasizes the notion that written and visual communications in the media are intrinsically tied to our individual and bodily experiences in the world, something that is present throughout Kruger's work. The appropriated photographs found in Kruger's work are posed, originating from stock images, and in this piece that aspect is highlighted through in the instructive-like, exaggerated hand gestures. This piece incorporates more color than her typical palette of black, white, and red, yet these colors remain, with each image of the series framed in red, a technique used throughout her work. This framing and the primary color washes heighten the sense of artifice in the posed images while softening their appearance to the viewer. This speaks to Kruger's strategy throughout her work, as she says: "I work with pictures and words because they have the ability to determine who we are, what we want to be, and what we become [. . .] I'm interested in *coupling* the ingratiation of wishful thinking with the criticality of knowing better. To use the device to get people to look at the picture, and then to displace the conventional meaning that the image usually carries with perhaps a number of different readings" (from an interview with Jeanne Siegel: Siegel 1987, 19).
*NIKKI KANE*

**RICHARD PRINCE**
(Panama 1949)

[7.5]
***Untitled (Cowboy)***
**1980–83**
Edition: from an edition of 2; chromogenic print
61 × 50.8 cm
Minneapolis, Walker Art Center
Gift of Lewis S. Baskerville, 2016

[7.6]
***Untitled (Cowboy)***
**1992**
Edition: 1/2; Ektacolor photograph
50.8 × 61 cm
Minneapolis, Walker Art Center
Gift of Barbara Gladstone, 2001

[7.7]
***Cowboys and Girlfriends***
**1992**
Edition: A.P. from the edition A–Z; Ektacolor print
50.8 × 61 cm each of 6
61 × 50.8 cm each of 6
Minneapolis, Walker Art Center
T. B. Walker Acquisition Fund, 2000

In the mid- to late-1970s, Richard Prince was working as an artist in New York and came to be associated with the group of artists known as the Pictures Generation, which included Sherrie Levine, Cindy Sherman, Louise Lawler, and Robert Longo. He moved to the city in 1973 and worked in the tear-sheet department at *Time Life*, where he made cuttings from magazines for the staff. After cutting this content, Prince was left with the sleek advertisements, which sparked his breakthrough artworks. He began to rephotograph these images to produce works that isolated and heightened their constructed, contrived nature and reframes our relationship to such ubiquitous imagery. His work incorporated familiar, aspirational commercial

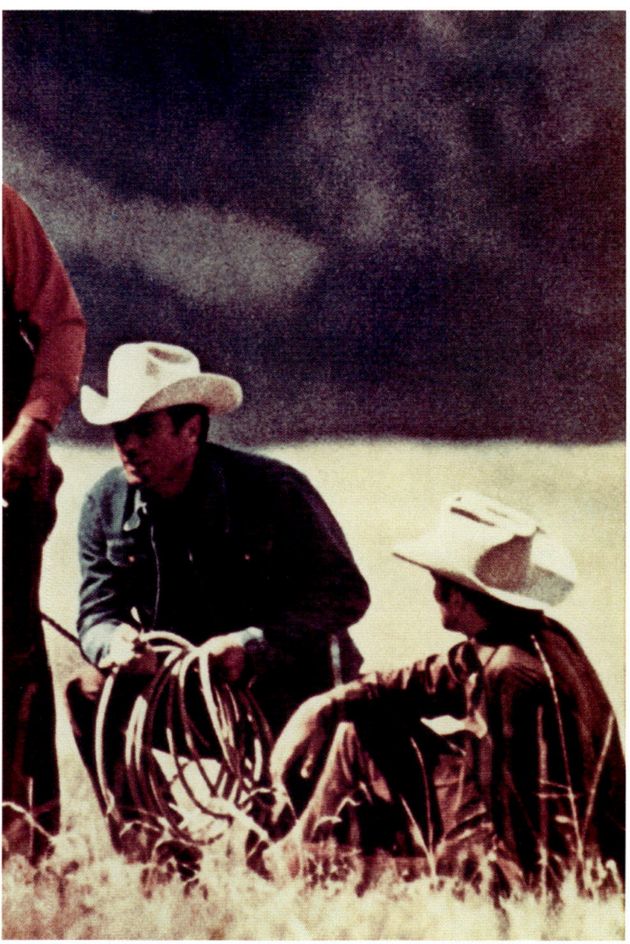

[7.5]

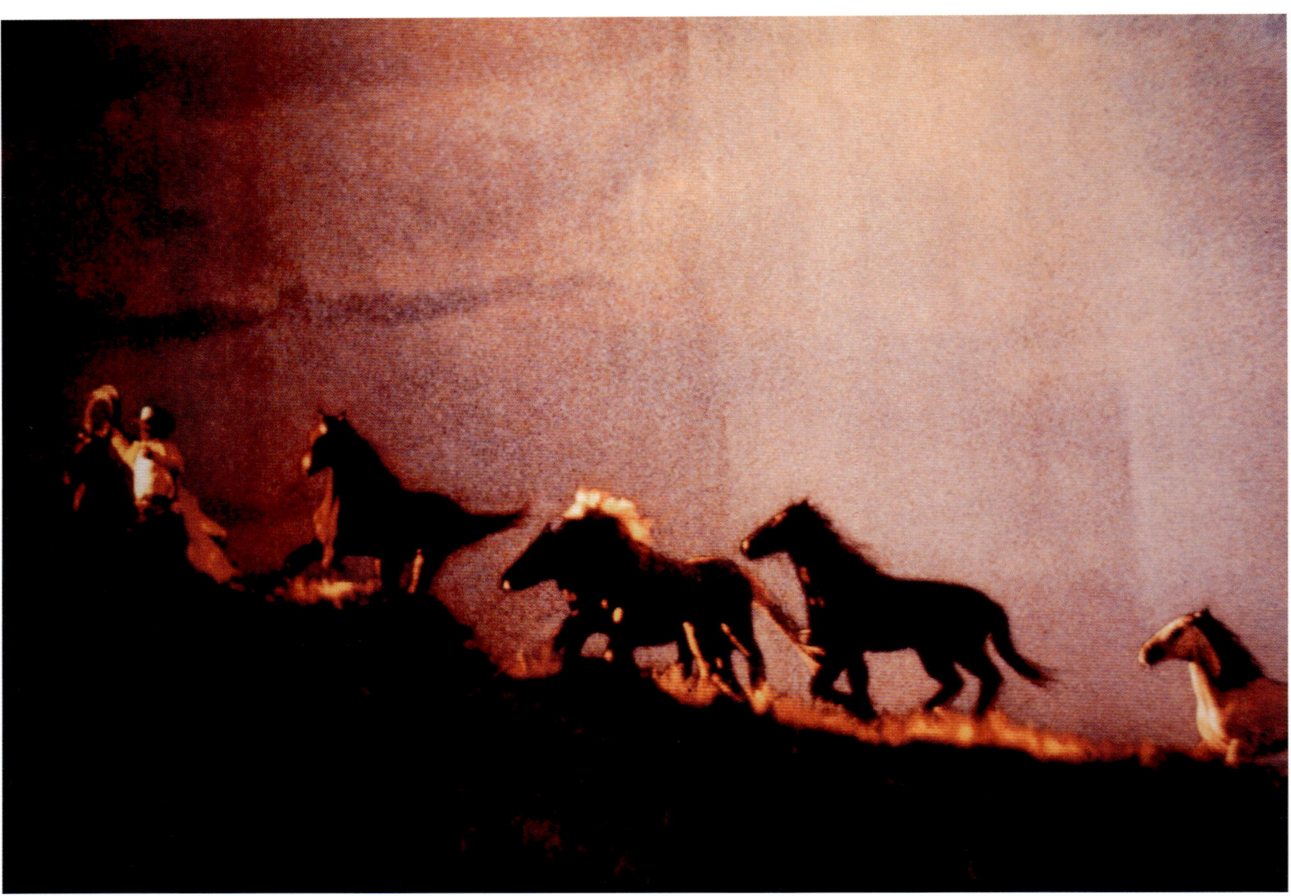

[7.6]

images of interiors, jewelry, cosmetics, and models. Prince's "deceptively casual gesture" technique of rephotographing "forever altered the history of contemporary art" by positing that someone else's work could be appropriated in this way and presented as one's own, a development of the readymade that tested the limits of copyright and legality (Spector 2007, 23–28).

Richard Prince has made use of his technique of rephotographing to work with a range of subject matter, but is perhaps most known for his images of cowboys. In his *Cowboy* series [7.5, 7.6], Prince rephotographed advertisements for Marlboro cigarettes, removing the text and blowing up the images. In doing so, Prince highlights the company's use of the figure of the cowboy as a representation of ideal American independence, freedom, and health (despite the effects of the product itself). The cowboy is the archetypal symbol of American masculinity, and in Prince's photographs he is clad in denim and a Stetson hat, lassoing and riding his horse. In *Cowboys and Girlfriends* (1992) [7.7], Prince combines this imagery with that from his *Girlfriends* series, in which he rephotographed and enlarged images from biker magazines in which motorcyclists' girlfriends are seen posing with and on the bikes, often scantily clad or with their breasts exposed. He presents these images without judgment, yet in bringing these figures together—and in including female figures alongside his cowboys—Prince amplifies our readings of masculinity in his work.

Curator and writer Nancy Spector notes that the "*Girlfriends* series is the female counterpart to the *Cowboys*, and the two are linked through their similar symbolic valences," whereby both figures of the cowboy and the biker speak to this notion of American freedom, escape, independence and autonomy. The magazine photographs of girlfriends, posing with the bike "photos serve as trophies for these dreams of self-sovereignty [. . .] a required prop in the biker's image of himself as independent, macho, relevant, and hip." In taking these photographs from the biker magazines and scaling them up, Prince reveals their awkwardness and vulnerability—in the snapshots' photo quality, in the poses and expressions of the models, and in the whole routine (Spector 2007, 41–42).

Prince's use of mass-media imagery has precedents in the work of, for example, Andy Warhol, Robert Rauschenberg, and Adrian Piper, yet his practice of rephotographing the photographs and making very little in the way of alterations places the primacy on the image itself. On his use of advertising, Prince has noted that "With advertising, the untruth was a fact," pointing to the space of projection and

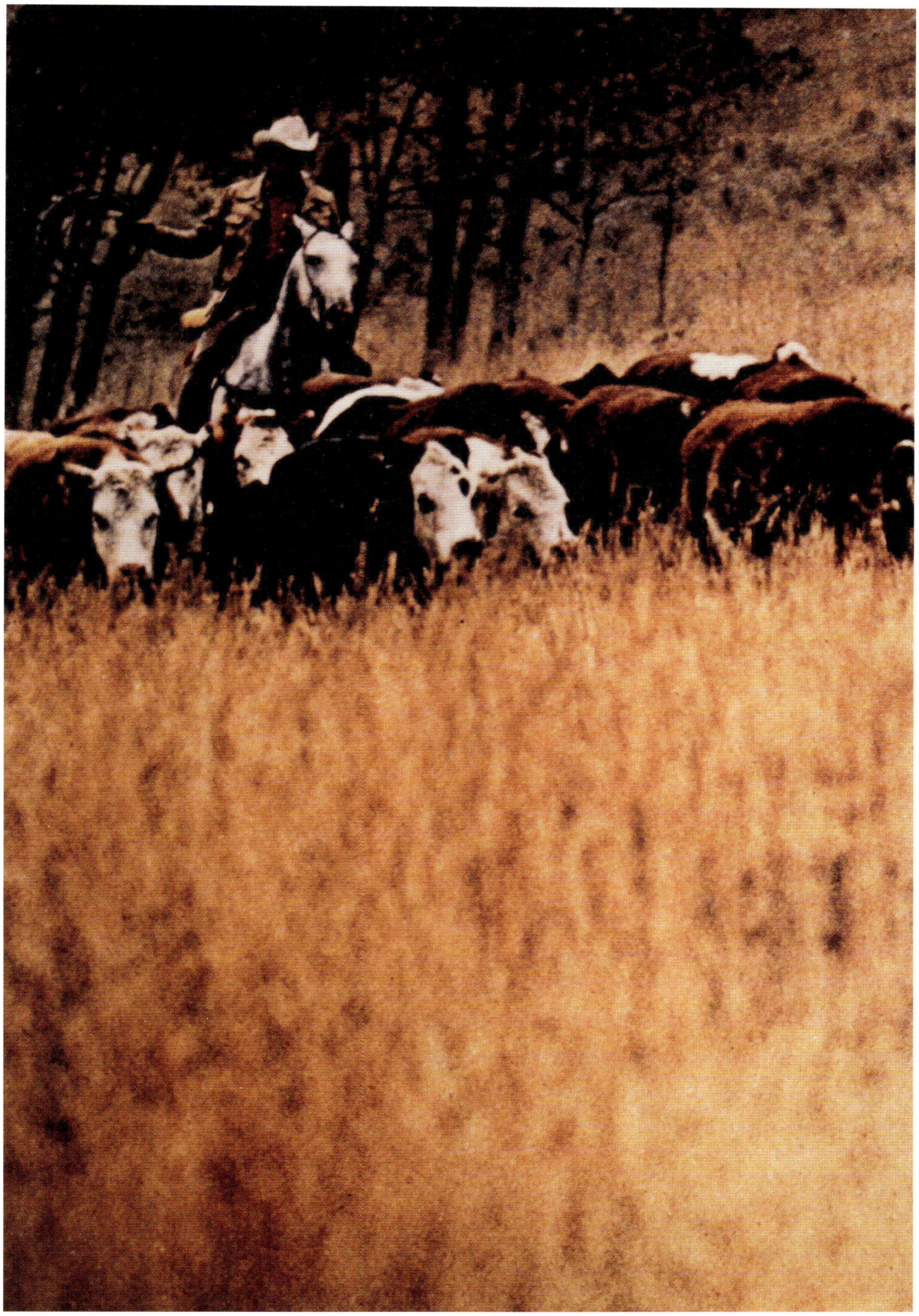

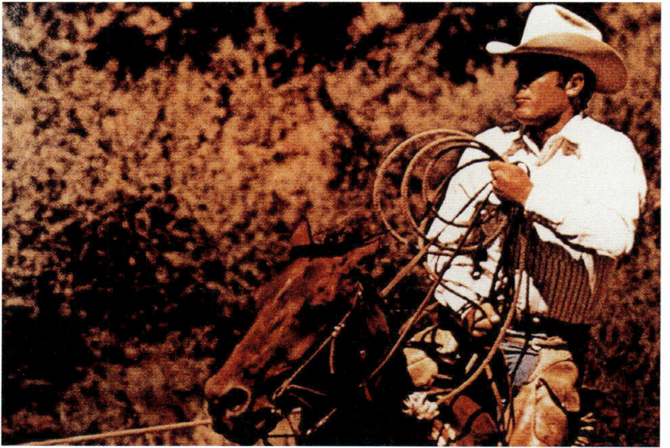

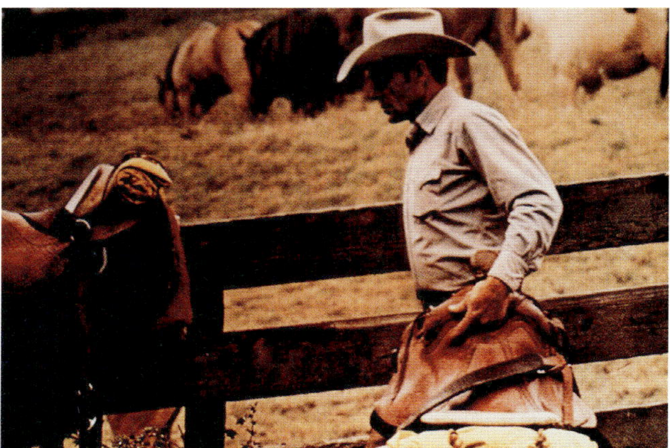



[7.7]

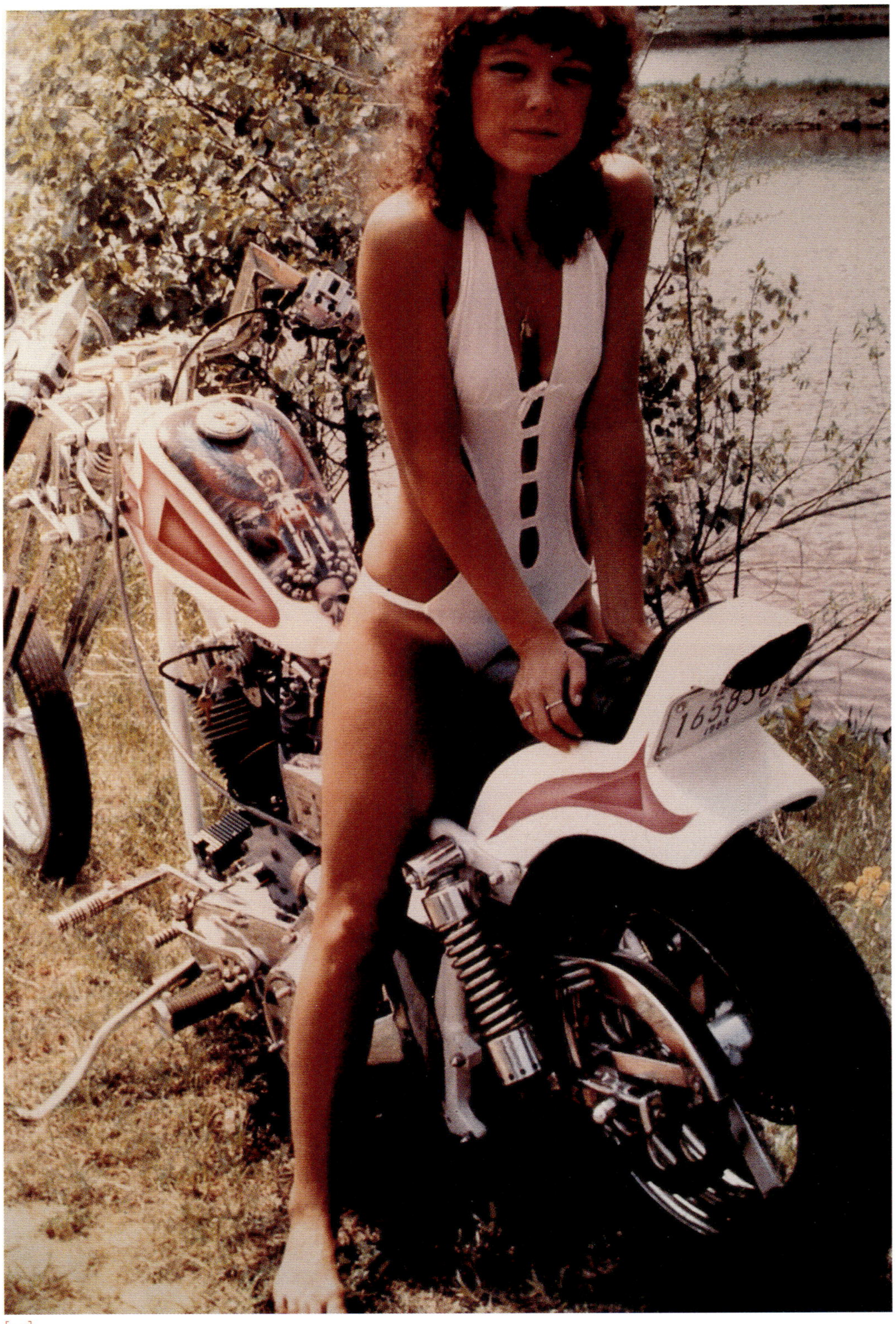

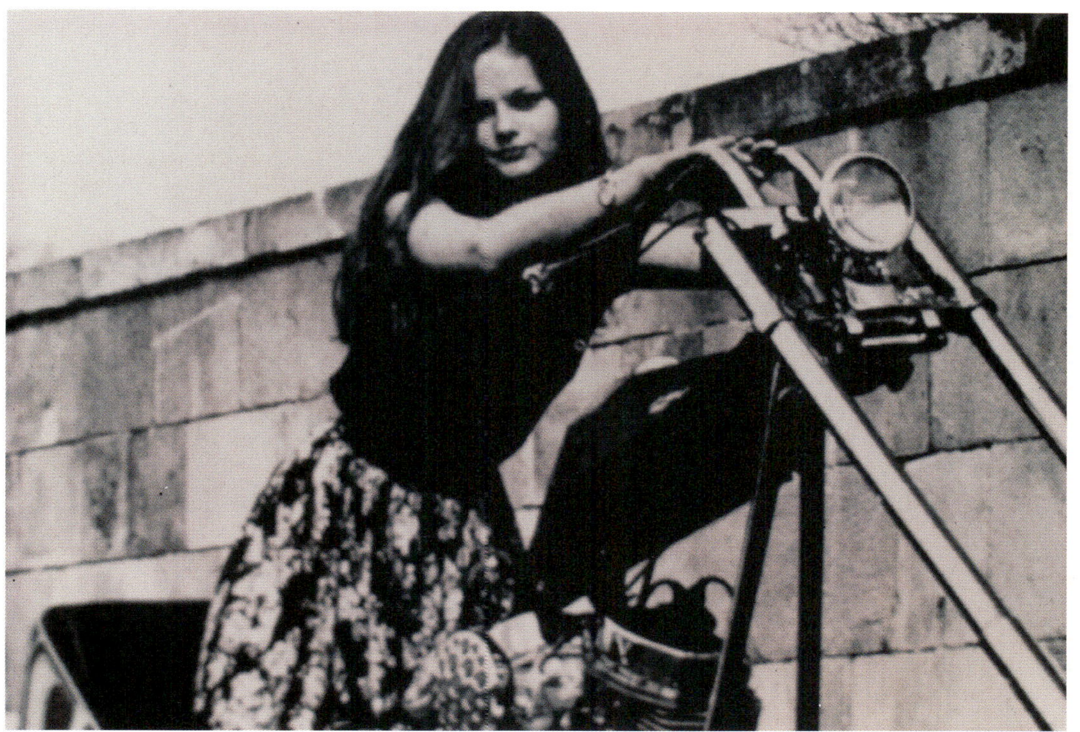

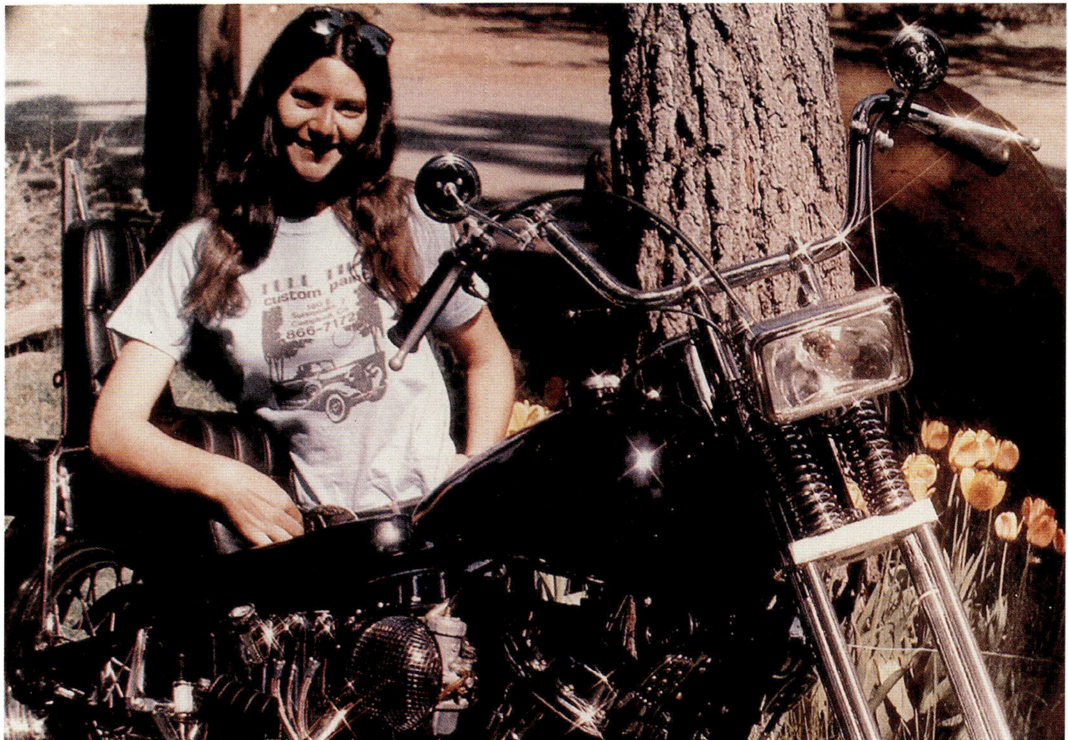



[7.7]

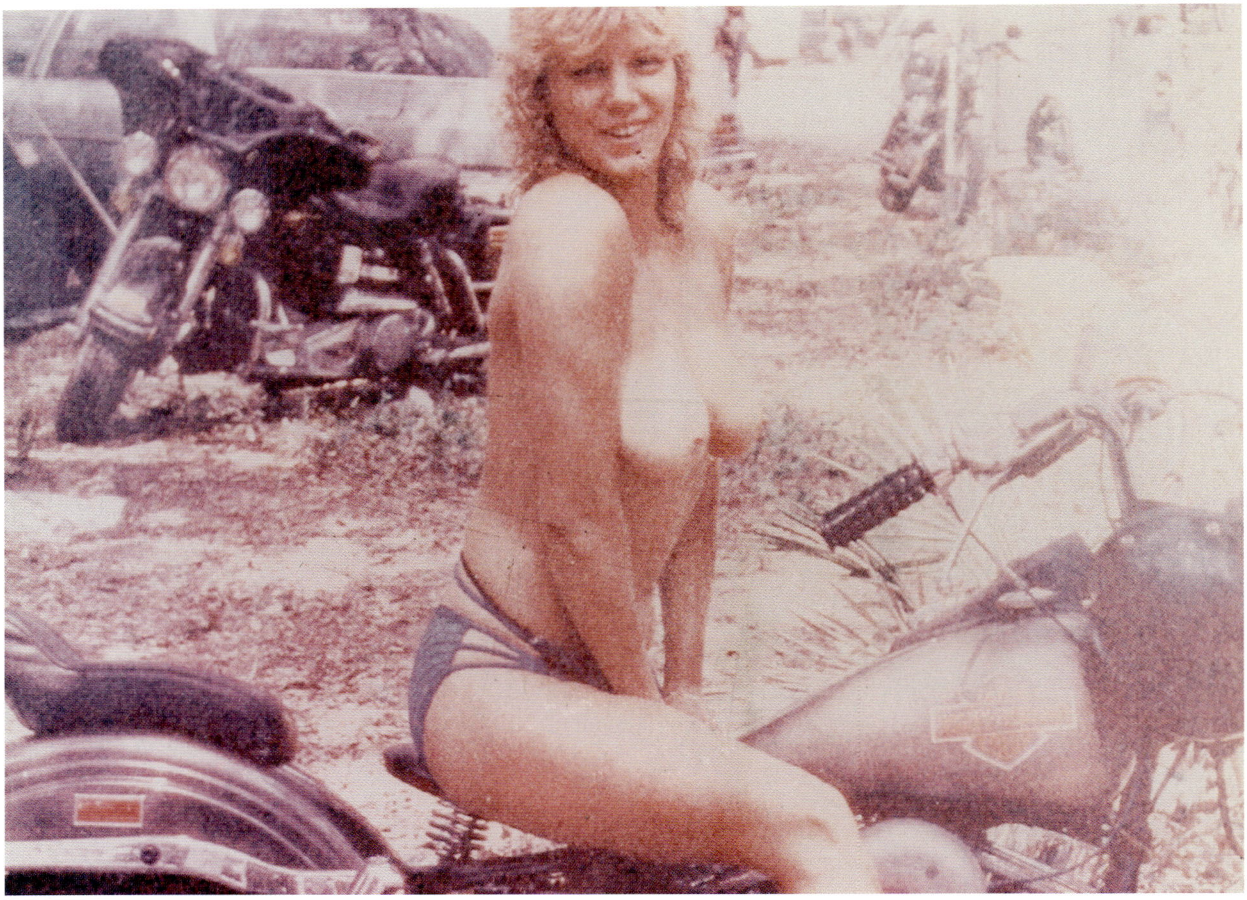

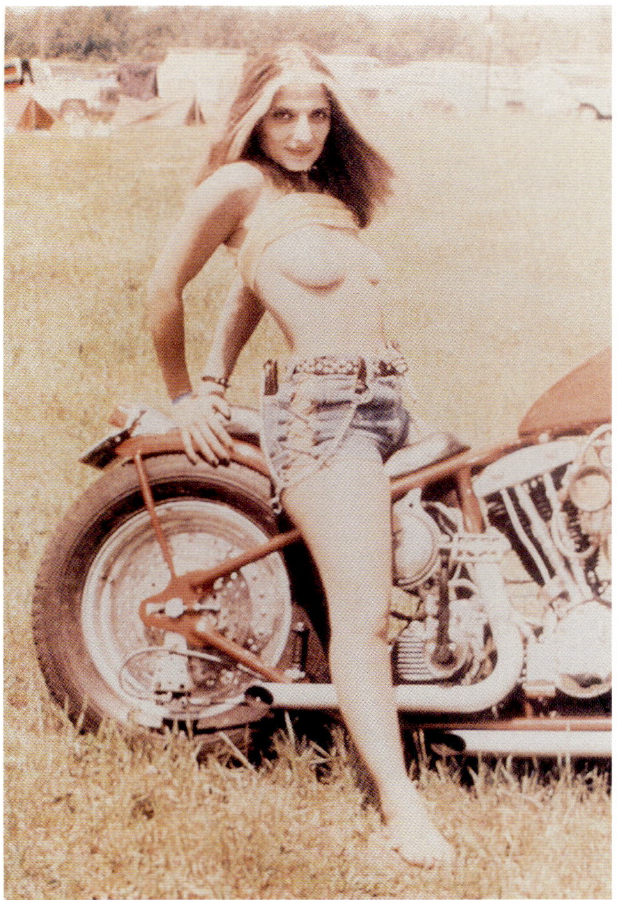

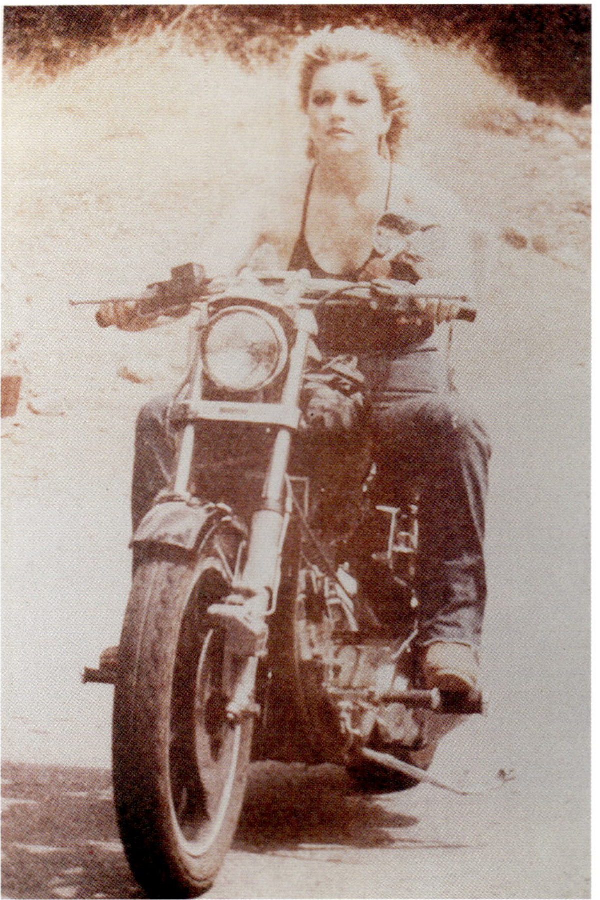

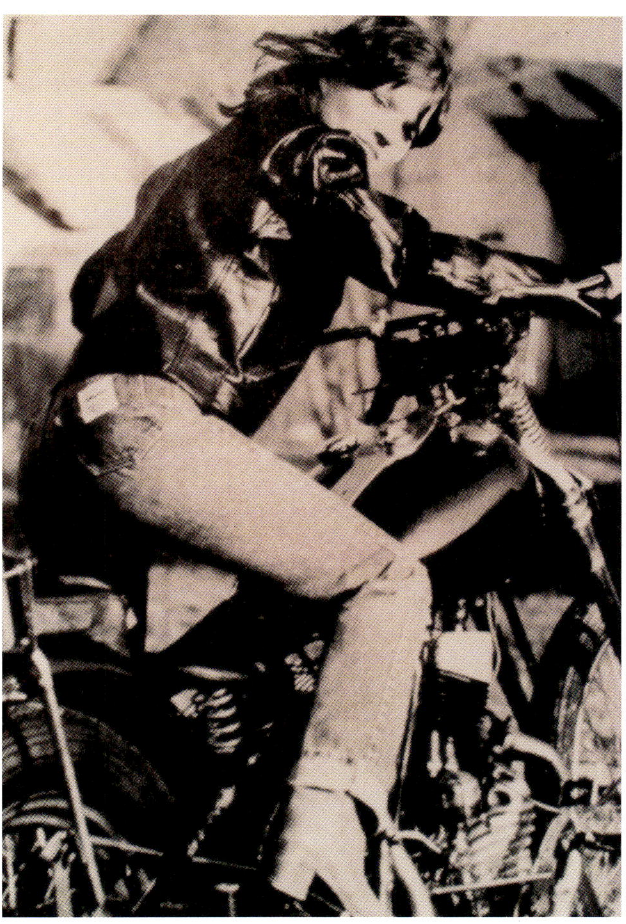

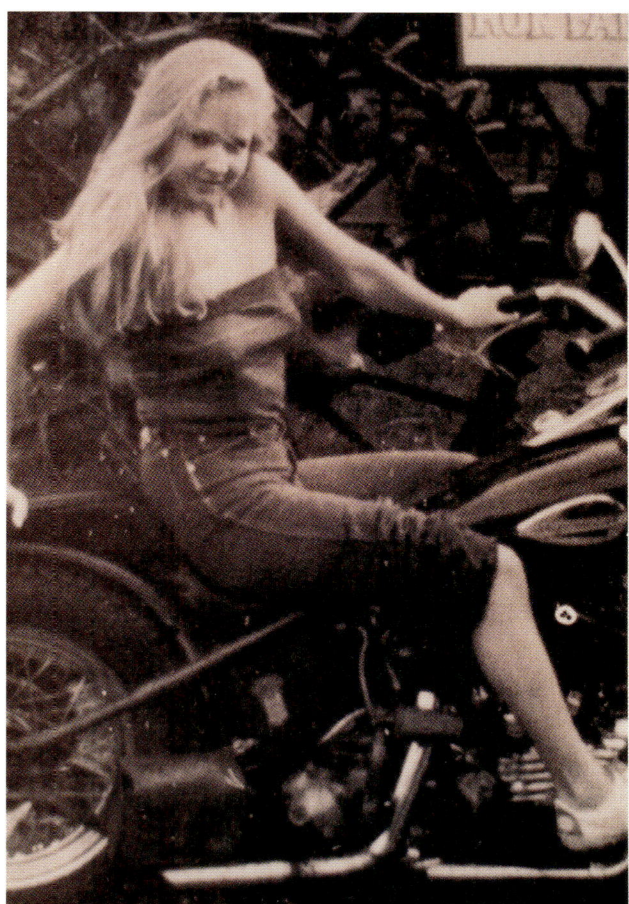

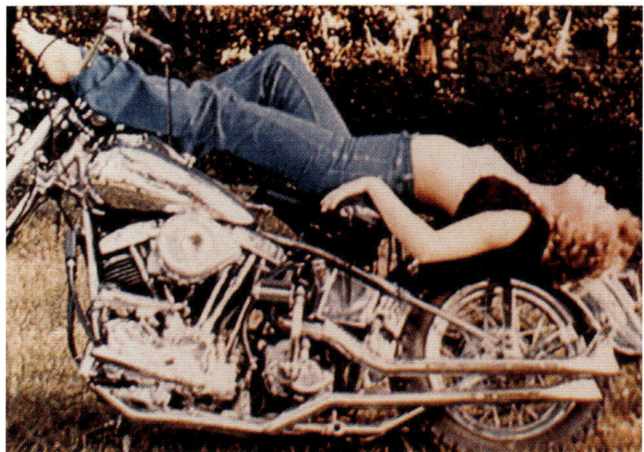

[7.7]

fantasy that his works highlight: "cowboys without Marlboros [. . .] Even though I'm aware of the classicism of the images, I seem to go after images that I don't quite believe. And, I try to re-present them even more unbelievably" (Heiferman 1988, 36).

Richard Prince's interest in icons of American rebellion, independence, and masculinity extends to muscle cars, and this work from 1989 is a key example of his series of modified and painted car hoods. Prince wanted to "paint something that gets painted in real life," and ordered the hood from a car magazine advert before making modifications. He squared off the shape and spray painted it using mostly primers, attempting to replicate the way these hoods are usually painted, especially by teenagers, and that gives the surface a sense of depth (Richard Prince 1997, Artist's statement in the Walker Art Center archives/files, Minneapolis).

This piece is presented hung on the wall, pointing to the context of painting, as well as to Prince's specific subject matter, being "at once paintings and anti-paintings that resonate between the poles of adolescent male fantasies of automotive speed and sexual power and the equally heroic delusions of modernist abstract painting" (Fogle 2005, 474).

*NIKKI KANE*

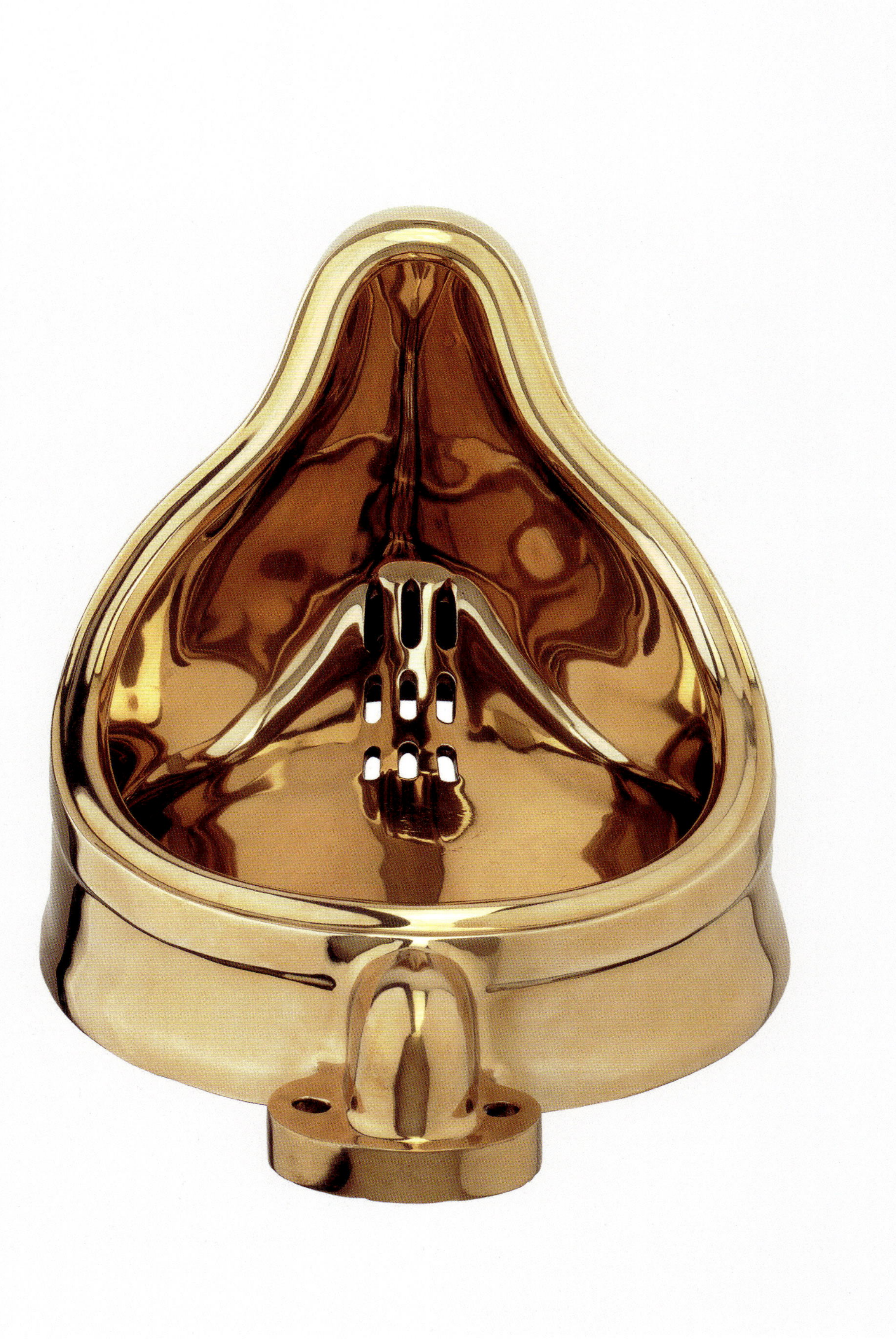



[7.8]

**SHERRIE LEVINE**
(Hazleton, Pennsylvania 1947)

[7.8]
***Fountain (after Marcel Duchamp: A.P.)***
**1991**
Edition: A.P. 1; edition of 6; bronze
36.8 × 36.2 × 63.5 cm
Minneapolis, Walker Art Center
T. B. Walker Acquisition Fund, 1992

Sherrie Levine moved to New York in 1975 and soon became a prominent figure in the art world there. She was one of five artists included in the now famous *Pictures* exhibition, organized by Douglas Crimp at Artists Space in 1977, whose title later expanded to describe a much larger group of artists, the *Pictures Generation*. Levine is closely associated with questions of authorship and both the production and reception of imagery. In 1981, she exhibited photographs of photographs by the influential American photographers Edward Weston (1886–1958) and Walker Evans (1903–75). This practice of re-producing the works of other artists has defined Levine's career, and extended across media to include painting and sculptural work as well as photography.

In 1917, Marcel Duchamp presented an upturned urinal as a work of art, calling into question the very definitions of sculpture and art. Sherrie Levine's 1991 *Fountain (after Marcel Duchamp: A.P.)* [7.8] continues to play with these questions: the ordinary readymade object that Duchamp inserted into the art institution is now itself recast—quite literally—as a precious art object, cast in bronze and polished to a high-shine finish. On this finish, Levine notes she "was interested in making references to Brancusi and Arp as well as to Duchamp" and on the work more broadly that she "liked it as an object because it's an object that has a function so closely identified with men, but the form is so feminine, so vessel-like" (Levine 1991, 19).

Levine's relationship with this historical artwork, and art history more broadly, then, is far more complex and layered than a straightforward of appropriation, or a simple one-liner. Her practice has been described as creation rather than an appropriation, emphasizing the meaning she produces through her material makings, whereby her "work operates in collusion with prior art," embracing it and bringing it into the fold of her provocations (Weinberg 2012, 8; Burton, Sussman 2012, 15).

In producing artworks that re-present other pieces, Levine confronts us with the tension between our wish to pin down and "own" images, and the absurdity—impossibility, even—in such claims (Burton 2012, 26). Indeed, in this confrontation, as we grapple with the implications of Levine's work, we might remember that, to an extent, "all art is based on other art"; she has just made it explicitly so (Weinberg 2012, 8). Critic Craig Owens pointed to this element of Levine's work in a 1983 essay in which he noted her work as demonstrating a "disrespect for paternal authority" and her practice being "less one of appropriation—a laying hold and grasping—and more one of expropriation," that is, of opening up and making freely available (Owens 1983, 73). While referring specifically to Levine photographs

of Weston's and Evans's photographs, this analysis can be extended to Levine's oeuvre more broadly, and specifically to *Fountain (after Marcel Duchamp: A.P.)*. After all, Duchamp is considered the "father" of twentieth-century avant-garde art, and specifically practices of appropriation and "readymades"; Levine's assumption of his seminal work along with that of fellow modern "master" Constantin Brancusi into her own work directly challenges the very notions of (patriarchal) lineage in art history.
*NIKKI KANE*

# BIOGRAPHIES

8.

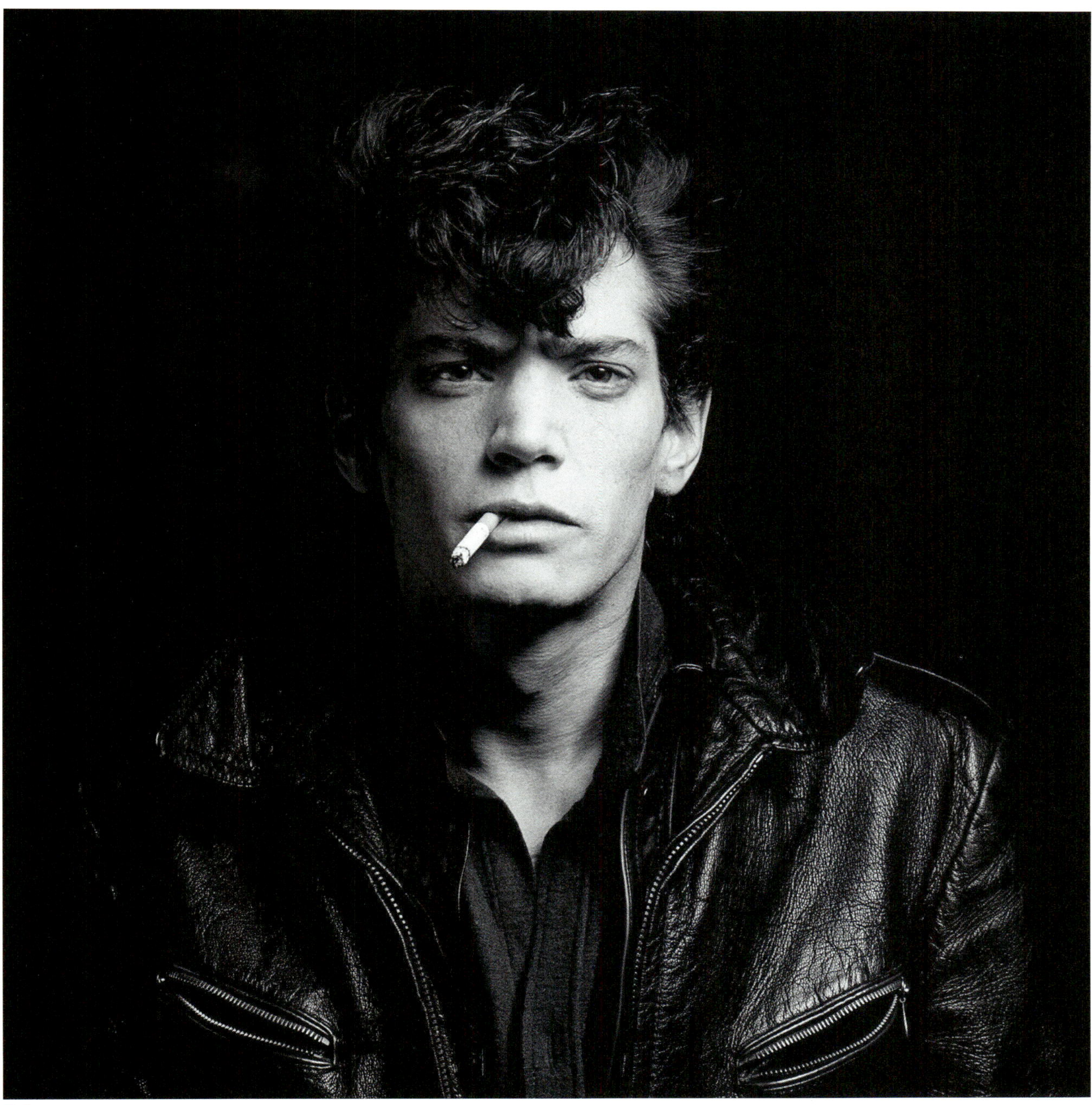



**ROBERT MAPPLETHORPE**
(New York 1946–Boston, Massachusetts 1989)

[8.1]
*Self-Portrait*
**1980**
Edition: XB from an edition of 15; gelatin silver print
50.8 × 40.6 cm
Minneapolis, Walker Art Center
Gift of the Robert Mapplethorpe Foundation, Inc., 2005

[8.2]
*Two Men Dancing*
**1984**
Edition: A.P. from an edition of 10; gelatin silver print
50.2 × 40.2 cm
Minneapolis, Walker Art Center
Gift of Richard Flood, 2006

Robert Mapplethorpe was a photographer known for his black-and-white photographs. In the 1960s, he attended the School for Applied Arts at the Pratt Institute in Brooklyn, where he began a long private and artistic partnership with the singer Patti Smith.

Mapplethorpe acquired a Polaroid camera in 1970 from artist and filmmaker Sandy Daley. From 1971, encouraged by the curator of the Metropolitan Museum's graphic print and photography section John McKendry, he devoted himself to photography. Supported in his work by collector Sam Wagstaff, Mapplethorpe soon became the enfant terrible of the New York cultural scene. In the mid-1970s, he began photographing his circle of friends and acquaintances—artists, musicians, socialites, and film stars. He also worked on commercial projects, creating album cover art, including covers for Patti Smith and Television, and a series of portraits and party pictures for *Interview* magazine. In the late 1970s, Mapplethorpe grew increasingly interested in documenting the New York S/M scene. The resulting photographs are shocking for their content and remarkable for their technical and formal mastery.

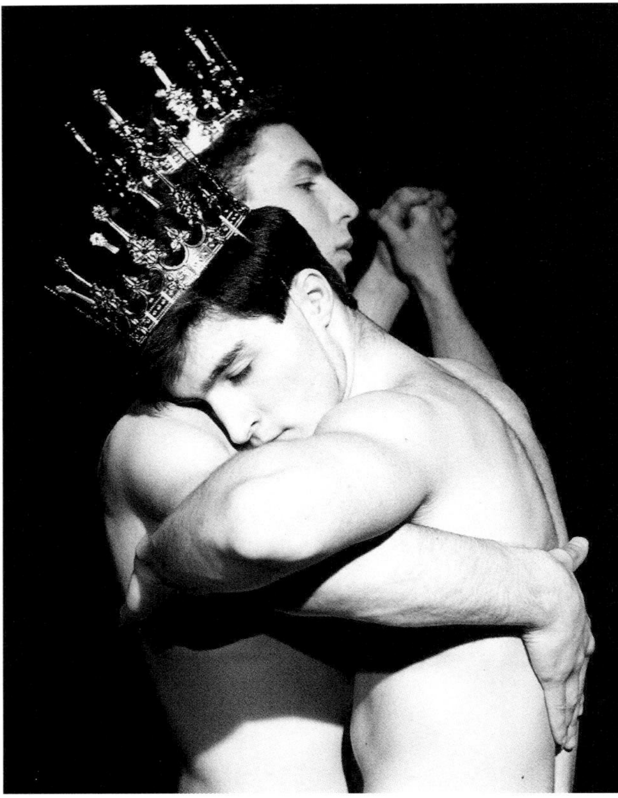



In 1980, Mapplethorpe began his collaboration with Lisa Lyon, world bodybuilding champion and inspiring muse of a series of shots that are configured as portraits—or, rather, figure studies—and seem to respect, and at the same time challenge, classic aesthetic canons. During the 1980s, he experimented with different formats and techniques (photoengraving as well as photos on platinum and linen).

In 1986, he designed sets for Lucinda Childs's dance performance, *Portraits in Reflection*, created a photogravure series for Arthur Rimbaud's *A Season in Hell*, and was commissioned by curator Richard Marshall to take portraits of New York artists for the book *50 New York Artists*. That same year he was diagnosed with AIDS. Despite the illness, he continued with his creations, widened the field of his photographic investigation, and established his Foundation with the mandate to promote and support photography at the institutional level as well as provide funding for AIDS/HIV medical research. In 1988, a year before his death, the Whitney Museum of American Art organized his first retrospective.

In *Self-Portrait* [8.1] Mapplethorpe portrays himself as the archetypal bad boy, with black leather jacket, dark shirt, cigarette hanging out of the corner of his mouth, a coolly appraising gaze, and a carefully coiffed 1950s hairstyle. Mapplethorpe was keen to promote this image of himself as cool and impervious to emotion. The composition helps to underscore this. The pose is wholly frontal and composed so that his mouth lies at the very center of the photograph.

The image *Two Men Dancing* [8.2] was part of a larger commercial commission that Mapplethorpe executed for a Dutch dance company. While the title of the photograph, *Two Men Dancing*, is self-explanatory, one may find meaning beyond the iconography. The crowns might remind one of a gay couple dancing like prom kings, upending the stereotypes of school proms as reinforcing traditional gender and sexual identifications.

*VINCENZO DE BELLIS*

**JENNY HOLZER**
(Gallipolis, Ohio 1950)

> [8.3]
> ***LAMENTS***
> **1989**
> carbon, graphite on paper
> 213.4 × 81.6 cm
> Minneapolis, Walker Art Center
> T. B. Walker Acquisition Fund, 1995

Jenny Holzer is a visual artist and writer who uses language to explore ways that words can manipulate and influence us. Her short texts, most of which she writes herself, range from inflammatory to introspective essays. While she considers her work political and is deeply engaged with such issues as feminism, poverty, nuclear proliferation, and AIDS, Holzer's texts express a range of viewpoints—or none at all. Always concerned with reaching a wide audience, she has placed her work in such public spaces as an electronic billboard in Times Square, the cable channel MTV, and the fronts of T-shirts and ball caps, but she has also worked in more traditional media, such as drawing, photography, and printmaking.

A native of Gallipolis, Ohio, Holzer originally hoped to be a painter. She studied at Ohio University in Athens, Ohio, and earned an MFA from the Rhode Island School of Design. After moving to New York City in 1977, she began using language as her medium and produced her first major series, *Truisms*—short, often provocative sentences that she printed on handbills and posted anonymously on buildings and walls around Manhattan.

In subsequent series, Holzer explores other methods of presentation. *Survival Series* (1983–85), which warned about the dangers of everyday living, were blazoned on enormous electronic signboards in public spaces, while *Living* (1981) was a group of short instructional texts first presented on bronze plaques to give them an institutional, authoritative look. In 1989, Holzer had twenty-eight texts from *Living* engraved on white granite benches for the Minneapolis Sculpture Garden, where they provide seating along one of the park's pathways.

The birth of her first child in 1989 inspired Jenny Holzer's *LAMENTS* series, perhaps her most personal and angst-ridden series. *LAMENTS* [8.3] was developed by the artist as a full body of thirteen texts engraved into a continuous row of stone sarcophagi that recounted what Holzer identified as "voices of the dead." These lamentations expressed the thoughts of one infant, two children, and ten adults before death. Each of these laments brings a preparatory drawing, in which, along with the full sentence, the artist also annotates the kind of stone and look of the marble that she would envision for that specific sentence.

In 1990, Holzer became the first woman to represent the United States at the Venice Biennale. Her installation of flashing LED signboards was awarded the Leone d'Oro for best pavilion. Since the mid-1990s, she has created dozens of outdoor light projections on buildings in cities ranging from Singapore to San Diego. Concurrent-

THERE IS NO ONE'S
SKIN UNDER
MY FINGERNAILS.
THERE IS NO ONE
TO WATCH
MY HAIR GROW.
NO ONE LOOKS AT
ME WHEN I WALK.
PEOPLE WANT ME
TO PAY MONEY FOR
EACH THING I GET.
I HAVE EVERY KIND
OF THOUGHT AND THAT
IS NO EMBARRASSMENT.
I LOOK AT MYSELF
WHEN I BATHE.
WHAT I GIVE
TO ALL THE PEOPLE
WHO DO NOT WANT
TO LIVE WITH ME
IS ARITHMETIC.
I COUNT INFANTS AND
PREDICT THEIR DAYS.
I SUBTRACT PEOPLE
KILLED FOR ONE
REASON OR ANOTHER.
I GUESS THE NEW
REASONS AND PROJECT
THEIR EFFICACY.
I DECORATE MY
NUMBERS AND
CIRCULATE THEM.

[8.3]

ly, the artist returned to painting with silkscreened canvases based on declassified, redacted government documents concerning the US wars in Iraq and Afghanistan. Holzer's deeply felt and formally inventive work has established her as one of the leading artists of her generation.
*VINCENZO DE BELLIS*

**ROBERT GOBER**
(Wallingford, Connecticut 1954)

[8.4]
***Newspaper***
**1992**
Edition: 2/10; photolithograph on paper, twine
10.8 × 40 × 35.6 cm
Minneapolis, Walker Art Center
T. B. Walker Acquisition Fund, 1994

Robert Gober's multilayered practice incorporates sculpture, drawing, photography, painting, and installation. Characterized by deliberate and painstaking making processes, Gober's work makes use of juxtapositions and handmade reproductions of familiar forms, rendering them strange. His work has often been discussed in relation to Surrealism due to its playful, dream-like qualities, and he has noted that a childlike perspective has informed a lot of his work (Robert Gober interviewed by Craig Gholson: Gholson 1989). As curator and critic, Johanna Burton has pointed out in Gober's work that "what we see is one object in the act of representing another object," where much of the fascination and experience of the work "lies somewhere in between" (Burton 2015, 12).
For Gober, humor is an important element in his work, describing it as "a way to let people enter into the piece, where you can give them more complicated and fraught material. It's a disarming device, but it's also a pleasure that comes with the piece" (Gholson 1989). As he notes, this humor is one element in his work that in fact often references complex questions of society and identity. Gober has also been involved in activism and his work has addressed social and political issues including the AIDS epidemic, religion, sexuality, and racism.
*Newspaper* (1992) [8.4] is one of several editions of works that Gober made in the form of newspapers, some, like this piece, stacked and tied with string, and others as individual sheets presented on gallery walls. While they have the initial appearance of standard newspapers, Gober has in fact produced pages through photolithography techniques to resemble newsprints. His pages include articles and images, some of which are real stories from real newspapers, and others that have been fabricated or altered for his works.
In this edition, along with two short news stories, there is a large photographic "advertisement" for bridal wear that occupies most of the visible page. However, on closer inspection, the advert appears somehow off— the "model" is somewhat un-model-like, and is, in fact, the artist himself in a wedding dress and wig. In pre-

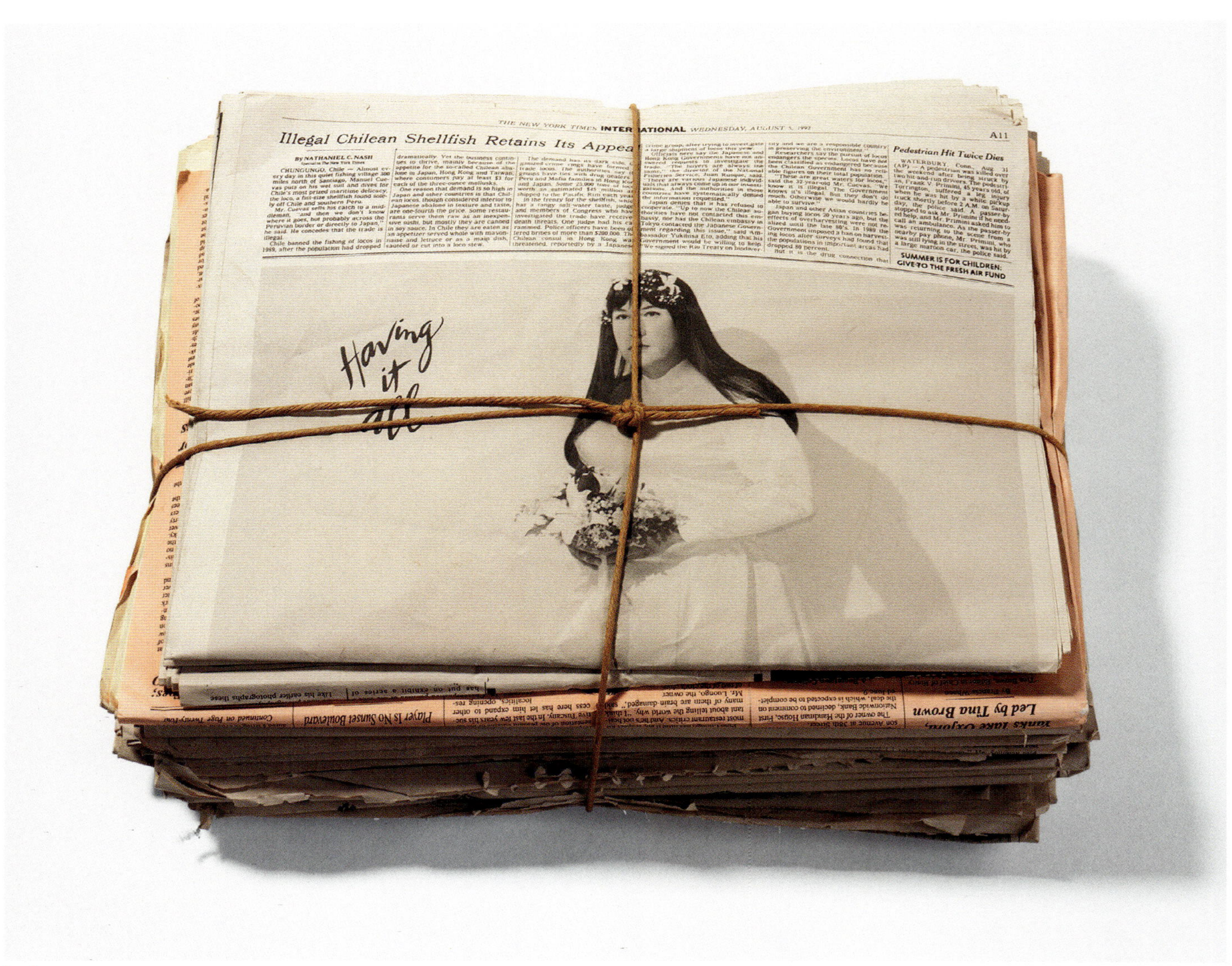



[8.4]

senting himself as a bride in the advertisement, Gober calls the "realities" presented in the media into question, while also raising questions about our expectations of gender and issues of marriage equality. Gober had invoked the imagery of the bride in an earlier sculptural piece too as part of an installation at Paula Cooper Gallery in New York in 1989, where an empty wedding dress on a metal support occupied the center of the gallery, surrounded by walls papered with a repeating pattern of a lynched black man and a sleeping white man, and handmade "bags" of cat litter set around the perimeter.

*NIKKI KANE*

**FELIX GONZALEZ-TORRES**
(Guáimaro, Cuba 1957–Miami 1996)

[8.5]
***"Untitled" (Last Light)***
**1993**
Edition: 14/24
light bulbs, extension cord, plastic light sockets, dimmer switch
Minneapolis, Walker Art Center
Gift of Gilbert and Lila Silverman, Detroit, Michigan, 2003
Published by A.R.T. Press, Los Angeles and Andrea Rosen Gallery, New York

Felix Gonzalez-Torres was born in Cuba and immigrated to the United States via Puerto Rico in 1979. He studied poetry and photography, which he employed in his art with utmost economy and subtlety to speak equally to the personal and the political with remarkable elegance and eloquence. Widely read in contemporary theoretical literature, the artist was also fiercely committed to political causes of the time—the heady years of the late 1980s and early 1990s when the so-called culture wars raged on. At the same time, he worked as a member of the activist artist collective Group Material and continued his utterly singular practice, which was anything but doctrinaire. Instead, during a lamentably short career, he turned art into a vanishing act.

In two of his best-known series, Gonzalez-Torres exhibited stacks of paper sheets to be taken home and piles of candies to be melted on tongues, both replenished magically and "endlessly." While making clear references to the industrial, obdurate objects of Minimalism (the most obvious Minimalist precedents for Gonzalez-Torres's works are Donald Judd's stacks or cubes and Carl Andre's floor pieces; the corner pieces are art-historically reminiscent of Robert Morris's benchmark installation at his one-person show at the Green Gallery, New York, in 1964, in which Morris installed a group of gray polyhedrons, including a corner piece), his stack pieces are printed with monochromatic colors, textual snippets, reproduced newspaper clippings, or photographs of natural landscapes, often of the sky. Each sheet in the stack in the Walker Art Center's collection is printed with an image of the calm surface of water. He also placed individually wrapped candies, intended to be consumed by viewers, in piles in the corners of rooms or spread them evenly on the floor. Distributing information or oblique poetics, the series were, and are, an implicit critique of the art market, questioning the very notions of commodification and ownership. The candy piles, with their oral associations, effectively conflated fears of contagion (AIDS) and the transubstantiation of the Eucharist.

In 1992, Gonzalez-Torres started making light strands—simple extension cords on which low-wattage lightbulbs are evenly spaced—that may be installed variably according to given spaces and as the owners see fit (in 1991, Gonzalez-Torres made *"Untitled" (March 5th) #2*, which consists of two lightbulbs attached separately at the ends of two extension cords, but did not start using multiple bulbs until 1992; most of the light strands have twenty-four or forty-two lightbulbs per string, and the Walker's light strand has twenty-four—see *Felix Gonzalez-Torres* 1997, 14). He made most of them in the next two years. Although they do not involve gifts in the way the stack pieces and candy piles do, their fluidity, openness, and formal simplicity are hallmarks of his practice.

In the opening sequence of Alain Resnais's 1959 film *Hiroshima, mon amour*, the female protagonist utters these words: "You are good for me because you destroy me" (Gonzalez-Torres discusses the film, directed by Alain Resnais and based on a script by Marguerite Duras, in an interview with Tim Rollins—see *Felix Gonzalez-Torres* 1993). Gonzalez-Torres, living at the end of the twentieth century and facing a cruel epidemic and institutionalized hate, saw artmaking as a necessary rejoinder to love, that terrible double-edged blessing and curse. And as we take part in the artist's

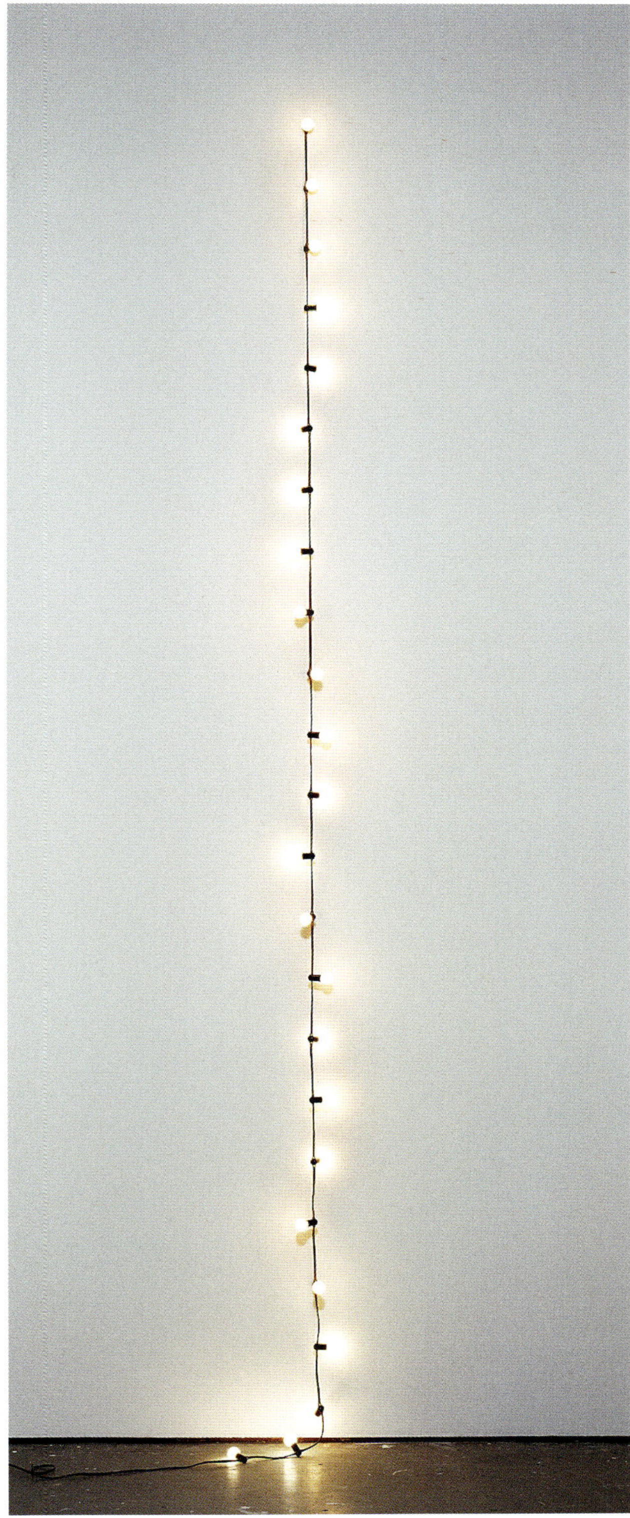

[8.5]

generous acts of giving or behold the gentle iridescent lights, we are reminded of how socially committed he was, how his art redefined beauty itself and, more than anything else, how his art speaks volumes about love.

DORYUN CHONG (revised version of text, published in *Bits and Pieces*, 2005, 241)

# MORE VOICES

9.

**JIMMIE DURHAM**
(Houston, Texas 1940)

[9.1]
***I WANT 2 BE MICE ELF***
**1985**
bone, wood, metal, mirror, paint, seashell
144.8 × 70.5 × 69.9 cm
Minneapolis, Private collection

Jimmie Durham is an artist, essayist, poet, and political activist. His artistic research focuses on the critical analysis and deconstruction of the founding concepts and symbols of Western thought and culture. Through different materials and artistic languages (installation, sculpture, video, writing), Durham overturns commonplaces and status symbols, opening up viewers to other and alternative perspectives, not always—indeed, almost never—matching those of dominant cultural thought.

In 1973, for example, the artist became an activist for American Indian Movement, an association in support of the rights of Native Americans. In this period he devoted himself almost exclusively to political activity, also becoming director of the International Indian Treaty Council and representative of the United Nations. After a decade of intense political activity, Durham moved to New York and got back in touch with the field of visual arts. He left the US again in 1987, moving to Cuernavaca, Mexico, then to Europe in 1994, where he has lived ever since. His nomadic existence became a crucial part of his work. The theme of the dynamism of the forms with which men respond to the most essential needs became central in his production together with the ongoing critical examination of the supposed unity of individual and cultural identity.

Among the recurring materials in Durham's sculpture, installations, and performative practice, we find stones and boulders, which often take on a symbolic value or perform a plastic action. In many of his works, the symbols of contemporaneity and well-being (furniture, refrigerators, cars, or planes) appear crushed under the weight of stones and boulders, which Durham described as references to architecture, a discipline that the artist critically interprets as a structure that deceives us to live in stability and which, in contrast with nature, instead creates an order that pushes men to an infinite repetitiveness of gestures and habits. In the early 1990s, the artist began to produce a series of sculptures by assembling heterogeneous materials and objects: salvaged elements of industrial origin, tools, and everyday consumer goods composed to form apparently arbitrary structures.

In *I WANT 2 BE MICE ELF* [9.1], Durham has incorporated several items typically associated with Native American art—an animal skull, a tree branch, and a seashell. But the resulting totem-like structure is hardly traditional. The side-mirror and reflectors are bits of modern refuse that situate the work firmly in the present. The placard nailed to the sculpture informs us that Durham rejects stereotypes about Native Americans; he will be himself. Despite addressing ideas relevant to his heritage, Durham refuses the category "Indian artist." He asserts, "I am Cherokee but my work is simply contemporary art, and for me it is vital that my work be seen as contemporary art without any qualifiers or labels" (http://artsmia.org/until-now/artworks/durham_miceelf.html).
*VINCENZO DE BELLIS*



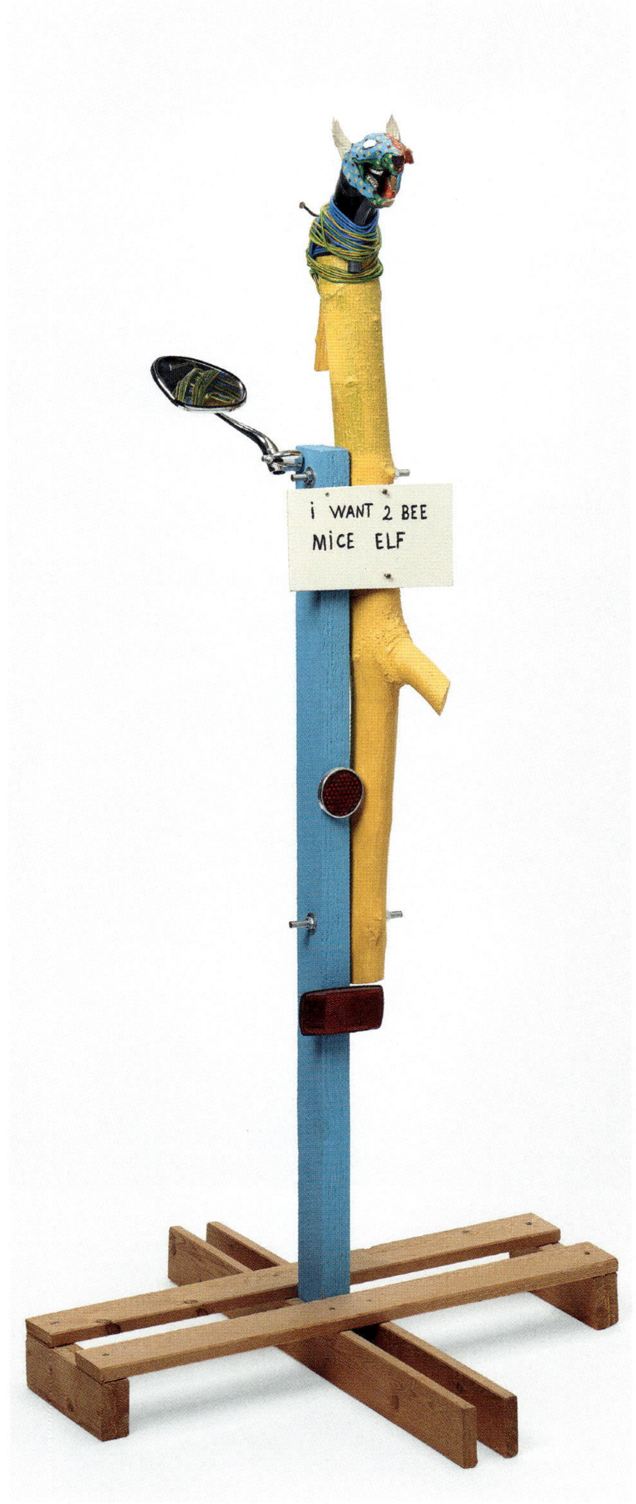


[9.1]

## HOCK E AYE VI/EDGAR HEAP OF BIRDS
(Wichita, Kansas 1954)

[9.2a]

***Building Minnesota: Ma-ka'ta I-na'-zin
(One Who Stands on the Earth)***
**1990**
enamel on aluminum
45.7 × 92.1 cm
Minneapolis, Walker Art Center

[9.2b]

***Building Minnesota: Ta-te' Hdi-da
(Wind Comes Home)***
**1990**
enamel on aluminum
45.7 × 92.1 cm
Minneapolis, Walker Art Center
All acquired in conjunction with the exhibition *Claim Your Color:
Hachivi Edgar Heap of Birds* (1990), 1993

[9.2c]

***Building Minnesota: Shakopee
(Little Six)***
**1990**
enamel on aluminum
45.7 × 92.1 cm
Minneapolis, Walker Art Center

For more than three decades, Hock E Aye Vi/Edgar Heap of Birds has worked as an artist, activist, and teacher. Based in Oklahoma City and on tribal land, where he has lived since 1981, Heap of Birds consistently creates works that confront repressed or unacknowledged histories of state and settler violence against Native communities in the United States. His work often draws parallels between historical violence and ongoing injustices today.

Across his drawings, prints, and spatial interventions—such as the steel parking signs that allude to the forced relocation of Native communities, including those in New York, to Oklahoma in the 1830s as part of the Trail of Tears—Heap of Birds harnesses the power of familiar forms and expressions for political ends.

His output is seamlessly linked to his life experiences: an ongoing series of abstract acrylic paintings, for example, is based on the natural canyon forms in his native Oklahoma, and his diaristic drawings use language to record memories, emotions, and encounters. His declarative public sculptures explore the history and culture of Native Americans, including that of the Cheyenne and Arapaho nations on whose tribal lands he has lived. The artist's extensive travels and many residencies have resulted in collaborative, community-based curatorial and educational projects that look at the human condition through the lens of regional politics, history, and geography.

In recent installations of monoprints and their corresponding "ghost prints," the artist culls poetic fragments from a wide range of sources, appropriating popular music, sayings taken from reservation so-cial gatherings, written accounts of historical events, and political speeches, among others. By transforming vernacular language into monumental works of art resembling grids of protest posters, Heap of Birds blurs the boundaries between aesthetics, pedagogy, and activism, creating a body of work that opens new critical perspectives on American histories and cultures.

In 1990, the Walker Art Center commissioned Heap of Birds to make a public piece in conjunction with its presentation of *Claim Your Color*, a traveling survey of his work. The artist's research led him to a signal event in state history: the US–Dakota Conflict, fought over a six-week period along the banks of the Minnesota River in the late summer of 1862. The chronicle of the conflict is an all too familiar one in American history: beginning with white settlements that encroached on native lands, it also features forced relocation, broken treaties, treachery, brutality, racism, and greed. It concluded with the largest mass execution in US history: thirty-eight Dakota men were hanged in late 1362, and two others in 1865 (the fighting, which claimed the lives of more than five hundred people on both sides, only ended when the Dakota were overpowered by an army of one thousand men led by Colonel Henry H. Sibley. A military tribunal condemned 3,030 Dakota men to death by hanging. All but forty had their sentences commuted by President Abraham Lincoln; of those, thirty-eight were executed on December 26, 1862, in Mankato, and two others, who were captured later, were hanged at Fort Snelling in November 1865).

Heap of Birds's *Building Minnesota* (1990) [9.3a-c], installed along a grassy stretch of parkland on the banks of the Mississippi River, was essentially a memorial to those executed after the conflict. It consisted of a sweeping arc of forty signs bearing the names of the executed men—given in both the original Dakota and an English translation—along with his date and place of death and a command to the viewer to "HONOR" (*Building Minnesota* was installed on West River Parkway in Minneapolis from March 10, 1990, through late summer 1991). The signs themselves are screenprinted aluminum panels bolted on green metal posts, a format that purposely mimics that of generic road signage and suggests that their messages are informational, cautionary, or both. *Building Minnesota* was placed near the site of one of the earliest white settlements in the state, where the rush of St. Anthony Falls was long ago redirected by a lock and dam and the riverbank bristles with power lines, grain elevators, and high-rises. The river itself is still a busy thoroughfare for barge traffic and an important source of power and water for the surrounding area. Heap of Birds's work thus links the events of 1862 with the commercial interests and economics that likely fueled them, as well as with a reverence for the land and its resources that is traditional in native cultures.

*JOAN ROTHFUSS* (revised version of text, published in *Bits and Pieces*, 2005, 263)

**HONOR**

# Ma-ka'ta I-na'-zin
## One Who Stands On The Earth

**DEATH
BY
HANGING**

DEC. 26, 1862, MANKATO, MN. - EXECUTION ORDER ISSUED BY
PRESIDENT OF THE UNITED STATES — **ABRAHAM LINCOLN**

© HACHIVI EDGAR HEAP OF BIRDS 1990

[9.2a]

**HONOR**

# Ta-te' Hdi-da
## Wind Comes Home

**DEATH
BY
HANGING**

DEC. 26, 1862, MANKATO, MN. - EXECUTION ORDER ISSUED BY
PRESIDENT OF THE UNITED STATES — **ABRAHAM LINCOLN**

© HACHIVI EDGAR HEAP OF BIRDS 1990

[9.2b]

**HONOR**

# Shakopee
## Little Six

**DEATH
BY
HANGING**

NOV. 11, 1865, FORT SNELLING, MN. - EXECUTION ORDER ISSUED BY
PRESIDENT OF THE UNITED STATES — **ANDREW JOHNSON**

© HACHIVI EDGAR HEAP OF BIRDS 1990

[9.2c]

## LORNA SIMPSON
(Brooklyn, New York 1960)

[9.3]
***Wigs (portfolio)***
**1994**
Edition: 2/15 plus 5 A.P.; waterless lithograph on felt
38 panels total, 21 with photos, 17 with text
182.9 × 411.5 cm
Minneapolis, Walker Art Center
T. B. Walker Acquisition Fund, 1995

Lorna Simpson trained in traditional photography techniques, but soon began to experiment with a conceptual approach, combining photographic images with text and then going on to incorporate installations, moving image, and collage into her practice. She became well known for her early work in the late 1980s and early 1990s that questioned notions of identity and representation. In these works, Simpson worked with strategies of portraiture, but played with the expectations of "showing and hiding" in the format (Gili 2002, 9–10). Much of this early work included the figure of a black woman, turned away from the camera or cut off somehow by the framing, to "play with the viewer's curiosity, with his/her desire to know who the figure in the picture was." In her later work she "decided to focus more on the absence of the figure," photographing architectural or interior settings (Lorna Simpson quoted in Fusco 1997, and in Novakov 1998, 172).

*Wigs (portfolio)* [9.3] dates from 1994, and is a key piece in Simpson's body of work that centers on images of black women's hair. This piece comprises twenty-one lithograph prints of photographs of wigs, on felt, accompanied by several small text panels, also printed onto felt. To produce the piece, Simpson visited shops in Fulton Mall in Brooklyn, where she is based, that sold a wide range of wigs and purchased a selection of these—those photographed include braided, curled, and waved hairstyles, as well as two wigs for dolls, and a merkin (https://www.moma.org/learn/moma_learning/lorna-simpson-wigs-1994). The wigs are all presented approximately to scale, provoking a physical connection with the viewer, a sense that these wigs could be placed on their heads (ibid.).

*Wigs* acts as a sort of transitional piece in Simpson's practice, marking the point where she began to remove the presence of the figure in her work. It was also her first work on felt, a key development in her work that built on the strategies of fragmentation already present in her early photographs and extended the materiality of these concerns. Many of her previous works presented close views of a figure, or of part of their body, often in series or split across frames. This approach has been read as representing an act of "defiance" or self-preservation of identity on the part of the photographed figure; or, as an artistic "gesture of refusal" on Simpson's part that works to expose and reject "prejudices inscribed within viewer's expectations" (Belisle 2011, 158–159).

In printing these images onto felt, Simpson continues her experimental and conceptual approach to the presentation of photo-

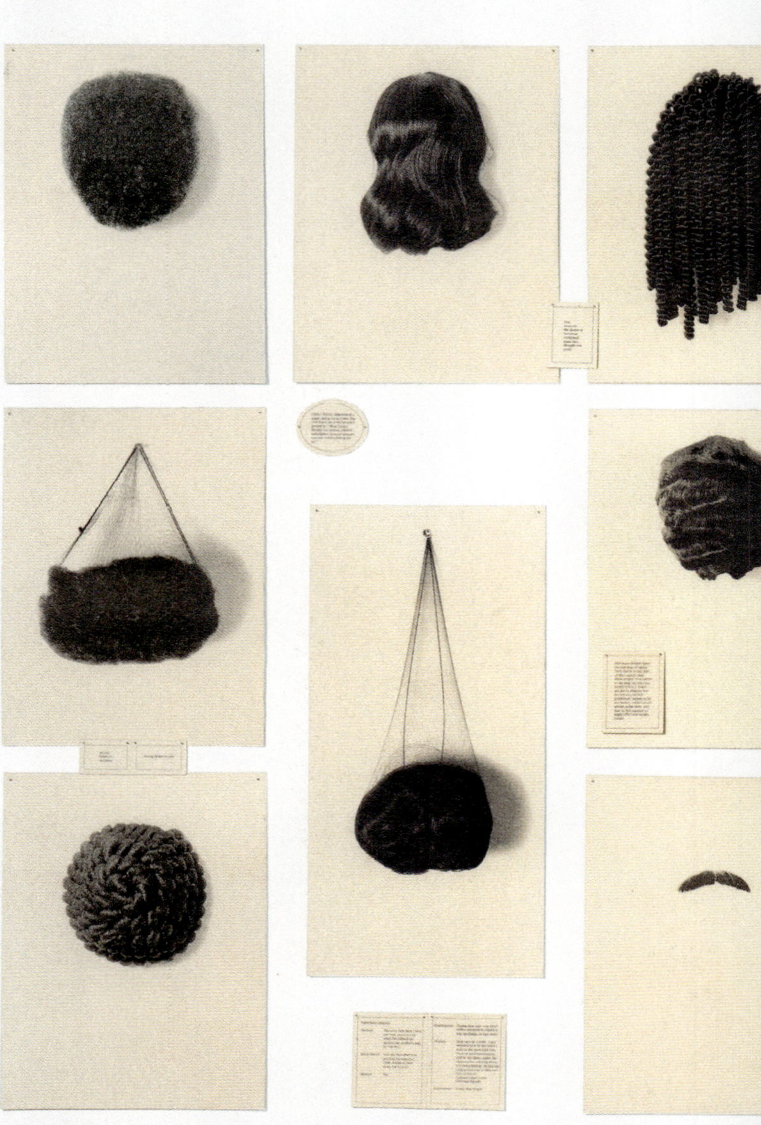

[9.3]

graphic work. In reflecting on this move to felt, which she continued to work with notably in her *Public Sex* series, Simpson says: "I continue to use it, because on a formal level, I got tired of the idea of photographs behind frames, behind glass. With the felt, it gives it a softer quality, the look of photogravure. They absorb light, rather than having all of these framing devices. The images are more seductive when they are photographic images printed on felt" (Lorna Simpson quoted in Novakov 1998, 176–177). Presenting images on felt also adds a sculptural quality to the work, with their texture, occasional overlaps of panels, and curves and curls of felt edges against the walls. Simpson has also observed that felt resembles "compressed hair" and so lends a haptic quality to work in terms of both its subject matter and its reception by a viewer.

In *Wigs*, we are presented with wigs hanging on a wall, with no bodies present. Simpson has noted that "This work came at a point where I wanted to eliminate the figure, or eliminate its presence from the work, but I still wanted to talk about that presence. So the wigs act as a surrogate for talking about the body or speaking about the presence of a person in the work" (https://www.moma.org/learn/moma_learning/lorna-simpson-wigs-1994).

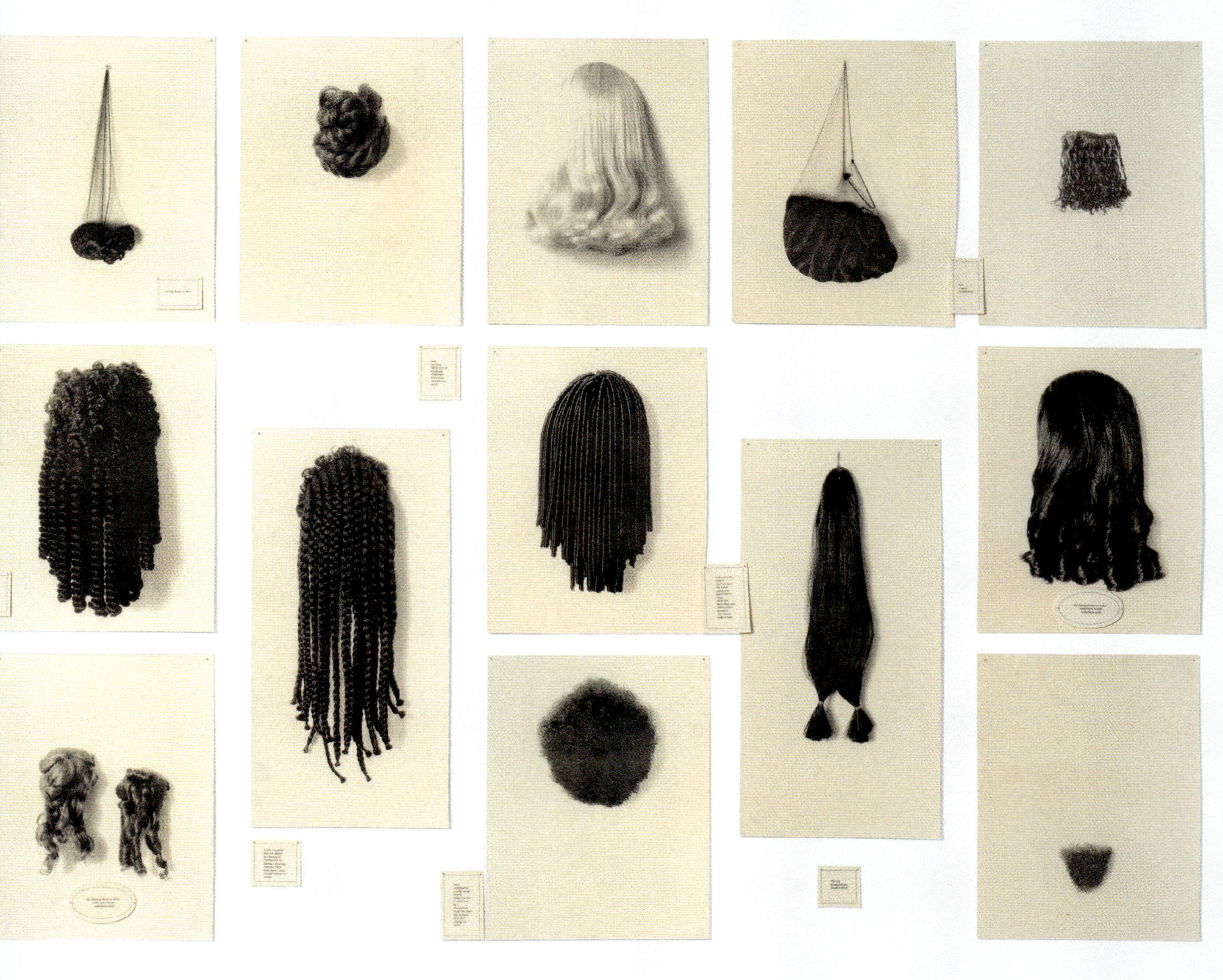

This points to the complex nature of the wigs as subject matter, and their relation to the body and questions of identity, which is further emphasized by the pieces of text that accompany the images.

These text fragments include short statements, such as "strong desire to decipher," "strong desire to blur," "first impressions are the most lasting," "the clothes make the man," "the leopard does not change its spots." There is also a note about a woman named "Truth" being asked to show her breasts as proof of her sex, and another about a light-skinned enslaved woman disguising herself as a male slaveowner to free herself and her darker-skinned husband. In these texts, we are confronted by the potentials of physical appearances as truth, deception, flexibility, freedom, and constraint, and their ties to race and gender.

Hair has particular connotations and complexities with relation to gender and race and is considered a "site where blackness seems to appear and adhere, a surface read as a sign." Its changeability and "potential for manipulation," though, means it is "more than just a static signifier continuous with the body; it becomes a tool for self-conscious signification" (Belisle 2011, 168). Simpson points out that "The wearer of the wigs can either become someone else or become closer to the person that one sees oneself to be. In terms of either embracing or cutting across a particular stereotype, or in terms of gender, blurring the lines between masculinity or femininity" (https://www.moma.org/learn/moma_learning/lorna-simpson-wigs-1994). The wigs in this piece, emphasized by the work's title, and the lack of any figures, are clearly removable and impermanent modes of emphasizing or shifting perceptions of oneself.

*NIKKI KANE*

**KERRY JAMES MARSHALL**
(Birmingham, Alabama 1955)

[9.4]
***Blind Ambition***
**1990**
acrylic, collage on canvas
218.8 × 142.2 cm
Minneapolis, Walker Art Center
Gift of RBC Wealth Management, in honor of John Taft, 2016

[9.5]
***"WE SHALL OVERCOME"***
**1998**
Edition: 1/5; relief print on paper
65.1 × 101.6 cm
Minneapolis, Walker Art Center
T. B. Walker Acquisition Fund, 1999

[9.6]
***"BLACK IS BEAUTIFUL"***
**1998**
Edition: 1/5; relief print on paper
6.1 × 101.6 cm
Minneapolis, Walker Art Center
T. B. Walker Acquisition Fund, 1999

[9.7]
***"BLACK POWER"***
**1998**
Edition: 1/5; relief print on paper
65.1 × 101.6 cm
Minneapolis, Walker Art Center
T. B. Walker Acquisition Fund, 1999

[9.8]
***"BURN BABY BURN"***
**1998**
Edition: 1/5; relief print on paper
65.1 × 101.6 cm
Minneapolis, Walker Art Center
T. B. Walker Acquisition Fund, 1999

[9.9]
***"BY ANY MEANS NECESSARY"***
**1998**
Edition: 1/5; relief print on paper
65.1 × 101.6 cm
Minneapolis, Walker Art Center
T. B. Walker Acquisition Fund, 1999

Details of Marshall's biography are emphasized in much of the writing on his work: he was born in Birmingham, Alabama, in 1955, a crucial time and location for the civil rights movements, and then moved with his family to Los Angeles in 1963, coinciding with a period turmoil in the city—Marshall notes that "LA was a pretty apocalyptic place in the late 1960s [. . .] In 1965, when the Watts Riots started, we no longer lived there, but I vividly remember when it all blew up" (Roelstraete 2012, 65). It was in LA that Marshall first began to develop his interest in art and drawing, tracing pictures and learning techniques from television and instructional books and then attending classes at the Otis Art Institute where Charles White was a teacher and became a great inspiration and mentor to Marshall. A recent exhibition and catalogue have emphasized the importance of mastery in Marshall's work, and this is evident in his accounts of

his early developments as an artist, where he was focused on learning a range of artistic techniques (*Kerry James Marshall* 2016, 79). "Mastering the art of figuration" was an early commitment for Marshall and, although he remained open to working with abstraction and also worked with collage, this was an important priority. From this early stage, Marshall was concerned with issues of representation and art history and considered mastering figurative techniques as an important step in being able to produce grand paintings that represented black figures, as a "counter-archive" to the pervasive Western canon of art that represents white bodies and produces the "impression that beauty is synonymous with whiteness" (Roelstraete 2012, 21, 28).

This large-scale canvas is one of Kerry James Marshall's early figurative paintings, created a decade after his 1980 *A Portrait of the Artist as a Shadow of His Former Self* that solidified his interests as an artist and pointed to the direction his work would take, which he describes as: "trying to establish a phenomenal presence that is unequivocally black and beautiful. It is my conviction that the most instrumental, insurgent painting for this moment must be of figures, and those figures must be black, unapologetically so" (Marshall 2016, 79).

*Blind Ambition* (1990) [9.4] is, on first appearance, a fairly sparse painting, but on closer inspection it is filled with subtle details and textures that point to issues of economic structures and success. It includes elements of collage, with panels of paper and pieces of tapes pasted across its canvas, along with acrylic paint depicting a single black figure wearing a business suit and a large ladder that outsizes the figure. At the bottom of the canvas, "AMBITION" is spelled out in red, some letters washed over in white, at the top, "SUCCESS" is barely visible, in painted-over gray-on-white. In the middle of the ladder, in small letters, "COURAGE" and "INDUSTRY" each sits atop a rung and faint traces of the outlines of figures can be seen beneath the paint in the spaces between each step on the ladder. The composition is completed with gold-filled circles in each corner, and a gold-colored ring and green paint splash in the left of the canvas.

Typical of Marshall's work, the outlines of the figure's features are picked out but are mostly flattened, and the skin of his face and hands is painted not in naturalistic shades of brown but black, with little shading or modelling visible. Marshall's use of black pigments has been discussed by curator Lanka Tattersall, who notes that his commitment to the "insertion of blackness into the field of art" and to highlighting the absence of black figures in Western art history is "carried through the literal matter—the pigments—of his paintings" (Tattersall 2016, 57–69). In *Blind Ambition* [9.4], this is highly contrasted with the off-white background of the canvas, and the pale pink panel behind his head.

Marshall's focus on painting—on figurative painting at that—seems at odds with the moves towards conceptual art, abstraction, and appropriation that dominated American art in the mid- to late twentieth century. However, while clearly focused on figuration and rooted in the experience and politics of black identity—"With everything that was going on in the streets at that time, how could a black person be concerned with an art for art's sake?" (Roelstraete 2012, 23)—Marshall's work is conscious and connected with other artistic practices. Critic and curator He.en Molesworth has pointed to the relationship

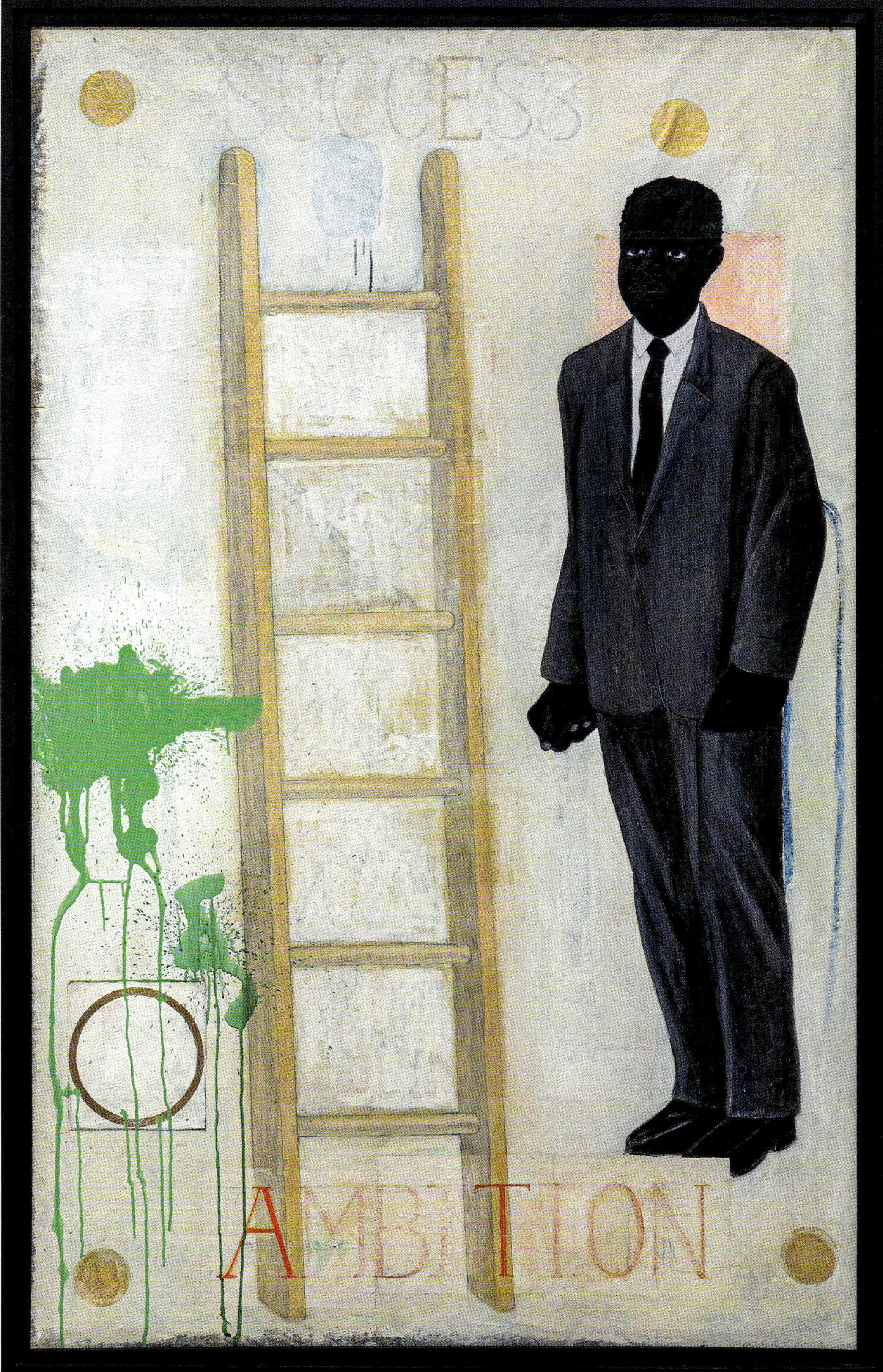




[9.4]

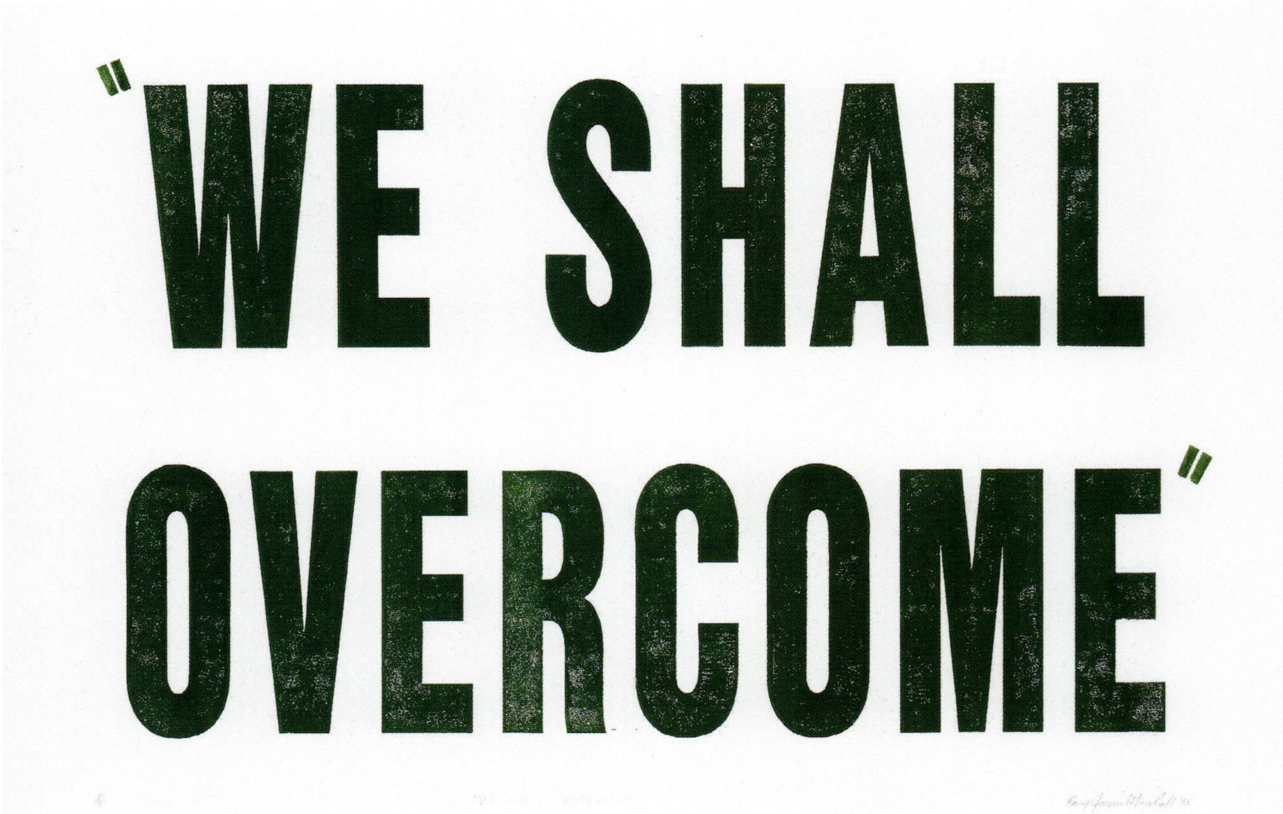

"WE SHALL OVERCOME"

[9.5]

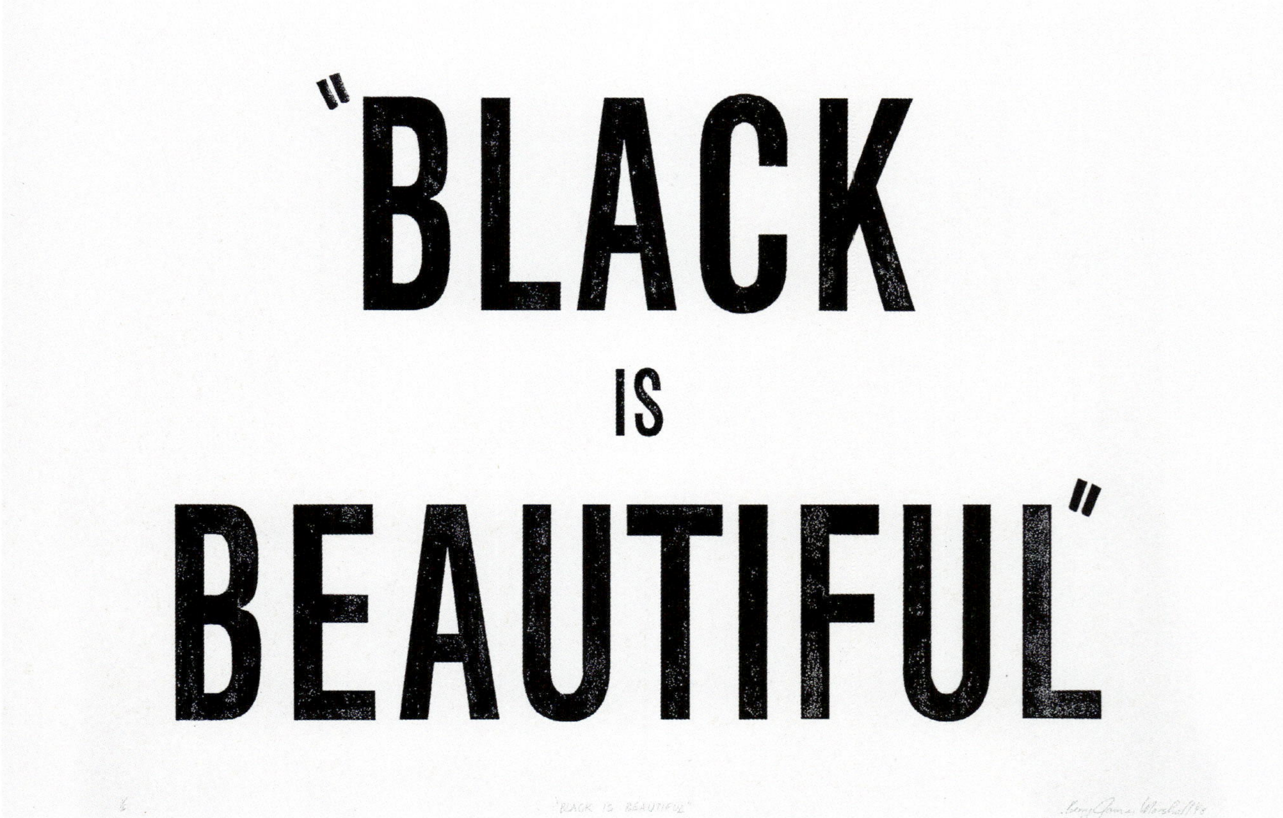

"BLACK IS BEAUTIFUL"

[9.6]

[9.7]

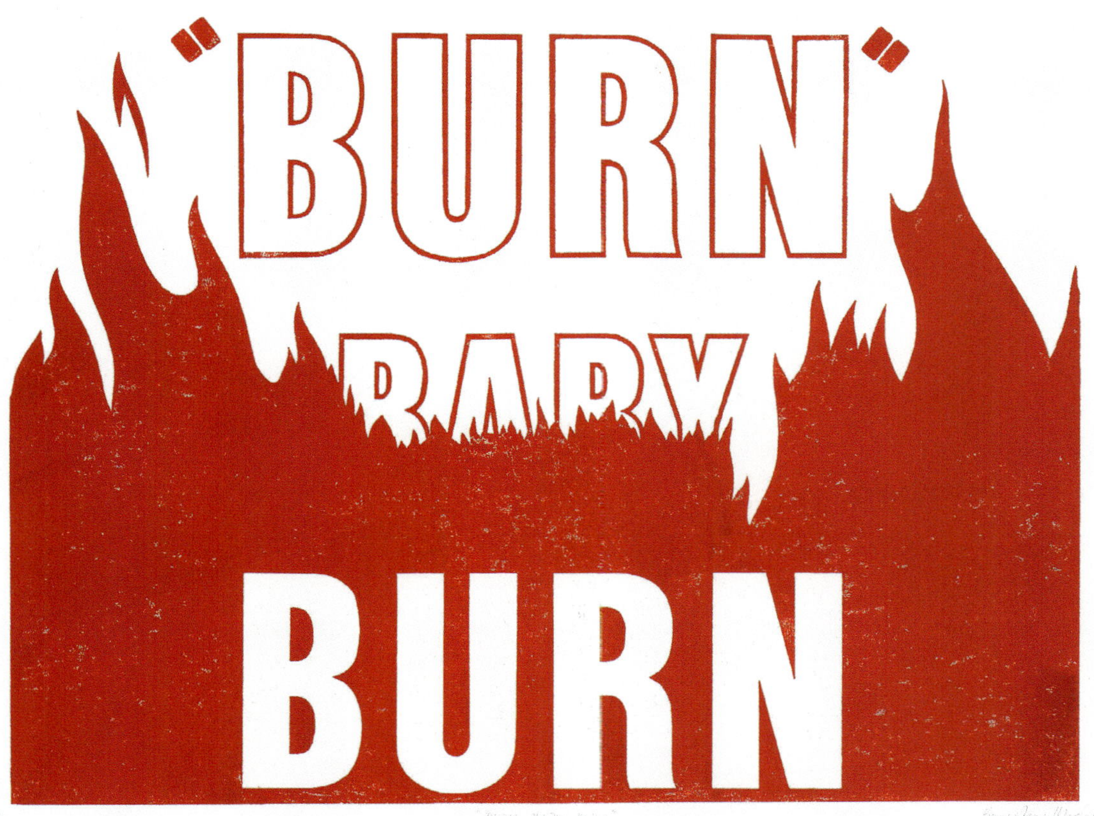





[9.8]

between Marshall and the artists of the "Pictures generation," noting that "Instead of reveling in the field of mass-produced imagery, Marshall appropriated fragments from the rich archive of Western painting. Much of his early work displayed a collage aesthetic, with Marshall composing his paintings from borrowed fragments and passages to subsume them into a new whole" (Molesworth 2016, 40). This speaks to Marshall's mastery of composition, where externally sourced imagery or texture is carefully interwoven with precisely plotted arrangements of figures, scenes, and objects. His compositions are controlled and restrained, yet full of detail, conveying his deep understanding of the history of painting and a distillation of the traditions of history painting, landscape, portrait, and genre painting. He aims for his paintings to be "straightforward," avoiding any possibility to "rest on a flourish, on some kind of trick" (Roelstraete 2012, 32–33). These are categories of painting with a long history over centuries of practice, and it is precisely Marshall's aim to situate his work within the lengthy history of Western art so that the images he creates become part of that history. This approach is shaped by generous and generative critique of the institutions of the museum and art history, one that hopes to help them better attend to their ideals (Roelstraete 2012, 27–28; Molesworth 2016, 37–39).

While Kerry James Marshall is primarily known and established as a painter, his practice extends to photography, installation, video, comic strips, and printmaking. The series of five prints included in this exhibition were produced as relief prints on paper, using specially designed stamps that were exhibited alongside the prints as part of a solo exhibition that toured in the US in 1998.

Each large print carries a phrase, in all capital letters, referencing the 1960s Civil Rights and Black Liberation movements: "BLACK IS BEAUTIFUL" [9.6], "BLACK POWER" [9.7], "WE SHALL OVERCOME" [9.5], "BY ANY MEANS NECESSARY" [9.9], "BURN BABY BURN" [9.8]. They are each printed in red, green, or black, colors that symbolize black nationalism and the Pan-African flag. These phrases, described by Marshall as "rallying cries to celebration and defiance," (Artist's statement, August 2, 1999, Walker Art Center Archives, quoted in Rinder 2005, 373) evoke a particular moment in time, while simultaneously speaking directly to society and activism today. When first exhibited in 1998, art historian Richard J. Powell reflected on the way the series (and accompanying stamps) spans across time. These concise statements capture the power and significance of language in civil rights movements, words that "had a particular cache and potency that, now, seem impossible to attain ever again," but that

"have an uncanny, undeniable presence in the here and now" (Powell 1998, 37). Their scale, simplicity, and use of reproducible printing techniques similarly both fix and monumentalize their messages, while pointing to their continuation. Now, over twenty years on from this exhibition, these words feel especially potent within our time of increasing racism and political turmoil, and in turn the resurgence of highly visible activism and awareness of historical movements.
*NIKKI KANE*

## GLENN LIGON
(New York 1960)

[9.10]
***Untitled (Stranger in the Village #16)***
**2000**
acrylic, coal dust, oil stick, glue, glitter, gesso on canvas
122.1 × 142.6 cm
Minneapolis, Walker Art Center
Butler Family Fund, 2000

Born and raised in the Bronx, New York, Glenn Ligon came to prominence in the early 1990s with works in which he painted and stenciled texts from African American literature onto canvas to challenge social-ly constructed conceptions of race and sexuality. This incorporation of text into his paintings was prompted by his experience as part of the Whitney Museum's Independent Study Program, which he participated in in 1985. Ligon's practice has developed to incorporate sculpture, audio, printmaking, and neon as well as works on canvas, but he has continued to work with texts, from a variety of sources, as a material. Since the late 1980s, Ligon has produced canvases featuring stenciled text extracts from the work of a variety of figures, including Zora Neal Hurston, Walt Whitman, Richard Pryor, and, as in this work, James Baldwin. From early on in this work, Ligon allowed and even encouraged the smudging of his stenciled words from his processes of working with stencils and oil sticks, playing with questions of legibility. This has continued to be an important element of Ligon's work that he has dealt with through the use of various materials and techniques, and also reflected on in interviews, for example noting in one that "Text demands to be read, and perhaps the withdrawal of the text, the frustration of the ability to decipher it, reflects a certain pessimism on my part about the ability and the desire to communicate" (Glenn Ligon quoted in Firstenberg 2001, 43).
While his early text canvases featured black text on white backgrounds, in *Untitled (Stranger in the Village #16)* [9.10] from 2000, both the text and the background of the canvas are black, with layers of coal dust added on top to distinguish the letters from the canvas. Ligon linked this material to the "gravity and weight" in Baldwin's text,

where its addition to the canvas "literally bulked up the text" (Ligon 2011, 161). He has also pointed to how this tied with questions of legibility: "It obscures the text while making it more present and sculptural. There is always that push/pull in the work, of the desire for legibility and disappearance of the text" (Glenn Ligon in Andrews 2005, 173).

The text on this canvas is an extract from Baldwin's 1955 essay "Stranger in the Village" where the writer describes his experiences of living in a small village in Switzerland, and with this an analysis of the effects of histories of colonialism on Africa, America, and Europe, and the nature of both witnessing and being a stranger, in any context. Ligon's "quotation" of this text in his work is inexact; some words are missing or cut off at the end of the canvas (Baerwaldt 2005, 7). This is characteristic of his use of source texts in his work, as a material within his pieces, as intrinsic as the paint or canvas, and not simply a subject a rendered. It also works to bring together the past and the present, and the personal and the communal.

Ligon's work has been described as making "personal the exploration of what may be considered historically weighted texts and images" and drawing attention to the "representation of self in relation to culture and history" (Baerwaldt 2005, 7). Baldwin's "Stanger in the Village" is both specific to its time and place, and incredibly pertinent to contemporary life in providing historical context as well as echoing the experiences of many people of color today. His nuanced, and loaded artworks have been described by art historian Darby English as addressing "the semantic of blackness without succumbing to the redundancy of merely reproducing the black body," drawing comparison with the likes of Kara Walker, David Hammons, Lorna Simpson, Carrie Mae Weems, and Gary Simmons (English 2005, 54).
*NIKKI KANE*

## MATTHEW BARNEY
(San Francisco 1967)

[9.11]
**selection from *Cremaster 2: The Drones' Exposition***
**1999**
video transfer from HDTV, nylon, acrylic, carpet inlay, laminated chromogenic prints, flags
film: 79:17 min.
12 photographs: 111.7 × 111.7 × 3.17 cm each
12 flags: *c.* 90 × 167 cm each
Minneapolis, Walker Art Center
Collection Walker Art Center and San Francisco Museum of Modern Art, T. B. Walker Acquisition Fund, 2000

Matthew Barney's career began, paradoxically, with a very profound absence. The night before his New York debut in 1991, he locked himself inside the gallery and began to climb. Using customized mountaineering equipment such as titanium ice screws and a climbing harness, he made his assault on the architecture. He ascended walls, moved across the ceiling, and finally descended into a basement gallery containing a sculptural tableau that included a weight-lifting bench cast from petroleum jelly housed

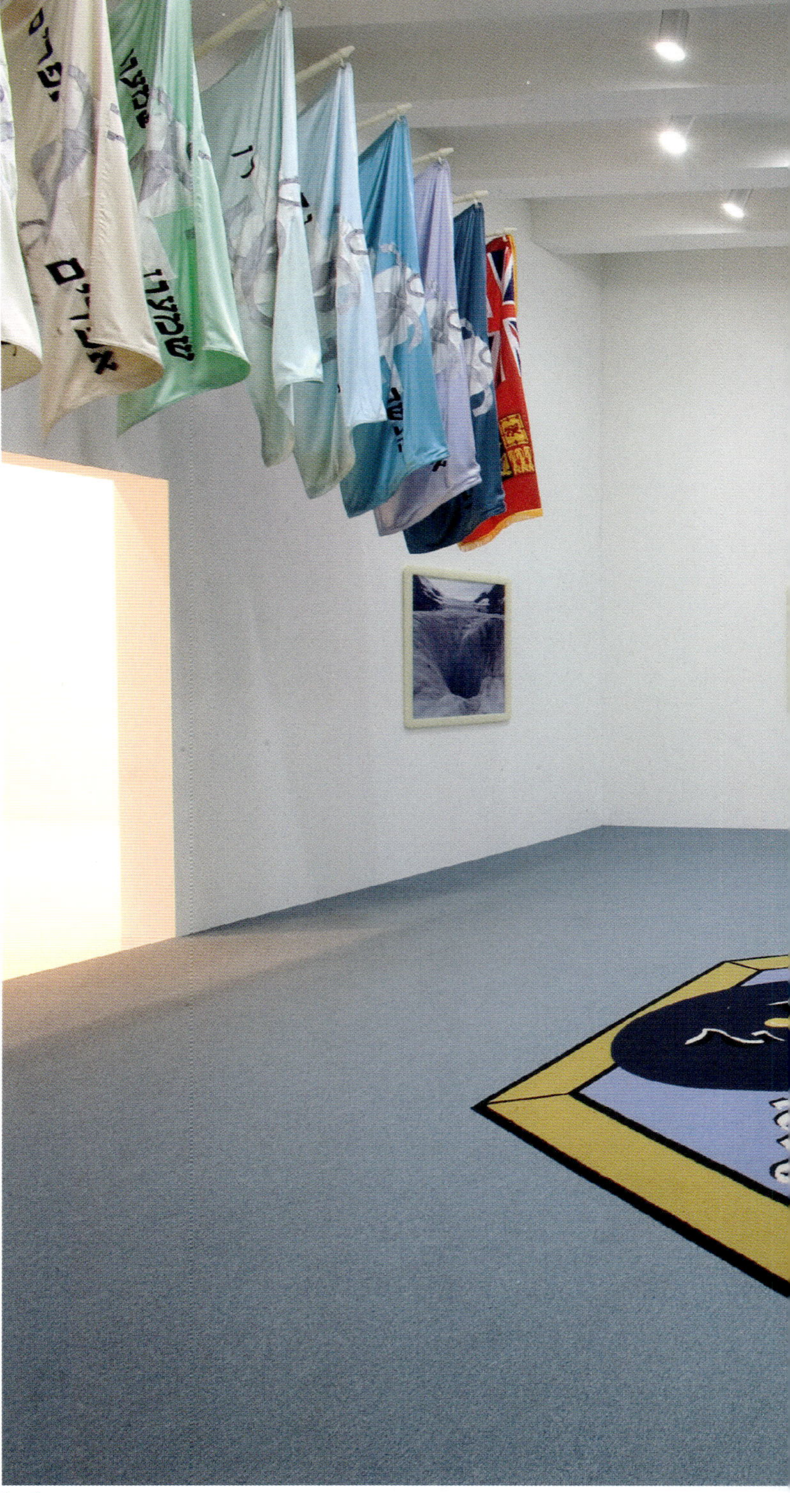

[9.11]

in an industrial refrigeration unit. The next day, visitors saw only a video of the artist's climb and the sculptural and performative residue of his presence. Barney might have left the building, but he opened a door onto a new aesthetic gambit: a powerful hybridization of sculpture, performance, and the moving image that has grown more complex since that first exhibition. Today, his universe is composed of a wildly complex pantheon of figures and forces, each of which overflows with narrative connotations and sculptural possibilities. Driving these intricate narratives is a systematic investigation into the generative nature of physical resistance in the

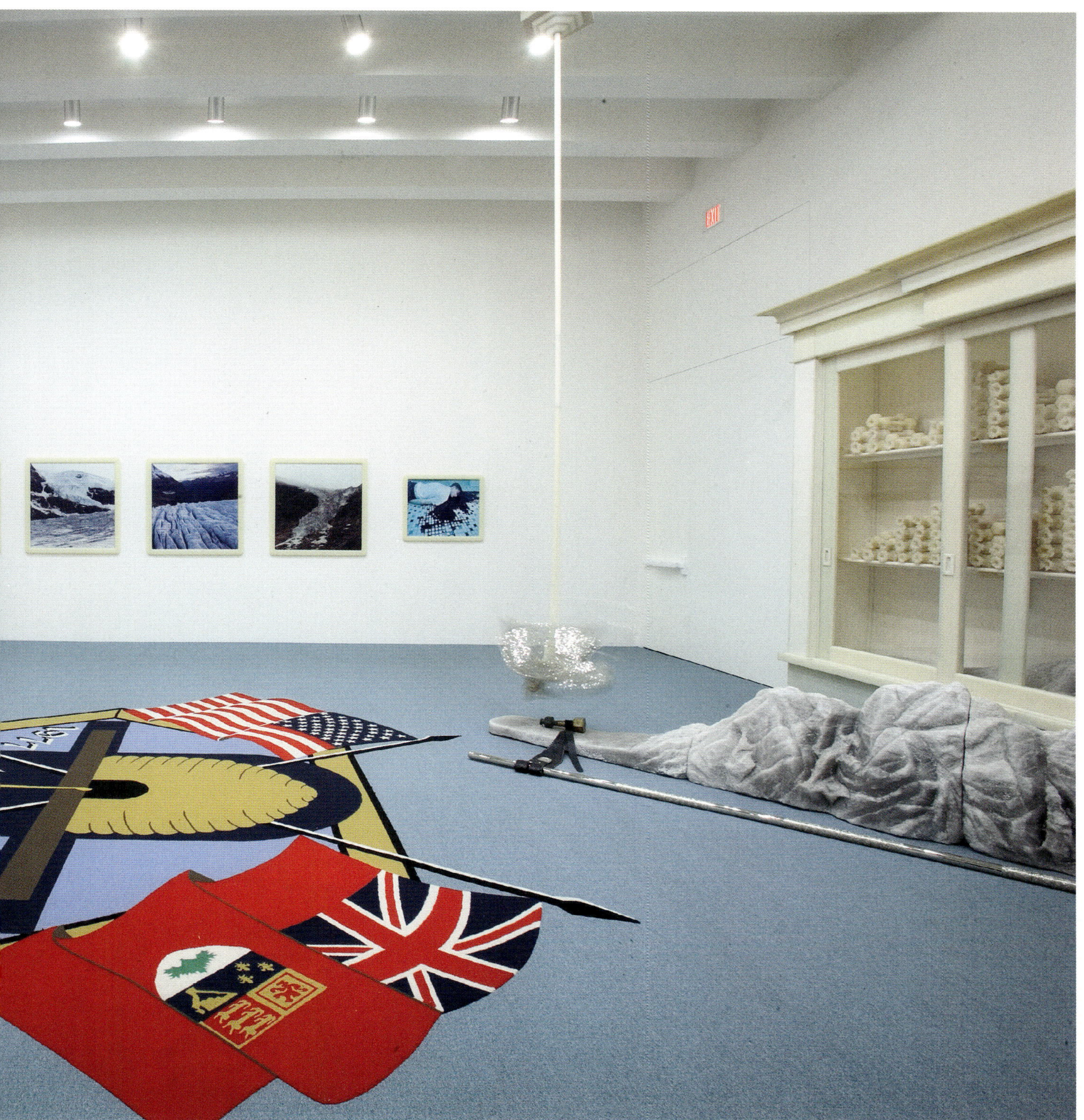

creation of form. In Barney's world, objects cannot take physical shape and narratives cannot develop without the struggle of a protagonist against an opposing force (Spector 2002, 2–91).

One of the artist's most astonishing contributions is his ability to expand the possibilities for sculpture—not only through his choice of such unorthodox materials as petroleum jelly and self-lubricating plastic, but through his insistence on the sculptural possibilities of both performance and film. Both aspects have their roots in a wide range of cultural references and artistic sources: for example, Barney has acknowledged a debt to Bruce Nauman, who used his own body to explore the limitations of his studio space in such videos as *Bouncing in a Corner No. 1* or *Slow Angle Walk (Beckett Walk)* (both 1968). Vito Acconci's notorious *Seedbed* (1972), with its hidden onanistic performance, also comes to mind, and it is impossible not to think of Richard Serra's thrown-lead pieces, whose dynamic forms were shaped by the surfaces they encountered (Richard Serra himself would play a central role in *Cremaster 3*. In one sequence, Serra throws liquid petroleum jelly into a wall along the rotunda of the Guggenheim Museum in a concatenation of Barney's materials with Serra's ear-

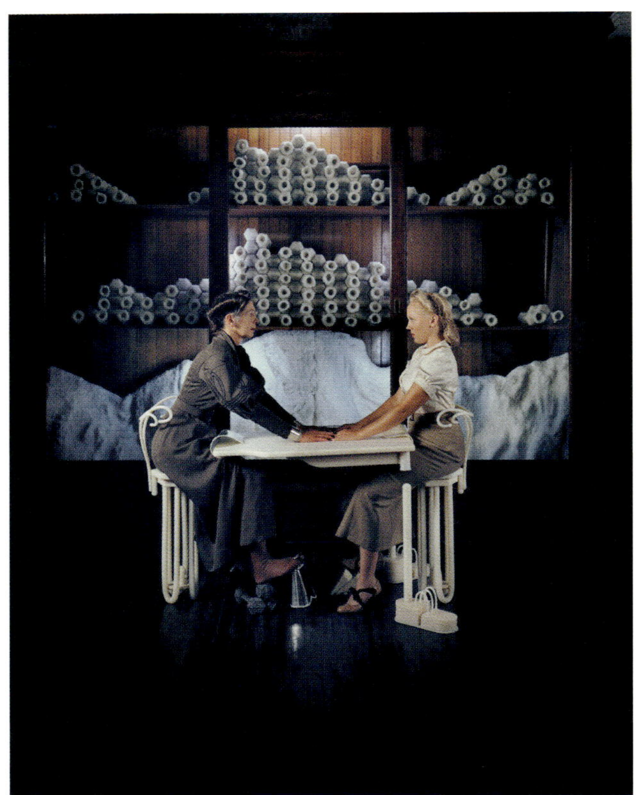

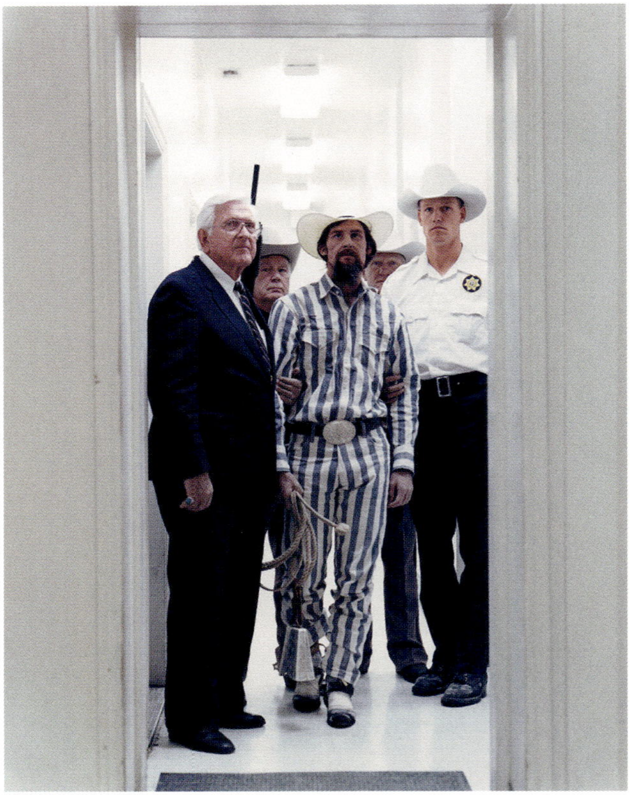

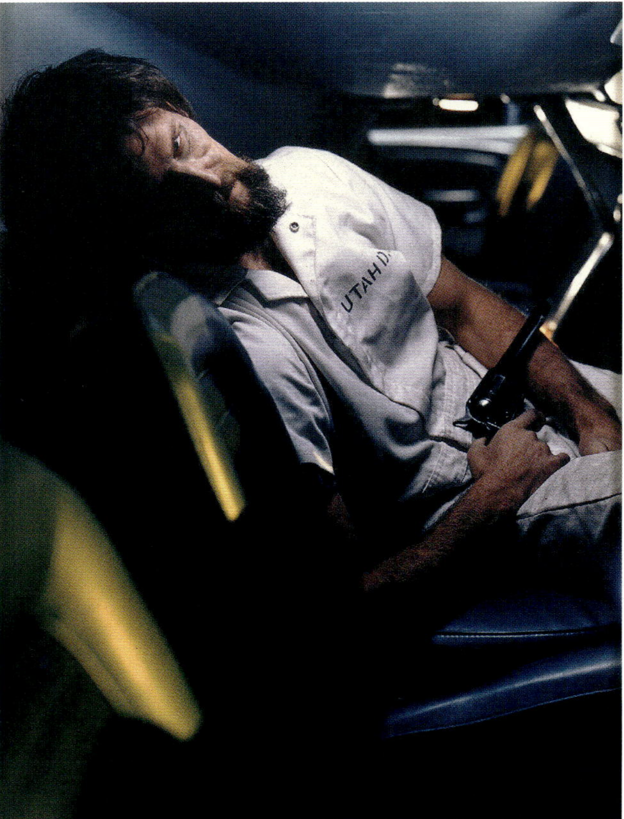

[9.11]

ly aesthetic endeavors). These art-historical progenitors are fused with references to the artist's childhood heroes, including the Oakland Raiders' legendary offensive lineman Jim Otto or escape artist Harry Houdini, both of whom tested the extreme physical thresholds of the body. When the visual and narrative influence of films such as Sam Raimi's *Evil Dead II* (1987) or Stanley Kubrick's *The Shining* (1980) are thrown into the mix, it becomes clear that we are not simply dealing with cultural bricolage but with a fundamentally hybrid conception of sculptural practice (on Barney's relationship to film, see Flood 1995, 21–35).

An operatic series of five epic films, Barney's monumental *Cremaster* cycle constitutes a biological, mythological, and topological recasting of classical mythopoetic narratives in the form of a series of phantasmic quests. As Nancy Spector suggests, "Born out of a performative practice in which the human body—with its psychic drives and physical thresholds—symbolizes the potential of sheer creative force, the cycle explodes this body into the particles of a contemporary creation myth" (Spector 2002, 5). It is the anatomy of the body itself that provides this creation myth with its title, as it refers to the cremaster muscle, which controls the raising and lowering of the testicles in response to such external stimuli as fear and changes in temperature. The entire cycle alludes to the moment in prenatal development just prior to the assignment of gender—an undifferentiated physical state that embodies the tension between stasis and dynamic movement. That moment provides the metaphorical superstructure for the endless sequence of expenditure and renewal of energy that permeates the narrative of the Cremaster cycle.

While linked by a certain repetition of themes, the five *Cremaster* films do not form a continuous narrative with repeating characters. Shot out of sequence, each of the installments centers around a series of ritualized athletic endeavors and magical transformations in which landscape and architecture are characters in the plot. Each film also has at its core a quest that, as in classical mythology, forces the central character to overcome a series of escalating challenges before reaching his goal. The protagonists (often played by Barney) are forced to engage in a range of physical tribulations, including Houdiniesque escapes, trials by tap-dancing, and heroic climbs across the proscenium of Budapest's Magyar Állami Operaház (State Opera House) and up the rotunda of New York's Guggenheim Museum. These challenges are played out in a narrative of subtle ascents and descents that mimics the movement of the cremaster muscle itself and are set in a sequence of topographies that moves from west to east: from Idaho (*Cremaster 1*, 1995), Utah and Alberta, Canada (*Cremaster 2*, 1999) [9.11], and New York (*Cremaster 3*, 2001) across the Atlantic to the Isle of Man (*Cremaster 4*, 1994) and Hungary (*Cremaster 5*, 1997). In addition to a video or film component, each Cremaster is also realized in the form of a multiple that includes sculptural objects housed in a vitrine of the artist's design; additional related sculptures, drawings, and photographs have often been shown at the debut of each film. As with his earliest works, these installations typically encompass a transformation of the architecture of the gallery into a complete, immersive design environment for viewing these films in which carpet, wall coverings, and even seating find themselves subject to Barney's sculptural vision (*Cremaster 2* premiered at the Walker Art Center in 1999 in an installation that included a large group of sculptural objects, many of which were used in the film), a suite of photographs, flags, drawings, and stadium seating designed and fabricated by the artist. The entire installation was acquired jointly by the Walker and the San Francisco Museum of Modern Art. The Walker also owns the special-edition film vitrines related to the other four *Cremaster* films).

The *Cremaster* project feeds on itself in a kind of systemic autophagy that is generative rather than destructive. The cycle builds a complex, closed system of references in which the epic play of forces can never come to a conclusion but is instead held in a moment of undetermined suspension just prior to resolution. In the end, it is the body itself, with its biological play of forces, that is at the center of this opus. Ovid's *Metamorphoses* opens with the words "Of bodies changed to various forms I sing." These are the unspoken lyrics to the imaginary soundtrack playing in the background of Barney's work.

*DOUGLAS FOGLE* (revised version of text, *published in Bits and Pieces*, 2005, 117–119)

## KARA WALKER

(Stockton, California 1969)

[9.12]

### *Do You Like Creme in Your Coffee and Chocolate in Your Milk?*

**1997**
watercolor, colored pencil, graphite on paper
29.5 × 20.8 cm each of 64
20.8 × 29.5 cm each of 2
Minneapolis, Walker Art Center
Justin Smith Purchase Fund, 1998

[9.13]

### *Cut*

**1998**
cut paper
223.5 × 137.2 cm
Minneapolis, Walker Art Center
Gift of Donna MacMillan, 2013

[9.14]

### *Testimony: Narrative of a Negress Burdened by Good Intentions*

**2004**
Video (black and white, silent), boxed with paper silhouette
8:49 minutes
Edition: 1/5
Minneapolis, Walker Art Center
Clinton and Della Walker Acquisition Fund, 2004

Working since the mid-1990s, Kara Walker has developed a formidable, and at times controversial, artistic practice that has seen her exhibit extensively and receive important accolades, including becoming one of the youngest ever recipients of the MacArthur "genius" award in 1997 at age 28. She is perhaps most known for her silhouette works, in which she creates complex scenes of paper cutout figures that present uncomfortable and often grotesque and violent interactions based in the antebellum southern United States. She has also produced many painted and drawn works, as well as films, that extend these scenes and her concerns with the complexity of racism and history in America. Following the announcement of Walker's MacArthur award, several older African American artists, notably Betye Saar and Howardena Pindell, publicly protested her receiving of the accolade, and her work more generally. For these figures, Walker's work perpetuated racist ideas and images, and was described by Saar as "revolting" and a "betrayal" (Gilman 2007, 27–36; Betye Saar quoted at http://www.pbs.org/wgbh/cultureshock/provocations/kara/3.html). This stance centered on Walker's use of pornographic and violent scenes that employed caricatures of African American figures, and that resisted easy readings or only "positive" depictions of black figures. Instead, in Walker's work, the figures of slave and the slaveowner are complicated and bound up in complex relations of desire, violence, and mastery.

The large series of drawings titled *Do You Like Creme in Your Coffee and Chocolate in Your Milk?* (1997) [9.12] was produced in part as a response to this very public criticism and controversy, to "try and construct my answers to the controversy" as Walker has described it, as well as in a broader "cathartic mode" following the birth of her child around the same period (Kara Walker in conversation with Philippe Vergne at the Walker Art Center Minneapolis in 2005, viewable at https://walkerart.org/magazine/kara-walker-with-philippe-vergne). This extensive body of works on paper incorporates drawn and water-colored images, as well as pieces of text that address and articulate Walker's relationship with history and with racism, and crucially implicates herself in this, for example in her writing of "acknowledging that perhaps I had Neglected (IGNORED) the racist (racialized) parts of myself + that needed real exploring" in one of the pages of the series. She extends these questions

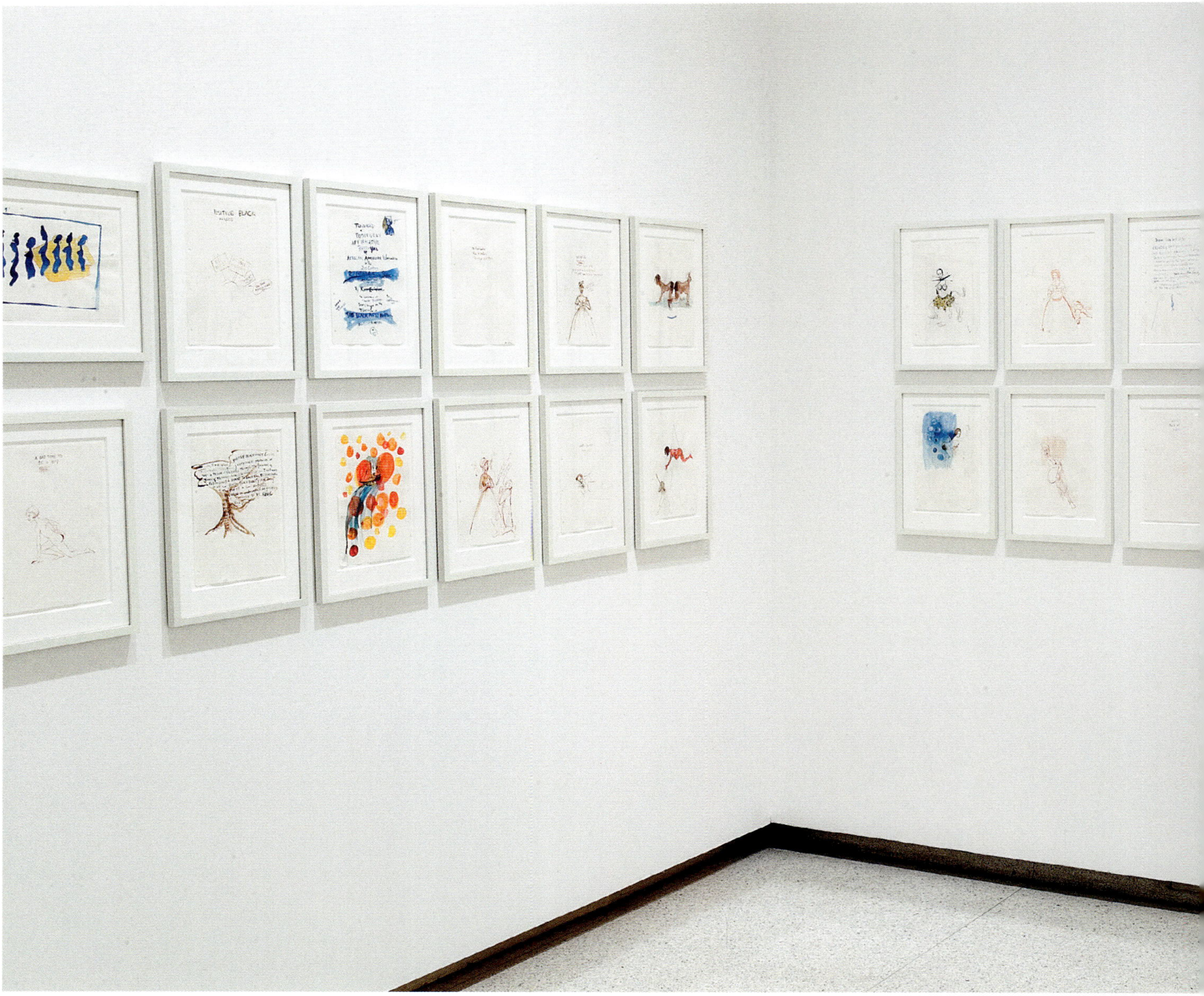

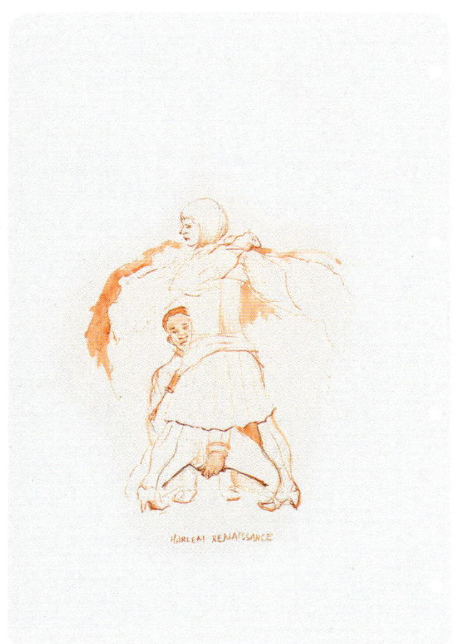

HARLEM RENAISSANCE


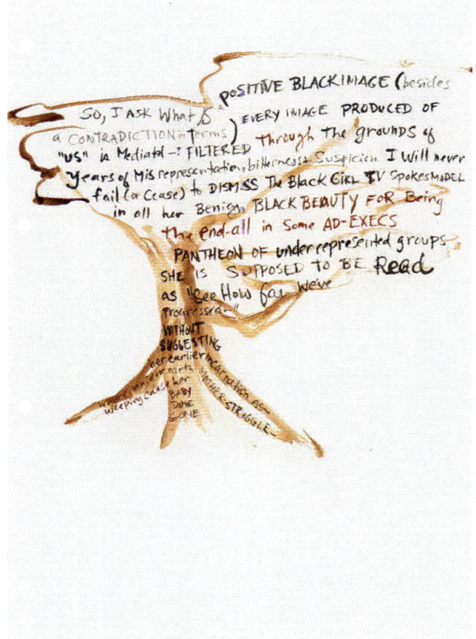

POSITIVE BLACK IMAGE (besides
So, I ASK What is a EVERY IMAGE PRODUCED OF
a CONTRADICTION in terms) through the grounds of
"US" is Mediated –? FILTERED
Years of Mis representation, bitterness + Suspicion. I Will never
fail (or cease) to DISMISS The Black Girl TV Spokesmodel
in all her Benign BLACK BEAUTY FOR Being
the end-all in Some AD-EXECS
PANTHEON OF under represented groups
SHE IS SUPPOSED TO BE Read
as "See How far We've
progressed-"
WITHOUT
SUGGESTING
her earlier incarnation as
her mother + struggle
weeping cause her
BABY
DONE
GONE

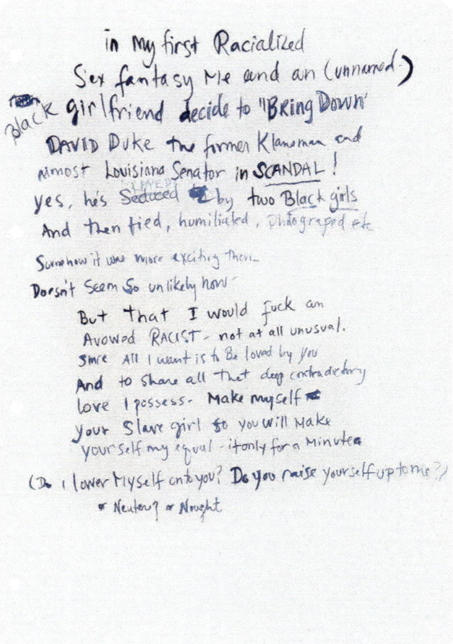

in My first Racialized
Sex fantasy Me and an (unnamed)
Black girlfriend decide to "Bring Down"
DAVID Duke the former Klansman and
almost Louisiana Senator in SCANDAL!
yes, he's Seduced by two Black girls
And then tied, humiliated, Photographed etc
Somehow it was more exciting Then—
Doesn't Seem So unlikely now—
But that I would fuck an
Avowed RACIST— not at all unusual.
Since All I want is to Be loved by you
And to share all That deep contradictory
love I possess— Make myself
your Slave girl So you will Make
yourself my equal—it only for a Minute
(Do i lower Myself onto you? Do you raise yourself up to
or Neuter? or Nought

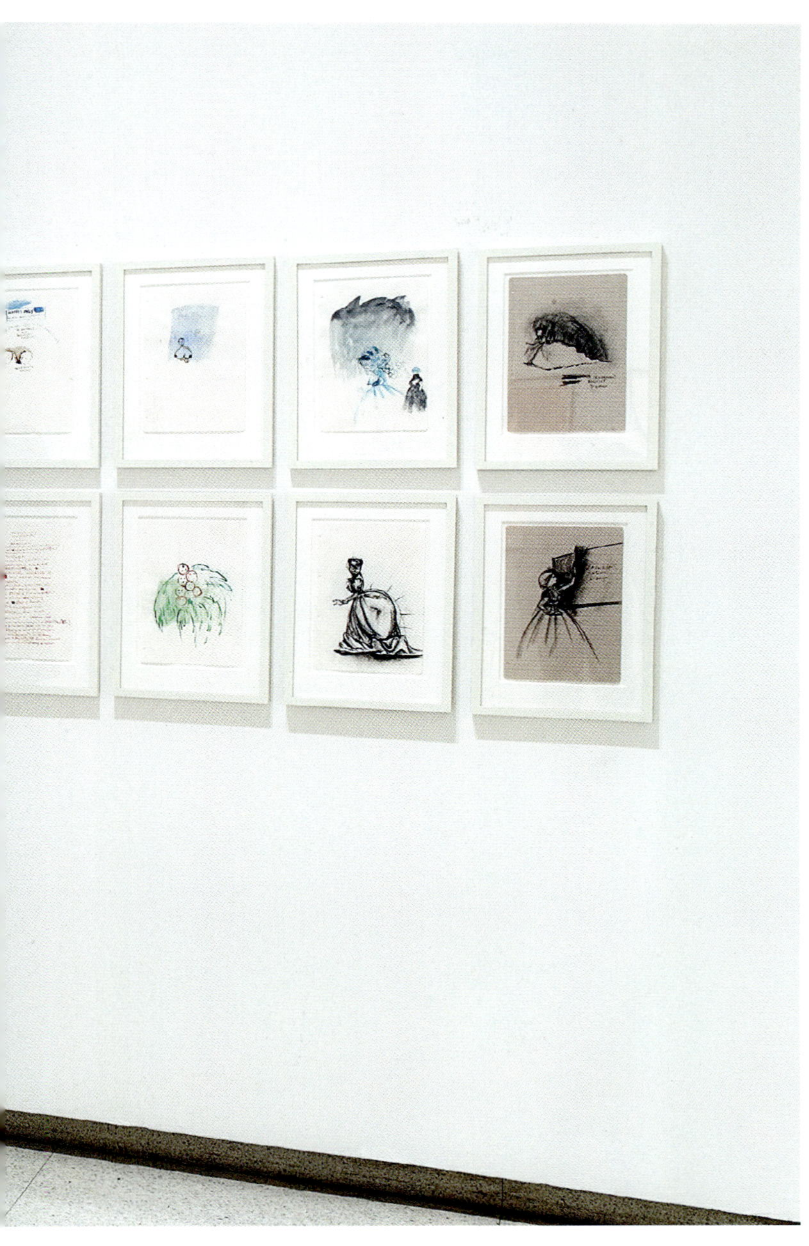

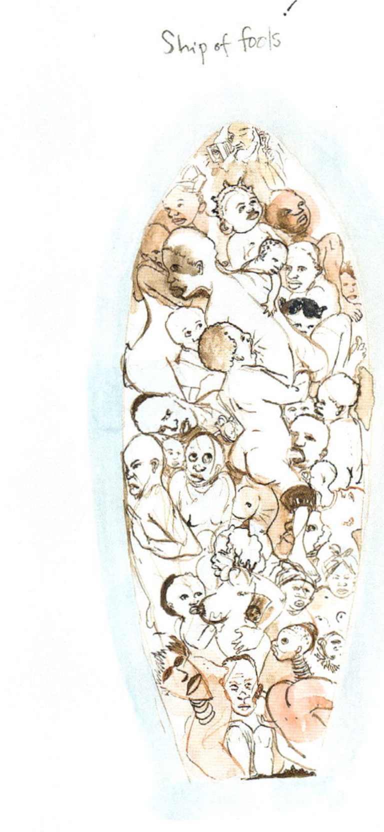


further, emphasizing the breadth of black experience—noting her own "BLACK, MIDDLE CLASS, Suburban, intergrated (RACE TRAITOR) experience" with which "any attempt [...] to Discover those links to the past would be forced and fakey"—and clearly problematizing the notion of singular "POSTIVE BLACK IMAGES" or even a "POSITIVELY AFFIRMATIVE PORTRAYAL of AFRICAN AMERICAN WOMANHOOD." These pieces of text directly address the charges against her in the controversy surrounding her award, and also get to the crux of Walker's work and its use of ambiguity and refusal to subscribe to simple narratives.

Across the series, these pieces of text are interwoven with drawings that present a range of motifs that Walker has used throughout her practice—the exaggerated caricatures of black slaves, white colonial figures in period clothes, ships, and violent and sexualized actions. As in her large-scale drawing and paintings, the use of watercolor and pencil here allow Walker to produce detailed depictions of her figures and their facial features and clothing, something not possible in the medium of silhouette cutouts, yet across both techniques, she demonstrates a skilled use of composition to create a sense of narrative. Similarly, the scale of this series—sixty-six pages—overwhelms with a scale and volume of challenging images, just like her large-scale cutout wall pieces.

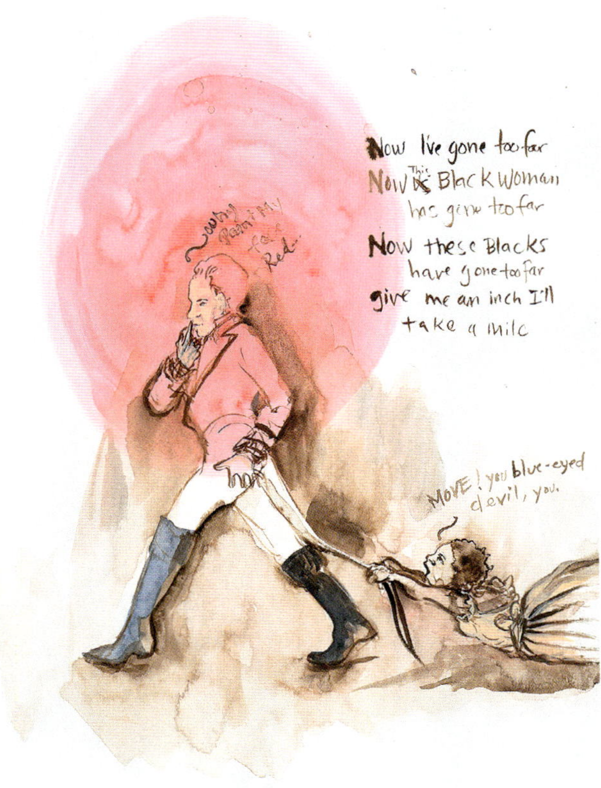




[9.12]

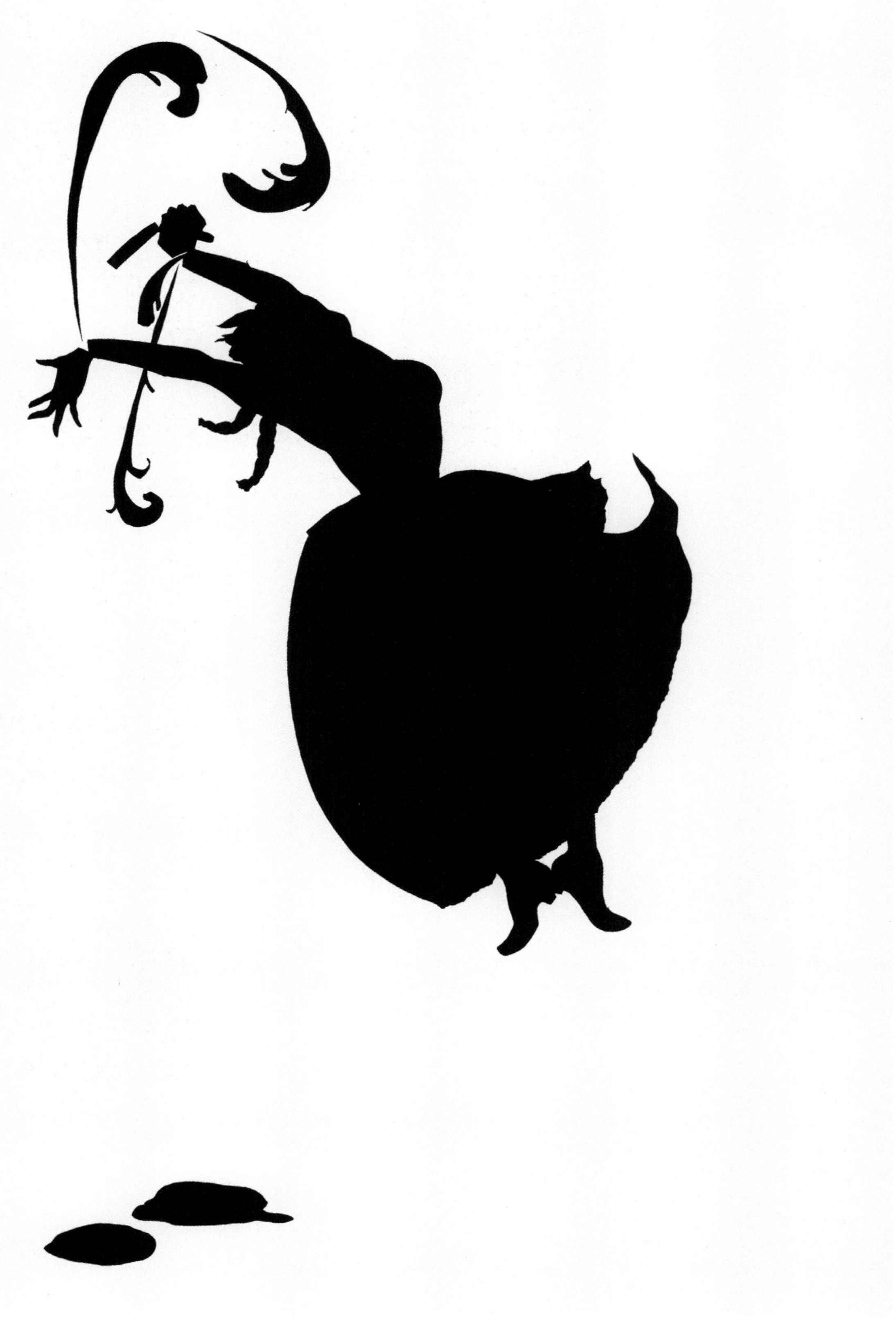

[9.13]

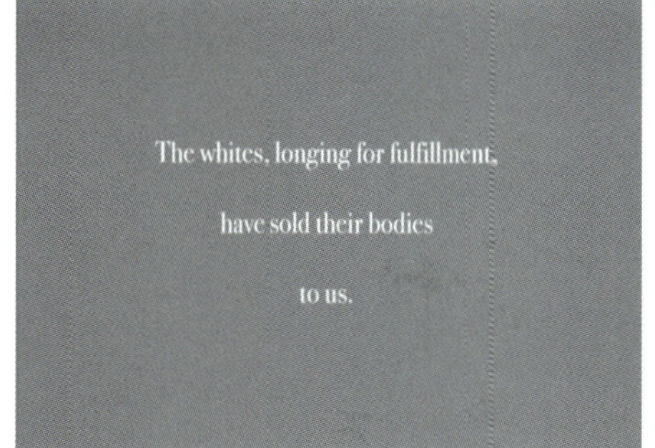


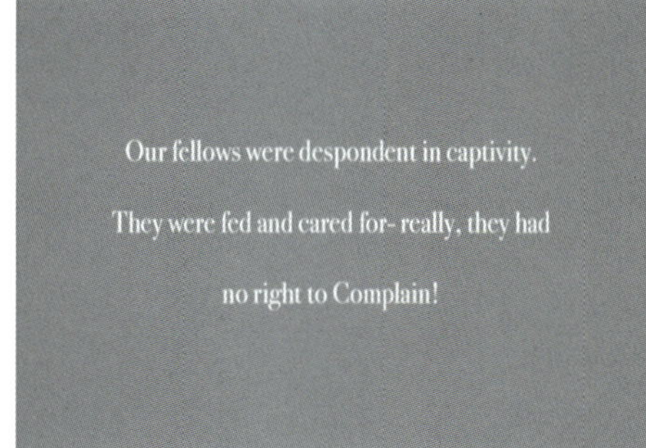


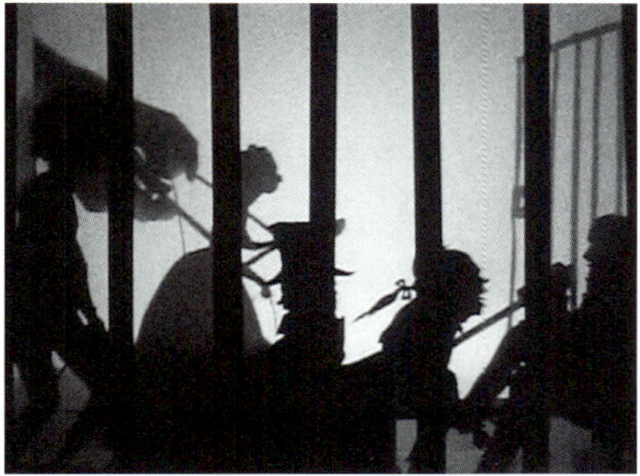

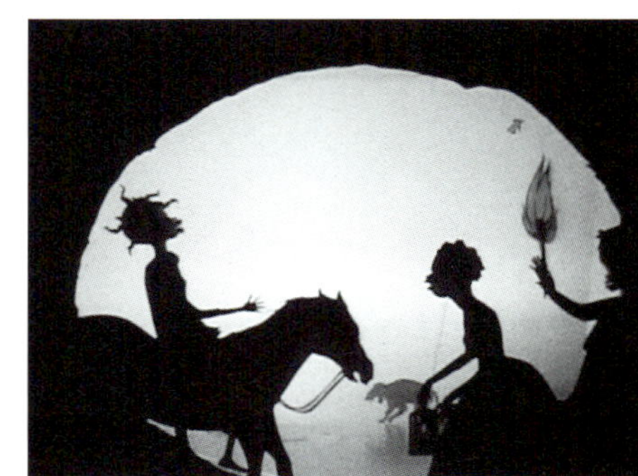

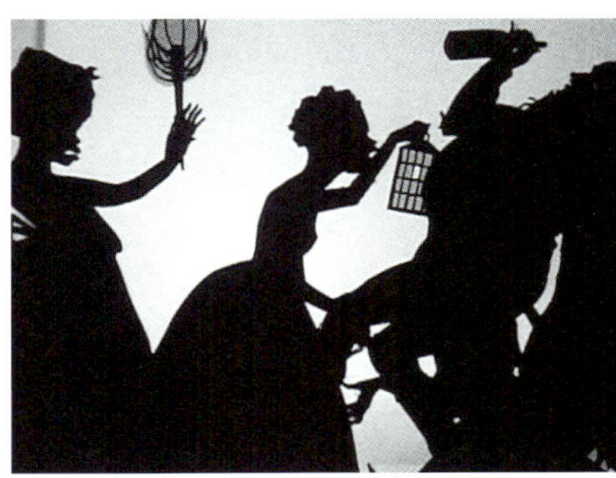

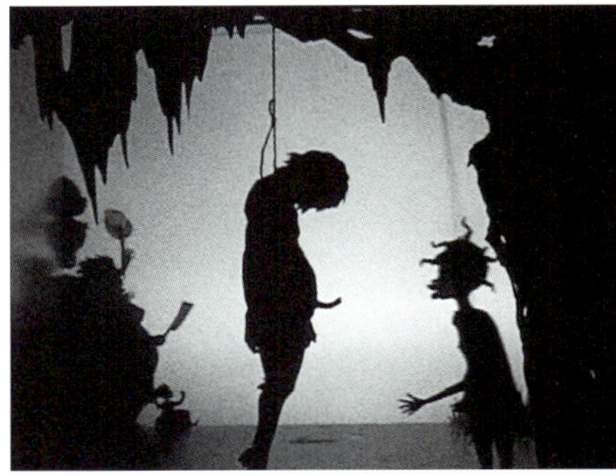

[9.14]

In *Cut* (1998) [9.13], the silhouette of a self-mutilated woman critically explores the past roles of women of color and the contemporary context of gender, represented through the life-size silhouette, cut from black paper and glued to a gallery wall. In this sense, the work visualizes Walker's personal experience as being an African American female artist in the public sphere. The woman sailing through space has slashed her wrists, with blood from the wounds gathered in piles beneath her. Though the work is simplified through the black silhouette form, it retains a complexity of meaning and representation of past histories regarding gender and race, and the contemporary definitions and constructions of identity. The work expresses Walker's complex experience of alienation as an African American female artist in a white, male-dominated art world.

In her film works, Walker continues to work with silhouettes and with text, "sort of repeating the themes of the wall work, but just doing it with time and sound, or the lack of," as she has described it (Kara Walker in conversation with Philippe Vergne at the Walker Art Center Minneapolis in 2005, viewable at https://walkerart.org/magazine/kara-walker-with-philippe-vergne). With the addition of these qualities, Walker has demonstrated her mastery of "pac[ing] discomfort." While her wall works have alluded to narrative, they also overwhelm by presenting many vignettes together; in the time-based medium of film, Walker employs narrative arcs to sustain the power of her scenes for the duration of the piece.

*Testimony: Narrative of a Negress Burdened by Good Intentions* (2004) [9.14] is a short, silent film that pairs silhouette puppets with text panels. It opens with a setting of the scene: "The Whites, longing for fulfilment, have sold their bodies to us," reads the first text. From here, Walker takes her silhouette characters on a violent journey that includes black slave figures whipping, imprisoning, chasing, sexually violating, and lynching white men. It concludes with the film's "negress" figure "performing fellatio on the lynched male body," and "the 'negress' face disintegrates into puddles of watercolor" (Green Fryd 2010, 150). This final act has been read as both a signifier of the presence of the artist in the film (throughout, her arms are visible moving the puppets), as the manipulator of the action on screen, and as an act in which the paint represents semen and thus marks the "negress" figure as "in control" yet she too is dissolved, "eliminated," "disintegrated" (Green Fryd 2010, 150). No one, therefore, is free of the trauma of slavery.

*NIKKI KANE*

# GOING WEST

10.

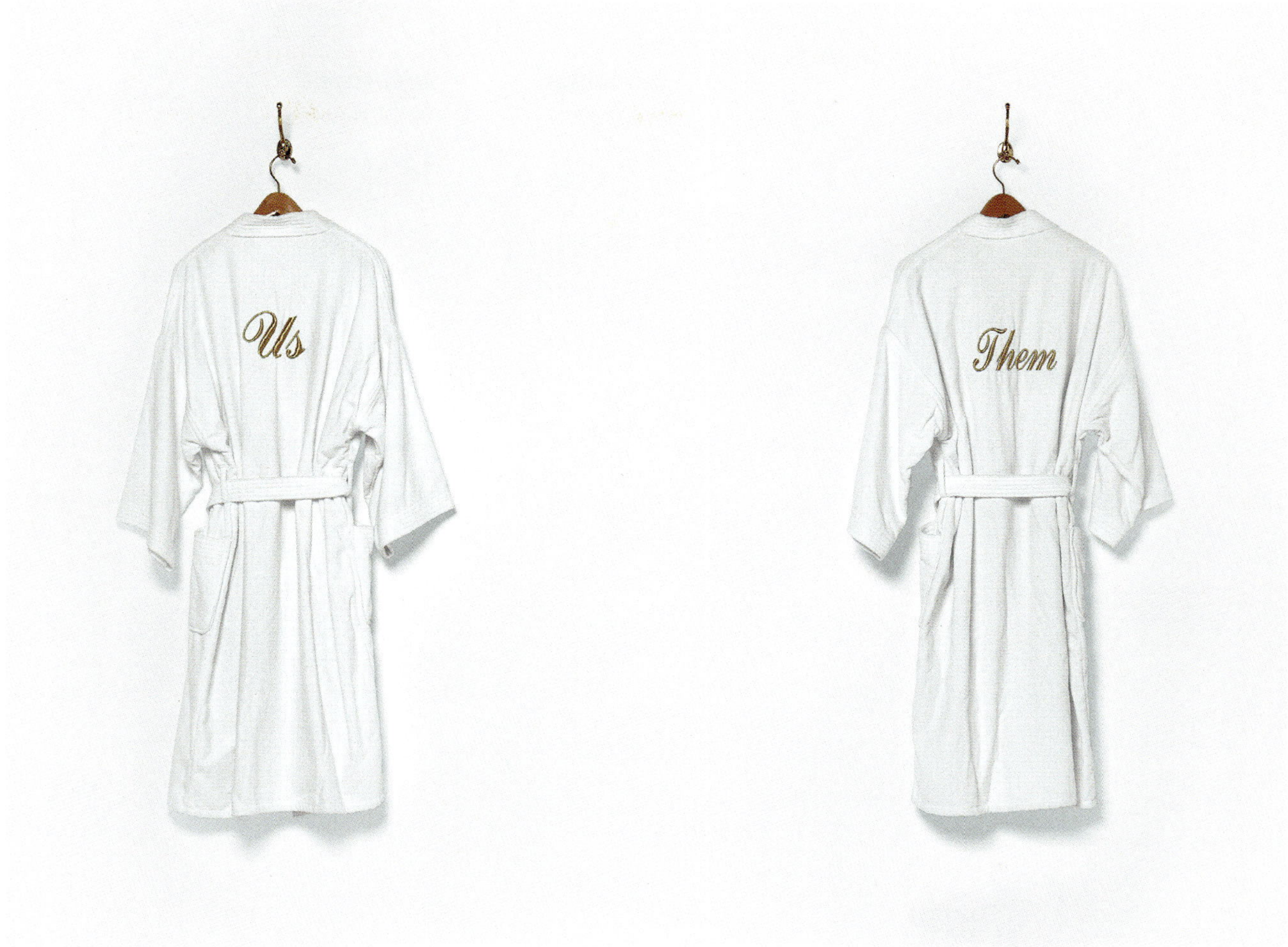



[10.1]

**GARY SIMMONS**
(New York 1964)

[10.1]
***Us and Them***
**1991**
Edition: 1/3
embroidered cotton robes, clothes hangers, coat hooks
121.9 × 66 × 1.3 cm each
Minneapolis, Walker Art Center
Anonymous gift, 2001

Gary Simmons is New York-born artist now living and working in Los Angeles. His practice uses icons and stereotypes of American popular culture to explore race, cultural politics, and memory. He has long remained interested in the intersection of the politics of racial identity and the idea of the past and the way in which the vagueness of time affects our understanding of the present. He is perhaps best known for his "erasure drawings" in which he draws in chalk on slate-painted panels or walls. He then smudges the work with his hands creating a ghostly effect. Even then, Simmons's practice also includes sculpture and installation, often employing references to cartoons, films, pedagogical settings, or even musical scores.

Upon receiving his MFA from the California Institute of the Arts in 1990, Simmons began working on the erasure drawings which would become his signature over the next few decades. At the same time, his work was still very much grounded in sculpture, through which he would often tackle issues of racial violence most directly and confrontationally through works that used objects and symbols of extreme violence in works such as *Duck, Duck, Noose* and *Klan Gate*.

Whether direct and confrontational or subtle and subversive, Simmons has always turned his attention toward that which is unseen, unspoken, or underrecognized, and asks us to reflect on culpability, history, and the courage to say what must be said.

Physically, *Us & Them* [10.1] is a soft, comfortable work. It is comprised of two white cotton robes, hanging invitingly on hooks waiting to be worn. The words *Us* and *Them* are embroidered in gold on the backs, which face the audience. The presentation is in keeping with the minimalist, object driven aesthetics of its moment. It seems welcomely simple. Hiding within this veneer of minimal, easy comfort is a deeply uncomfortable and rough subject.

In this work, Simmons is asking the viewer to effectively choose which robe to wear. In offering us this choice, in asking us to take a side Simmons reveals our own affiliation between two camps. The language of "us" and "them" not only directly establishes an in-group and an out-group but does so in a way that mirrors the kinds of language used to continue racial discrimination. The question forces viewers to confront their own standing within systemic racism and confront the reality of which side they have been placed compared to what they may choose.

The relationship between the words, subject matter, and tactile comfort of the robes opens further questions that are not initially apparent through its presentation. The material of cotton plays a central role, suggesting not only the comfort and luxury previously mentioned, but also the role that enslaved people played in the history of this material, and its pivotal role in the history of the United States as both an agricultural product and symbol of its historic oppression of Black people. It suggests that underneath the decisions and effects surrounding language lies an uncomfortable history that we would be willing to wear without thinking.

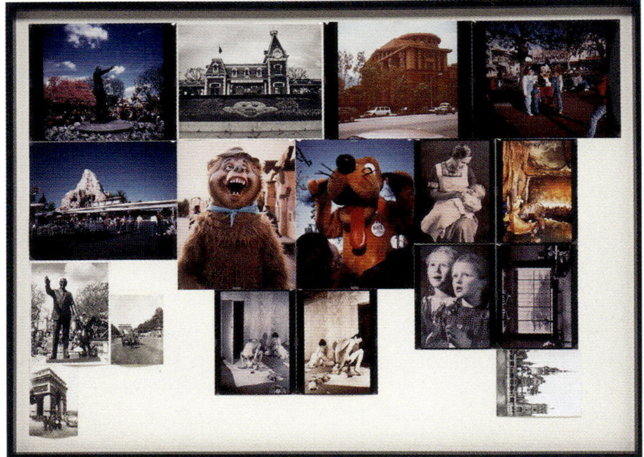

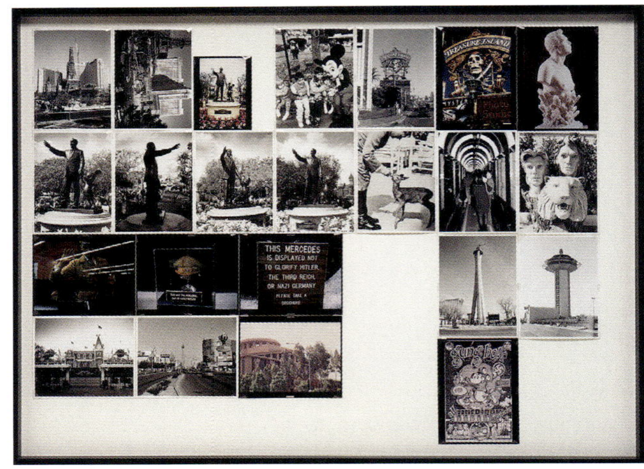

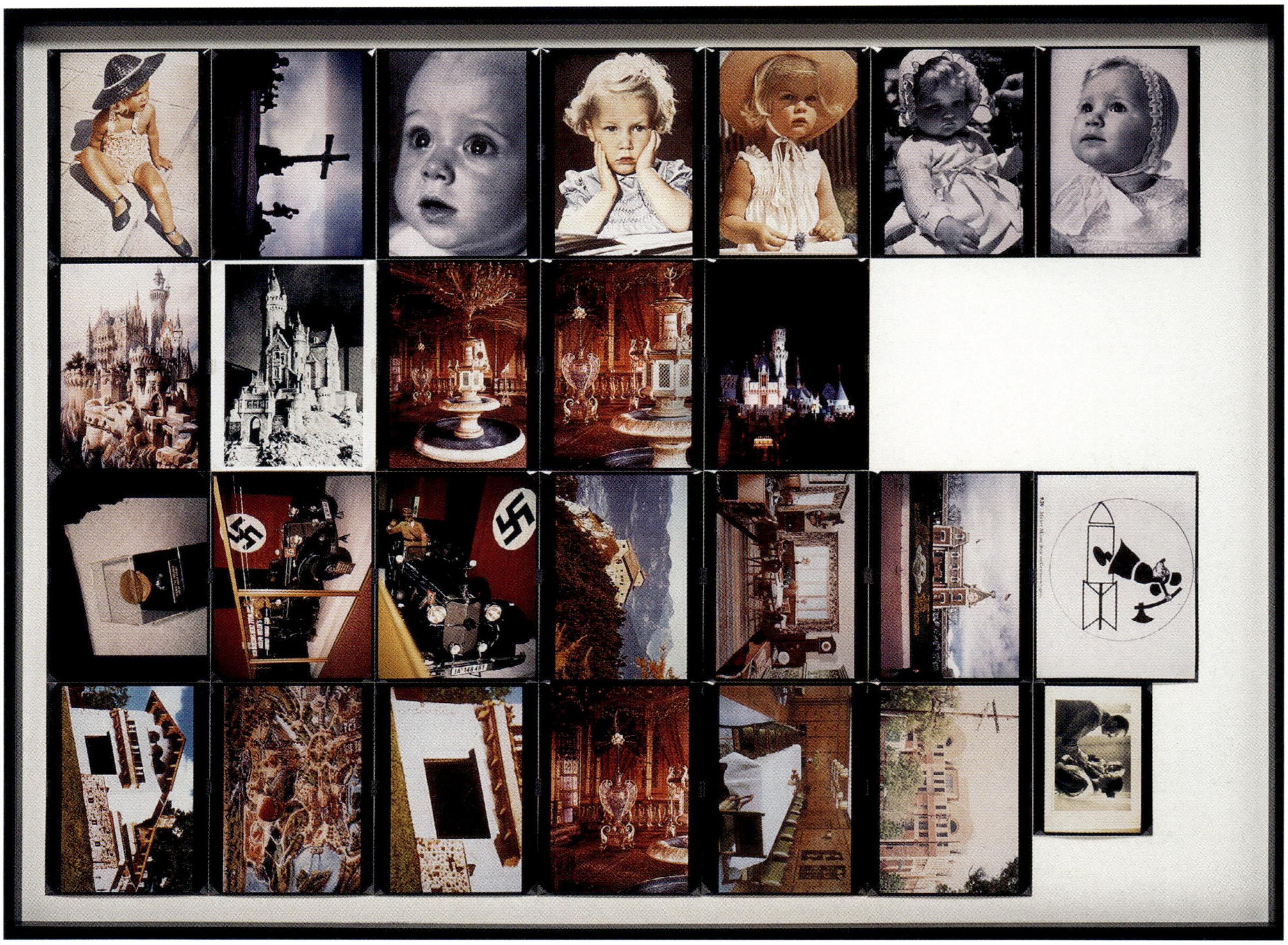

[10.2]

Perhaps the final provocation of this work was best expressed by artist and curator Charles Gaines who, upon showing this work in the show *Theater of Refusal: Black Art and Mainstream Criticism* (1993), asks, "Is it true, however, that aesthetic judgments are different from social/political ones? Can [critics] separate [their] feelings about racism from [their] aesthetic judgments, particularly aesthetic judgments about a work whose subject is race?" *Us & Them* asks to see differently and, in doing so, to complicate our own feelings of identity, belonging, and ultimately the line between aesthetics and politics.

*WILLIAM HERNANDEZ-LUEGE*

**PAUL MCCARTHY**
(Salt Lake City, Utah 1945)

[10.2]
***Documents***
**1995–99**
color photographs
157.5 × 218.4 × 8.3 cm each of 8
Minneapolis, Walker Art Center
T. B. Walker Acquisition Fund, 2001

To label Paul McCarthy's years of artistic output as "a body of work" would strain the use of the phrase. With its presumptions of a neatly wrapped-up oeuvre, the phrase is hopelessly inappropriate to describe the breadth of forms his practice has taken: a hole in the wall that is a film, gagging-on-hot dogs performances, giant inflatable sculptures—let alone buffoonery about Osama bin Laden and the Queen of England. Yet the "body of work" metaphor would also be misplaced in suggesting a summary of the more literal corpora that inhabit McCarthy's world. Here bodies inexorably gush—puking, shitting, bleeding, ejaculating, and giving birth in clownish acts of debauchery and depravity, slapstick sex, and sordid secrets.

McCarthy studied at the University of Utah in the late 1960s, making door-size paintings with black oil and using rags and his hands as surrogate brushes. Several of the thirteen short films collected as *Black and White Tapes* (1970/75–1993)—made while continuing his studies in California—extend a kind of perverse painting practice. In *Face Painting—Floor, White Line* (1972), for example, the artist drags himself across his studio floor, pouring paint in front of him, while in another tape he petulantly flogs walls with a paint-soaked sheet. Of these films, *Ma Bell* (1971) is most prescient of what was to come in McCarthy's guise as a performer. While smothering each

page of a Los Angeles telephone directory to make something resembling an oil-and-cotton wool lasagna, he began cackling and muttering, seemingly with no forethought, acting in character for the first time.

McCarthy's trademark live performances often become well-lubricated, penis-fixated, tragicomic epics—some would last five hours or more—through an increasingly fluent language of costumes, props such as rubber masks and dolls, and foodstuffs like ketchup, mayonnaise, and raw meat. Deranged, improvised, yet repetitive tableaux were tempered with feral desire, castration narratives, and Oedipal trauma. In works such as *Meat Cake* (1974), *Doctor* (1978), *Monkey Man* (1980), and *Popeye, Judge and Jury* (1983), gender-morphing grotesques that mashed up the human with the non-human drew as much on the no-budget teen "slasher" movie as on the ambivalent heritage of the clown. Unlike the real blood-and-guts of the Vienna Actionists—who were concerned with quasi-religious rituals of communion and redemption—McCarthy dredged below the veneer of the "perfect" family and "proper" behavior with a knowingly bankrupt symbolism. In this primordial semiotic universe,

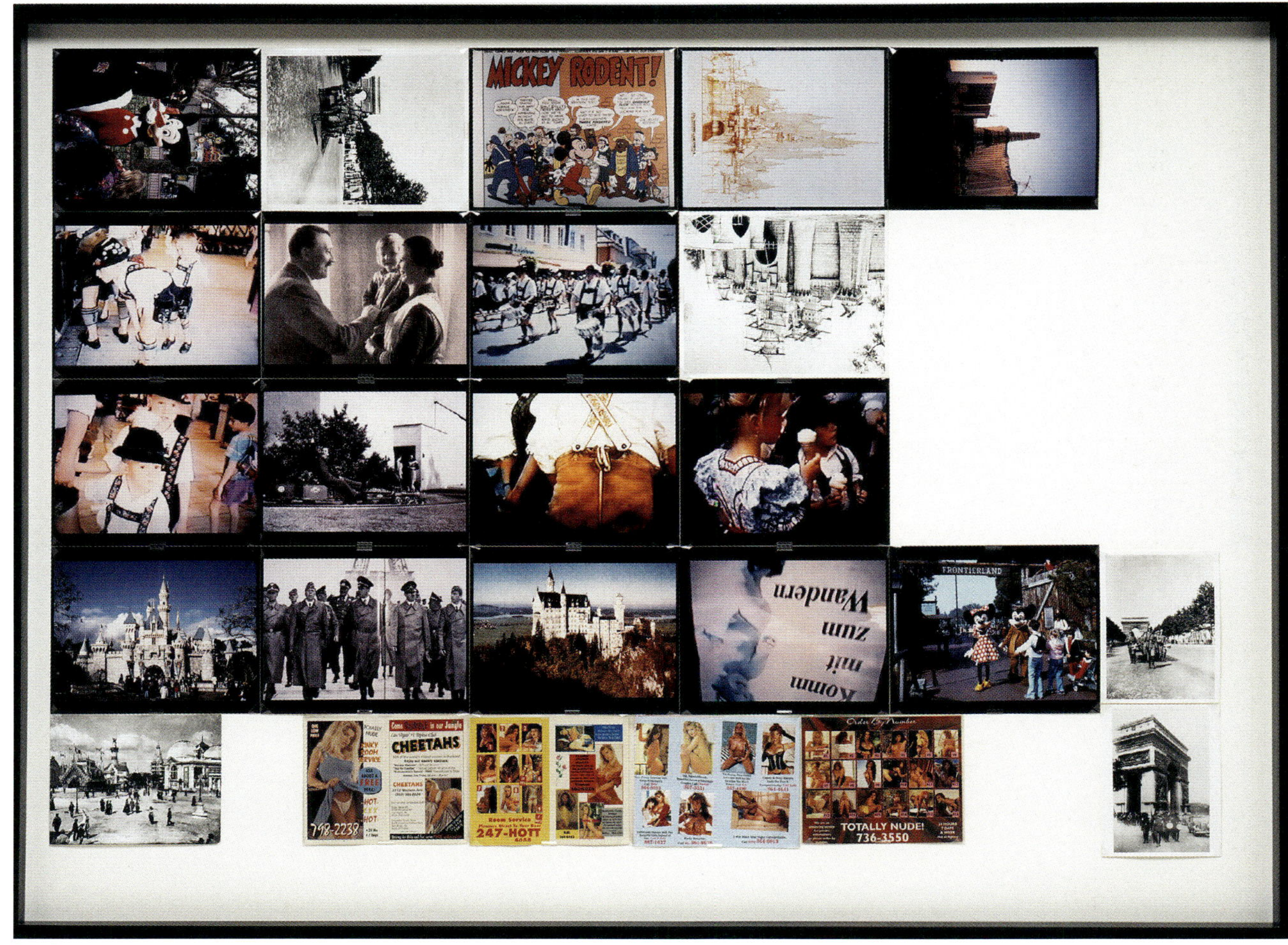



[10.2]

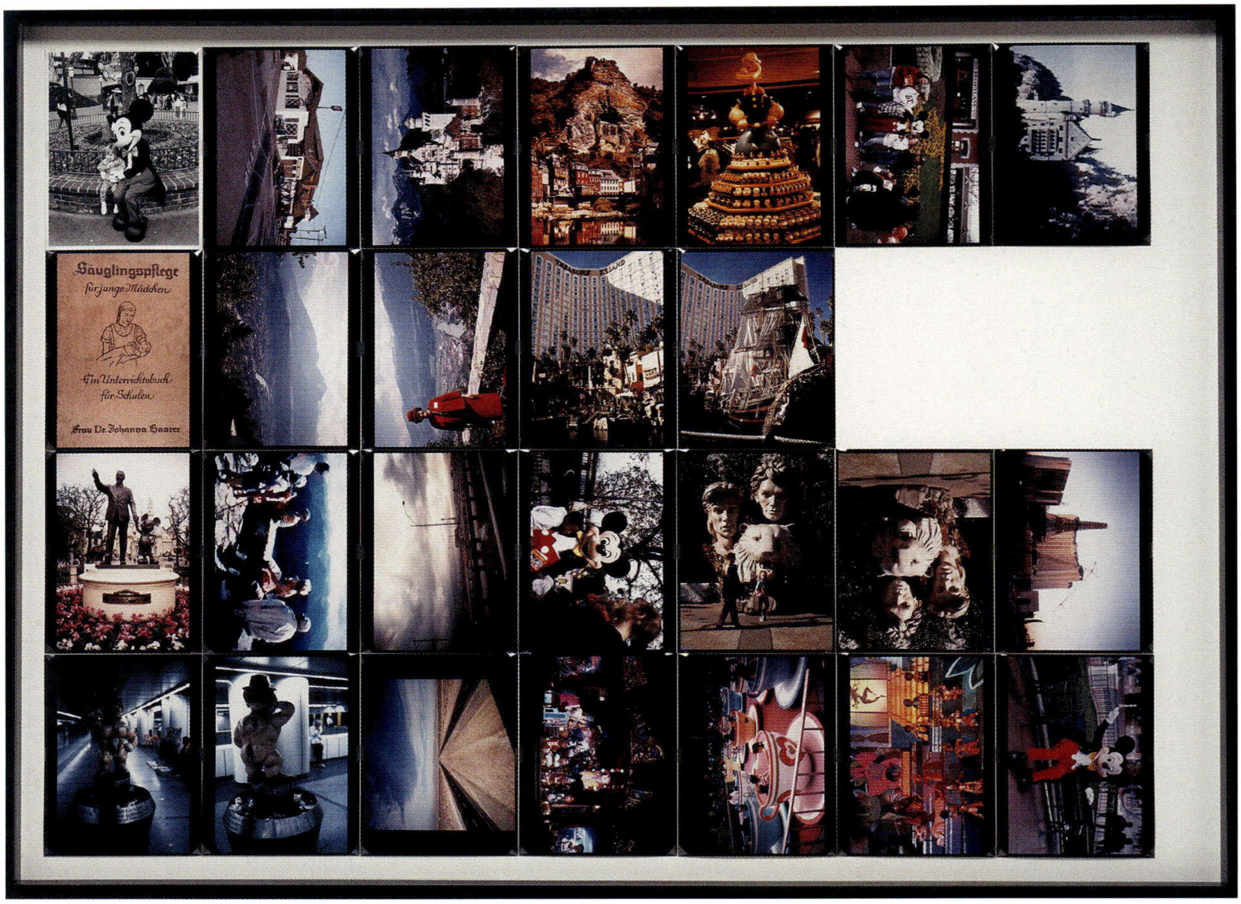
Säuglingspflege
für junge Mädchen
Ein Unterrichtsbuch
für Schulen
Frau Dr. Johanna Haarer

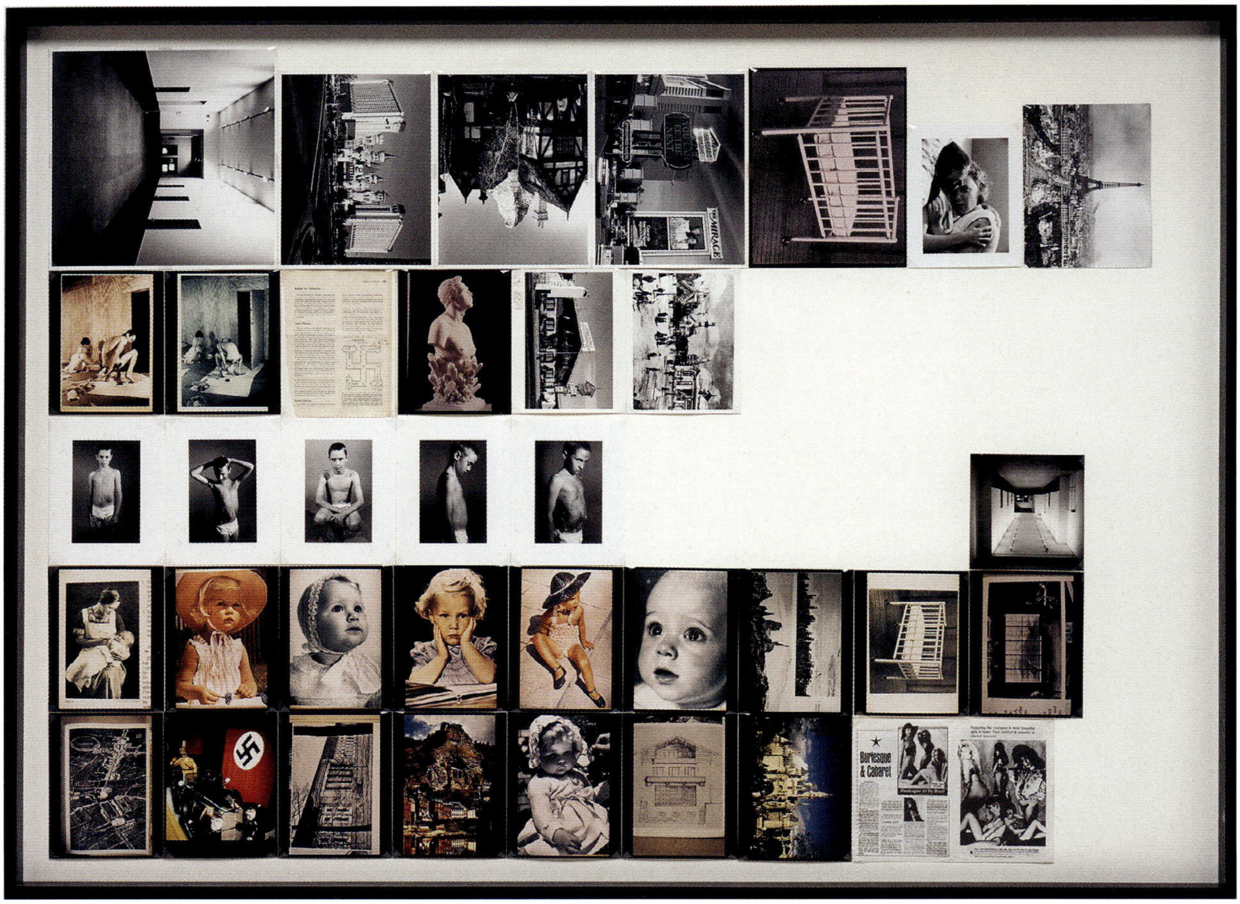
MIRAGE
Burlesque
& Cabaret

[10.2]

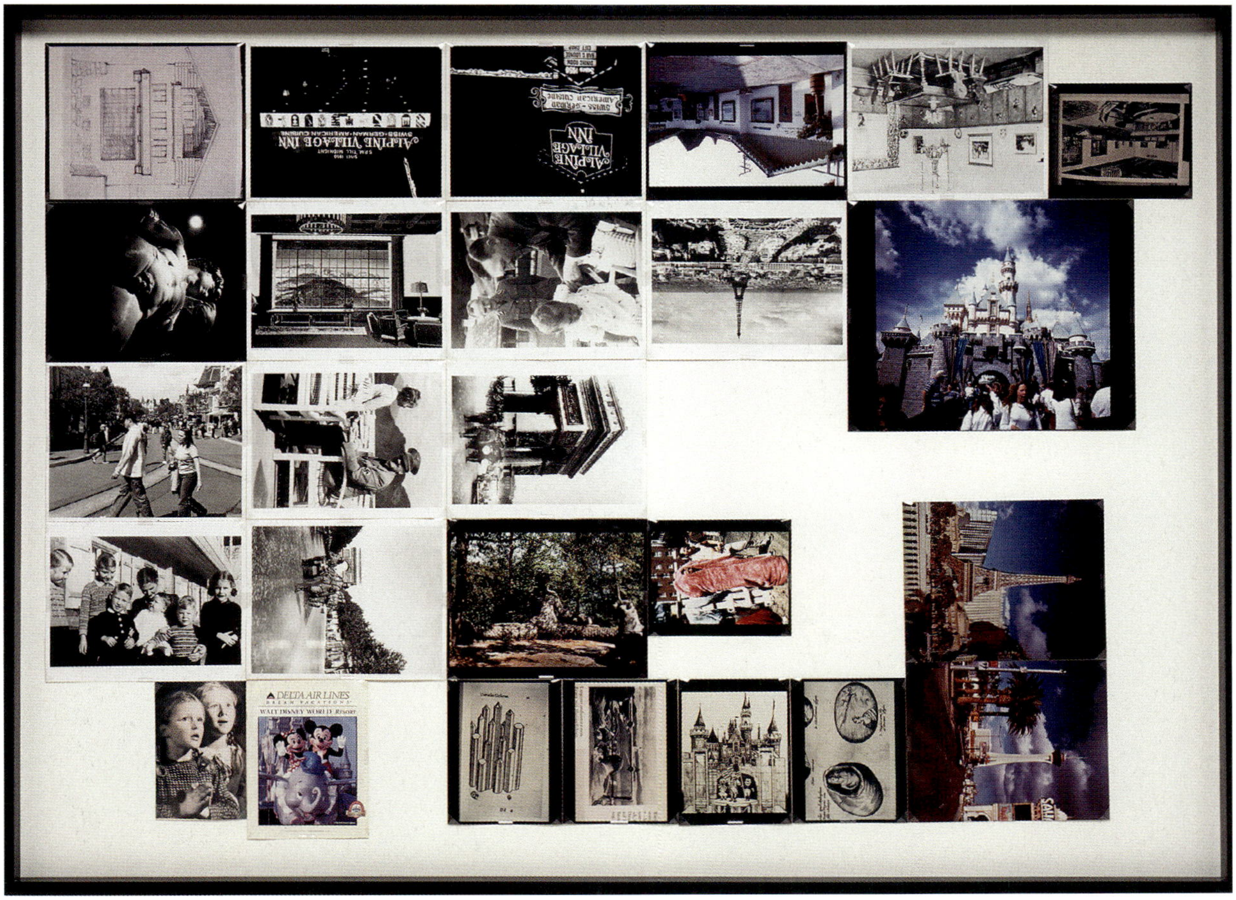

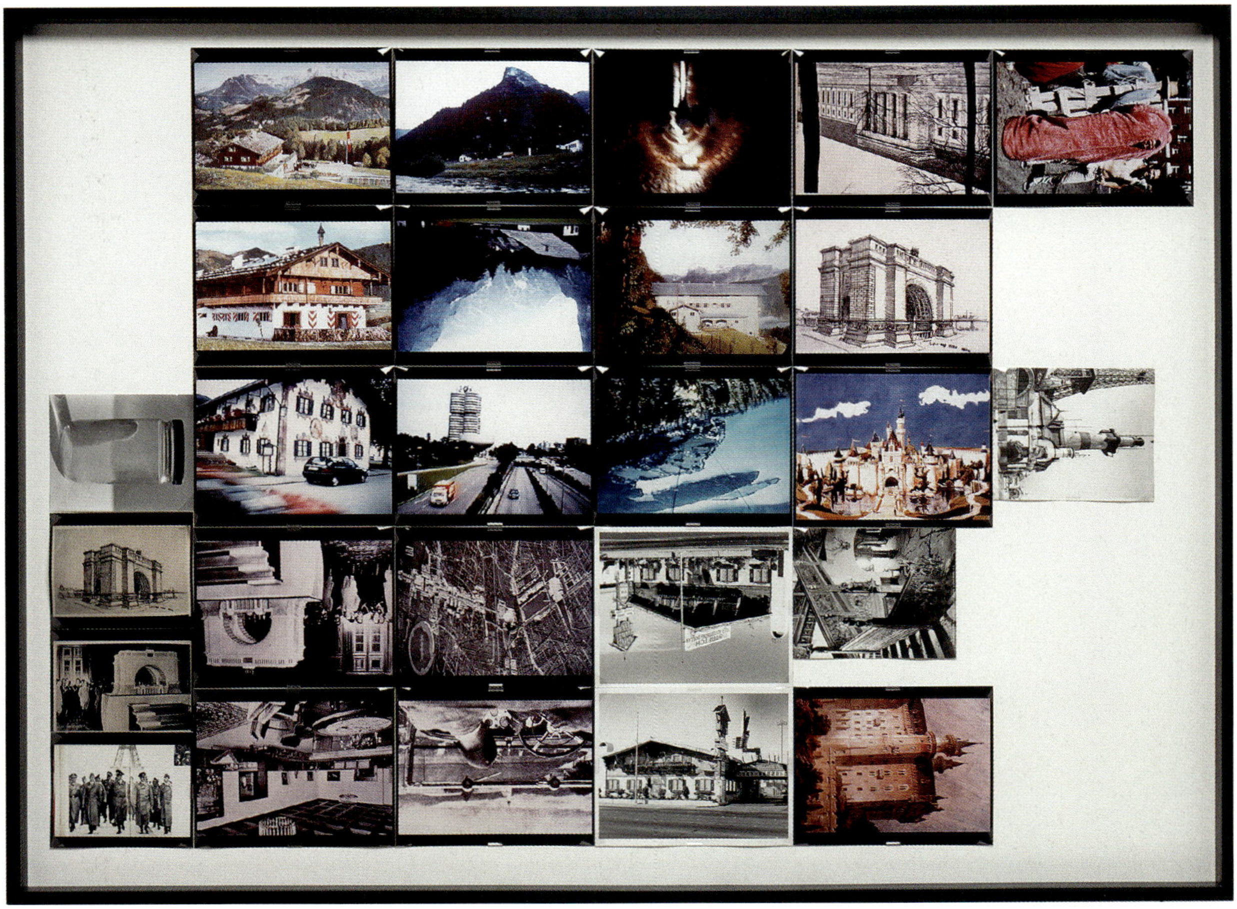

[10.2]

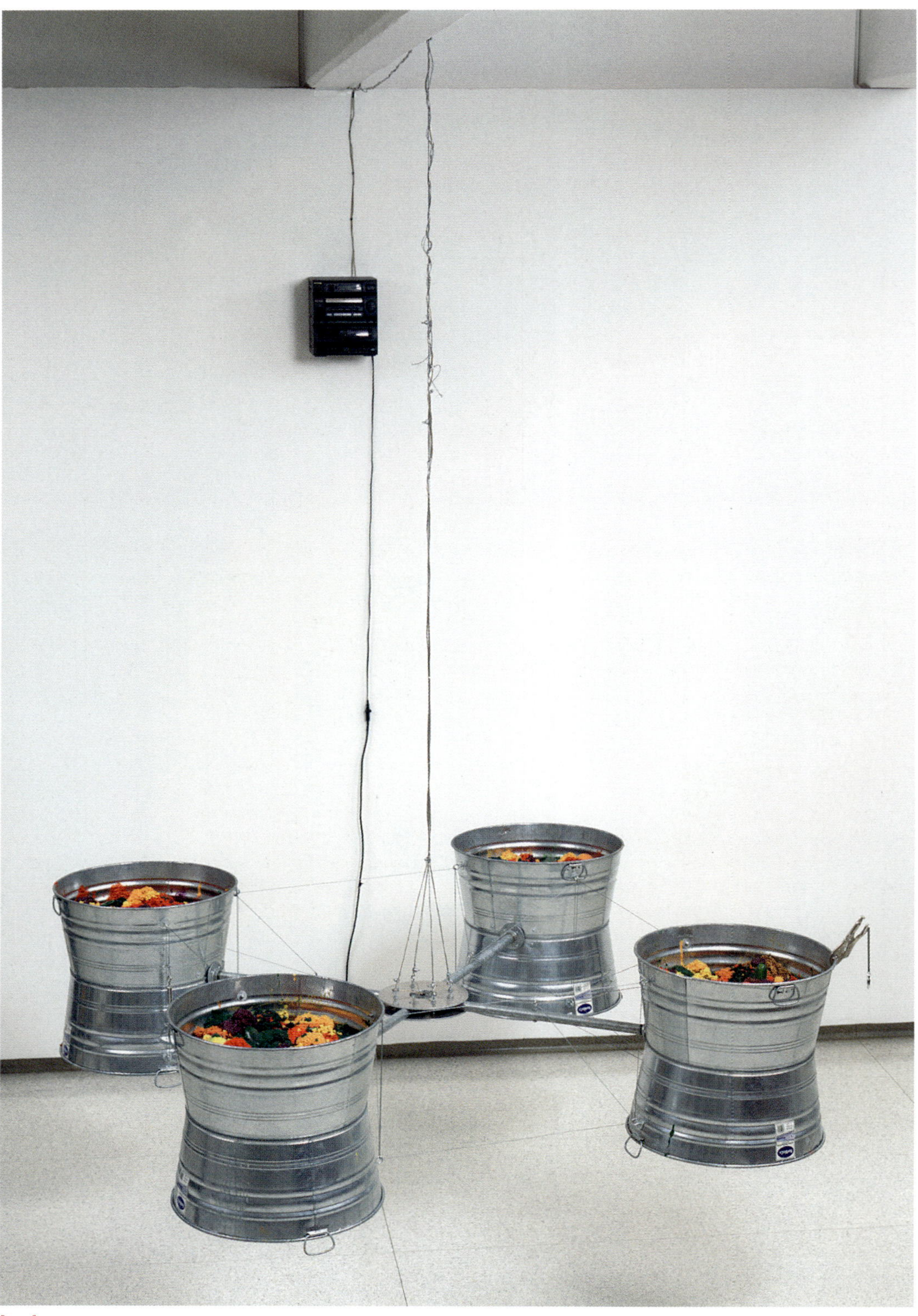

"Daddy's Sauce" was capable of representing both diaper-filling excrement and the taboos of incestuous desire.

McCarthy ceased live work in 1984, feeling that his performances had become too theatrical, too vaudevillian (he had preferred a small, invited audience). Focusing on the way in which history and folktales are framed by theme parks, television, and Hollywood, his vocabulary as a visual artist crystallized into a world in which kinetic mannequins depicted tree fornication and bestiality, and fluffy sculptures sported preposterous penises.

*Documents* (1995–99) [10.2] is a photographic series prompted by an invitation to McCarthy to guest edit an issue of the French magazine *Documents sur l'art* and shown as part of the 2000 Walker Art Center-organized exhibition *Let's Entertain*. Like a visual scrapbook of installation works such as *Bavarian Kick* (1987), *Rear View* (1991), *Heidi* (with Mike Kelley, 1992), *Pinocchio Pipenose Householddilemma* (1994), and *Mechanized Chalet* (1999), *Documents'* eight panels of photographs abut apparent charm with latent malevolence. The work operates within a culture where the legacy of Nazi terror in World War II Europe can emerge as easily via the camp "Do-Re-Mi" of the movie *The Sound of Music* as it can in the defense of O. J. Simpson. A shot of a Bavarian castle, which might adorn a chocolate box, is put on the same visual field with one of a waxwork Hitler waving merrily from his car. The fiberglass peaks of Disney's Magic Kingdom clash with Tirolean postcard views, and giant busts of an aptly Wagnerian Siegfried and tiger-taming Roy encounter snapshots of Albert Speer's master plans or greet a Mickey mascot.

The status of the photograph as a document, as the unquestioned bearer of truth, becomes desperately muddled in these juxtapositions, which suggest that Disney's corporatization of childhood is just as tyrannical as Hitler's repurposing of Teutonic folklore. As the artist has written of this piece: "The initial premise was to investigate Hitler's Germany; the Paris, France, Exposition of 1900; Las Vegas, Nevada; and Disneyland, Anaheim, California, each location being a particular vision of Utopia and constituting a geographical straight line from East to West" (Artist's statement, circa 2001, Walker Art Center Archives). The pitch-perfect, pitch-black tone of *Documents* seems to elude, just barely, the impression that it has a lesson to teach—it is already too embroiled in conspiracy to parse any blame. *MAX ANDREWS* (revised versione of text, published in *Bits and Pieces*, 2005, 380)

## MIKE KELLEY
(Detroit 1954–Los Angeles 2012)

[10.3]
### *Four Part Butter-Scene N'Ganga*
### 1997
galvanized washtubs, pigmented vermiculite, plastic fruits and vegetables, cable, speaker wire, audio system, CD, adjustable wrench, locking pliers
63.5 × 281.9 × 281.9 cm
Minneapolis, Walker Art Center
T. B. Walker Acquisition Fund, 1997

Starting in the late 1970s, Mike Kelley produced a funny, nasty, transgressive, sharp body of work that takes as its target notions of taste, morality, authority, and social responsibility and addresses the American social and psychological condition. Kelley grew up in a working-class community in the suburbs of Detroit, where he became involved with the counterculture scenes of rock and free jazz—from noise-rock pioneers Iggy and the Stooges to cosmic jazz musician Sun Ra—that became ideal critical tools for subverting ideological orders. Kelley moved to Los Angeles in 1976, and it was there, as a student at CalArts, that he produced a series of performance works in which he collapsed his interest in popular culture with an acute awareness of art history, including such movements such as Dada, Futurism, Fluxus, and Viennese Actionism; artists like Vito Acconci, Guy de Cointet, La Monte Young, and Öyvind Fahlström; and events such as the Destruction in Art Symposium (London, 1966). Based on the urge to overcome the limitations projected on sculpture by a postminimal, postconceptual art discourse, his early performances (first realized at the Los Angeles Contemporary Exhibitions space in 1978) consisted of the artist manipulating handmade props that might also be seen as performative sculpture.

If the earliest performances were merely organized around nonsensical recitations and incantations about the objects Kelley built and their fluctuating meanings, over the years they became longer and more scripted, involving collaborators such as artist Tony Oursler and the band Sonic Youth. The performances also provided an early structure for the core content of Kelley's work: an attempt to give shape to his unforgiving representation of the American psyche and its obsessions with religion, national history, education, adolescence, sexual identity, and the role of gender in the structure of social practices. These performances and their props have defined a unique visual language as well as a methodology relying on a distrust of conventional aesthetics, both of which are still at play in his work today.

In the sculpture *Four Part Butter-Scene N'Ganga* (1997) [10.3], four washtubs full of brightly colored, mysteriously textured gooey stew and plastic fruits and vegetables are connected by a fixture of pipe and wire. At its base, each washtub is attached to a second, inverted tub that houses a speaker emitting excerpts from the soundtrack of the violently erotic "butter scene" in Bernardo Bertolucci's 1972 film *Last Tango in Paris*. The entire construction is suspended from the ceiling in an × shape. The tubs themselves are estimations of "n'ganga pots," cauldrons containing a fetid stew used in Santería rituals. According to Kelley, "The n'ganga is considered the repository of enslaved tortured souls who are bound to carry out the evil spirits of the magician [. . .] the n'ganga stew is the limitless erotic made manifest [. . .] it is the pot which gives chaos its form and, in doing so, limits it" (Kelley 1996, 21). The sculpture reflects on the fear of the unknown, of the different. Starting with a 1989 news item about the abduction of a twenty-one-year-old white college student from Texas by a drug-smuggling gang who practiced black magic, Kelley takes this source to the next level by connecting it to Bertolucci's film, an "icon" of cultural and sexual aggression in which an aging American man (Marlon Brando) has his way with a young French woman (Maria Schneider). Sexuality and otherness constitute the American "ecology of fear" that Kelley is referring to in this X-rated and X-shaped installation.

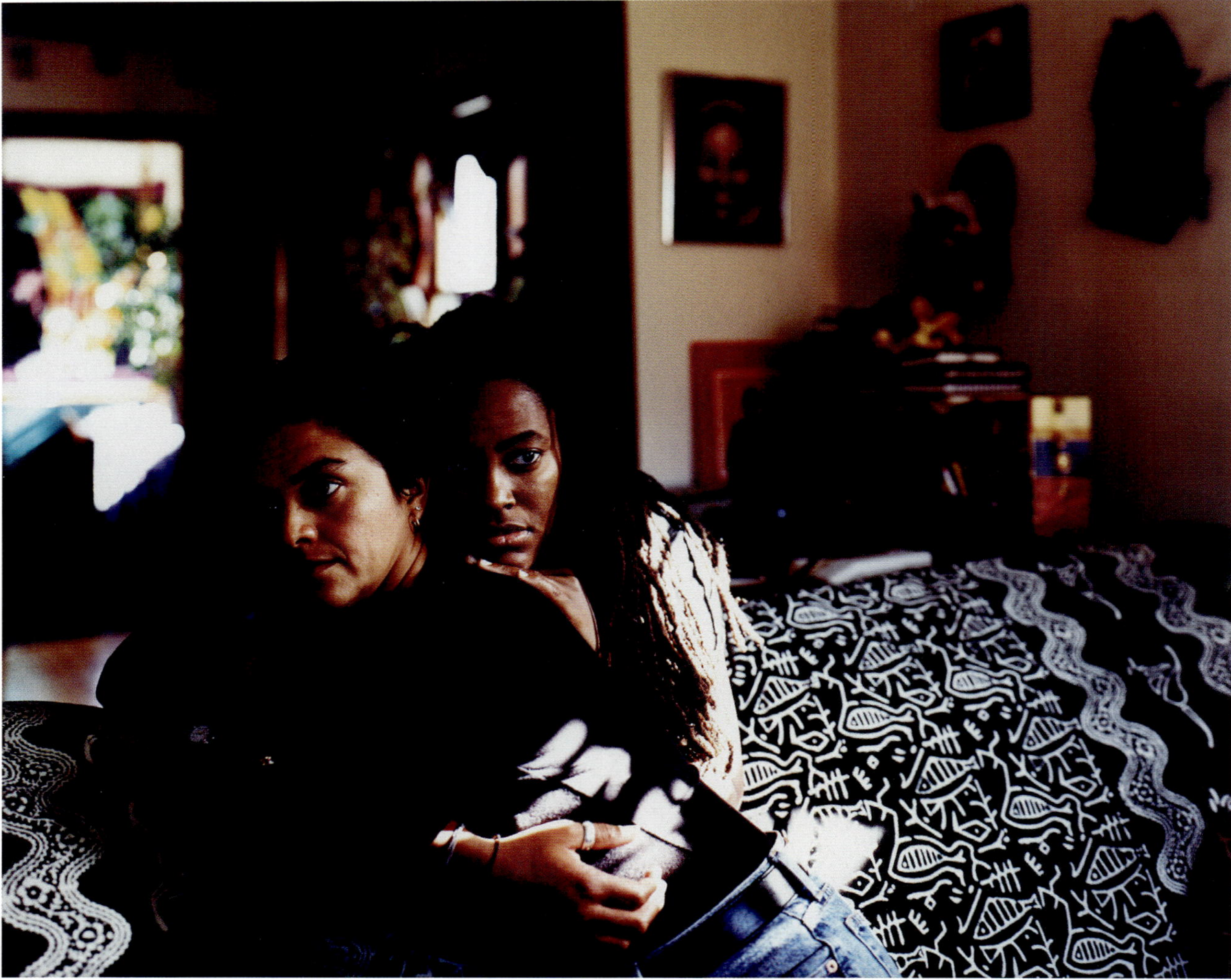

[10.4]

The formal aspect, whether the X-shaped mobile or the binary structure of the inverted washtubs, appeared in Kelley's work as early as the "demonstrational" sculptures or performance-related diagrams of the late 1970s. Such a shape, answering neither to the abstract code nor to the figurative tradition, has been analyzed by art historian Howard Singerman as a testimony to Kelley's knowledge of structuralism and the writings of Claude Lévi-Strauss: "The binary operation is, for structuralism, the 'smallest common denominator of all thoughts'; appropriately, it is marked in structuralism's formal diagrams by an encircled X. The × lies at the center of the world and it builds the world in its image, through its repetition. But if it is the world's core—its content—it is also, as Kelley insists, empty. The center is not one but two, not presence but absence" (Singerman 1993). *Four Part Butter-Scene N'Ganga* [10.3] seems to be an anomaly that mirrors acknowledged foundations of cultural dysfunction through a formal structure that resists any identifiable categorization.

Kelley's work provides a topography of the American subject as it develops through social, personal, political, and historical spaces. Informed by his knowledge of subversive countercultures, vernacular traditions, high art, and psychology, the work elaborates a methodology of watchful disrespect that leads the viewer to reconsider hidden, familiar things—what Sigmund Freud named the Uncanny—that have undergone repression only to reemerge again (Kelley 2003, 70–99).
*PHILIPPE VERGNE* (revised version of text, published in *Bits and Pieces*, 2005, 312–314)

**CATHERINE OPIE**
(Sandusky, Ohio 1961)

[10.4]
***Norma & Eyenga, Minneapolis, Minnesota***
**1998**
Edition: 1/5; chromogenic print
103.2 × 128.6 cm
Minneapolis, Walker Art Center
Clinton and Della Walker Acquisition Fund, 1999

[10.5]
***Tammy Rae & Kaia, Durham, North Carolina***
**1998**
Edition: 1/5; chromogenic print
103.2 × 128.6 cm
Minneapolis, Walker Art Center
Clinton and Della Walker Acquisition Fund, 1999

Catherine Opie's entire artistic career can be seen as one long photographic road trip across this continent in search not of the American dream but rather a dream of an idea of community. Her works—whether the extremely formal, color-saturated portraits of friends in the lesbian and gay leather community of Los Angeles that brought her to the art world's attention in 1993 or those documenting that city's ubiquitous concrete highway overpasses, mini-malls, and architectural façades—are each animated by a single question: How does one create a portrait of a community? This question provides the motivating impetus behind Opie's *Domestic* series. These portraits of lesbian couples, families, and friends in their households, taken in 1998 as the artist embarked on a three-month odyssey in an RV to nine different cities across the country, were an attempt to "document the lesbian dream" (quoted in Ferguson 2000, 48). The catalyst for this series could be found in an earlier work, *Self-Portrait/Cutting* (1993), a color photograph of the artist isolated against a lush green backdrop with her bare back turned toward the viewer. This was, however, a self-portrait with a difference, as Opie's back became a surface for a naïve, childlike line drawing—cut into her skin with a razor—depicting two women holding hands in front of a house. It is paradoxically a heartbreakingly sweet image, notable for its ability to transform what might seem like a violent act into a beautiful one. As she suggests, this image is "about an idealistic view of what domesticity is, and what I want from

it" (quoted in Allen 1998, 2). This desire became the basis for her *Domestic* series, which expands our understanding of how families can be constructed by presenting its lesbian subjects in a powerful and dignified manner in the realm of a profoundly recognizable American domesticity.

Communities can also be portrayed in terms of the architectural spaces they inhabit, as the artist demonstrated in 2001 when she began a year-long residency project at the Walker Art Center. The resulting body of work was a series of fourteen large-scale color photographs of icehouses—indigenous, ad hoc architectural structures that populate the winter landscape of Minnesota. Like one of Italo Calvino's "invisible cities," these recreational fishing outposts manifest themselves organically on the frozen lakes, creating temporary, seasonal communities that cut across social distinctions. In the spring, these ice villages disappear as quickly as they had appeared, their citizens dispersing to their other lives. Under Opie's meticulous

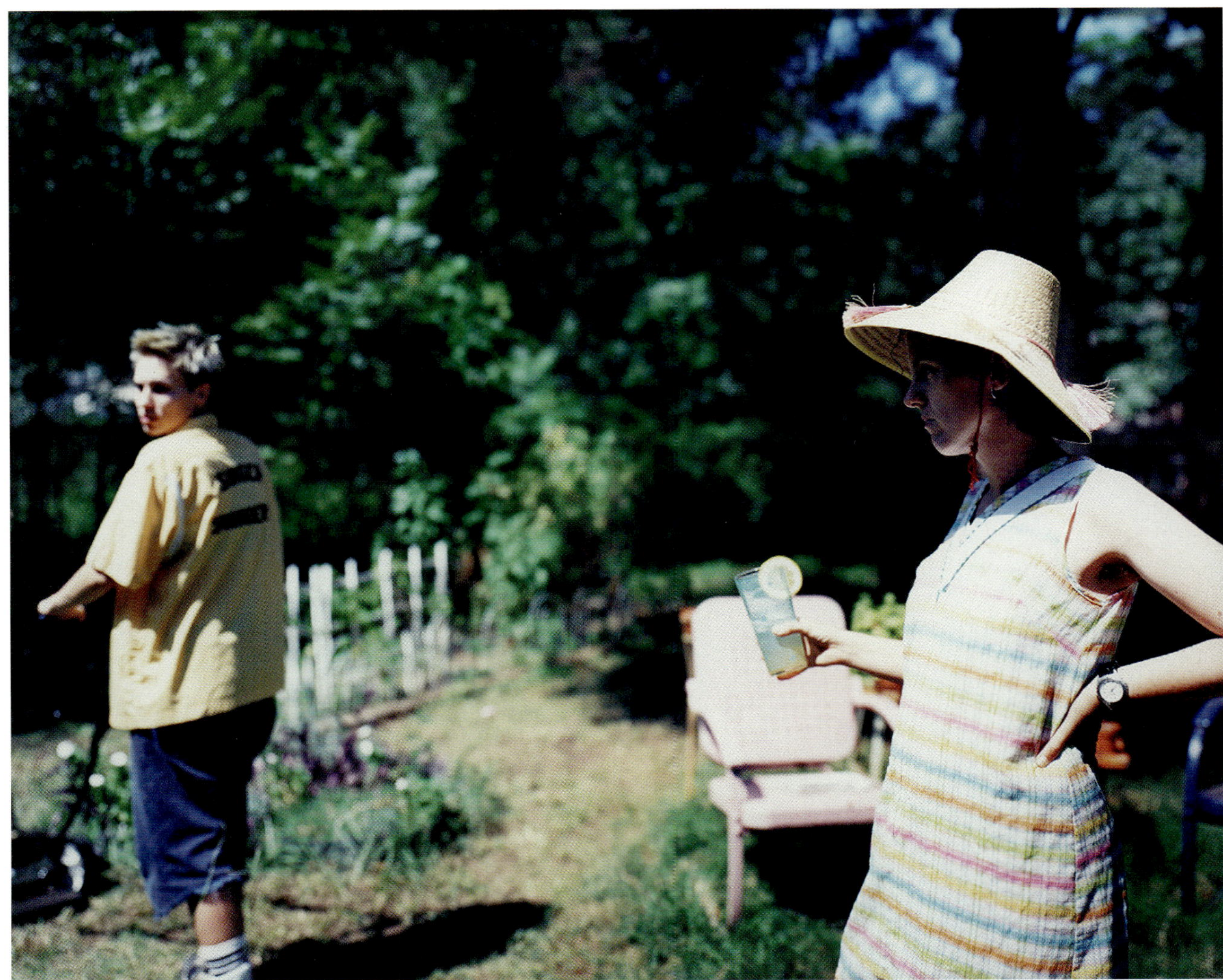



[10.5]

lens, the colorful shacks respire from foreground to background along a horizon line that from image to image never wavers. Devoid of human presence, these almost abstract, minimal structures become anthropomorphic markers of their inhabitants, who use them to fish, socialize, and while away the winter hours. Taken together, the two bodies of work present divergent, if complementary, methods for documenting their respective communities and can take their place in the documentary tradition in American photography dating back to the work of Robert Frank and Walker Evans, who both took their own road trips in search of America. Opie has adapted those formal techniques and social thematics to her own subjects, enlisting the genres of architectural and portrait photography in order to trace the diverse, shifting contours of the conceptual horizon line of the American community.

*DOUGLAS FOGLE* (revised version of text, published in *Bits and Pieces*, 2005, 442)

## MARK BRADFORD

(Los Angeles 1961)

[10.6]
***Analog***
**2004**
oil and paper on canvas
318.8 × 318.5 cm
Minneapolis, Walker Art Center
T. B. Walker Acquisition Fund, 2006

Mark Bradford is a painter who lives and works in Los Angeles, California. He is best known for paintings that incorporate collage techniques and a wide range of materials. His practice involves highly physical processes in which he manipulates the surface of works by cutting, tearing, soaking, and sanding, creating a range of textures and gradations. While most recognizable for this very formal practice, his work is also driven by conceptual concerns that affect the choice of materials, the scale of the piece, and the process by which it is made.

Bradford says of his work: "Think about all the white noise out there in the street: all the beepers and blaring culture— cell phones, amps, chimed-out wheels, and synthesizers. I pick up a lot of that energy in my work, from the posters, which act as memory of things pasted and things past. You can peel away the layers of papers and it's like reading the streets through signs."

After Graduating from the California Institute of the Arts, Bradford received his first solo exhibition at the Walter & McBean galleries, part of the San Francisco Art Institute, in 1998. He received wide public success after participating in the 2006 Whitney Biennial at the Whitney Museum of American Art, where he won the Bucksbaum Award. He continued to attract widespread acclaim, featuring in solo exhibitions at major museum in the United States, and representing the country at the 57th Venice Biennale with his solo exhibition *Tomorrow is Another Day*. His work is found in collections worldwide.

*Analog* [9.18], at first glance, appears as a tan series of stripes comprised of red and black shapes. To the left of the canvas lie five large white empty spaces which, almost like a footprint, walk their way down the composition from top to bottom. Upon closer inspection the painting is comprised of many layers of other materials which have been meticulously stacked on top of each other seemingly in no particular pattern. The various black and brown bands, red slips of paper, and black squares are interwoven so that no single element can come to the foreground. The resulting effect resembles a topographical map, or even an aerial view, of a city center.

While its forms are abstract, *Analog* can be read as a landscape painting. To create this work, Bradford built up the canvas with discarded materials such as printed billboard images and end papers for hair treatments. He then weathered and tore the surface with a sander to expose unintended layers and juxtapositions of color. By pulling material residue of his neighborhood into the painting, Bradford probes its character and alludes to the area's informal economic patterns, social networks, culture, and communities. Rather than create an actual map of the city, Bradford's conceptual map functions like a map-making machine. It aggregates these advertisements, billboard images, and other miscellaneous materials and then processes them into a single matrix upon which they are layered and then sanded down to access the archive just beneath the surface.

*Analog*, ultimately, can be seen as a map of the memory of a place. Like our own memories, it is comprised of fragments layered one upon another in bits and pieces until it forms a whole. Bradford makes it a map by demonstrating this process of accumulation and assimilation and by undoing the process itself. Bradford sands down the components of the painting until the method of its creation is transparent and navigable. It is a painting which seems to know itself and presents itself to the viewer in a way that resembles how we might come to know ourselves: one layer at a time.

*WILLIAM HERNANDEZ-LUEGE*

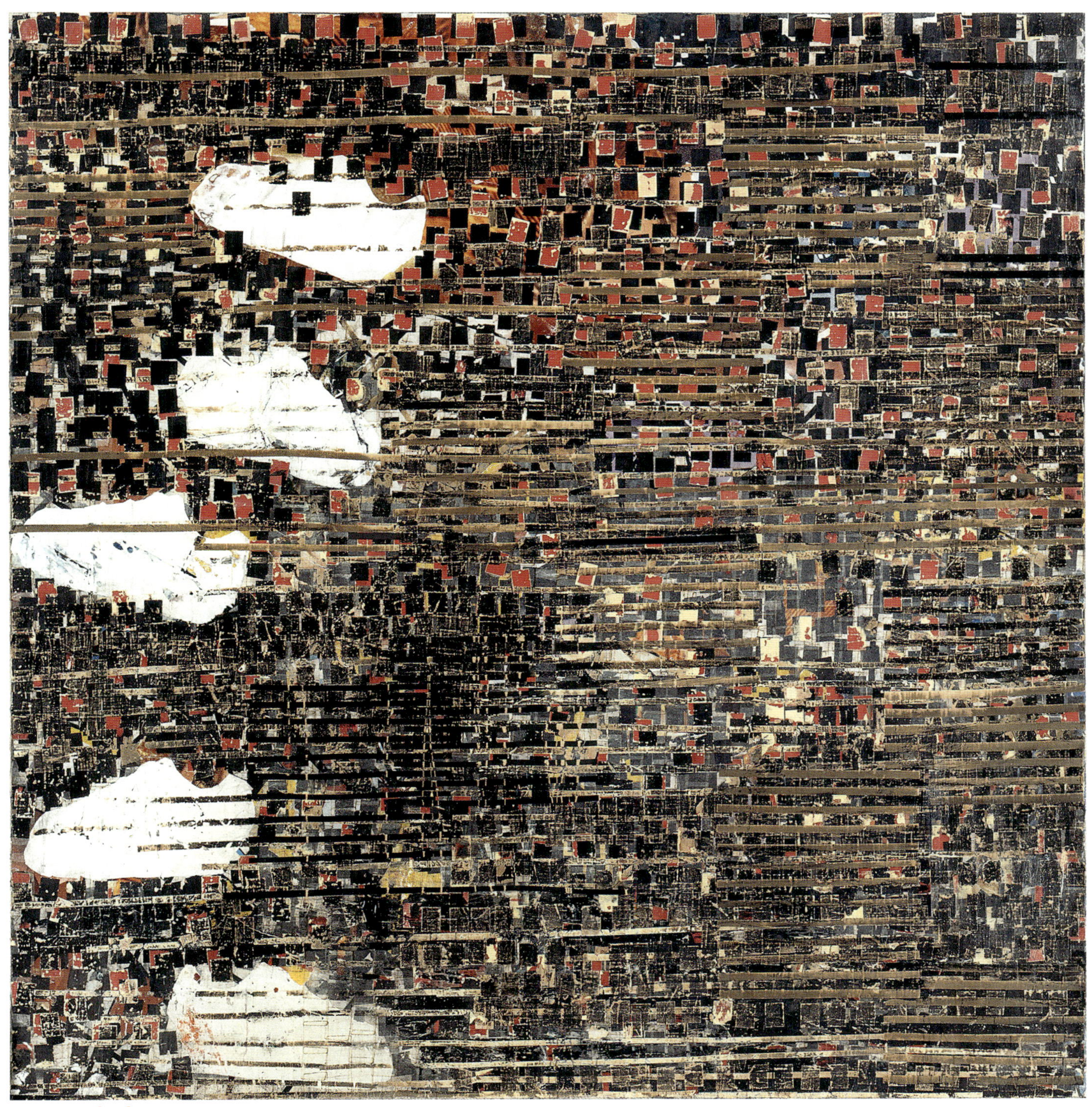

[10.6]

LUDOVICA SEBREGONDI

LUDOVICA SEBREGONDI

# CHRONOLOGY 1961–2001

## 1961

**JANUARY 20**
At noon on January 20, as per the US Constitution, President David "Ike" Eisenhower's term comes to an end. It is Inauguration Day, or Day One. John F. Kennedy (JFK) is sworn in as the thirty-fifth president of the US. ↓

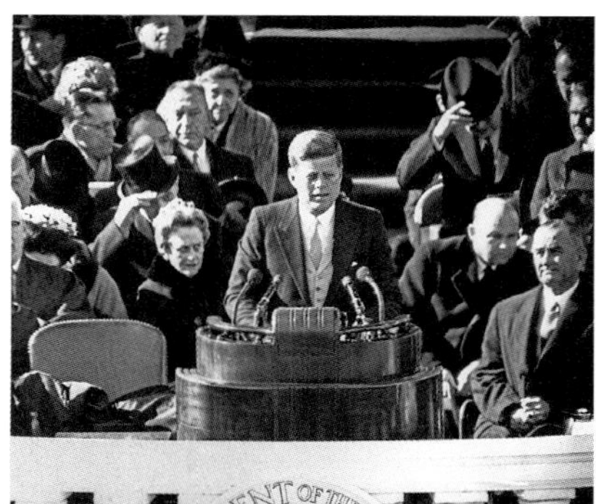

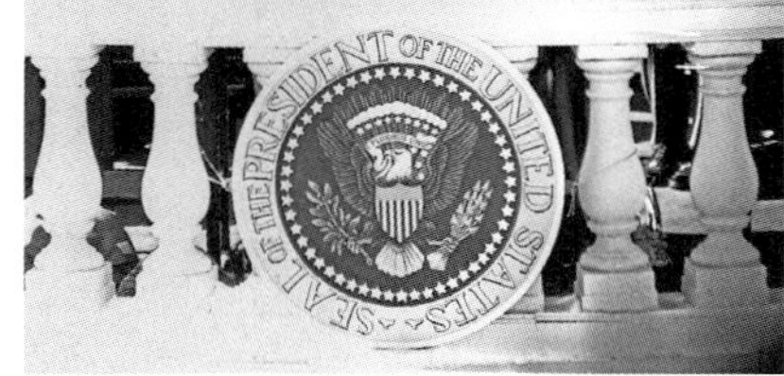

**APRIL 12**
Russian astronaut Yuri Gagarin is the first human in outer space, remaining in orbit for 1 hour and 48 minutes.

**APRIL 17**
The "Bay of Pigs" invasion fails in its attempt to overthrow Fidel Castro's government by using a group of CIA-trained Cubans who are either killed or captured.

**MAY 4**
The first Freedom Ride begins in Washington. These are civil rights protests in which blacks and whites travel together—unsegregated—on Greyhound buses, breaking the laws of the states that impose racial segregation on public transportation. The aim is to challenge the nonenforcement of the Supreme Court's ruling that declared that segregated buses were unconstitutional. The first Freedom Ride arrives in New Orleans on May 17, after traveling through Virginia, North and South Carolina, Georgia, Tennessee, Alabama, Mississippi, and Louisiana. The buses are assailed and attacked along the way. ↓

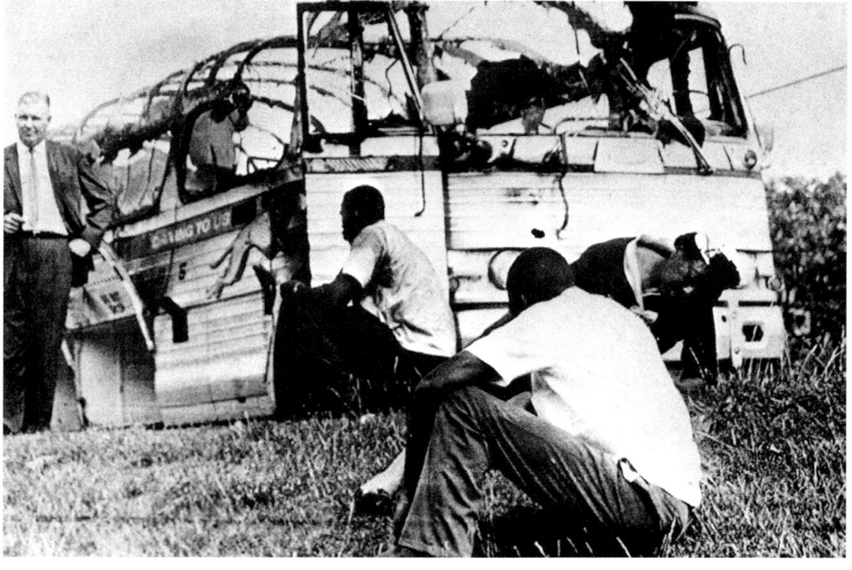

**MAY 31–JUNE 2**
President Kennedy and First Lady Jacqueline Lee Bouvier travel to Europe. While in Paris, Jackie is the center of attention for her elegance and sophistication. JFK refers to himself during a press call as "the man who accompanied Jacqueline Kennedy to Paris." Jackie is indeed a style icon, and her pale-hued two-piece suits, three strands of pearls, kitten heels, and pillbox hat created by Roy Halston Frowck make up the look she would wear at every official event, from Inauguration Day to Dallas.

**JUNE 3–4**
Kennedy is in Vienna. Due to the turbulent world situation (Cuba, Laos, Berlin), talks with Soviet Premier Nikita Khrushchev go nowhere. In an interview, Kennedy declares: "Now we have a problem in making our power credible, and Vietnam looks like the place."

**AUGUST 12–13**
To stop people from crossing over to the West, East Germany—with the help of the Soviet Union—begins building the Berlin Wall under cover of night. The wall is 155 kilometers long and divides the city into two sectors: East (under Soviet control) and West (under the influence of the Western powers).

**DECEMBER 11**
President John Fitzgerald Kennedy is committed to maintaining the independence of South Vietnam, and the first American helicopters arrive in Saigon (Ho Chi Minh City) along with four hundred soldiers.

## 1962

**JULY 9**
Bob Dylan records "Blowin' in the Wind," and adds it to the studio album *The Freewheelin' Bob Dylan* when it is released the following year. The line "How many roads must a man walk down before you call him a man?" becomes the manifesto of young antiwar protesters. ↓

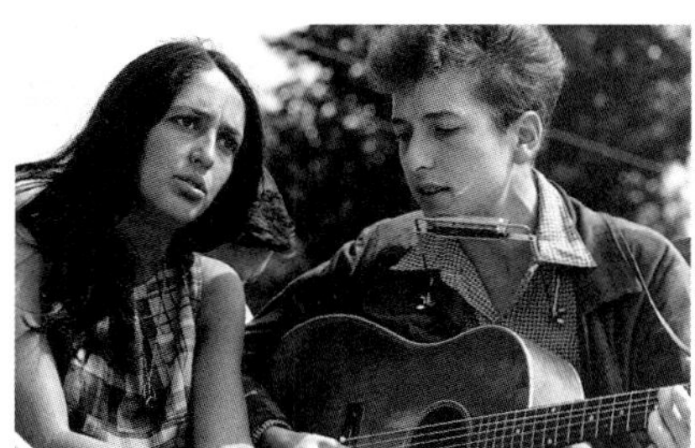

AUGUST 5
Marilyn Monroe dies.

OCTOBER 11
Pope John XXIII convenes the Vatican Council II, which comes to a close on December 8, 1965.

OCTOBER 14–28
Confrontation between the US and the USSR over the secret installation in Cuba of Soviet missile bases with nuclear missiles capable of reaching Washington DC and other cities in the US. Cold War tensions are at an all-time high, with serious risk of nuclear conflict. Despite the Soviet Union's denials, proof is provided that the missiles are on the island and the Soviet Union must publicly announce the dismantling of Cuban bases, while the US vows to conditionally withdraw its nuclear missiles from Turkey and Italy.

**NOVEMBER–DECEMBER**
***Jasper Johns* is the first exhibition organized by Ileana, Leo Castelli's ex-wife, in the Paris gallery opened with her husband Michael Sonnabend.** ↓

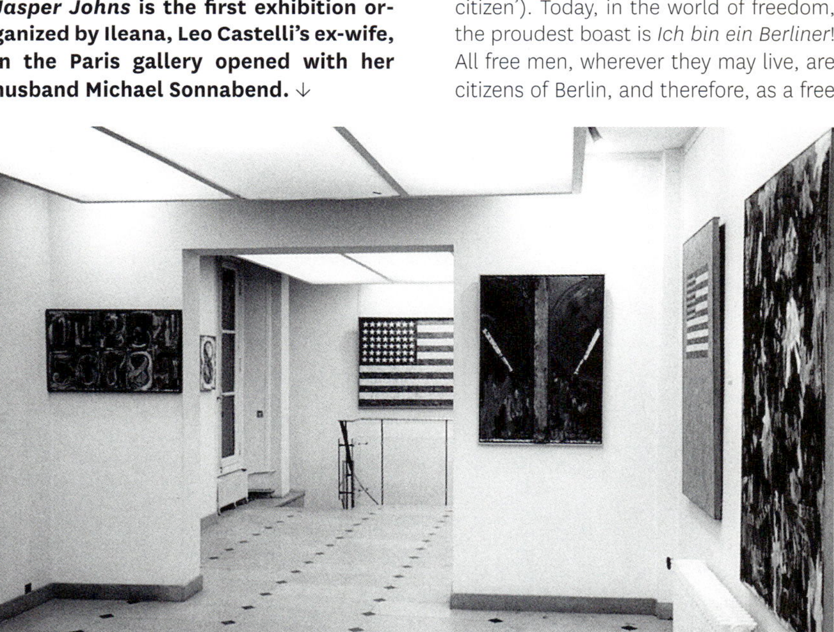

**Mark Rothko (along with Adolph Gottlieb, Philip Guston, and Robert Motherwell) cuts ties with Sidney Janis, who had shown the works of the Pop artists in his gallery.**

## 1963

MAY 2–10
In Birmingham, Alabama, civil rights protesters are attacked by police deploying ferocious police dogs.

**JUNE 5–30**
**Roy Lichtenstein show at the Galerie Ileana Sonnabend. After the opening Ileana writes the following to Leo Castelli: "There is an accumulative effect which by now has made a deep stir in the art world. The most invraisemblable conservative critics have come in to shake their canes at us! We're in for a marvelous massacre!"**

JUNE 26
During a speech delivered in West Berlin before a huge crowd, Kennedy utters some of his most famous words: "Two thousand years ago, the proudest boast was *civis Romanus sum* ('I am a Roman citizen'). Today, in the world of freedom, the proudest boast is *Ich bin ein Berliner!* All free men, wherever they may live, are citizens of Berlin, and therefore, as a free man, I take pride in the words *Ich bin ein Berliner!*"

AUGUST 28
March on Washington for Jobs and Freedom in favor of civil rights, with over

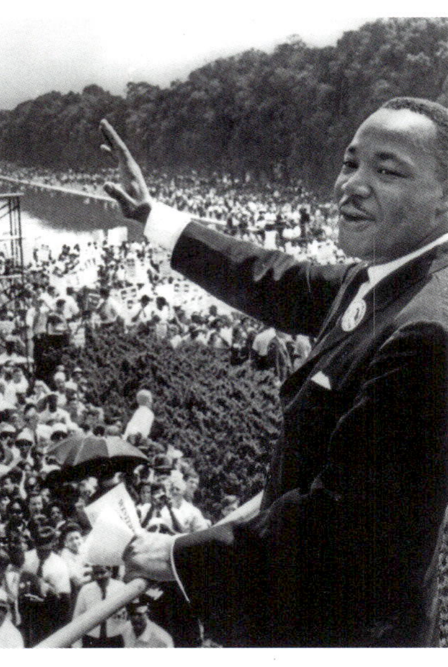

250,000 participants demanding the end of racial segregation. Performing on the stage set up in front of the Lincoln Memorial are Mahalia Jackson, Joan Baez, Peter, Paul and Mary, Bob Dylan, among others. The last of the ten speakers, Martin Luther King Jr., delivers his memorable "I Have a Dream" speech. ↑

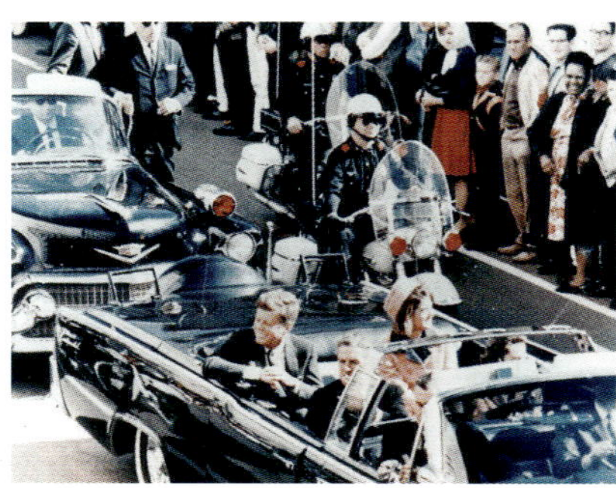

NOVEMBER 22
President Kennedy is assassinated in Dallas. Less than two hours after Kennedy's death, Vice President Lyndon B. Johnson takes the oath of office on Air Force One as it prepares to fly Jackie and her husband's casket back to Washington. Johnson is the thirty-sixth president of the US. ↑

NOVEMBER 24
Lee Harvey Oswald is accused of Kennedy's assassination and arrested within hours of the shooting. He is shot and killed by Jack Ruby live on television as he is being transferred to the county jail.

**In 1963, Andy Warhol moves his studio to 231 East 47th Street: decorated with tin foil by the photographer Billy Name and covered with silver paint, it is dubbed the "Silver Factory."**

Betty Friedan publishes *The Feminine Mystique*, a "deliberate plan centered on persuasion and conditioning that resulted in millions of American women being segregated in the American suburbs."

## 1964

Military intervention in Vietnam escalates as antiwar protests and marches continue to grow around the world. President Lyndon Johnson orders the first bombing of North Vietnam.

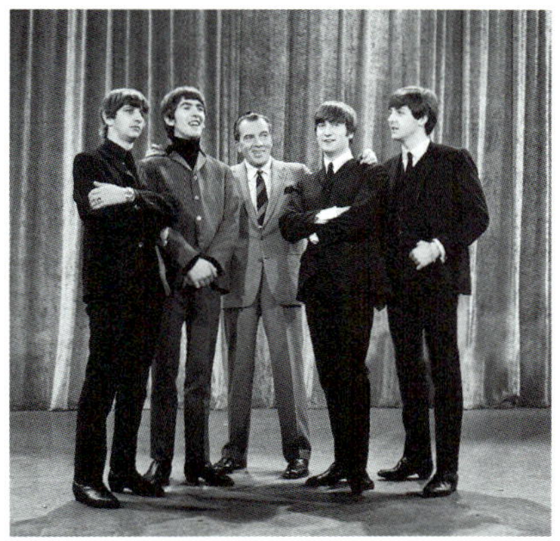

FEBRUARY 7
The Beatles arrive in the US for their first American tour. They perform on the *Ed Sullivan Show* and the broadcast draws a record audience. ↑

**JUNE 18**
**As part of the Merce Cunningham Dance Company's world tour, Story is performed at the Teatro La Fenice in Venice, under the musical direction of John Cage, with props, costumes, and lighting by Robert Rauschenberg. For the entire tour, Rauschenberg creates new scenes—using objects found locally, or "living sets"—for every performance.**

**JUNE 20**
**At the 32nd Venice Biennale, the Grand Prize for Painting is awarded to artist Robert Rauschenberg, not without causing an uproar. It is the first time that an American artist has been chosen for the award. Alan**

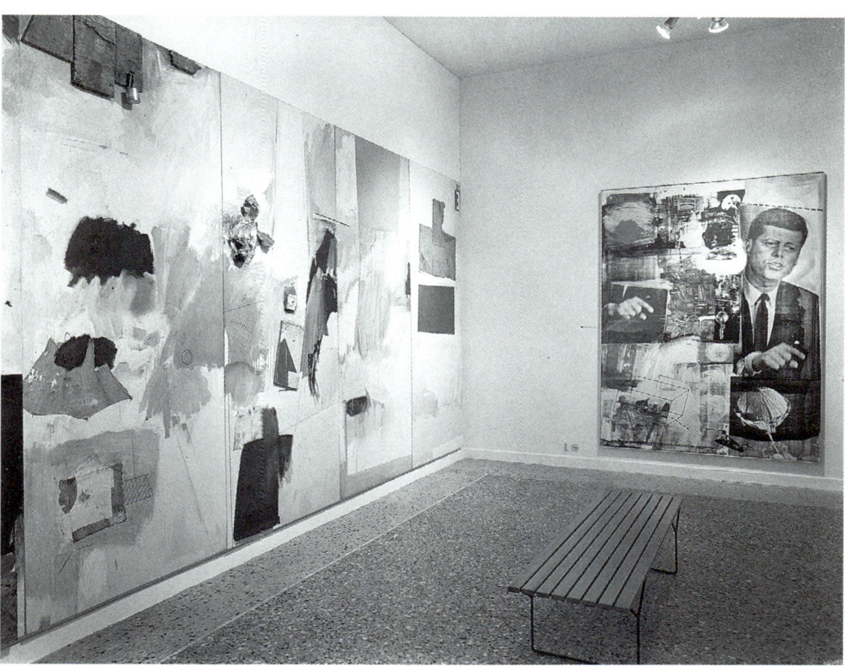

**Solomon is the US Commissioner, and he organizes the exhibition with the support of Leo Castelli (whose gallery represents Rauschenberg and Jasper Johns) and Ileana Sonnabend. The ninety-nine works are exhibited in two venues: the national US pavilion at the Giardini and the former US Consulate at San Gregorio, with two parallel exhibitions, Quattro pittori germinali. Four Germinal Painters (Morris Louis, Kenneth Noland, Robert Rauschenberg, Jasper Johns) and Quattro artisti più giovani. Four Younger Painters (John Chamberlain, Claes Oldenburg, Jim Dine, Frank Stella). On view in the US Pavilion is a single work by Rauschenberg, Stop Gap, while the other twenty-one are at the former consulate. At the last minute, to put an end to the dispute, Solomon transfered three more works to the official pavilion.** ↑

**JUNE 20–OCTOBER 18**
**In the Biennale catalogue, the Secretary General Gian Alberto Dell'Acqua declares that for the first time the US's participation in the Venice Biennale is "official in nature."**

JULY 2
President Lyndon B. Johnson (familiarly referred to as LBJ) signs the Civil Rights Act, which outlaws discrimination on the basis of race, sex, religion or national origin, and mandates equal access to public places, employment, and federal economic programs. To describe his presidency, LBJ uses the expression "the Great Society," which is implemented by way of a vast legislative plan. Momentous social and political reforms are launched.

SUMMER
The writer Ken Kesey, in a school bus decorated with psychedelic images, crosses the US along with a group of friends nicknamed the Merry Pranksters, including Neal Cassady, a key figure in the Beat Generation. They hand out amphetamines and LSD and organize jam sessions: it is the start of the hippie movement.

SEPTEMBER
The magazine *Ebony*, aimed at African Americans, publishes a picture of the Black activist Malcolm X in his home as he peers through the curtains while holding a shotgun. Determined to defend his family and himself, this is his reaction to the death threats he has been receiving. The image becomes popular and inspires, for instance, the cover of the album *By All Means Necessary* by Boogie Down Productions (1988). ↓



NOVEMBER 3
On Election Day, which since 1845 falls on

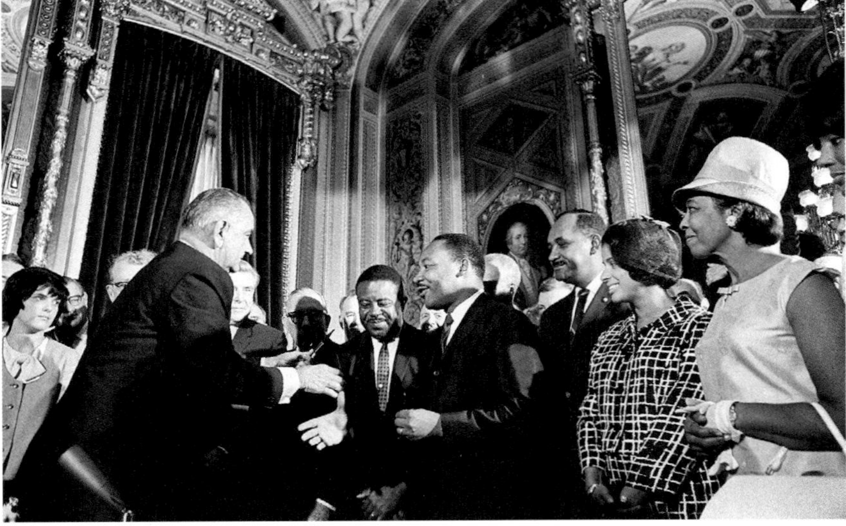

"the Tuesday next after the first Monday in the month of November," Johnson is confirmed president, winning against his ultra-conservative adversary Barry Goldwater.

## 1965

FEBRUARY 21
Malcolm X is murdered in the Audubon Ballroom in New York by the members of the Nation of Islam (NOI), a group he had once been a member of.

MARCH 7–25
Protest marches in Alabama, from Selma to Montgomery, in favor of the voting rights of African Americans. The first of these takes place on March 7 and, though peaceful, it is violently repressed by the police. In the second march, one of the protesters is killed by segregationists; however, a federal judge also recognizes the right of citizens to march—guaranteed by the First Amendment in the Constitution—on public roads. The third march makes it all the way to the courthouse in Montgomery, the capital of Alabama, escorted by the army. The marches start out with six hundred protesters, who grow to about twenty-five thousand. Martin Luther King delivers one of his most famous speeches. ↓

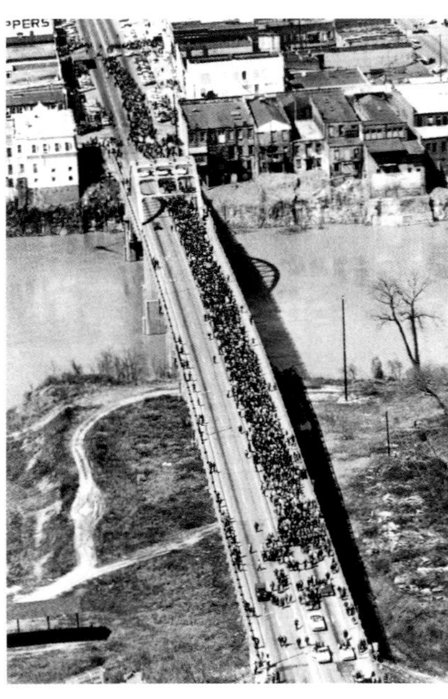

AUGUST 6
Lyndon B. Johnson—in part also because of the bloody marches in Alabama—signs the Voting Rights Act, strongly supported by Martin Luther King. The law prohibits racial discrimination in voting: up to then, the right to vote could be denied based on insufficient wealth or illiteracy. Language tests and other obstacles that kept people from registering to vote are outlawed. The new law has an immediate impact and in a short amount of time 250,000 Black voters are registered to vote. ↑

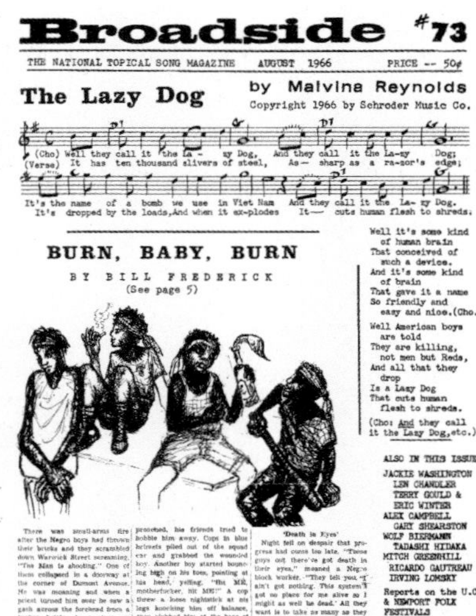

# Broadside #73

THE NATIONAL TOPICAL SONG MAGAZINE    AUGUST 1966    PRICE -- 50¢

### The Lazy Dog
by Malvina Reynolds
Copyright 1966 by Schroder Music Co.

(Cho) Well they call it the La-zy Dog, And they call it the La-zy Dog;
(Verse) It has ten thousand slivers of steel, As— sharp as a ra-zor's edge;
It's the name of a bomb we use in Viet Nam And they call it the La-zy Dog.
It's dropped by the loads, And when it ex-plodes It— cuts human flesh to shreds.

**BURN, BABY, BURN**
BY BILL FREDERICK
(See page 5)

Well it's some kind of human brain That conceived of such a device. And it's some kind of brain That gave it a name So friendly and easy and nice.(Cho.

Well American boys are told They are killing, not men but Reds, And all that they drop Is a Lazy Dog That cuts human flesh to shreds.

(Cho: And they call it the Lazy Dog, etc.)

ALSO IN THIS ISSUE
JACKIE WASHINGTON
LEN CHANDLER
TERRY GOULD &
ERIC WINTER
ALEX CAMPBELL
GARY SHEARSTON
WOLF BIERMANN
TADASHI HIDAKA
MITCH GREENHILL
RICARDO GAUTREAU
IRVING LOMSKY

Reports on the U.C. & NEWPORT FOLK FESTIVALS

There was small-arms fire after the Negro boys had thrown their bricks and they scrambled down Warwick Street screaming, "The Man is shooting." One of them collapsed in a doorway at the corner of Dumont Avenue. He was moaning and when a priest turned him over he saw a gash across the forehead from a broken bottle. As a siren approached, his friends tried to hobble him away. Cops in blue helmets piled out of the squad car and grabbed the wounded boy. Another boy started bouncing high on his toes, pointing at his head, yelling, "Hit ME, motherfucker, hit ME!" A cop threw a loose nightstick at his legs knocking him off balance, then clubbed him at the base of the neck.

'Death in Eyes'
Night fell on despair that progress had come too late. "These guys out there've got death in their eyes," moaned a Negro block worker. "They tell you 'I ain't got nothing. This system's got no place for me alive so I might as well be dead.' All they want is to take as many as they can along with them."

AUGUST 11–16
The police abuse of a young African American triggers the "Watts Riots" in the Watts neighborhood of Los Angeles. Dozens die and property is heavily damaged. The following year, in 1966, singer-songwriter Bill Frederick will write the song "Burn, Baby, Burn." ↑

AUGUST 30
Bob Dylan releases the album *Highway 61 Revisited*. US Route 61 connects Minnesota, where Dylan was born, with the Mississippi delta, cutting across the US from north to south. It is also known as the Blues Highway. The first song on the album, "Like a Rolling Stone," already released as a single, has been hailed as "the greatest song in the history of rock music," and the anthem of a generation.

SEPTEMBER 29
The National Endowment for the Arts, an independent federal agency offering economic support to artistic projects, is established.

OCTOBER 3
Johnson signs the Immigration and Nationality Act, the law on immigration, which reforms the entrance quota for the US, no longer based on "race," but on nationality instead. It also prohibits denial of a visa based on "sex, nationality, place of birth, or place of residence."

Sony markets the Portapak, the first portable video camera, leading to the birth of Video Art.

**OCTOBER 4**
**Pope Paul VI makes a fourteen-hour visit to New York and the UN. Over a million people follow him through Manhattan, Bronx, and Queens. Nam June Paik makes a film, then at the Café au Go Go in Greenwich Village he makes his first video: *Café Gogo, 152 Bleecker Street, October 4 and 11, 1965*.**

NOVEMBER
In the essay "How to Make a March/Spectacle," the poet and writer Allen Ginsberg coins the expression "Flower Power" to describe the symbolic action of handing

flowers to police officers, journalists, and onlookers as an act of protest against the Vietnam War.

**DECEMBER**
**As part of its Christmas card program, MoMA turns to Robert Indiana, who is inspired by one of his own previous works for the word LOVE in capital letters inside a square with the letter O tilted.**

## 1966

NOW (National Organization for Women) is founded, its stated goals being the economic, civil, and political equality of women. It was to become the largest feminist organization in the US.

The Black Panther Party, a revolutionary organization theorizing armed violence in self-defense against police brutality, is founded in Oakland (California).

Mao Zedong announces the Great Chinese Proletarian Cultural Revolution.

**SEPTEMBER 15**
**Andy Warhol's *Chelsea Girls*, filmed at the Hotel Chelsea in Manhattan, is released. This underground film is also a huge commercial success. Twelve vignettes, each about thirty minutes long, candidly and graphically describe one of Warhol's friends.**

## 1967

JANUARY 14
The *Human Be-In* (subtitled *A Gathering of the Tribes*), the hippie movement's first rock festival, is held at the Golden Gate Park Polo Fields in San Francisco. It is attended by around twenty to thirty thousand people. "All of San Francisco's rock groups" perform, including Santana, Jefferson Airplane, and The Grateful Dead.

**JANUARY 29–FEBRUARY 8**
**For three days, as part of *Angry Arts Week Against the War*, about two dozen actors and poets move around New York: the anti-Vietnam War protest is transformed into happenings, performances, and poetry readings. Flyers are handed out with images depicting the atrocities committed by Americans and the effects of napalm.**

APRIL AND OCTOBER
Huge protest marches against the Vietnam War take place in Washington, New York, and San Francisco.

SUMMER
The Summer of Love gatherings bring around 100,000 people to the Haight-Ashbury district in San Francisco, where they share the music, psychedelic

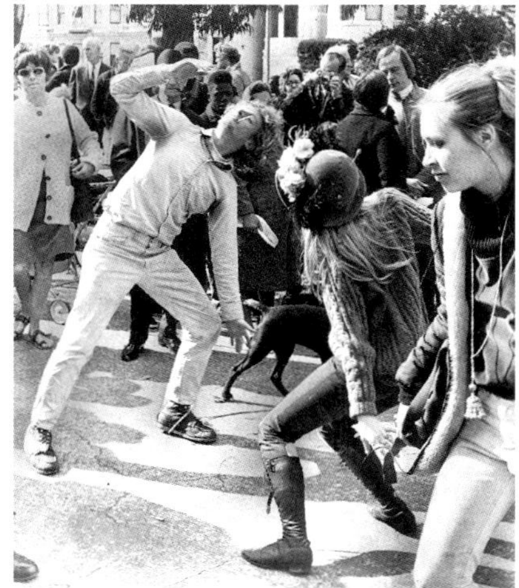

drugs, clothes, and antimilitary ideologies of the hippies, a term used to define youth counterculture. Members are also known as "flower children." Scott McKenzie sings "If you're going to San Francisco / Be sure to wear some flowers in your hair / If you're going to San Francisco / You're gonna meet some gentle people there / For those who come to San Francisco / Summertime will be a love-in there…" ↙

## 1968

JANUARY 30–31
On the occasion of the Vietnamese New Year, known as *Tết*, Vietcong and the North Vietnamese launch a surprise attack on the South: the attack reaches Saigon and breaches the US Embassy. The threat is repelled, but public opinion in America is shaken.

MARCH 31
Johnson announces a pause in the bombing campaign north of the 17th parallel, his willingness to begin peace negotiations, and the fact that he does not intend to seek the nomination of his party for another presidential term.

APRIL 4
The Rev. Martin Luther King, leader of the movements against racial discrimination, is assassinated. ↓

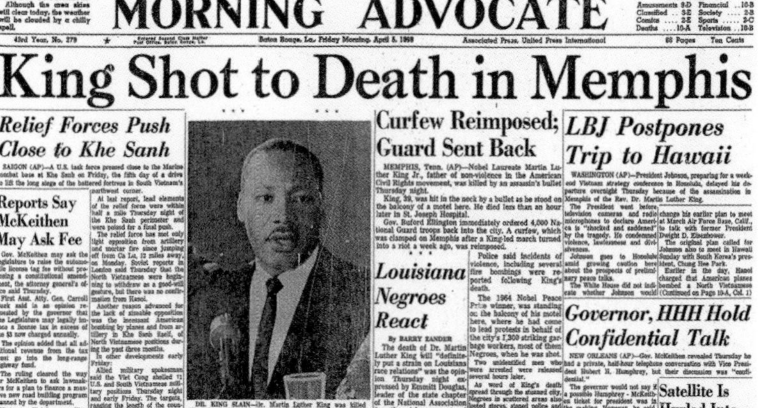

GOOD MORNING
Although the area skies will clear today, the weather will be clouded by a chilly spell.

# MORNING ADVOCATE

THE INDEX
Amusements 9-D  Financial ..10-B
Classified .... 3-E  Society .... 2-B
Comics .... 2-E  Sports ..... 2-C
Deaths ....10-A  Television ..10-B

43rd Year, No. 279  ★  Entered Second Class Matter Post Office, Baton Rouge, La.  Baton Rouge, La., Friday Morning, April 5, 1968  Associated Press, United Press International  68 Pages  Ten Cents

# King Shot to Death in Memphis

## Relief Forces Push Close to Khe Sanh

SAIGON (AP)—A U.S. task force pressed close to the Marine combat base at Khe Sanh on Friday, the fifth day of a drive to lift the long siege of the battered fortress in South Vietnam's northwest corner.

### Reports Say McKeithen May Ask Fee

Gov. McKeithen may ask the legislature to raise the automobile license tag fee without proposing a constitutional amendment, the attorney general's office said Thursday.

## Curfew Reimposed; Guard Sent Back

MEMPHIS, Tenn. (AP)—Nobel Laureate Martin Luther King Jr., father of non-violence in the American Civil Rights movement, was killed by an assassin's bullet Thursday night.

King, 39, was hit in the neck by a bullet as he stood on the balcony of a motel here. He died less than an hour later in St. Joseph Hospital.

Gov. Buford Ellington immediately ordered 4,000 National Guard troops back into the city. A curfew, which was clamped on Memphis after a King-led march turned into a riot a week ago, was reimposed.

## Louisiana Negroes React

By BARRY ZANDER

The death of Dr. Martin Luther King will "definitely put a strain on Louisiana race relations" was the opinion Thursday night expressed by Emmitt Douglas, leader of the state chapter of the National Association for the Advancement of Colored People, and echoed by many civil rights move-

## LBJ Postpones Trip to Hawaii

WASHINGTON (AP)—President Johnson, preparing for a week-end Vietnam strategy conference in Honolulu, delayed his departure overnight Thursday because of the assassination in Memphis of the Rev. Dr. Martin Luther King.

(Continued on Page 10-A, Col. 1)

## Governor, HHH Hold Confidential Talk

NEW ORLEANS (AP)—Gov. McKeithen revealed Thursday he had a private, half-hour telephone conversation with Vice President Hubert H. Humphrey, but their discussion was "confidential."

### Satellite Is Hurled Into Wrong Orbit

DR. KING SLAIN—Dr. Martin Luther King was killed Thursday in Memphis, Tenn., in a downtown hotel. He was taken to a Memphis hospital after being shot in the neck and was pronounced dead.  —AP wirephoto

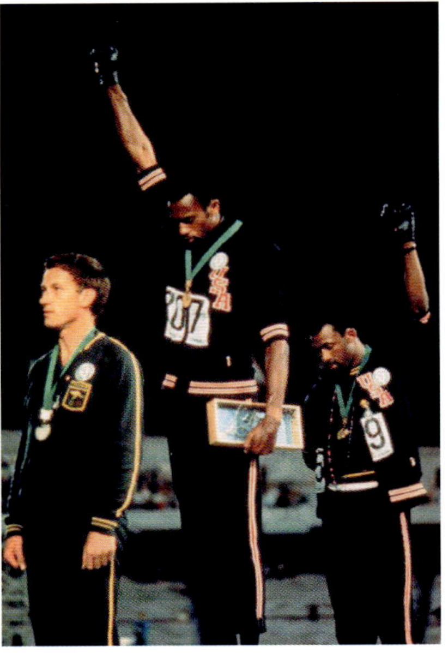

APRIL 11
Johnson signs the Civil Rights Act or Indian Civil Rights Act prohibiting discrimination in housing, whether selling or renting.

MAY 3
Protests against traditional society begin in Paris and then spread throughout Europe and to the United States—especially the University of California at Berkeley

## JUNE 3
**Andy Warhol is shot by actor Valerie Solanas, a radical feminist and artist and a regular guest at the Factory.**

JUNE 5–6
Overnight in Los Angeles, Robert (Bob) Kennedy, John Kennedy's younger brother and Democratic Party candidate for the presidential elections, is shot. He was a supporter of civil rights, and against the Vietnam War.

## JUNE 19
**The opening of the 34th Venice Biennale is marred by a protest gathering artists and students.**

## JUNE 27–OCTOBER 6
**documenta 4 opens in Kassel, presented as "The Youngest documenta Ever." During the opening artists and demonstrators stage a violent protest.**

AUGUST 20
Soviet troops and tanks, along with the Warsaw Pact countries of Poland, East Germany, Hungary, and Bulgaria, invade Czechoslovakia and get as far as the capital. It is the end of the so-called "Prague Spring," a season of democratization and reform guided by Alexander Dubček.

## OCTOBER 2
**Marcel Duchamp dies in Neuilly-sur-Seine. From 1913 he was often in the US, where he moved permanently in 1942 because of the war, and where he became a citizen in 1955.**

OCTOBER 16
At the Games of the XIX Olympiad in Mexico City, as they received their medals for the 200-meter race, two African American athletes, Tommie Smith (gold) and John Carlos (bronze), stand on the podium with their heads bowed while they raise their black-gloved fists (symbolizing Black Power). They are suspended from the US team and banned from the Olympic Village. ↑

## 1969

## JANUARY 18–APRIL 6
**The exhibition *Harlem on My Mind. Cultural Capital of Black America, 1900–1968* held at the Metropolitan Museum in New York causes a stir because it does not include the works of African American artists, but rather photographs and other documentation of the everyday life of the Black community.**

JANUARY 20
The transition takes place between Lyndon B. Johnson and Richard Nixon, who moves into the White House as the thirty-seventh president of the US. His top foreign policy aide is National Security Adviser Harry Kissinger.

## JANUARY
**The Art Workers' Coalition (AWC), made up of actors, filmmakers, writers, and critics is established in New York. Its main goal is to put pressure on the city museums for a more inclusive exhibition policy regarding African American and women artists, allow free admission for those who cannot afford to visit museums, and involve the artists themselves in the planning of exhibitions.**

JUNE 28–JULY 3
A revolt takes place at the Stonewall Inn, a gay bar in Greenwich Village, New York. When the bar is raided by the police the customers react violently, giving rise to the gay rights movement. ↓

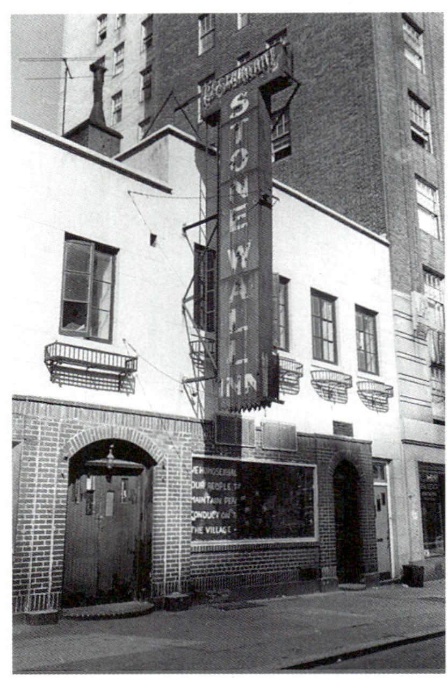

JULY 14
The movie *Easy Rider* is released. Directed by Dennis Hopper, it stars Hopper himself along with Peter Fonda and Jack Nicholson. The film follows a trip from Los Angeles to New Orleans by two bikers on their choppers, and portrays the hippie counterculture. ↓

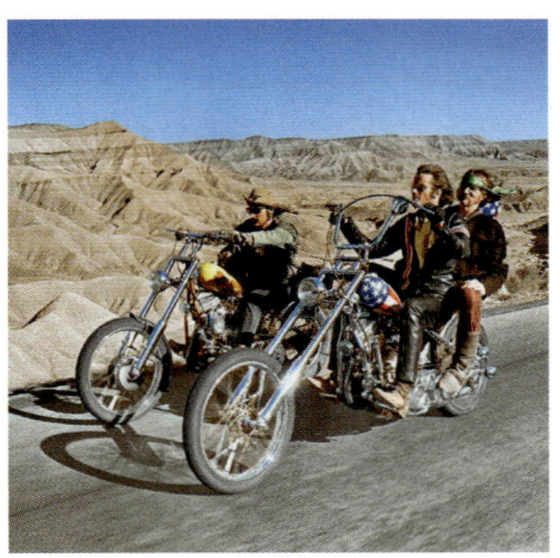

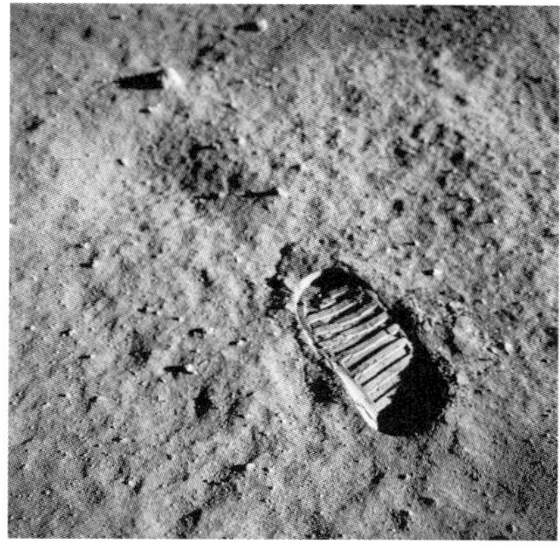

## JULY 21

With the Apollo 11 Mission Americans put a man on the moon. Neil Armstrong and Edwin Aldrin take the first moonwalk. Armstrong utters the famous words: "That's one small step for man, one giant leap for mankind." Robert Rauschenberg is invited to witness the launch at Cape Canaveral, on July 16, which inspires him to produce the lithographs *Stoned Moon* (1969–70), *Stoned Moon Drawing* (1969), as well as collages and drawings for *Stoned Moon Book* (1970). ↑


The Woodstock music festival is held in Bethel, New York State. It is estimated that half a million people attended the rock concert also known as "3 Days of Peace & Rock Music." Woodstock becomes a symbol of the American hippie counterculture, which also includes opposition to the Vietnam War, enshrined, among other things, by the pacifist slogans "Put Flowers in Your Guns" and "Make Love, not War." Among others, the performances by Janis Joplin, Joe Cocker, and Jimi Hendrix remain in the collective imagination today. ↓

## 1969, OCTOBER 18

*New York Painting and Sculpture. 1940–1970* opens at the Metropolitan Museum of Art, the MET's first contemporary art exhibition. Curated by Henry Geldzahler, over four hundred works by forty-three artists retrace the most important trends since 1940.

## 1969 END

Warhol and the English journalist John Wilcock found the cinema, fashion, art, and culture magazine *Interview*, dubbed *The Crystal Ball of Pop*.

## 1970

One of the photographs taken in 1969 by the army photographer Ron L. Haeberle in the village of My Lai in South Vietnam—where American soldiers massacred over three hundred defenseless civilians, including women, children, and the elderly—is chosen for the poster *Q. And babies? A. And babies.* produced by MoMA and the Art Workers' Coalition. The question and answer printed on the poster, taken from a televised interview with a soldier who was there when it happened, tersely confirm the killing of children.

APRIL
The US invades Cambodia.

## MAY 18

Following violent clashes between protesters and police in early May, during which many are killed or injured, members of the artistic community meet at the Loeb Student Center at NYU demanding that museums and galleries be closed on May 22 in protest "against repression, sexism, and war."

SUMMER
After marrying the Greek shipowner Aristotle Onassis in 1968, Jackie Kennedy vacations on Capri and the Amalfi Coast where she sports a completely different look from when she was in the White House: low-heeled thong sandals made by local artisans, cigarette or bell-bottom pants, dark top, a scarf tied around her head, and large sunglasses. She also often uses a Gucci handbag that will later be named after her.

JUNE 28
First New York City Pride March, one year after the Stonewall Inn riots, with thousands of young people marching from Greenwich Village to Sheep Meadow and Central Park to uphold "the new strength and pride of gay people."

## 1971

FEBRUARY 5
Following the boom of the New Economy, the NASDAQ (National Association of Securities Dealers Automated Quotation) is founded in New York. It is the index for the most important electronic trading on the US Stock Market.

JULY 3
Jim Morrison, front man for the Doors and poet, is found dead in Paris. Two months earlier Jimi Hendrix and Janis Joplin had died. All of them were aged twenty-seven.

AUGUST 15
Nixon announces the suspension of the gold standard, or the fixed conversion of

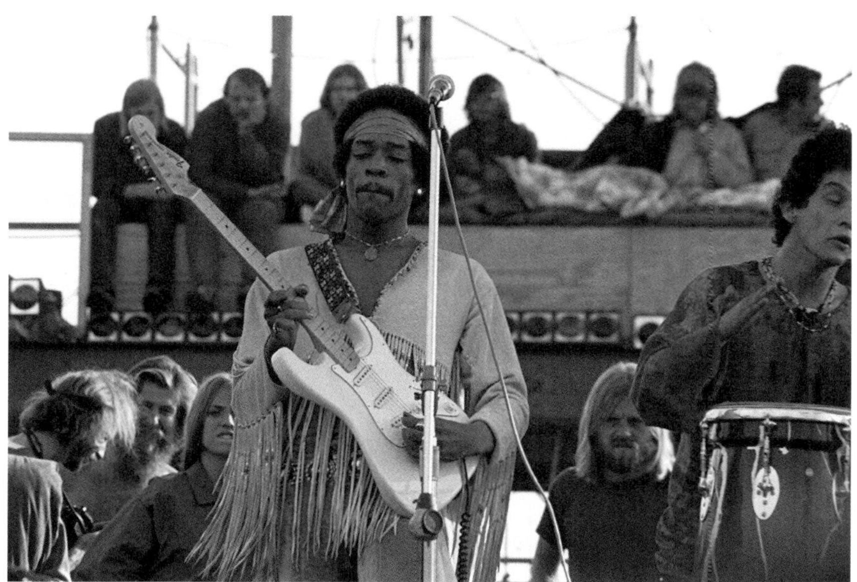

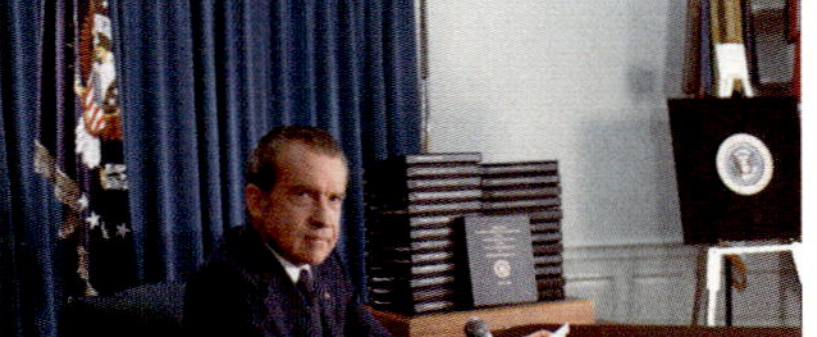

dollars to gold at a fixed value, which had been in place since the 1944 agreement underwritten in the American town of Bretton Woods by the victorious allies of World War II.

## 1972

### JUNE
The Watergate scandal erupts, related to the cover-up—investigated and reported on by Bob Woodward and Carl Bernstein, two young journalists from the *Washington Post*—of the break-in at the Democratic National Committee headquarters.

### NOVEMBER 7
Richard Nixon is reelected president of the US. He visits China and paves the way for mutual diplomatic acknowledgment in 1979.

## 1973

### JANUARY 22
*Roe vs. Wade*: historic Supreme Court ruling, which affirms the principle of a woman's freedom to choose whether to have an abortion.

### JANUARY 27
The Paris Peace Accords formally put an end to the Vietnam War. US troops leave the country. Fifty-eight thousand Americans, and one and a half million Vietnamese had died. For the Vietnamese the war is not yet over.

### FEBRUARY 27
Native Americans occupy Wounded Knee in South Dakota, where the first massacre of the Lakota people took place in 1890. The occupation ends on May 8, seventy-one days after the start of the protest, and with the death of two activists.

### SEPTEMBER 11
Chile undergoes a military coup led by General Augusto Pinochet and backed by the US. President Salvador Allende dies.

### OCTOBER 6–25
The Yom Kippur War between Israel and a coalition of Arab states led by Egypt and Syria begins with an attack on Israel on the holy day of Yom Kippur. It ends with a UN-brokered ceasefire on October 22, thanks in part to the mediation of Henry Kissinger.

### FALL
**Theme Song by Vito Acconci is produced in Florence by art/tapes/22, the first Video Art production company in Europe, founded the previous year by Maria Gloria Conti Bicocchi at 22 Via Ricasoli. Acconci, "who came for a day and stayed three weeks," made four other works (Home Movies, Full Circle, Come Back, Indirect Approche). Ballroom, Acconci's last public performance, takes place at the Galleria Schema at 17 Via della Vigna Nuova.**

**Allan Kaprow makes the video titled Then in the art/tapes/22 studio in collaboration with the Galleria Multipla in Milan. He produces Third Routine in 1974.**

## 1973–74

Oil crisis: OPEC countries raise the price of oil in response to the Yom Kippur War. The price of oil rises fourfold.

## 1974

### AUGUST 9
Nixon—the first and only US president ever to do so—resigns because of the Watergate scandal. Vice President Gerald R. Ford (1974–77) becomes the new US president. ↑

**John Baldessari makes the video The Italian Type in New York for art/tapes/22, in collaboration with Castelli-Sonnabend Videotape and Films founded that year.**

## 1975

### SPRING
**Critic Rosalind Krauss leaves Artforum and founds October, a magazine published by the Massachusetts Institute of Technology Press. The new periodical will have a profound impact on the art world.**

### APRIL 30
The last Americans hurriedly abandon Saigon by helicopter while the Vietcong enter the city, determining the end of the Vietnam War. It is the US's first ever military–political defeat. ↓

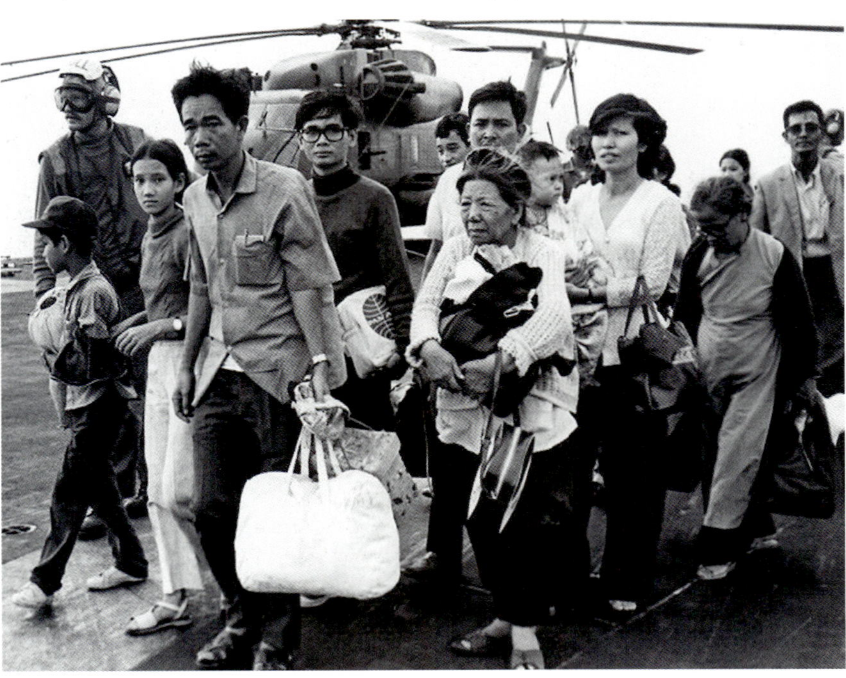

Dara Birnbaum, who is in Florence for a year, first approaches Video Art at art/tapes/22 and is a regular guest of the Galleria Schema and of the Zona art space.

## 1976

### FEBRUARY 8

*Taxi Driver*, directed by Martin Scorsese, is released in the US. Robert De Niro plays Travis Bickle, a Vietnam War veteran who is scarred by his experiences and finds it impossible to go back to life as it was before. He lives in solitude, working as a taxi driver at night in New York, where he runs into "whores, skunk pussies, buggers, queens, fairies, dopers, junkies, sick, venal." The young man, obsessed by his ghosts, becomes a vigilante. ↓

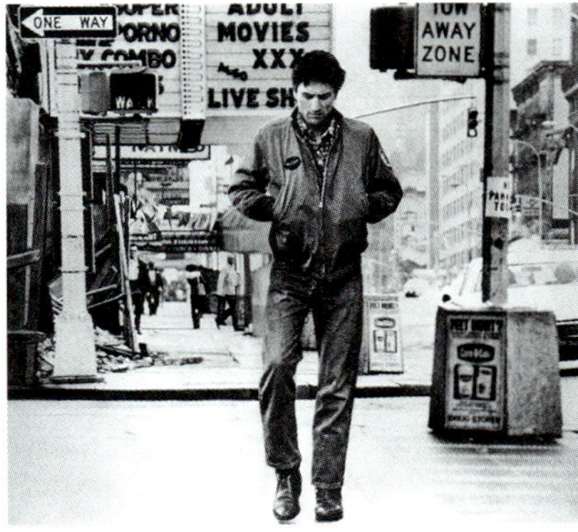


### SEPTEMBER 9
Mao Zedong dies.

### SEPTEMBER 11–NOVEMBER 7
*Robert Rauschenberg* exhibition at Forte di Belvedere in Florence.

## 1977

### JANUARY 17
**Gary Gilmore, guilty of two brutal murders, is executed in Utah. Refusing to appeal his sentence, he is the first American citizen to undergo capital punishment after a ten-year federal moratorium. Utah allows its prisoners on death row to choose how they want to be executed, and Gilmore chooses firing squad, based on the Mormon principle that a sinner must shed his own blood to be able to obtain salvation. Inspired by the case, Norman Mailer writes *The Executioner's Song* (1979) and Matthew Barney makes *Cremaster 2* (1999).**

### JANUARY 20
The Democrat James E. (Jimmy) Carter, former governor of Georgia, beats the incumbent president Gerald Ford and is sworn in as thirty-ninth president of the US. He loses the next election after only one term in office (1977–81).

### FEBRUARY
**The twentieth anniversary of the Leo Castelli Gallery is celebrated in Frank Stella's studio in New York. Leo Krausz, aka Leo Castelli, is surrounded by his artists: Oldenburg, Flavin, Rosenquist, Sonnier, Ruscha, Weiner, Kosuth, Daphnis, Barry, Serra, Judd, Warhol, Rauschenberg, Morris, Lichtenstein, Poppy Johnson (the only woman), Scarpitta, and Waldman. In his *Diaries*, Andy Warhol writes about it: "Cabbed with Vincent down to Frank Stella's studio ($ 2.75), a party for Leo Castelli's twenty years in the art business [. . .] just the kind of party I hate because they're all like me, so similar, and so peculiar, but they're being so artistic and I'm being so commercial that I feel funny [. . .] All the artists I've known for years are with their second wives."**

### APRIL 26
Studio 54 opens in Manhattan, a club whose habitués include—until it closes in 1980—artists, writers, actors, and singers such as Woody Allen, John Belushi, Truman Capote, Martha Graham, Michael Jackson, Liza Minnelli, John Travolta, Grace Jones,

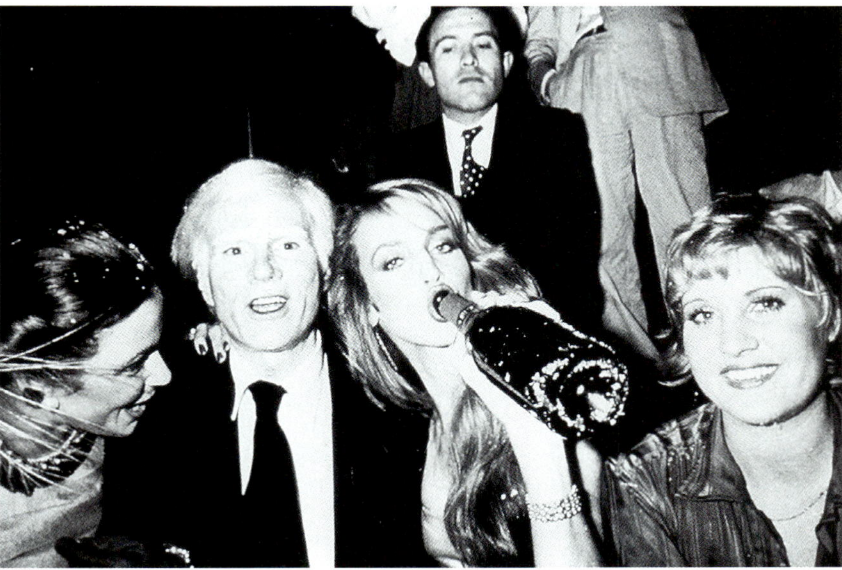

Michael Jackson, Elton John, and, above all, Andy Warhol. ↑

### AUGUST 16
Elvis Presley, the King of Rock and Roll, dies in Memphis at the age of 42.

## 1978

### OCTOBER 16
Polish cardinal Karol Wojtyła is elected pope and takes the name John Paul II. He will play an important role in the collapse of the Communist regimes.

### NOVEMBER 13
The Village People releases the single "YMCA," whose title refers to the acronym for Young Men's Christian Association: the gyms annexed to these hostels are places where gay people can meet. The song is an anthem for the gay movement. ↓

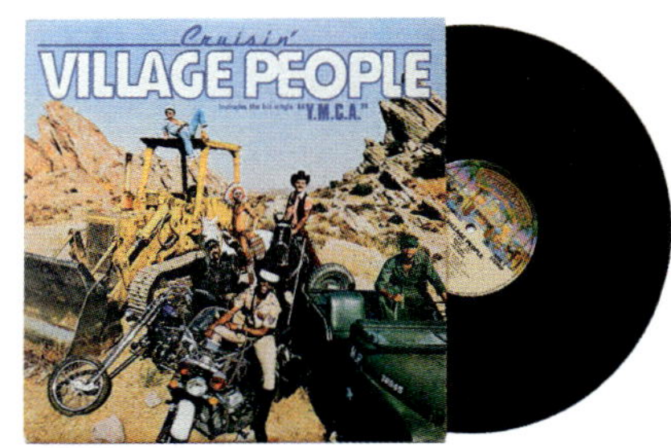


## 1979

### JANUARY
The Shah of Iran Reza Pahlavi leaves Iran following the Islamic Revolution led by the Ayatollah Khomeini. New oil crisis.

MAY
A nondefinitive version of *Apocalypse Now*, directed by Francis Ford Coppola, wins the Palme d'Or at the Cannes Film Festival. The director declares, "My film is not about Vietnam, it *is* Vietnam." ↓

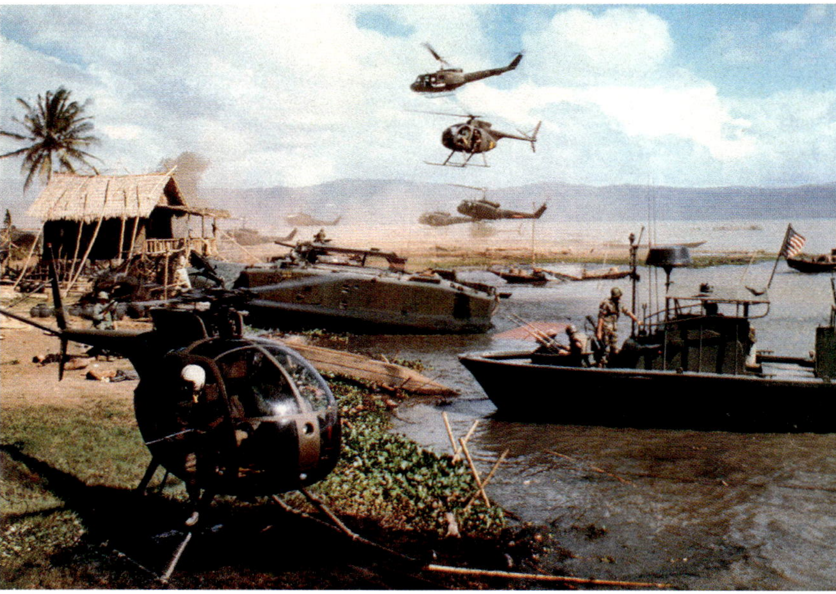

1980, NOVEMBER 4–1981, JANUARY 20
The US Embassy in Teheran is overrun by students and fifty-two members of staff are held hostage (it is the so-called "hostage crisis"). The hostages are not freed until Ronald Reagan takes office.

DECEMBER 25
Soviet troops invade Afghanistan.

## 1980

**JANUARY 1**
**The Real Estate Show opens. The squatted exhibition is organized by the group of New York artists COLAB in a vacant city-owned commercial building in the East Village. The show is an example of what can be organized in parts of the city that have no spaces devoted to art. It is shut down by the authorities.**

JULY 19–AUGUST 3
Sixty-five countries, including the US, Chi-na, Japan, Canada, and West Germany, boycott the Moscow Olympics as a sign of protest against the Soviet invasion of Afghanistan.

NOVEMBER 4
On Election Day, the battle is between Republican Ronald Reagan and the incumbent Democrat president Jimmy Carter. Just a few days before, during their last debate, Reagan asked the voters the following rhetorical question: "Are you better off today than you were four years ago?" The high cost and limited supply of gas, the truck drivers' strike, and the subsequent shortage of goods, unemployment, the fifty-two American citizens being held hostage in the US Embassy in Teheran influence the vote, making Carter one of very few one-term presidents.

DECEMBER 8
John Lennon is shot four times by a fan named Mark Chapman. The Beatle was returning to his home in New York with his wife Yoko Ono.
CNN (Cable News Network), the first American news-based network, is inaugurated, and MTV is launched.

## 1981

JANUARY 20
The Republican Ronald Reagan is sworn in as fortieth president of the US. His vice president is George H. W. Bush. Reaganomics, the name for the economic policies implemented during his presidency (which ended on January 20, 1989), is mainly based on cuts to public spending, deregulation, and the containment of inflation. Similar choices are made in the United Kingdom by the Conservative Prime Minister Margaret Thatcher (1979–90), whose ideology comes to be known as Thatcherism. ↓

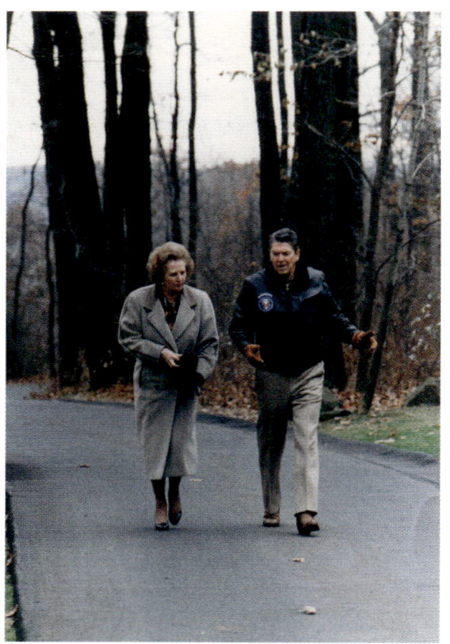

MAY 13
An attempt is made to assassinate John Paul II in Saint Peter's Square in Rome.

JUNE
The existence of a new disease, Acquired Immune Deficiency Syndrome-AIDS, is acknowledged. The US reports the first AIDS-related deaths, and the AIDS epidemic influences the art world. Governments around the world fail to respond to the problem and the political culture is permeated by a deep sense of homophobia.

DECEMBER 12–13
Overnight in Poland, the government of General Wojciech Jaruzelski imposes martial law, suspends constitutional rights, cancels the Gdańsk Agreement, and imprisons leader Lech Wałęsa and about a thousand other militant members of Solidarność (Solidarity), the independent, self-governing free trade union backed by the Catholic church.

## 1982

**JUNE 30–SEPTEMBER 12**
**Barbara Kruger represents the US at the 40th Venice Biennale.**

OCTOBER 1
Helmut Kohl, leader of the CDU (conservative, Christian Democrat, and pro-European party), is elected Chancellor of West Germany.

OCTOBER 22
*First Blood* is released in US movie theaters. Sylvester Stallone plays the part of an ex-member of the Green Berets, US Army Special Forces, and a Vietnam veteran who embodies the drama of a country emerging defeated from war and of soldiers incapable of settling into a peaceful life. ↓

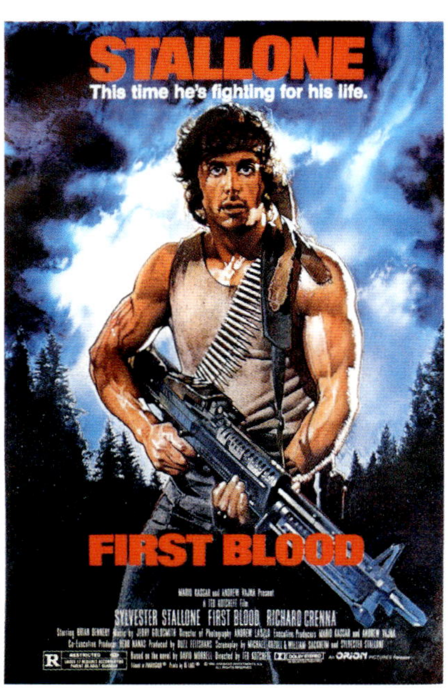


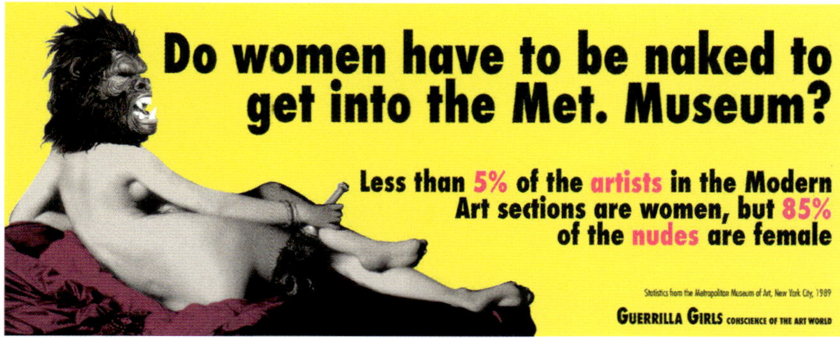


## 1983

MARCH 23
Ronald Reagan announces the beginning of the Strategic Defense Initiative. The plan is dubbed "Star Wars" in the US.

MAY 20
A group of French researchers directed by Luc Montagnier publishes an article in *Science* announcing the discovery of a new virus, HIV, which causes AIDS. The previous year the American researcher Robert Gallo had identified the viral origin of the epidemic.

Motorola, a company based in the Chicago suburbs, manufactures the first cell phone.

## 1984

**MAY 17–AUGUST 19**
**The Museum of Modern Art in New York opens with *An International Survey of Recent Painting & Sculpture* curated by Kynaston McShine. It showcases the outstanding vitality of the output by the younger generation of artists. Nevertheless, only thirteen of them are women, and there are very few artists of color, none of whom are women.**

## 1985

JANUARY 20
Ronald Reagan is sworn in for his second term after being reelected in November.

## SPRING
**The Guerrilla Girls, a group of women artists fighting for gender equality in the artistic world as well as other contexts, is founded in New York in response to the discriminatory choices made toward the artists of the exhibition *An International Survey of Recent Painting & Sculpture* held the previous year. ↑**

Mikhail Gorbachev is the new leader of the Soviet Union. He seeks political detente with the US and also aims to cut military expenditure.

## 1986

APRIL 26
A serious accident occurs at the Chernobyl Nuclear Power Plant in the Soviet Union.

*Platoon*, written and directed by Oliver Stone, is released. The film is autobiographical and retraces the director's dramatic experience as a volunteer in Vietnam in 1967–68.

## 1987

**FEBRUARY 22**
**Andy Warhol dies suddenly in New York following gallbladder surgery.**

MARCH
The AIDS Coalition to Unleash Power (ACT UP) is founded in New York, promoting the fight against AIDS and committed to implementing policies to help the sick. The critic Douglas Crimp is a member of the group.

JUNE 12
During his speech at the Brandenburg Gate on the occasion of the 750th anniversary of the founding of Berlin, Ronald Reagan famously tells Mikhail Gorbachev to "Tear down this wall!"

DECEMBER
Douglas Crimp dedicates *October*'s issue (no. 43) to *Aids Cultural Analysis/Cultural Activism*: the dramatic crisis of the art world due to AIDS is analyzed by specialists and activists fighting for PWA–People with Aids.

**MAY 9**
**Leo Castelli donates Rauschenberg's 1955 masterpiece *Bed* to the MoMA. The piece is worth ten million dollars.**

JUNE 4
In Beijing, students demanding democracy occupy Tiananmen Square, which leads to a massacre.

NOVEMBER 9
The Berlin Wall is brought down and the West German border is reopened. ↓

JUNE 23
A march is held in San Francisco on the occasion of the Sixth International Conference on AIDS, aimed at sensitizing the public about the disease and demanding more funding for the sick.

**JUNE 27–SEPTEMBER 30**
**At the 44th Venice Biennale, the Golden Lion for best national representation goes to the US Pavilion, and for the first time ever to a woman, Jenny Holzer.**

AUGUST 2
One hundred thousand Iraqi men and three hundred armored tanks invade Kuwait by order of the nationalist leader Saddam Hussein. The United Nations calls for the withdrawal of forces.

SEPTEMBER
The documentary film *Paris is Burning*, directed by Jennie Livingston, is presented at the Toronto International Film Festival, and the following year at the Sundance Film Festival. Filmed over a six-year period, it presents a series of interviews to document the New York drag balls in which homosexuals, transgender individuals, and African American and Latin American drag queens compete against each other.

OCTOBER 3
Reunification of Germany after the fall of the Berlin Wall. Helmut Kohl is the chancellor of a united Germany.

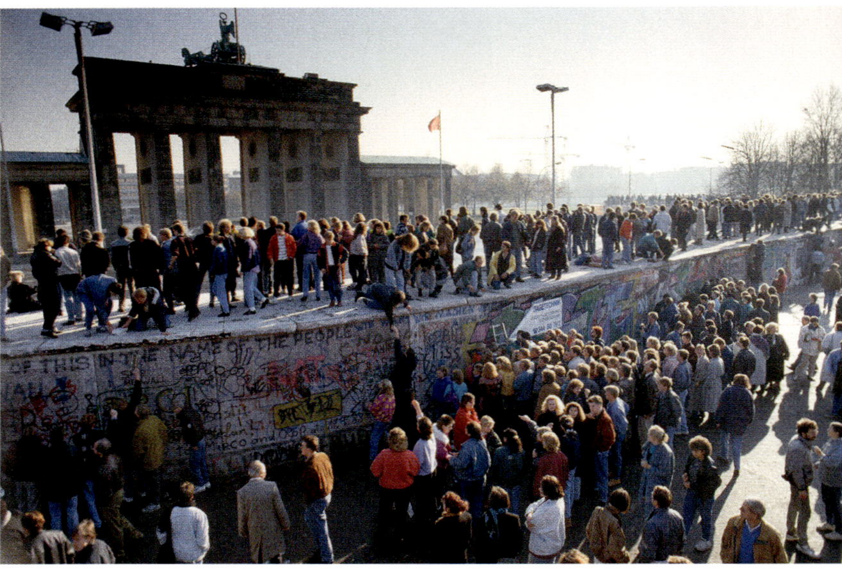

## 1988

**JUNE**
**At the 43rd Venice Biennale, the US Pavilion is devoted to *Jasper Johns. Work From 1974–1986*. The artist, who was first exhibited at the Biennale in 1958, is awarded the Golden Lion.**

## 1989

JANUARY 20
Republican George H. W. Bush is sworn in as the forty-first president of the US.

CERN announces the birth of the World Wide Web (WWW), open to all from the mid-1990s.

## 1990

**Douglas Crimp, along with the artist Adam Rolston, publishes *Aids Demo Graphics* chronicling ACT UP's "artistic activism" in the fight against AIDS.**

APRIL
Madonna launches the video for "Vogue," which leads to the craze for vogueing, a dance that is popular in gay clubs in America and imitates the poses of male and female models in the magazine *Vogue*.

## 1991

JANUARY 16–17
When the UN deadline runs out, the United States, at the head of an international coalition, orders the aerial bombing of Iraqi stations: it is the start of Desert Storm, the First Gulf War.

MARCH 3
An African American cab driver named Rodney King is brutally beaten by Los Angeles police for not stopping during a high-speed chase. An amateur video of the event is broadcast by the media.

The Soviet Union collapses.

## 1992

### APRIL
The acquittal of the police officers who brutally beat Rodney King leads to violent rioting in April–May 1992, with over fifty deaths.

### JULY 21
**Sonic Youth releases its seventh album, *Dirty*. The front cover features a crocheted orange stuffed toy, and the booklet includes other plush toys, all of which are by Mike Kelley, an old friend of the group's bass guitarist and singer, as well as visual artist, Kim Gordon.**

### NOVEMBER 3
William Jefferson (Bill) Clinton—former governor of Arkansas—is elected president of the US. He will be reelected to a second term in 1996. His reforms are progressive: lower taxes for lower incomes, higher taxes for higher incomes; the right to maternity and sick leave (without pay); gay men and lesbians allowed to serve in the armed forces, provided people "Don't ask, don't tell." Health care reform, overseen by First Lady Hillary Clinton, fails. If it had succeeded it would have been extended to 39 million citizens then without health care.

## 1993

The European Union is founded in Maastricht.

### DECEMBER
The movie *Philadelphia*, a film that shines a spotlight on discrimination against people with AIDS, is released. Director Jonathan Demme; actors Tom Hanks and Denzel Washington; music by Bruce Springsteen ("Streets of Philadelphia"). →

Toni Morrison is the first African American author to win the Nobel Prize in Literature.

## 1994

Kurt Cobain, frontman for Nirvana, dies of a self-inflicted gunshot wound to the head. The group Nirvana symbolizes the grunge movement and goes from being a phenomenon limited to the Seattle area to the emblem of the so-called Generation X across the world.

## 1995

The Srebrenica massacre takes place in Yugoslavia, during which about seven thousand Bosnian Muslims are murdered or deported.

### JULY 28
**The Venice Dance Biennale awards the Golden Lion for Career Achievement to Merce Cunningham.**

## 1996

### FEBRUARY 8
The Telecommunications Act deregulates the US communications market, letting anyone enter any communications business, whether it be telephone, television, journalism, or the Internet.

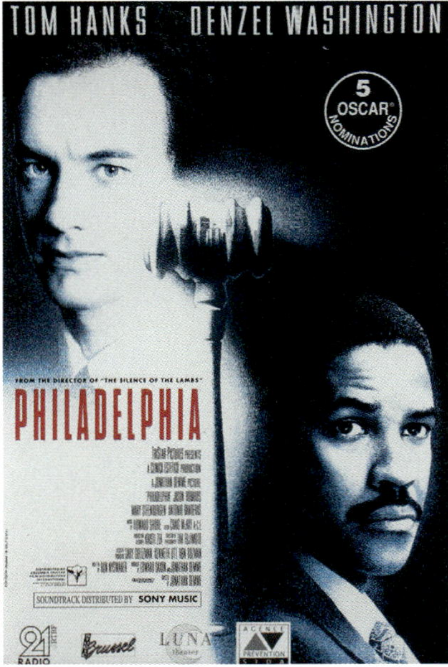


### SEPTEMBER 22–26
**As part of the Florence Biennale, Jenny Holzer presents her xenon light projections on the banks of the Arno.**

### OCTOBER 7
Australia-born Rupert Murdoch creates the international Fox News Channel (Fox News or FNC), a 24-hour news channel. Fox News Channel CEO is Roger Ailes, previously a political consultant for Richard Nixon, Ronald Reagan, and George H. W. Bush. The channel says that its news is "fair and balanced," while it is actually a mouthpiece for the aggressive Republican politician Newt Gingrich.

### NOVEMBER 5
Bill Clinton is reelected president of the United States. ↓

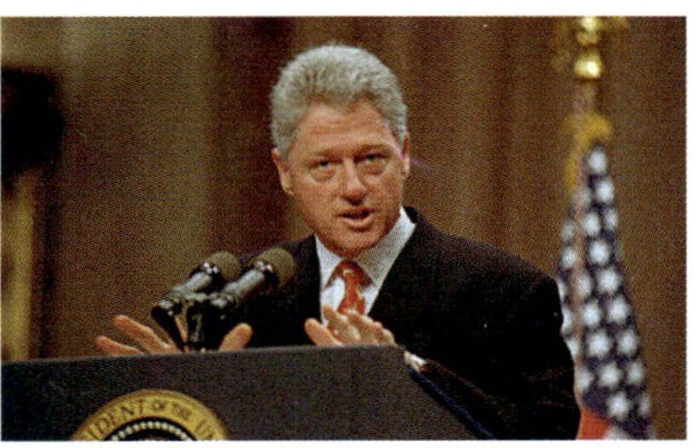

## 1997

### JANUARY 20
Bill Clinton is sworn in as president for a second term.

### SEPTEMBER 27
Two Stanford University PhD students, Larry Page and Sergey Brin, found Google, a company promoting the idea of a research engine for the Internet based on a new algorithm of links between websites.

**Agnes Martin wins the Golden Lion at the 47th Venice Biennale.**

## 1998

The scandal known as Sexgate follows in the wake of the sexual relationship between President Clinton and White House intern Monica Lewinsky. Clinton denies having any relationship with Lewinsky—a claim which is subsequently disproven—and he is found guilty of perjury.

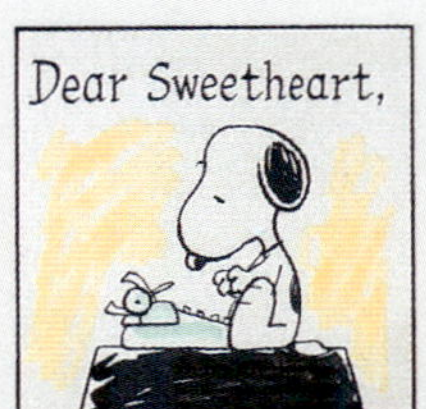
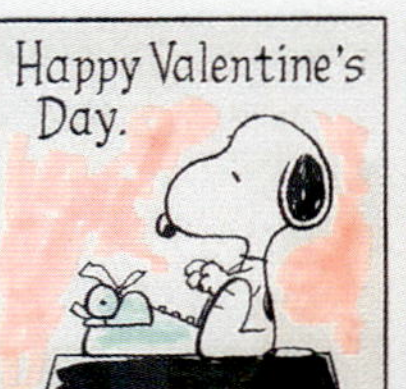
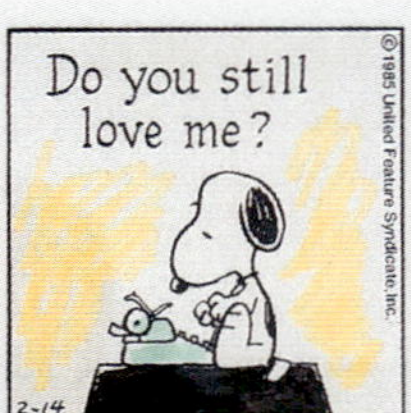
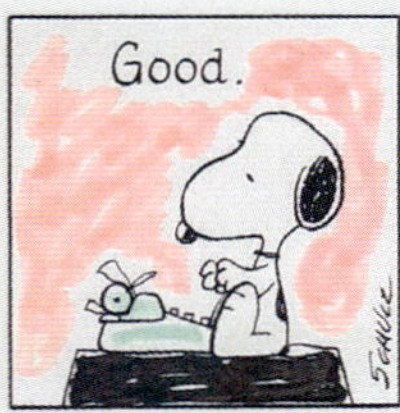


## 1999

FEBRUARY
Clinton is impeached by the House of Representatives but acquitted by the Senate.

APRIL 11
Guest star for *The Simpsons*' tenth-season episode "Mom & Pop Art" is Jasper Johns, who plays himself and even lends his voice to the show. Created by Matt Groening, the series is a caustic satire of society and life in the US, and is still running today. ↓

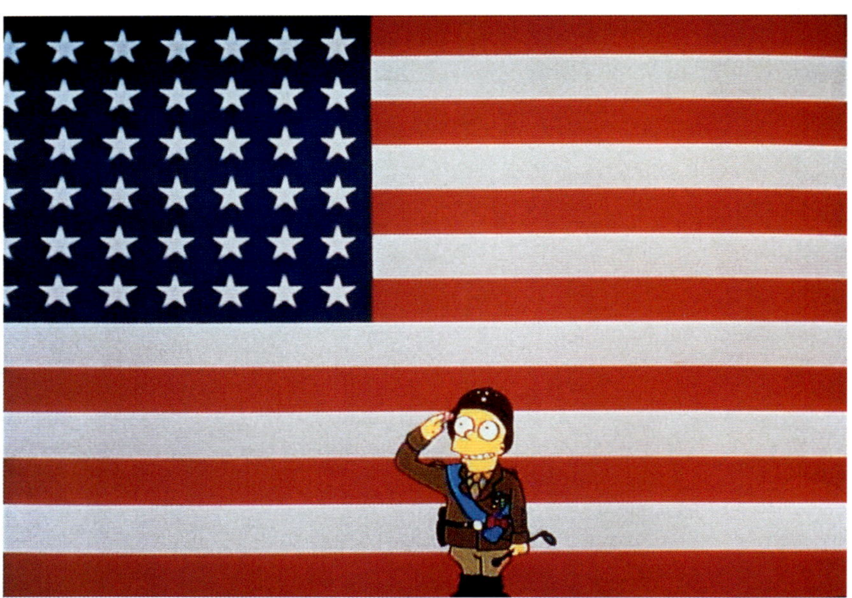

**JUNE 13–NOVEMBER 7**
**Harald Szeemann is the curator of the 48th Venice Biennale, for which he chooses the theme *dAPERTutto*. The Golden Lion goes to Louise Bourgeois and Bruce Nauman.**

**SEPTEMBER 21**
**At the Teatro del Rondò di Bacco in Florence's Palazzo Pitti, on the occasion of Pitti Immagine, Matthew Barney's *Cremaster 2* is given its European debut, thanks to the collaboration between Pitti Immagine Discovery and the Walker Art Center in Minneapolis. Matthew Barney and Richard Flood, chief curator of the Walker Art Center, are in attendance. →**

## 2000

FEBRUARY 13
*Peanuts* is published for the last time (one day after the death of its creator, Charles M. Schulz). It began on October 2, 1950 and continued uninterrupted with daily comic strips and a full panel every Sunday. ↑

NOVEMBER 7
Vice President Al Gore loses the presidential elections by a handful of votes. Florida's ballots have to be recounted.

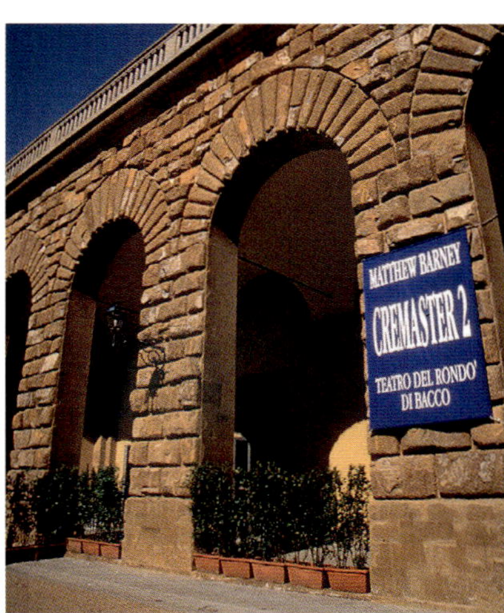


## 2001

JANUARY 20
George W. Bush, son of George H. W. Bush, is sworn in as the forty-third president of the US. Dick Cheney is vice president. ↓

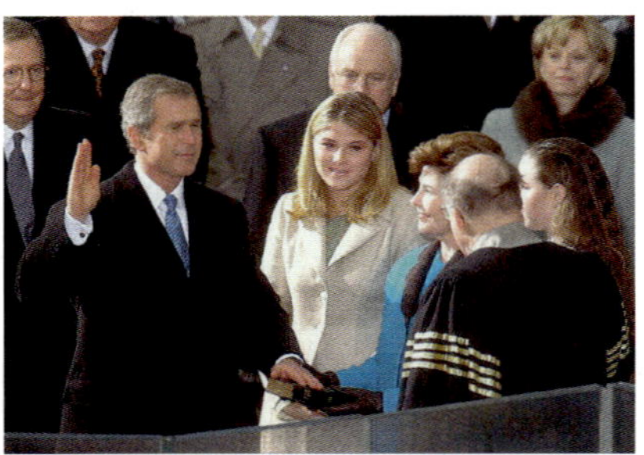

**JUNE 10–NOVEMBER 4**
**The 49th Venice Biennale is titled *Platea dell'Umanità—Plateau of Humankind—Plateau der Menschheit—Plateau de l'Humanité*: the US Pavilion is assigned to Robert Gober, a sensitive interpreter of the American psyche. The Golden Lion goes to Richard Serra and Cy Twombly.**

AUGUST 31–SEPTEMBER 8
Over the course of the Third World Conference "against racism, racial discrimination, xenophobia, and related forms of intolerance," held in Durban, South Africa, the term "Afro-descendant" becomes the official term to indicate the descendants of Africans deported to the American continent during the Atlantic slave trade.

SEPTEMBER 11
Four commercial planes are hijacked by suicide terrorists and members of Al Qaeda: two of them crash into the Twin Towers in New York. A third one aims for the Pentagon, and a fourth—perhaps intended for the White House or the Capitol—crashes in Pennsylvania. Almost three thousand people die in the worst attack on American soil since Pearl Harbor. The war on terrorism officially begins. ↗

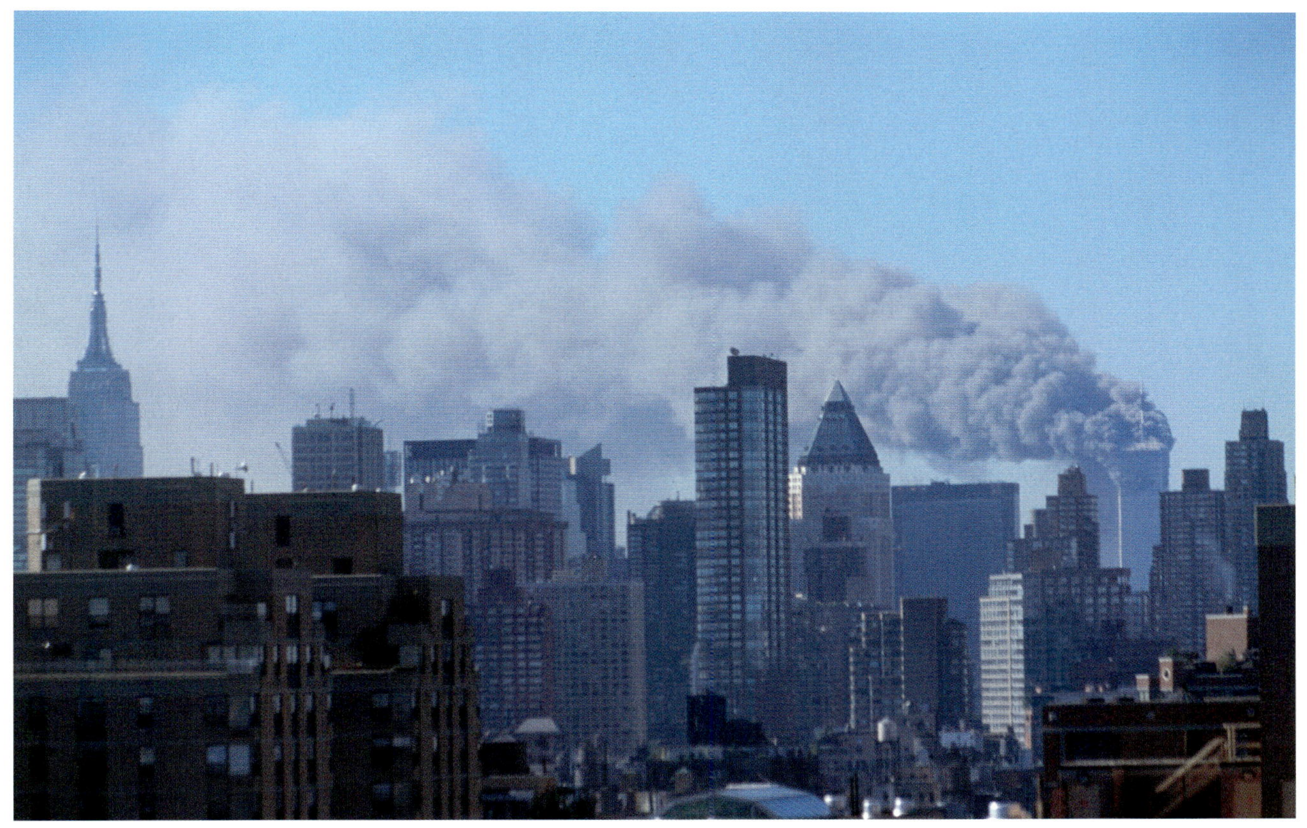

**Bill Viola declares, "The weapon used in 9/11 was the image and not the plane."**

OCTOBER 7
The War in Afghanistan begins when the Northern Alliance troops invade the territories controlled by the Taliban, a name used in the West to indicate fundamentalists in Afghanistan and Pakistan. The US and NATO offer military support. Bush justifies the invasion as a response to the September 11 terrorist attacks, and the country's determination to fight Al Qaeda and eliminate Bin Laden.

OCTOBER 26
With the Patriot Act, whose stated aim is to combat terrorism, law enforcement and intelligence services are granted more powers, while citizens' privacy is decreased.

NOVEMBER 12
Kabul is abandoned by the Taliban and is taken over by the Northern Alliance troops. The British and Americans back the new government.

# BIBLIOGRAPHY


ALBERRO 2010
Alexander Alberro. "Picturing Relations: Images, Texts, and Social Engagement." In *Barbara Kruger*, edited by Alexander Alberro, Martha Gever, Miwon Kwon, and Carol Squiers, 193–200. New York: Rizzoli International Publications, 2010.

ALLEN 1998
Rachel Allen. "Lesbian Domesticity: An Interview with Catherine Opie." In *Los Angeles Forum for Architecture & Urban Design Newsletter*, 2. Spring 1998.

ALTSHULER 1994
*The Avant-Garde in Exhibition. New Art in the 20th Century*. New York: Harry N. Abrams Inc., 1994.

ANDREWS 2005
Stephen Andrews. "Glenn Ligon: in Conversation." In *Glenn Ligon. Some Changes*, edited by Marie-Lynn Hammond, 173. Catalogue for the exhibition (Toronto, The Power Plant, June 25–September 5, 2005). Toronto: The Power Plant, 2005.

*Andy Warhol* 1988
*Andy Warhol: Death and Disasters*. Catalogue for the exhibition (Houston, Menil Collection, October 21–January 8, 1989). Houston: Fine Arts Press—Menil Collection, 1988.

ANFAM 1998
David Anfam. *Mark Rothko: The Works on Canvas*. Volume 1. New Haven: Yale University Press, 1998.

ASHTON 1977
Dore Ashton. "Agnes Martin and…" In *Agnes Martin: Painting and Drawings 1957–1975*, edited by the Arts Council of Great Britain, 13. Catalogue for the exhibition (London, Hayward Gallery, 1977). London: Arts Council of Great Britain, 1977.

ASHTON 1983
Dore Ashton. *About Rothko*. New York: Oxford University Press, 1983.

AUPING 2015
Michael Auping. "The Phenomenology of Frank. 'Materiality and Gesture Make Space.'" In *Frank Stella: A Retrospective*, edited by Michael Auping, 15–39. New York: Whitney Museum of American Art, 2015.

BAERWALDT 2005
Wayne Baerwaldt. Introduction. In *Glenn Ligon. Some Changes*, edited by Marie-Lynn Hammond, 7. Catalogue for the exhibition (Toronto, The Power Plant, June 25–September 5, 2005). Toronto: The Power Plant, 2005.

BAKER 1988
Kenneth Baker. *Minimalism. Art of Circumstance*. New York: Abbeville Press, 1988.

BASUALDO 2017
Carlos Basualdo. "Blossoming of The Bride. On Walkaround Time." In *Merce Cunningham. Common Time*, edited by Fionn Meade and Joan Rothfuss, 145–154. Catalogue for the exhibition (Minneapolis, Walker Art Center, February 8–July 30, 2017; Chicago, Museum of Contemporary Art, February 11–April 30, 2017). Minneapolis: Walker Art Center, 2017.

BELISLE 2011
Brooke Belisle. "Felt Surface. Visible Image." In *Photography & Culture* 4, 2 (July 2011): 158–178.

BOIS 1999
Yve-Alain Bois. "Kelly's Trouvailles. Findings in France." In Yve-Alain Bois, *Ellsworth Kelly: The Early Drawings 1948–1955*, 12–35. Catalogue for the exhibition (Cambridge, Massachusetts, Harvard, University Art Museum, March 6–May 16, 1999; Atlanta, High Museum of Art, June 8–August 15, 1999; Chicago, Art Institute, September 11–December 5, 1999; Winterthur, Kunstmuseum, January 15–March 19, 2000; Munich, Stadtische Galerie im Lenbachhaus, April 1–May 28, 2000; Bonn, Kunstmuseum, June 29–August 27, 2000). Harvard: University Art Museums, 1999.

BOIS 2005
Yve-Alain Bois. "A Drawing that is Habitable." In *Fred Sandback*, edited by Friedemann Malsch and Christiane Meyer-Stoll, 27–38. Catalogue for the exhibition (Vaduz, Kunstmuseum Liechtenstein, November 18, 2005–February 19, 2006; Edinburgh, Fruitmarket Gallery, March 18–May 14, 2006; Graz, Neue Galerie am Landesmuseum Joanneum, June 23–September 3, 2006). Ostfildern: Hatje Cantz Verlag, 2005.

BOSWELL 1999
Peter Boswell. "Theater of Light and Shadow." In *2000BC: The Bruce Conner Story, Part II*, edited by Joan Rothfuss and Michelle Piranio. Minneapolis: Walker Art Center, 1999, 54

VAN BRUGGEN 1990
Coosje van Bruggen. *John Baldessari*. New York: Rizzoli International Publications, 1990.

BRYAN-WILSON 2007
Julia Bryan-Wilson. "Hard Hats and Art Strikes: Robert Morris in 1970." In *The Art Bulletin* 89, 2 (June 2007): 333–359.

BURTON 2012
Johanna Burton. "Sherrie Levine. Beside Herself." In *Sherrie Levine. Mayhem*, edited by Johanna Burton and Elisabeth Sussman, 26. Catalogue for the exhibition (New York, Whitney Museum of American Art, November 10, 2011–January 29, 2012). New Haven: Yale University Press, 2012.

BURTON 2015
Johanna Burton. "Behind the Scenes." In *Robert Gober: 2000 Words*, edited by Karen Marta, 12. Athens: Deste Foundation for Contemporary Art, 2015.

BURTON, SUSSMAN 2012
Johanna Burton & Elisabeth Sussman. Introduction. In *Sherrie Levine. Mayhem*, edited by Johanna Burton and Elisabeth Sussman, 15. Catalogue for the exhibition (New York, Whitney Museum of American Art, November 10, 2011–January 29, 2012). New Haven: Yale University Press, 2012.

*Carolee Schneemann* 2015
*Carolee Schneemann. Kinetic Painting*. Catalogue for the exhibition (Salzburg, Muse-


"

um der Moderne Salzburg, November 21, 2015–February 28, 2016), edited by Sabine Breitwieser. Munich: Prestel, 2015.

*Carolee Schneemann* 2018
*Carolee Schneemann. Uncollected Texts 1956–1980*, edited by Brandon W. Joseph. Brooklyn, NY: Primary Information, 2018.

CELANT AND IPPOLITOV 2004
Germano Celant and Arkady Ippolitov. *Robert Mapplethorpe and the Classical Tradition. Photographs and Mannerist Prints*. Catalogue for the exhibition (Berlin, Deutsche Guggenheim, July 24–October 17, 2004; St. Petersburg, Hermitage, December 8, 2004–January 16, 2005; New York, The Solomon R. Guggenheim Museum, July 1–August 28, 2005). New York: Guggenheim Museum, 2004.

CHEVRIER 1992
Jean-François Chevrier. "Dual Reading." In *Walker Evans & Dan Graham*, edited by Jean-François Chevrier et al., 16. Catalogue for the exhibition (Rotterdam, Witte de With Center for Contemporary Art / Museum Boijmans van Beuningen, August 29–October 11, 1992; Marseille, Direction des Musées, November 6, 1992–January 10, 1993; Münster, Westfälische Landesmuseum für Kunst und Kulturgeschichte, January 31–March 21, 1993; New York, Whitney Museum of American Art, December 17, 1993–March 17, 1994). New York: Whitney Museum of American Art, 1992.

CHONG 2005
Doryun Chong. "Donald Judd." In *Bits & Pieces Put Together to Present a Semblance of Whole. Walker Art Center Collections*, edited by Joan Rothfuss and Elizabeth Carpenter. Minneapolis: Walker Art Center, 2005.

COMPTON 1987
Michael Compton. "Mark Rothko. The Subjects of the Artist." In *Mark Rothko. 1903–1970*, 50. Catalogue for the exhibition (London, Tate Gallery, June 17–September 1, 1987). London: Tate Gallery, 1987.

COTTER 1998
Holland Cotter. "Agnes Mart n." In *Art Journal* 57, 3 (Autumn 1998): 77–80.

CRIMP 1979
Douglas Crimp. "Pictures." In *October* 8 (Spring 1979): 75–88.

CUNNINGHAM 1969
Merce Cunningham. *Changes: Notes on Choreography*, edited by Frances Starr. New York: Something Else Press, 1969.

DANTO 2009
Arthur C. Danto. *Andy Warhol*. New Haven & London: Yale University Press, 2009.

*Dara Birnbaum* 1995
*Dara Birnbaum*. Catalogue for the exhibition (Vienna, Kunsthalle, October 8 ottobre–November 19, 1995), edited by Dara Birnbaum, Eleonora Louis, and Toni Stooss. Vienna: Die Kunsthalle, 1995.

DAVIS 2017
Ben Davis. "How Merce Cunningham Danced Art History in a New Direction." In *Artnet News* 7 (April 2017). Available at https://news.artnet.com/exhibitions/merce-cunningham-common-time-869543.

DE DUVE 2001
Thierry de Duve. "Dan Graham et la critique de l'autonomie artistique." In *Dan Graham. Œuvres 1965–2000*, editd by Marianne Brouwer, 49–67. Catalogue for the exhibition (Porto, Museu de Arte Contemporânea de Serralves, January 13–March 25, 2001; Paris, Musée d'art moderne de la ville de Paris, June 21–October 14, 2001; Otterlo, Kröller-Müller Museum, November 21, 2001–February 10, 2002; Helsinki, Kiasma—Museum of Contemporary Art, May 18–Augutst 18, 2002). Paris: Paris-Musées, 2001.

DEMOS 2010
T. J. Demos. *Dara Birnbaum. Technology/Transformation: Wonder Woman*. London & Cambridge, Mass.: Afterall Books, The MIT Press, 2010.

DIACONO 1975
Mario Diacono. *Vito Acconci. Dal testo-azione al corpo come testo*. New York: Out of London Press—A. H. Minters Publications, 1975.

EKLAND 2009
Douglas Ekland. "The Jump. Appropriation and its Discontents." In Douglas Ekland, *The Pictures Generation 1974–1984*, 118–199. Catalogue for the exhibition (New York, Metropolitan Museum of Art, April 21–August 2, 2009). New Haven & London: Yale University Press, 2009.

ELLEGOOD 2017
Anne Ellegood. *Jimmie Durham. At the Center of the World*. Catalogue for the exhibition (Los Angeles, Hammer Museum, January 29–May 7, 2017; Minneapolis, Walker Art Center, June 22–October 8, 2017; New York, Whitney Museum of America Art, November 3, 2017–January 28, 2018; Saskatoon, Remai Modern, March 23–August 12, 2018), edited by Anne Ellegood. Munich: Prestel, 2017.

ENGBERG 2005
Siri Engberg. "Frank Stella." In *Bits & Pieces Put Together to Present a Semblance of Whole. Walker Art Center Collections*, edited by Joan Rothfuss and Elizabeth Carpenter, 530–533. Minneapolis: Walker Art Center, 2005.

ENGLISH 2005
Darby English. "Glenn Ligon: Committed to Difficulty." In *Glenn Ligon. Some Changes*, edited by Marie-Lynn Hammond, 31–77. Catalogue for the exhibition (Toronto, The Power Plant, June 25–September 5, 2005). Toronto: The Power Plant, 2005.

*Environments* 1961
*Environments, Situations, Spaces*. Catalogue for the exhibition (New York, Marta Jackson Gallery, May 25–June 23, 1961). New York: Martha Jackson Gallery/David Anderson Gallery, 1961.

EVANS 2009
Sarah Evans. "There's No Place Like Hallwalls. Alternative-space Installations in

an Artists' Community." In *Oxford Art Journal* 32, 1 (2009): 97–119.

*FELIX GONZALEZ-TORRES* 1993
*Felix Gonzalez-Torres*, edited by William S. Bartman. New York: A.R.T. Press, 1993.

*FELIX GONZALEZ-TORRES* 1997
*Felix Gonzalez-Torres. Catalogue Raisonné. Volume II*, edited by Dietmar Elger. Ostfildern: Cantz Verlag, 1997.

FERGUSON 2000
Russell Ferguson. "How I Think. An Interview with Catherine Opie." In *Catherine Opie*, edited by Kate Bush, 48. Catalogue for the exhibition (London, The Photographer's Gallery, August 9–September 24, 2000; Chicago, Museum of Contemporary Art, November 18, 2000–February 4, 2001). London: The Photographer's Gallery, 2000.

FIRSTENBERG 2001
Lauri Firstenberg. "Neo-Archival and Textual Modes of Production. An Interview with Glenn Ligon." In *Art Journal* 60, 1 (Spring 2001): 42–47.

FLOOD 1995
Richard Flood. "Notes on Digestion and Film." In *Matthew Barney. Pace Car for the Hubris Pill*, edited by Matthew Barney and Gracia Lebbink, 21–35. Catalogue for the exhibition (Rotterdam, Museum Boijmans van Beuningen, October 21, 1995–January 1, 1996; Bordeaux, CAPC Musée d'art contemporain, January 26–April 8, 1996; Bern, Kunsthalle, May 17–June 23, 1996). Rotterdam: Museum Boijmans Van Beuningen, 1995.

FOGLE 2005
Douglas Fogle. "Richard Prince." In *Bits & Pieces Put Together to Present a Semblance of Whole. Walker Art Center Collections*, edited by Joan Rothfuss and Elizabeth Carpenter, 474. Minneapolis: Walker Art Center, 2005.

FOSTER 1989
Hal Foster. "Atrocity Exhibition." In *Robert Longo*, edited by Howard N. Fox, 52. Catalogue for the exhibition (Los Angeles, Los Angeles County Museum of Art, October 1–December 31, 1989; Chicago, Museum of Contemporary Art, February 17–April 22, 1990; Hartford, Wadsworth Atheneum, June 9–September 2, 1990). New York: Rizzoli, 1989.

FOSTER 1996
Hal Foster. *The Return of the Real: The Avant-Garde at the End of the Century*. Cambridge, Massachusetts: MIT Press, 1996.

FOX 1989
Howard N. Fox. "In Civil War." In *Robert Longo*, edited by Howard N. Fox, 12-31. Catalogue for the exhibition ((Los Angeles, Los Angeles County Museum of Art, October 1–December 31, 1989; Chicago, Museum of Contemporary Art, February 17–April 22, 1990; Hartford, Wadsworth Atheneum, June 9–September 2, 1990). New York: Rizzoli, 1989.

FRYD 2010
Vivien Green Fryd. "Bearing Witness to the Trauma of Slavery in Kara Walker's Videos. *Testimony, Eight Possible Beginnings*, and *I was Transported*." In *Continuum* 24, 1 (February 2010): 145–159.

FUSCO 1997
Coco Fusco. "Lorna Simpson." In *BOMB* 61 (October 1997). Available at https:/bombmagazine.org/articles/lorna-simpson/.

*Gary Simmons* 2002
*Gary Simmons*. Catalogue for the exhibition (Chicago, Museum of Contemporary Art, February 16–May 19, 2002), edited by Thelma Golden. New York: Studio Museum in Harlem, 2002.

*Gary Simmons* 2012
*Gary Simmons. Paradise*. Bologna: Damiani, 2012.

GELDZAHLER 1963
Henry Geldzahler. Interview with Ellsworth Kelly. In *Paintings, Sculptures and Drawings by Ellsworth Kelly*, no page numbers. Catalogue for the exhibition (Washington, DC, Washington Gallery of Modern Art, December 11, 1963–January 26, 1964; Boston, Institute of Contemporary Art, February 1–March 8, 1964). Washington: Washington Gallery of Modern Art, 1963.

GHOLSON 1989
Craig Gholson. "Robert Gober." In *BOMB* 29 (October 1989). Available at https://bombmagazine.org/articles/robert-gober/

GILI 2002
Marta Gili. "Knots: Notes toward a Disappearance." In *Lorna Simpson*, edited by M. Gili, E. Joo, and L. Camhi, 9–38. Catalogue for the exhibition (Salamanca, Centro de Arte de Salamanca, 2002). Salamanca: Consorcio Salamanca, 2002.

GILMAN 2007
Sander L. Gilman. "Confessions of an Academic Pornographer." In *Kara Walker. My Complement, My Enemy, My Oppressor, My Love*, edited by Philippe Vergne, 27–36. Catalogue for the exhibition (Minneapolis, Walker Art Center, February 17–May 13, 2007; New York, Whitney Museum of American Art, November 11, 2007–February 3, 2008; Los Angeles, UCLA Hammer Museum, February 17–May 11, 2008). Minneapolis: Walker Art Center, 2007.

GOLDSTEIN 1999
Ann Goldstein. "Bring in the World." In *Barbara Kruger. Thinking of You*, edited by Anna Goldstein, 32-34. Catalogue for the exhibition (Los Angeles, Museum of Contemporary Art, October 17, 1999–February 13, 2000; New York, Whitney Museum of American Art, July 13–October 22, 2000). Los Angeles, Cambridge, Mass., & London: MIT Press, 1999.

*Hachivi Edgar Heap of Birds* 1990
*Hachivi Edgar Heap of Birds. Claim your Color*. Catalogue for the exhibition (Lawrence, Lawrence Arts Center, September 30–October 19, 1989; Minneapolis, Walker Art Center, March 4–May 6, 1990; New York, Exit Art, September 8–October 6, 1990; San Jose, San Jose

Museum of Art, October 15–December 3, 1990), edited by Jeanette Ingberman. New York: Exit Art, 1990.

HASKELL 1984
Barbara Haskell. *Blam! The Explosion of Pop, Minimalism, and Performance 1958–1964*. Catalogue for the exhibition (New York, Whitney Museum of American Art, September 20–December 2, 1984). New York & London: W. W. Norton & Company, 1984.

HASKELL 1992
Barbara Haskell. "Agnes Martin: The Awareness of Perfection." In *Agnes Martin*, 106. Catalogue for the exhibition (New York, Whitney Museum of American Art, November 6, 1992–January 31, 1993). New York: H. N. Abrams, 1992.

HAUS 2003
Mary Haus. "Robert Longo." In *Artforum* 41, 7 (March 2003): 238–239.

HEIFERMAN 1988
Marvin Heiferman. "Richard Prince interview with Marvin Heiferman." In *BOMB* 24 (July 1988). Available at https://bombmagazine.org/articles/richard-prince/.

HUROWITZ 2009
Sharon Coplan Hurowitz. *John Baldessari. A Catalogue Raisonné of Prints and Multiples, 1971–2007*. Introduction by Wendy Weitman. Manchester, Vt: Hudson Hill Press, 2009.

INDIANA 1999
Gary Indiana. "The War at Home." In *Barbara Kruger. Thinking of You*, edited by Anna Goldstein, 10. Catalogue for the exhibition (Los Angeles, Museum of Contemporary Art, October 17, 1999–Februrary 13, 2000; New York, Whitney Museum of American Art, July 13–October 22, 2000). Los Angeles, Cambridge, Mass., & London: MIT Press, 1999.

JENKINS 1999
Bruce Jenkins. "Explosion in a Film Factory." In *2000 BC: The Bruce Conner Story, Part II*, edited by Joan Rothfuss and Michelle Piranio. Minneapolis: Walker Art Center, 1999

*Jenny Holzer* 2015
*Jenny Holzer. War Paintings*. Catalogue for the exhibition (Venice, Museo Correr, May 7–November 22, 2015), edited by Kristen Asp. Köln: König, 2015.

*Jimmie Durham* 2012
*Jimmie Durham. A Matter o,ᶠ Life and Death and Singing*. Catalogue for the exhibition (Antwerp, MuHKA, May 24–November 18, 2012), edited by Anders Kreuger. Geneva: JRP Ringier Kurstverlag, 2012.

*Jimmie Durham* 2014
*Jimmie Durham, Waiting to be Interrupted. Selected Writings 1993–2012*, edited by Jean Fisher. Milan: Mousse Publishing, 2014.

*John Baldessari* 2010
*John Baldessari. A Print Retrospective from the Collections of Jordan D. Schnitzer and His Family Foundction*. Catalogue for the exhibition (San Francisco, Fine Arts Museums, July 9–November 8, 2009). Portland: Jordar Schnitzer Family Foundation and San Francisco: Fine Arts Museums of San Francisco, 2010.

JOSELIT, SIMON, AND SALECL 1998
David Joselit, Joan Simon, and Renata Salecl. *Jenny Holzer*. London: Phaidon Press, 1998.

JUDD 1999
Donald Judd. "Specific Objects 1965." In *Art in Theory 1900–1990. An Anthology of Changing Ideas*, edited by Charles Harrison and Paul Wood, 809–812. Oxford: Blackwell, 1999.

KELLEY 1996
Mike Kelley. "Land-O-Lakes/Land-O Snakes." In Kentaro Ichihara, *Mike Kelley. Anti-Aesthetic of Excess and Supremacy of Alienation*, 21. Catalogue for the exhibition (Tokyo, Wako Works of Art, November 22–December 27 1996). Tokyo: Wako Works of Art, 1996.

KELLEY 1997
Mike Kelley. "Missing Time. Works on Paper 1974–1976, Recons dered." In *Mike Kelley, 1985–1996*, edited by José Leb-

rero Stals. Catalogue for the exhibition (Barcelona, Museu d'Art Contemporani, January 24–March 31, 1997; Malmö, Rooseum. Center for Contemporary Art, April 25–June 15, 1997; Eindhoven, Stedelijk Van Abbemuseum, June 5–Auguts 21, 1997). Barcelona: Museu d'Art Contemporani, 1997.

KELLEY 2003
Mike Kelley. "Playing with Dead Things. On the Uncanny (1993)." In Mike Kelley, *Foul Perfection. Essays and Criticism*, edited by John C. Welchman, 70–99. Cambridge, Mass. & London: MIT Press, 2003.

*Kerry James Marshall* 2016
*Kerry James Marshall. Mastry*, edited by Helen Molesworth. Catalogue for the exhibition (Chicago, Museum of Contemporary Art, April 23–September 25, 2016). New York: Skira/Rizzoli, 2016.

KLOSTY 1975
James Klosty. *Merce Cunningham*. New York: Saturday Review Press, 1975.

LAMARCHE-VADEL 1980
Bernard Lamarche-Vadel. "Interview: Richard Serra & Bernard Lamarche-Vadel." In Richard Serra, Clara Weyergraf, *Richard Serra. Interviews, Etc. 1970–1980*, 142. New York: The Hudson River Museum, 1980.

LARSON 1974
Philip Larson. Interview with Roy Lichtenstein. *Johns, Kelly, Lichtenstein, Motherwell, Nauman, Rauschenberg, Serra, Stella. Prints from Gemini G.E.L.*, 16–18. Catalogue for the exhibition (Minneapolis, Walker Art Center, August 17–September 29, 1974), Minneapolis: The Center, 1974.

LEA 2015
Sarah Lea. "Joseph Cornell. Wanderlust." In *Joseph Cornell. Fernweh*, edited by Sarah Lea, Sabine Haag, Jasper Sharp, 26-38. Catalogue for the exhibition (London, Royal Academy of Arts, July 4–September 27, 2015; Vienna, Kunsthistorisches Museum, October 20,

2015–January 10, 2016). London: Royal Academy of Arts, 2015.

LEVINE 1991
Sherrie Levine. "The Anxiety of Influence. Head On. A Conversation between Sherrie Levine and Jeanne Siegel." In *Sherrie Levine*, edited by Bernhard Bürgi, 19. Catalogue for the exhibition (Zürich, Kunsthalle, November 3, 1991–January 5, 1992). Zürich: Kunsthalle, 1991.

LEWITT 1967
Sol LeWitt. "Paragraphs on Conceptual Art." In *Artforum* 5, 10 (Summer 1967): 79–83.

LIGON 2011
Glen Ligon. "A Body of Work. An Interview with Patricia Bickers." In *Yourself in the World. Selected Writings and Interviews*, edited by Scott Rothkopf, 161. Published on the occasion of the exhibition (New York, Whitney Museum of American Art, March 10–June 5, 2011; Los Angeles, Los Angeles County Museum of Art, October 23, 2011–January 22, 2012; Fort Worth, Modern Art Museum, February–May 2012). New Haven: Yale University Press, 2011.

LINKER 1994
Kate Linker. *Vito Acconci*. New York: Rizzoli International Publications, 1994.

*Louise Nevelson* 1980
*Louise Nevelson. Atmospheres and Environments*, introduction by Edward Albee. New York: C. N. Potter, 1980.

*Louise Nevelson* 2007
*The Sculpture of Louise Nevelson. Constructing a Legend*, edited by Brooke Kamin Rapaport. New York & New Haven: Yale University Press, 2007.

*Mapplethorpe* 1992
*Mapplethorpe*. Catalogue for the exhibition (Humblebaeck, Louisiana Museum February 8–May 24, 1992; Hamburg, Museum fur Kunst und Gewerbe, June 26–August 20, 1992; Venice, Palazzo Fortuny, August 30–December 13, 1992), edited by Germano Celant. Milan: Electa, 1992.

*Mapplethorpe* 2018
*Robert Mapplethorpe. Pictures*. Catalogue for the exhibition (Porto, Fundação de Serralves, September 20, 2018–January 6, 2019), edited by João Ribas and Maria Ramos. Porto: Fundação de Serralves, 2018.

*Mark Bradford* 2013
*Mark Bradford. Through Darkest America by Truck and Tank*. London: White Cube, 2013.

*Mark Rothko* 1987
*Mark Rothko. 1903–1970*, edited by Diane Waldman. Catalogue for the exhibition (London, Tate Gallery, June 17–September 1, 1987). London: Tate Gallery, 1987.

MARSHALL 2016
Kerry James Marshall. "Shall I Compare Thee…?" In *Kerry James Marshall. Mastry*, edited by Helen Molesworth, 71–79. Catalogue for the exhibition (Chicago, Museum of Contemporary Art, April 23–September 25, 2016). New York: Skira/Rizzoli, 2016.

*Martha Rosler* 1998
*Martha Rosler. Positions in the Life World*. Catalogue for the exhibition (Birmingham, Ikon Gallery, December 5, 1998–January 30, 1990; Vienna, Generali Foundation, May 12–August 8, 1999; Barcellona, Museu d'Art Contemporani de Barcelona, October 19, 1999–January 9, 2000; New York, New Museum of Contemporary Art, June 13–Otober 18, 2000), edited by Catherine de Zegher. Cambridge, Mass.: MIT Press, 1998.

*Martha Rosler* 2009
*Martha Rosler. La casa, la calle, la cocina / The House, the Street, the Kitchen*. Catalogue for the exhibition (Granada, Centro José Guerrero, January 29–April 12, 2009). Granada: Diputación Provincial de Granada, 2009.

MCEVILLEY 2005
Thomas McEvilley. "Fred Sandback. Nothing Outside Factuality." In *Fred Sandback*, edited by Friedemann Malsch and Christiane Meyer-Stoll, 55–65. Catalogue for the exhibition (Vaduz, Kunstmuseum Liechtenstein, November 18, 2005–February 19, 2006; Edinburgh, Fruitmarket Gallery, March 18–May 14, 2006; Graz, Neue Galerie am Landesmuseum Joanneum, June 23–September 3, 2006). Ostfildern: Hatje Cantz Verlag, 2005.

*Merce Cunningham* 1997
*Merce Cunningham. Fifty Years*, account and comment by David Vaughan, edited by Melissa Harris. New York: Aperture, 1997.

*Merce Cunningham* 1998
*Merce Cunningham. Dancing in Space and Time*, edited by Richard Kostelanetz and Jack Anderson. New York: De Capo Press, 1998.

*Merce Cunningham* 2017
*Merce Cunningham. Common time*, edited by Fionn Meade and Joan Rothfuss. Minneapolis: Walker Art Center, 2017.

MEYER-STOLL 2005
Christiane Meyer-Stoll. Introduction. In *Fred Sandback*, edited by Friedemann Malsch and Christiane Meyer-Stoll, 14. Catalogue for the exhibition (Vaduz, Kunstmuseum Liechtenstein, November 18, 2005–February 19, 2006; Edinburgh, Fruitmarket Gallery, March 18–May 14, 2006; Graz, Neue Galerie am Landesmuseum Joanneum, June 23–September 3, 2006). Ostfildern: Hatje Cantz Verlag, 2005, p. 14

MOLESWORTH 2016
Helen Molesworth. "Thinking of a Mastr Plan. Kerry James Marshall and the Museum." In *Kerry James Marshall. Mastry*, edited by Helen Molesworth, 27–43. Catalogue for the exhibition (Chicago, Museum of Contemporary Art, April 23–September 25, 2016). New York: Skira/Rizzoli, 2016.

MORGAN AND JONES 2009
Jessica Morgan and Leslie Jones. *Pure Beauty. John Baldessari*. London: Tate Publishing, 2009.

MORRIS 1968
Robert Morris. "Anti Form." In *Artforum* 6, 8 (April 1968): 33–35.

*Most Serene Republics* 2008
*Most Serene Republics. Edgar Heap of Birds*. Catalogue for the exhibition (Washington, National Museum of the American Indian, Smithsonian Institution, June 6–September 30, 2007), edited by Kathleen Ash-Milby and Truman T. Lowe. Washington, D.C.: National Museum of the American Indian, 2008.

MOTHERWELL 1993
Robert Motherwell. "Robert Motherwell on Joseph Cornell." In *Joseph Cornell's Theater of the Mind. Selected Diaries, Letters, and Files*, edited by Mary Ann Caws, 13-15. New York: Thames and Hudson, 1993.

MÜLLER 1972
Grégoire Müller. *The New Avant-Garde: Issues for the Art of the Seventies*. New York: Praeger Publishers, 1972.

MULVEY 1975
Laura Mulvey. "Visual Pleasure and Narrative Cinema." In *Screen* 16, 3 (October 1975): 6–18.

MULVEY, SNAUWAERT, AND DURANT 1995
Laura Mulvey, Dirk Snauwaert, and Mark Alice Durant. *Jimmie Durham*. London: Phaidon, 1995.

MUNRO 1979
Eleanor Munro. *Originals: American Women Artists*. New York: Simon & Schuster, 1979.

NAM JUNE PAIK 2019
Nam June Paik. *We are in Open Circuits. Writings by Nam June Paik*, edited by John G. Hanhardt, Gregory Zinman, and Edith Decker-Phillips. Cambridge, Mass.: MIT Press, 2019.

*Nam June Paik* 2019
*Nam June Paik*. Catalogue for the exhibition (London, Tate Modern, October 17, 2019–February 9, 2020), edited by Sook-Kyung Lee and Rudolf Frieling. London: Tate Publishing, 2019.

*Nam June Paik* 2000
*The Worlds of Nam June Paik*. Catalogue for the exhibition (New York, The Solomon R. Guggenheim Foundation, February 11–April 26, 2000), edited by John G. Hanhardt. New York: Guggenheim Museum, 2000.

NORVELL 2001
Patsy Norvell. *Recording Conceptual Art. Early Interviews with Barry, Huebler, Kaltenbach, Lewitt, Morris, Oppenheim, Siegelaub, Smithson and Weiner*, edited by Patricia Norvell and Alexander Alberro. Oakland: University of California Press, 2001.

NOVAKOV 1998
Anna Novakov. "Public Sex. In Conversation with Lorna Simpson." In *Atlántica: Revista de arte y pensamiento* 19 (1998): 172–178.

O'DOHERTY 1973
Brian O'Doherty. *American Masters. The Voice and the Myth. Hopper, Davis, Pollock, De Kooning, Rothko, Rauschenberg, Wyeth, Cornell*. New York: Ridge Press/Random House, 1973.

OLDENBURG 1966
Claes Oldenburg. "Extracts from the Studio Notes (1962–64)." In *Artforum* 4, 5 (January 1966): 32–33.

OLDENBURG 1967
Claes Oldenburg. *Store Days*. New York, Villafranche-sur-Mer & Frankfurt am Main: Something Else Press, 1967.

OSTROW 2000
Saul Ostrow. "Saul Ostrow and Frank Stella." in *BOMB* 71, Spring, 2000: 28–35

OWENS 1983
Craig Owens. "The Discourse of Others. Feminists and Postmodernism." In *The Anti-Aesthetic. Essays on Postmodern Culture*, edited by Hal Foster, 57–81. Washington: Bay Press, 1983.

*Paul McCarthy* 2003
*Blockhead + Daddies Bighead. Paul McCarthy at Tate Modern*. Catalogue for the exhibition (London, Tate Modern, May 19–October 26, 2003), edited by Paul and Karen McCarthy. London: Tate Publishing, 2003.

*Paul McCarthy* 2004
*Paul McCarthy. Brain Box Dream Box*, edited by Eva Meyer-Hermann. Dusseldorf: Richter Verlag, 2004.

*Paul McCarthy* 2006
*Paul McCarthy. Head Shop, Shop Head. Works 1966–2006*. Catalogue for the exhibition (Stockholm, Moderna Museet, June 17–September 3, 2006; Aarhus, ARoS, February 3–May 6, 2007; Ghent, Stedelijk Museum voor Actuele Kunst, October 12, 2007–February 17, 2008). Stockholm: Moderna Museet; & Göttingen: Steidl, 2006.

*Paul McCarthy* 2000
*Paul McCarthy*. Catalogue for the exhibition (Los Angeles, Museum of Contemporary Art, November 12, 2000–January 21, 2001; New York, New Museum of Contemporary Art, February 22–May 13, 2001), introduction by Lisa Phillips. New York: New Museum; & Ostfildern: Hatje Cantz, 2000.

PAXTON 1997
Steve Paxton. "Rauschenberg for Cunningham and Three of His Own." In *Robert Rauschenberg. A Retrospective*, edited by Walter Hopps and Susan Davidson, 261. Catalogue for the exhibition (New York, Guggenheim Museum, September 19, 1997–January 7, 1998). New York: Guggenheim Museum, 1997.

PHILLIPS 2003
Lisa Phillips. Introduction. In *Cindy Sherman. Centerfolds*, 5–7. New York: Skarstedt Fine Art, 2003.

POWELL 1998
Richard J. Powell. "Lamentations from the Hood." In *Kerry James Marshall. Mementos*, 37. Catalogue for the exhibition (Chicago, The Renaissance Society at the University of Chicago, May 6–June 28, 1998). Chicago: The Renaissance Society at the University of Chicago, 1998.

*Primary Structures* 1966
*Primary Structures. Younger American and British Sculptors*, edited by Kynaston McShine. Catalogue for the exhibition (New York, The Jewish Museum, April 27–June 12, 1966). New York: The Jewish Museum, 1966.

PRINTZ 1988
Neil Printz. "Painting Death in America." In *Andy Warhol: Death and Disasters*, 16–21. Catalogue for the exhibition (Houston, Menil Collection, October 21, 1988–January 8, 1989). Houston: Fine Arts Press—Menil Collection, 1988.

*Projected Art* 1966
*Projected Art*. Catalogue for the exhibition (New York, Finch College Museum of Art, December 8, 1966–January 8, 1967). New York: Finch College Museum of Art, 1966.

RAGHEB 2005
J. Fiona Ragheb. "Dan Flavin." In *Bits & Pieces Put Together to Present a Semblance of Whole. Walker Art Center Collections*, edited by Joan Rothfuss and Elizabeth Carpenter, 214. Minneapolis: Walker Art Center, 2005.

RESPINI 2012
Eva Respini. "Will the Real Cindy Sherman Please Stand Up?" In Eva Respini, *Cindy Sherman*, 12–53. Catalogue for the exhibition (New York, Museum of Modern Art, February 26–June 11, 2012). New York: MoMA Publications, 2012.

RESPINI 2016
Eva Respini. "ON DEFIANCE. Experimentation as Resistance." In *Aperture* 225 (Winter 2016): 100–107.

RINDER 2005
Lawrence Rinder. In *Bits & Pieces Put Together to Present a Semblance of Whole. Walker Art Center Collections*, edited by Joan Rothfuss and Elizabeth Carpenter, 373. Minneapolis: Walker Art Center, 2005.

*Robert Indiana* 1968
*Robert Indiana*. Catalogue for the exhibition (Philadelphia, Institute of Contemporary Art of the University of Pennsylvania, April 17–May 7, 1968). Philadelphia: Falcon Press, 1968.

*Robert Indiana* 1998
*Robert Indiana. Rétrospective 1958–1998*. Catalogue for the exhibition (Nice, Musée d'art moderne et d'art contemporain, June 26–November 22, 1998). Nice: GS Éditions, 1998.

*Robert Indiana* 2012
*Robert Indiana. New Perspectives*, edited by Allison Unruh, preface by Robert Storr. Ostfildern: Hatje Cantz, 2012.

*Robert Indiana* 2013
*Robert Indiana. Beyond Love*. Catalogue for the exhibition (New York, Whitney Museum of American Art, September 26, 2013–January 5, 2014), edited by Barbara Haskell. New York: Whitney Museum of American Art, 2013.

*Robert Rauschenberg* 2016
*Robert Rauschenberg*, edited by Leah Dickerman and Achim Borchardt-Hume. Catalogue for the exhibition (London, Tate Modern, December 1, 2016–April 2, 2017; New York, MoMA, May 21–September 17, 2017; San Francisco, SFMoMA, Novembre18, 2017–March 25, 2018). New York & London: Tate Publishing, 2016.

ROELSTRAETE 2012
Dieter Roelstraete. "An Argument for Something Else. Dieter Roelstraete in conversation with Kerry James Marshall." In *Kerry James Marshall: Painting and Other Stuff*, edited by Nav Haq, 11–34. Antwerp: Ludion, 2012.

ROSENTHAL 1993
Mark Rosenthal. *Artists at Gemini G.E.L.: Celebrating the 25th Year*. New York: Harry N. Abrams Inc., 1993.

ROSLER 1981
Martha Rosler. *3 Works. Critical Essays on Photography and Photographs*. Halifax, N.S.: Press of the Nova Scotia College of Art and Design, 1981.

ROTHFUSS 2005
Joan Rothfuss. "Andy Warhol." In *Bits & Pieces Put Together to Present a Semblance of Whole. Walker Art Center Collections*, edited by Joan Rothfuss and Elizabeth Carpenter, 573–574. Minneapolis: Walker Art Center, 2005.

SANDBACK 2005
Fred Sandback. "Notes." In *Fred Sandback*, edited by Friedemann Malsch and Christiane Meyer-Stoll, 90. Catalogue for the exhibition (Vaduz, Kunstmuseum Liechtenstein, November 18, 2005–February 19, 2006; Edinburgh, Fruitmarket Gallery, March 18–May 14, 2006; Graz, Neue Galerie am Landesmuseum Joanneum, June 23–September 3, 2006). Ostfildern: Hatje Cantz Verlag, 2005.

SCHNEEMANN 2002
Carolee Schneemann. *Imaging Her Erotics. Essays, Interviews, Projects*. Cambridge, Mass.: MIT Press, 2002.

SERRA 1970
Richard Serra. "Play It Again, Sam." In *Arts Magazine* 44, 4 (February 1970): 24–27.

*Shock of the News* 2012
*Shock of the News*, edited by Judith Brodie. Catalogue for the exhibition (Washington, National Gallery of Art, September 23, 2012–January 27, 2013). London: Lund Humphries, 2012.

SIEGEL 1987
Jeanne Siegel. "Barbara Kruger. Words and Pictures. Interview." In *Arts Magazine* 61, 10 (June 1987): 17–21.

SINGERMAN 1993
Howard Singerman. "Charting Monkey Island with Lévi-Strauss and Freud." In *Mike Kelley. Catholic Tastes*, edited by Elisabeth Sussman. Catalogue for the exhibition (New York, Whitney Museum of American Art, November 5, 1993–February 20, 1994). New York: Whitney Museum of American Art & H. N. Abrams, 1993.

*Sixteen Americans* 1959
*Sixteen Americans*, edited by Dorothy C. Mill-

er. Catalogue for the exhibition (New York, Museum of Modern Art, December 16, 1959–February 14, 1960). New York: The Museum of Modern Art & Doubleday, 1959.

SMITH 2005
Daniel Smith. "Conner Films." In *Bits & Pieces Put Together to Resemble a Whole: Walker Art Center Collections*, edited by Elizabeth Carpenter and Joan Rothfuss. Minneapolis: Walker Art Centre, 2005

SPECTOR 2002
Nancy Spector. "Only the Perverse Can Still Save Us." In *Matthew Barney: The Cremaster Cycle*, edited by Nancy Spector, 2–91. Catalogue for the exhibition (Cologne, Museum Ludwig, June 6–September 1, 2002; Paris, Musée d'Art Moderne de la Ville de Paris, October 10, 2002–January 5, 2003; New York, Solomon R. Guggenheim Museum, February14–May 11, 2003). New York: Solomon R. Guggenheim Museum, 2002.

SPECTOR 2007
Nancy Spector. "Nowhere Man." In *Richard Prince*, edited by Nancy Spector, 23–28. Catalogue for the exhibition (New York, Solomon R. Guggenheim Museum, September 28, 2007–January 9, 2008; Minneapolis, Walker Art Center, March 22–June 15, 2008; London, Serpentine Gallery, Summer 2008). New York: Guggenheim Museum, 2007.

SUSSLER 1990
Betsy Sussler, "Sarah Charlesworth." In *BOMB* 30 (January 1990). Available at https://bombmagazine.org/articles/sarah-charlesworth/.

SWENSON 1963
Gene R. Swenson. "What is Pop Art? Interview." In *ARTnews* 63, 7 (November 1963): 142.

TATTERSALL 2016
Lanka Tattersall. "Black Lives, Matter." In *Kerry James Marshall. Mastry,* edited by Helen Molesworth, 57–69. Catalogue for the exhibition (Chicago, Museum of Contemporary Art, April 23–September 25, 2016). New York: Skira/Rizzoli, 2016.

TILLMAN 1999
Lynne Tillman. "Interview with Barbara Kruger." In *Barbara Kruger. Thinking of You*, edited by Anna Goldstein 190. Catalogue for the exhibition (Los Angeles, Museum of Contemporary Art, October 17, 1999–February 13, 2000; New York, Whitney Museum of American Art, July 13–October 22, 2000). Los Angeles, Cambridge, Mass., & London: MIT Press, 1999.

TOMKINS 2002
Calvin Tomkins. "Profiles. Man of Steel." In *The New Yorker*, August 5, 2002: 57.

TRUITT 1984
Anne Truitt. *Daybook. The Journal of an Artist*. New York: Penguin, 1984.

TUCHMAN 1970
Phyllis Tuchman. "An Interview with Carl Andre." In *Artforum* 8, 6 (June 1970): 55–61.

VAUGHN 1989
David Vaughn. "The Fabric of Friendship: Jasper Johns in conversation with David Vaughn." In *Dancers on a Plane. John Cage, Merce Cunningham, Jasper Johns*, edited by Judy Adam, 55, 137–142. Catalogue for the exhibition (London, Anthony d'Offay Gallery, October 31–December 2, 1989). London: Anthony d'Offay Gallery, 1989.

VAUGHAN 1998
David Vaughan. "Merce Cunningham's Walkaround Time [1982]." In *Merce Cunningham. Dancing in Space and Time*, edited by Richard Kostelanetz, 66–70. New York: Da Capo Press, 1998.

VERGNE 2005
Philippe Vergne. "Carl Andre." In *Bits & Pieces Put Together to Present a Semblance of Whole. Walker Art Center Collections*, edited by Joan Rothfuss and Elizabeth Carpenter, 102. Minneapolis: Walker Art Center, 2005.

*Vito Acconci* 2001
*Vito Acconci. Writings, Works, Projects*, edited by Gloria Moure. Barcelona: Polígrafa, 2001.

WALDMAN 1989
Diane Waldman. *Jenny Holzer*. Catalogue for the exhibition (New York, The Solomon R. Guggenheim Museum, December 12, 1989–February 11, 1990). New York: The Solomon R. Guggenheim Foundation—H. N. Abrams, 1989.

WALDMAN 1997
Diane Waldman. *Jenny Holzer*. Catalogue for the exhibition (New York, The Solomon R. Guggenheim Museum). New York: The Solomon R. Guggenheim Foundation—H. N. Abrams, 1997.

WALLACE, KEZIERE 1979
Ian Wallace & Russell Keziere. "In Conversation with Bruce Nauman." In *Vanguard* 8, 1 (February 1979): 18.

WEINBERG 2012
Adam D. Weinberg. Foreword. In *Sherrie Levine. Mayhem*, edited by Johanna Burton and Elisabeth Sussman, 8. Catalogue for the exhibition (New York, Whitney Museum of American Art, November 10, 2011–January 29, 2012). New Haven: Yale University Press, 2012.

WOLF 2007
Sylvia Wolf. *Polaroids. Mapplethorpe*. Munich & New York: Prestel, 2007.

# PHOTO CREDITS

*Exhibited works*

All works Collection Walker Art Center, Minneapolis unless otherwise noted.

©/®/TM The Andy Warhol Foundation for the Visual Arts, Inc. by SIAE 2021, figs. 3.2–3.13, p. 31;
© 1960 by Henmar Press Inc. Used by permission of C.F. Peters Corporation. All rights reserved, figs. 21.1a-c;
© 1966 Claes Olbenburg, fig. 3.14;
© 1998 Kate Rothko Prizel & Christopher Rothko / ARS, New York, fig. 1.3;
© 1999 Matthew Barney, photo Chris Winget, courtesy Gladstone Gallery, New York and Brussels, fig. 9.11;
© 2021 Fred Sandback Archive, fig. 4.8;
© Agnes Martin by SIAE 2021, fig. 4.10;
© Barbara Kruger. Courtesy the artist and the Walker Art Center, Minneapolis, fig. 7.4;
© Bruce Nauman by SIAE 2021, fig. 5.1;
© Carl Andre by SIAE 2021, fig. 4.4;
© Carolee Schneemann by SIAE 2021. Courtesy Electronic Arts Intermix (EAI), New York, fig. 6.1;
© Catherine Opie. Courtesy the artist and the Walker Art Center, figs. 10.4–10.5;
© Cindy Sherman. Courtesy the artist and the Walker Art Center, Minneapolis, fig. 7.3;
© Conner Family Trust, San Francisco, fig. 1.5;
© Dan Flavin by SIAE 2021, fig. 4.2;
© Ellsworth Kelly Foundation, courtesy Matthew Marks Gallery, figs. 1.6–1.9;
© Estate of Anne Truitt, Bridgeman Images, fig. 4.9;
© Estate of Louise Nevelson, fig. 1.4;
© Estate of Roy Lichtenstein, fig. 3.15;
© Felix Gonzalez-Torres. Courtesy of the Felix Gonzalez-Torres Foundation, fig. 8.5;
© Frank Stella by SIAE 2021, fig. 4.1;
© Gary Simmons. Courtesy the artist and the Walker Art Center, Minneapolis, fig. 10.1;
© Glenn Ligon. Courtesy the artist and the Walker Art Center, Minneapolis, fig. 9.10;
© Jasper Johns by SIAE 2021, fig. 2.3;
© Jenny Holzer by SIAE 2021, fig. 8.3;
© John Baldessari, figs. 5.2–5.3;
© Kara Walker, figs. 9.12, 9.14;
© Kara Walker. Courtesy the artist and the Walker Art Center, Minneapolis, fig. 9.13;
© Kerry James Marshall. Courtesy of the artist and the Jack Shainman Gallery, New York, figs. 9.4–9.9;
© Lorna Simpson. Courtesy the artist and Hauser & Wirth, fig. 9.3;
© Mark Bradford. Courtesy the artist and the Walker Art Center, Minneapolis, fig. 10.6;
© Mike Kelley. Courtesy the artist and the Walker Art Center, Minneapolis, fig. 10.3;
© Paul McCarthy. Courtesy the artist and Hauser & Wirth, fig. 10.2;
© Richard Prince, fig. 7.5;
© Richard Prince. Courtesy the artist and the Walker Art Center, Minneapolis, figs. 7.6–7.7;
© Richard Serra by SIAE 2021, fig. 4.5;

© Robert Gober, courtesy Matthew Marks Gallery, fig. 8.4;
© Robert Indiana by SIAE 2021, fig. 3.1;
© Robert Longo. Courtesy the artist and the Walker Art Center, Minneapolis, fig. 7.2;
© Robert Mapplethorpe Foundation. Used by permission, figs. 8.1–8.2;
© Robert Morris by SIAE 2021; fig. 4.6;
© Robert Rauschenberg Foundation by SIAE 2021, figs. 2.2, p. 171 top;
© Sherrie Levine. Courtesy the artist and the Walker Art Center, Minneapolis, fig. 7.8;
© Sol LeWitt by SIAE 2021, fig. 4.3;
© The Estate of Sarah Charlesworth, and Paula Cooper Gallery, New York, fig. 7.1;
© The Joseph and Robert Cornell Memorial Foundation by SIAE 2021, figs. 1.1–1.2;
© Vito Acconci by SIAE 2021. Courtesy Electronic Arts Intermix (EAI), New York, fig. 6.3;
Courtesy of Dara Birnbaum and Electronic Arts Intermix (EAI), New York, fig. 6.4;
Art © Judd Foundation by SIAE 2021, fig. 4.7;
Courtesy Electronic Arts Intermix (EAI), New York, figs. 2.4–2.5, 5.3, 6.2, 6.5;
Courtesy of Martha Rosler and Electronic Arts Intermix (EAI), New York, fig. 6.6;
Hock E Aye/Edgar Heap of Birds, figs. 9.2a-c.

*Essays and chronology*

© 2021. Digital image Whitney Museum of American Art / Licensed by Scala, p. 39 top;
© Archivio storico art tapes 22_Firenze, courtesy Maria Gloria Bicocchi, p. 14 top;
© Guerrilla Girls, courtesy guerrillagirls.com, p. 179 top;
A.F. ARCHIVE / Alamy Stock Photo, p. 182 top;
AA Film Archive / Alamy Stock Photo, p. 181 bottom;
American Photo Archive / Alamy Stock Photo, p. 178 right;
Barb Economon for Walker Art Center, Minneapolis, p. 35 top;
Bridgeman Images, pp. 172 left, 183 top;
Cameraphoto Epoche / © Vittorio Pavan, p. 171 top;
Cameron Wittig for Walker Art Center, Minneapolis, p. 41;
CBW / Alamy Stock Photo, p. 177 bottom;
Collection Christophel / Alamy Stock Photo, pp. 177 left, 179 bottom;
Courtesy Archivio Pitti Immagine, p. 182 bottom left;
Courtesy, Artists Space, New York. Photo: James Dee, p. 35 bottom;
Courtesy Jenny Holzer / Art Resource, New York, p. 18;
Courtesy Walker Art Center, Minneapolis, p. 36 top;
Dan Dennehy for Walker Art Center, Minneapolis, p. 39 bottom;
Eric Sutherland for Walker Art Center, Minneapolis, p. 25 bottom;

Gene Pittman for Walker Art Center, Minneapolis, p. 36 bottom;
Granger, NYC. / Alamy Stock Photo, p. 169 top;
Library of Congress, pp. 174 middle, 181 right, 183;
kpa Publicity Stills / Alamy Stock Photo, p. 177 top;
Media Punch / Alamy Stock Photo, pp. 169 left, 175 bottom;
Moviestore Collection / Alamy Stock Photo, p. 178 left;
National Archives, p. 169 bottom;
Niday Picture Library / Alamy Stock Photo, p. 172 top;
Nippon News / Alamy Stock Photo, p. 182 top right;
Norbert Michalke / Alamy Stock Photo, p. 180;
Photo © Gianni Melotti, Firenze, pp. 14, 17;
Photo courtesy the Oldenburg van Bruggen Studio, © 1988 Claes Oldenburg and Coosje van Bruggen, photo: Attilio Maranzano; p. 26;
Photograph: Shunk-Kender © J. Paul Getty Trust. Getty Research Institute, Los Angeles (2014.R.20). Gift of the Roy Lichtenstein Foundation in Memory of Harry Shunk and Janos Kender, p. 170 left;
Pictorial Press / Alamy Stock Photo, p. 170 top;
Pictures From History / Alamy Stock Photo, p. 176 bottom;
Pierre Barlier / Alamy Stock Photo, pp. 174 top, 182 bottom;
Photo by Nicole Baster on Unsplash, p. 20;
Public domain, pp. 171 right, 172, 173 bottom;
Records / Alamy Stock Photo, p. 171 bottom;
Rolphe Dauphin for Walker Art Center, Minneapolis, p. 25 top;
World History Archive / Alamy Stock Photo, pp. 170 right, 176 top.

Every reasonable attempt has been made to identify owners of copyrights. Errors or omissions notified to the publisher will be corrected in subsequent editions.

*reproduction*
Opero S.r.l., Verona

*printing*
Grafiche DueGi, San Martino B.A. (VR)

*for*
Marsilio Editori® S.p.A., Venice